Social Support Measurement and Intervention

SOCIAL SUPPORT MEASUREMENT AND INTERVENTION

A GUIDE FOR HEALTH AND SOCIAL SCIENTISTS

EDITED BY

Sheldon Cohen

Lynn G. Underwood

Benjamin H. Gottlieb

A PROJECT OF THE FETZER INSTITUTE

OXFORD
UNIVERSITY PRESS

2000

OXFORD
UNIVERSITY PRESS

Oxford   New York
Athens   Auckland   Bangkok   Bogotá   Buenos Aires   Calcutta
Cape Town   Chennai   Dar es Salaam   Delhi   Florence   Hong Kong   Istanbul
Karachi   Kuala Lumpur   Madrid   Melbourne   Mexico City   Mumbai
Nairobi   Paris   São Paulo   Singapore   Taipei   Tokyo   Toronto   Warsaw

and associated companies in
Berlin   Ibadan

Copyright © 2000 Oxford University Press

Published by Oxford University Press, Inc.
198 Madison Avenue, New York, New York, 10016

Oxford is a registered trademark of Oxford University Press

Library of Congress Cataloging-in-Publication Data
Social support measurement and intervention : a guide for health and
social scientists / edited by Sheldon Cohen, Lynn G. Underwood,
Benjamin H. Gottlieb.
p.   cm.
A project of the Fetzer Institute.
Includes bibliographical references and index.
ISBN 978-0-19-512670-9
1. Social networks—Therapeutic use—Research.
I. Cohen, Sheldon, 1947– .   II. Underwood, Lynn.
III. Gottlieb, Benjamin H.   IV. Fetzer Institute.
R726.5.S623   2000
362.1'042—dc21   99-43200

Printed in the United States of America
on acid-free paper

SC: For my parents, Ruth S. and Harry F. Cohen

LU: With love to my daughters Anna, Michelle, and Zoë

BG: For my sweet son Avery Julian Gottlieb

Preface

In the winter of 1991, Lynn G. Underwood of the Fetzer Institute invited a small interdisciplinary group of scientists working in the area of psychosocial factors in disease and clinical epidemiology to a meeting in Chicago. The purpose of the meeting was to discuss activities the institute might sponsor that would contribute to improving the methodological rigor and overall quality of research examining the connections between psychological and social factors and health outcomes.

One conclusion of the Chicago meeting was that state-of-the-art techniques for measuring psychosocial concepts were slow to disseminate to the wide interdisciplinary group of investigators working in this area. In particular, psychosocial measures are often chosen because of their availability or visibility rather than because they are the most appropriate for answering investigators' specific questions. Similarly, while there was considerable work addressing strategies for intervening to change psychological and social factors thought to affect disease outcomes, there was little structured information available regarding how one should go about designing such interventions. It was decided that edited volumes that provided theoretical bases for measurement and intervention and helped researchers and clinicians choose appropriate measurement and intervention strategies would be an effective means of improving research and clinical work in these areas. The initial volume, *Measuring Stress: A Guide for Health and Social Scientists* (Oxford University Press, 1997), addressed the conceptualization and measurement of stress.

Encouraged by the success of the stress volume, the Fetzer Institute initiated plans for a second volume, this one to focus on social support measurement and intervention. There has been much interest in how we might most effectively tap the resource of human relationships as we think about improving the health of people and communities. Surgery, procedures, and pharmaceuticals, although valuable and important, are not our only response to health care needs. Researchers and practitioners alike have devised and implemented interventions that utilize social support. We are hoping, in this text, to enable individuals to more effectively design interventions to address disease and improve well-being that draw on our human capacity to care for one another.

We decided that the social support volume should reflect a variety of specific approaches to social support, help to integrate these approaches, and in the process be useful to social and medical scientists alike. The specific purpose of the volume is to serve as a state-of-the-art resource for selecting social support measures and designing social support interventions in relation to physical and psychiatric health in humans. We expect that the book will be used primarily as a resource for those conducting research in this area and as a guide for those designing interventions. Moreover, we thought that, like the stress volume, this volume is well suited for use in graduate courses in psychology, psychiatry, sociology, social work, nursing, and epidemiology. It includes discussions of how social support is conceptualized, the pathways through which the social environment might influence the onset and progression of psychiatric and physical illness, the alternative methods of measuring and mobilizing social support, and how to decide on appropriate measures and interventions. Our intent is to provide valuable information for audiences with a wide range of expertise: to aid those without extensive experience but at the same time provide sufficient information for experts to select state-of-the-art measurement instruments and design appropriate and effective support interventions.

We begin by providing a theoretical orientation to the study of social support and its relation to health. Then, in part II, each chapter provides a conceptual underpinning of the approach it addresses and discusses the important measures within the approach, the kinds of studies each is appropriate for, and the various costs and benefits of each alternative measure. In part III, we provide a general overview of the issues in designing and evaluating support interventions and separate chapters on each of three intervention approaches. Finally, we end with the insightful comments of an outside reviewer and one of the editors.

We are indebted to the Fetzer Institute for its generous support of this endeavor. We express our gratitude to the contributors to this volume, who persevered in the face of editorial onslaught and produced exceptional products in a relatively constrained time frame. A Senior Scientist Award from the National Institute of Mental Health supported Sheldon Cohen's (MH00721) participation. We are also indebted to James House, Karen Rook, and Alan Vaux, who served as reviewers and provided outstanding feedback and stimulation. We sincerely appreciate their help and note that it is we and not they who are responsible for any errors or misinterpretations. We also want to thank Heidi Matteo, who worked so hard in putting this book together; our editor, Joan Bossert; and the staff of Oxford University Press for their support and professionalism.

Pittsburgh, PA	S. C.
Kalamazoo, MI	L. U.
Guelph, Ontario	B. G.

Contents

Contributors   xi

Part I. Theoretical and Historical Perspectives

1. Social Relationships and Health   3
   SHELDON COHEN
   BENJAMIN H. GOTTLIEB
   LYNN G. UNDERWOOD

Part II. Social Support Measures

2. Social Support Theory and Measurement   29
   BRIAN LAKEY
   SHELDON COHEN

3. Measuring Social Integration and Social Networks   53
   IAN BRISSETTE
   SHELDON COHEN
   TERESA E. SEEMAN

4. Measuring Perceived and Received Social Support   86
   THOMAS A. WILLS
   ORI SHINAR

5. Measuring Relationship Properties and Interactions
   Relevant to Social Support   136
   HARRY T. REIS
   NANCY COLLINS

Part III. Social Support Interventions

6. Selecting and Planning Support Interventions   195
   BENJAMIN H. GOTTLIEB

7. Support Groups   221
   VICKI S. HELGESON
   BENJAMIN H. GOTTLIEB

8. One-to-One Support Interventions:
   Home Visitation and Mentoring   246
   JOHN ECKENRODE
   STEPHEN HAMILTON

9. Optimizing Support in the Natural Network   278
    CAROLYN E. CUTRONA
    VALERIE COLE

Part IV. Implications

10. Social Support Measurement and Interventions:
    Comments and Future Directions   311
    KAREN S. ROOK
    LYNN G. UNDERWOOD

Index   335

Contributors

Ian Brissette, Department of Psychology, Carnegie Mellon University, Pittsburgh, PA 15213.

Sheldon Cohen, Department of Psychology, Carnegie Mellon University, Pittsburgh, PA 15213.

Valerie Cole, St. John Fisher College, Rochester, NY 14618.

Nancy Collins, Department of Psychology, University of California, Santa Barbara, Santa Barbara, CA 93106.

Carolyn E. Cutrona, Department of Psychology, Iowa State University, Ames, IA 50011.

John Eckenrode, Human Development and Family Studies, Cornell University, Ithaca, NY 14853,

Benjamin H. Gottlieb, Department of Psychology, University of Guelph, Guelph, Ontario, Canada N1G 2W1.

Stephen Hamilton, Human Development and Family Studies, Cornell University, Ithaca, NY 14853.

Vicki S. Helgeson, Department of Psychology, Carnegie Mellon University, Pittsburgh, PA 15213.

Brian Lakey, Department of Psychology, Wayne State University, Detroit, MI 48202.

Harry T. Reis, Department of Psychology, University of Rochester, Rochester, NY 14627.

Karen S. Rook, Department of Psychology and Social Behavior, University of California, Irvine, Irvine, CA 92697.

Teresa E. Seeman, Division of Geriatrics, UCLA School of Medicine, Los Angeles, CA 90095.

Ori Shinar, Department of Epidemiology and Social Medicine, Albert Einstein College of Medicine of Yeshiva University, Bronx, NY 10461.

Lynn G. Underwood, Fetzer Institute, 9292 West KL Avenue, Kalamazoo, MI 49009.

Thomas A. Wills, Department of Epidemiology and Social Medicine, Albert Einstein College of Medicine of Yeshiva University, Bronx, NY 10461.

PART I

Theoretical and Historical Perspectives

1

Social Relationships and Health

Sheldon Cohen
Benjamin H. Gottlieb
Lynn G. Underwood

I. Approaches to Studying Social Support and Health
   A. The Sociological Tradition
   B. The Cognitive Tradition and the Stress-Buffering Hypothesis
   C. The Interpersonal Process Tradition
   D. The Intervention Tradition
II. How Social Relationships Influence Health
   A. Main Effect Model
   B. Stress-Buffering Model
   C. Threshold or Gradient?
III. Research Directions
   A. Support Measures
   B. Support Interventions
IV. Goals and Organization
   A. Outline of Measurement Chapters
   B. Outline of Intervention Chapters
V. Conclusion

The importance of social relationships in the treatment of disease and the maintenance of health and well-being has drawn the attention of scientists and practitioners across a large number of behavioral science and medical disciplines. Prospective population studies have established associations between measures of interpersonal relationships and mortality, psychiatric and physical morbidity, and adjustment to and recovery from chronic diseases (reviews by Berkman, Vaccarino, & Seeman, 1993; Broadhead et al., 1983; S. Cohen, 1988; S. Cohen & Wills, 1985; Helgeson, S. Cohen, & Fritz, 1998; House, Landis, & Umberson, 1988; Reifman, 1995). Interventions designed to alter the social environment and the individual's transactions with it have been successful in facilitating psychological adjustment, aiding recovery from traumatic experiences, and even in extending life for persons with serious chronic disease (e.g., Andersen, 1992; Fawzy et al., 1990; Spiegel, Bloom & Kraemer, 1989).

However, increases in social contact, social interaction, and the provision of social resources are not always health protective. Comprehensive reviews of this literature suggest that many of the characteristics of social environments and relationships that are presumed to be beneficial are not associated with better health (S. Cohen & Wills, 1985; Schwarzer & Leppin, 1989). Moreover, attempts to improve health and well-being by planned interventions have had mixed success (Bourgeois, Schulz, & Burgio, 1996; Coates & Winston, 1983; Cowan & Cowan, 1986; Helgeson & Cohen, 1996; Hughes, 1988; Lavoie, 1995). In short, the associations between social relationships and health are complex, and it is challenging to design successful social interventions. It is the premise of this book that the design of effective studies and interventions requires careful consideration of the processes occurring in social relationships, the determinants of health outcomes, and their mutual relations.

This book emphasizes the importance of beginning the planning of studies and interventions with a theory of how social relationships are linked to health. On the measurement side, we discuss different ways of conceiving and measuring people's interactions with others. We argue that appropriate conceptualization of relationships and social interactions is central to the development and testing of theories of how our interpersonal lives influence our health. We also address the choice of measures to aid in designing and evaluating support interventions. On the intervention side, we discuss the importance of explicitly testing a theory of the intervention. We emphasize that a support intervention has to focus on emotions, cognitions, and behaviors that prior research has shown to be consequential for health and adjustment. We also encourage the use of intervention as a quasi-experimental technique for testing theories about how the social environment influences health.

Even the casual reader may have noticed that until this point we have emphasized the role of social relationships and have generally avoided the popular term *social support*. Social support is often used in a broad sense, referring to any process through which social relationships might promote health and well-being. This book adopts this view of support but also identifies different processes through which social relationships can influence health. We categorize these processes into two groups. One type of process involves the provision or exchange of emotional, informational, or instrumental resources in response to the perception that others are in need of such aid. These needs are often associated with acute or chronic stressful experiences such as illness, life events, developmental transitions, and addiction. In this model, the term *social support* is used to refer to the social resources that persons perceive to be available or that are actually provided to them by nonprofessionals in the context of both formal support groups and informal helping relationships.

The other type of process we address focuses on the health benefits that accrue from participation in one or more distinct social groups. The hypothesis here is that others can influence cognitions, emotions, behaviors, and biological responses in manners beneficial to health and well-being through interactions that are not explicitly intended to exchange help or support. Examples of pathways through which these benefits might occur are the effects of human relationships on the diversity of our self-concepts, feelings of self-worth and personal control, and conformity to behavioral norms that have implications for our health.

This book focuses primarily on characteristics of social relationships that are thought to maintain or promote psychological and physical health. However, even these select characteristics have the potential for harm. For example, those with more close friends and family members have more opportunities for interpersonal conflict than their relatively isolated counterparts. Moreover, the provision of aid in the face of a crisis can have detrimental effects on a recipient when the source or type of aid is inappropriate. Hence, in discussing each social concept and in planning interventions, we also address potentially harmful social and psychological processes.

This chapter begins with a history of the theoretical perspectives on the importance of social relationships for health and well-being. It then presents a series of models that explain how social factors can influence health and discusses the challenges facing the field in regard to the development of measurements and interventions. The chapter concludes with an overview of the remainder of the volume.

APPROACHES TO STUDYING SOCIAL SUPPORT AND HEALTH

The Sociological Tradition

One hundred years ago, Durkheim (1897/1951) postulated that the breakdown in family, community, and work ties that occurred when workers migrated to industrial areas would be detrimental to psychological well-being. The breakdown in social ties was thought to produce a loss of social resources and a reduction in social constraints based on well-defined norms and social roles (Brownell & Schumaker, 1984; Heller, 1979). Durkheim (1897) found that suicides were more prevalent among those with fewer social ties, and other sociologists found similar increases in social disorganization and behavior problems among uprooted populations, including immigrants (Thomas & Znaniecki, 1920) and those forced to leave their communities to find work (Park & Burgess, 1926).

Interest in the relations between social ties and psychological well-being was rekindled in the 1970s and 1980s. Several studies found that those who participated in their community and the larger society were in better mental health than their more isolated counterparts (e.g., Bell, LeRoy, & Stephenson, 1982; Miller & Ingram, 1979; review in S. Cohen & Wills, 1985). Social network participation, known as *social integration*, was generally measured in terms of the diversity of relationships one participated in. Relationships assessed in a typical social integration measure included spouse, close family member, friend, neighbor, and social and religious group member. The more types of relationships persons reported, the greater their level of social integration.

At the same time, social epidemiologists were using similar social integration measures in their studies of the role of social ties in physical morbidity and mortality. In a seminal study, Berkman and Syme (1979) examined the association between social integration and mortality in a 9-year follow-up of residents of Alameda County, California. Those who were more socially integrated at the outset of the study lived longer than their counterparts who had fewer types of social ties. Increased longevity among socially integrated persons has since been replicated in several large prospective epidemiologic studies (e.g., Blazer, 1982; Cerhan & Wallace, 1997; House, Robbins, & Metzner, 1982; Schoenbach, Kaplan, Fredman, & Kleinbaum, 1986; Vogt, Mullooly, Ernst, Pope, & Hollis, 1992). Moreover, socially integrated persons have also been found to be less likely to have heart attacks (Kaplan et al., 1988), less likely to develop upper respiratory illness when experimentally exposed to a common cold virus (S. Cohen et al., 1997), and more likely to survive breast cancer (Vogt et al.; Funch & Marshall, 1983; reviewed in Helgeson et al., 1997). The health risks associated with lower levels of social integration are comparable in magnitude to the risks associated with cigarette smoking, high blood pressure, and obesity and are still significant after controlling for these and other traditional risk factors (House et al., 1988).

There is still some controversy about which characteristics of social networks are essential to health. Social integration, whether defined as having a diverse range of relationships (S. Cohen et al., 1997; Thoits, 1983) or involvement in a range of social activities (e.g., House et al., 1982), has received the most support, while number of network members has proved less important. However, there are other structural dimensions of social networks that may have a bearing on health and deserve more systematic investigation (e.g., Wellman, 1985; See chapter 3 of this book).

The Cognitive Tradition and the Stress-Buffering Hypothesis

In 1976, physician and epidemiologist John Cassel and psychiatrist Sidney Cobb argued that those with strong social ties were protected from the potential pathogenic effects of stressful events. Cassel (1976) thought that stressors which placed persons at risk for disease were often characterized by confusing or absent feedback from the social environment. In contrast, the impact of the stressors was mitigated or precluded among individuals whose networks provided them with consistent communication of what is expected of them, support and assistance with tasks, evaluation of their performance, and appropriate rewards (Cassel, 1976). Similarly, Cobb (1976) thought that major life transitions and crises placed people at risk. He argued that those who interpreted communications from others as signifying that they were cared for and loved, esteemed and valued, and that they belonged to a network of mutual obligation were protected. He thought that this protection occurred because these perceptions facilitated coping and adaptation.

In 1985, Cohen and Wills reviewed more than 40 correlational studies designed to test the hypothesis that social support protected persons from the negative psychological consequences of life stress. They concluded that consistent evidence for stress-buffering was found among studies in which the social support measure assessed the perceived availability of social resources that were suited to ("matched") the needs elicited by the stressful event. The exact parameters on which stressful events and support resources need to match were elaborated by S. Cohen and McKay (1984), as well as by Cutrona and her colleagues (Cutrona & Russell, 1990). There was also evidence that emotional and esteem support provided protection against a wide range of different stressful events (S. Cohen & Wills, 1985). An essential component of these approaches has been that it is the *perception* that others will provide resources when they are needed that is key to stress-buffering (also see Wethington & Kessler, 1986). In short, the data suggest that whether or not one actually receives support is less important for health and adjustment than one's beliefs about its availability.

Chapter 4 includes a discussion of issues that have arisen in the study of stress-buffering and their implications for measurement. They include more careful measurement of the functions and sources of perceived and received support, as well as evaluations of their adequacy and sufficiency.

The Interpersonal Process Tradition

Over the last 20 years, interest in the design of effective social support interventions has spawned research on the dynamics involved in the expression and receipt of social support for those in stressful circumstances. The earliest approaches involved attempts to develop detailed classification schemes of various aspects of the support that is exchanged between people, in both dyadic and group contexts. These schemes were based on the self-reports of those providing or receiving support. For example, based on interviews with a sample of low-income, sole-support mothers, Gottlieb (1978) developed a set of 26 categories of informal helping behaviors that he organized into four classes: emotionally sustaining behaviors, problem-solving behaviors, indirect personal influence, and environmental action. This scheme provided the foundation for Barrera, Sandler, and Ramsay's (1981) Inventory of Socially Supportive Behaviors, which has been widely used as a tool to gauge the mobilization of network support.

At the same time, Levy (1979) studied support groups in several U.S. towns and cities, including groups focused on behavioral control, personal growth, support and coping, and counteracting stigma. He also developed a classification of the supportive exchanges that occur in mutual aid self-help (MASH) groups based on members' reports of supportive processes. Of the scheme's 28 categories, Levy found that the 9 most frequently occurring helping exchanges involved empathy, mutual affirmation, explanation, sharing, morale building, self-disclosure, positive reinforcement, personal goal setting, and catharsis. Other proposals for categories of support-intended behaviors (types of social resources) include emotional, informational, and tangible support (House & Kahn, 1985); esteem, belonging, informational, and tangible support (S. Cohen & McKay, 1984); and esteem, network (companionship), informational, tangible, and emotional support (Cutrona, Suhr, & MacFarlane, 1990). (See the review of alternative typologies in Cutrona and Russell, 1990.)

Others have examined how support is elicited and provided. For example, Cutrona and her colleagues (Cutrona et al., 1990) developed a framework that describes support elicitation strategies that differ in their directness and specificity. To communicate the kind of support desired, individuals can directly complain about the stressful situation they are grappling with, express doubt about their own coping abilities, or elicit support indirectly through nonverbal emotional displays. Barbee (1990) developed a framework for classifying how support is provided. Using scenarios and laboratory-based behavioral observation methods, she identified four types of "cheering-up" strategies, two reflecting efforts to actively provide problem- and emotion-focused support, and two reflecting efforts to help the recipient avoid or escape from the problem or the feelings it provokes.

Other work has addressed the interactional context in which support occurs and how it might influence the unfolding of the support process. For example, Barbee (1990) has examined how the two parties' moods affect the kinds of support that arise. She found that subjects in an induced positive mood tended to approach a partner's distress by offering suggestions, whereas those who were in a negative mood tended to engage in such avoidant behaviors as withdrawal and changing the subject. She also examined the helper's attributions regarding the controllability and importance of a stressful circumstance. Helpers who regarded the problem as controllable tended to be dismissive, while those who regarded the problem as uncontrollable tended to offer suggestions about how to cope with the problem or the feelings it provoked.

The contrasting effects of support solicited by would-be recipients and support spontaneously tendered by providers have been studied by Eckenrode and Wethington (1990). Among the benefits of receiving support from network members without explicitly requesting it are the preservation of self-esteem and a reinforced sense of intimacy and dependability in the relationship with the provider. Moreover, Eckenrode and Wethington (1990) observe that, by their very nature, some stressors are more visible to network members, allowing them to intervene earlier and without being asked to do so. Other stressors may be invisible to the network, either because they are actively concealed because of the embarrassment or stigma associated with them or because they are chronic in nature and therefore less likely to be noticed and interpreted as a cue to render support. Similarly, Steinberg and Gottlieb (1994) have shown that hidden messages underlying the support process, such as expectations of repayment, often undermine any positive effects of support.

The work discussed in this section provides evidence that the materialization and benefits of social support are strongly influenced by many personal, relational, situational, and emotional characteristics of the interactional context. Many contemporary studies use intensive diary techniques that allow on-line monitoring of social interactions to assess these processes. An overview of recent studies and techniques is provided in chapter 5.

The Intervention Tradition

Two of the most frequently quoted early investigators of social support admonished the social science community to act on the epidemiological evidence linking social ties to health by planning programs aimed to augment the support people exchange with others. John Cassel (1976) urged his audience to "attempt to improve and strengthen the social supports rather than reduce the exposure to the stressors" (p. 479); Sydney Cobb (1976) echoed his message and added that "we should start now to teach all our patients, both well and sick, how to give and receive social support" (p. 312).

Early network-centered interventions aimed to increase the responsiveness and upgrade the helping skills of informal community caregivers. Targets of these outreach programs included informal helping agents such as teachers, police, family physicians, and clergy. For example, Weisenfeld and Weis (1979) trained hairdressers to use a set of core helping skills while at the same time discouraging the use of helping tactics that were deemed to be less constructive. Compared to a control group of hairdressers who were equally motivated but did not have the time to participate in the training, those who participated altered their helping behaviors in the ways recommended by the program.

In a similar vein, D'Augelli, Vallance, Danish, Young, and Gerdes (1981) implemented a much larger and more ambitious initiative in two rural counties of Pennsylvania. The program planners recruited individuals who had been functioning as informal helpers in their own social networks and taught them the same kinds of generic helping skills the hairdressers in the previous study had learned. In addition, they trained them in crisis intervention and life development skills. This project also found evidence that the trainees adopted the helping skills they were taught. However, the evaluation stopped short of assessing the effects of the training on the intended beneficiaries, namely, those citizens who received the trainees' support.

The second approach to early support interventions also began in the late 1970s. It entailed the creation of support groups for people who had experienced a range of acute life events and crises, including bereavement, natural disasters, marital separation, and the transition to parenthood. Numerous short-term groups were designed to offer intensive, albeit temporary, support to these populations at risk.

One of the first and most carefully evaluated support groups was convened for bereaved women. It revealed that a sequence of one-to-one support from a veteran widow followed by participation in a group composed of widows hastened the participants' emotional and social adjustment (Vachon, Lyall, Rogers, Freedman-Letofsky, & Freeman, 1980). Other early examples include groups for new parents (McGuire & Gottlieb, 1979), for the parents of premature infants (Minde et al., 1980), and for women diagnosed with metastatic breast cancer (Spiegel, Bloom, & Yalom, 1981).

The third approach to mobilizing support involved the creation of one-to-one mentoring and coaching programs, in which a key supporter was drawn either from the beneficiary's existing social network or grafted onto it. A familiar example of a program involving mentors drawn from the general community is Big Brothers and Big Sisters. This organization attempts to compensate for the absence of one parent by recruiting and matching volunteers who provide companionship, guidance, and emotional support to children in single-parent households. An example of a widely known coaching initiative offered by public health departments is the encouragement of a spouse or partner's participation in birth and parenting preparation classes (Wideman & Singer, 1984). The idea is that the coach's presence will not only communicate caring and solidarity with the expectant mother but also serve an analgesic function during labor and delivery. In fact, one of the most widely cited pioneering support interventions was conducted in the maternity unit of the Social Security Hospital in Guatemala City. A female companion was randomly assigned to accompany and render support to half the expectant mothers who were admitted for their first delivery (Sosa, Kennell, Klaus, Robertson, & Urrutia, 1980). The untrained companion soothed and encouraged the mothers and made them more physically comfortable. Compared with mothers who received the maternity unit's routine medical care, those mothers assigned a birth companion experienced fewer serious complications during labor and delivery and required less than half the time from admission to delivery. In addition, during the hour after the baby's birth, these mothers stayed awake longer and stroked, talked to, and smiled at their infants more than the control group.

The chapters in the intervention section of this volume testify to the fact that these early initiatives have spurred much experimentation with support groups (see chapter 7) and one-to-one strategies of marshaling support (see chapter 8). This is not to say that interventions in the natural network have been neglected, compared with strategies of marshaling new social ties. Rather, as chapter 9 reveals, such interventions have shifted from teaching helping skills to effecting changes in the social network's overall structure or in patterns of interaction between certain members in order to optimize the expression of support or to reduce the likelihood that it will miscarry.

HOW SOCIAL RELATIONSHIPS INFLUENCE HEALTH

In general, social support is thought to affect mental and physical health through its influence on emotions, cognitions, and behaviors (S. Cohen, 1988). In the case of mental health, social support is thought to maintain regulation of these response systems and prevent extreme responses associated with dysfunction. This regulation occurs through communication of what is expected, of appropriate norms, of rewards and punishments, and through the provision of coping assistance (Caplan, 1974; Cassel, 1976; Thoits, 1986). Social support is also thought to play a role in the risk for, progression of, and recovery from physical illness. In this case, the hypothesis is that social relationships influence behaviors with implications for health such as diet, exercise, smoking, alcohol intake, sleep, and adherence to medical regimens. Moreover, the failure to regulate emotional responses also contributes to psychological problems and can trigger health-relevant changes in the responses of the neuroendocrine, immune, and cardiovascular systems (S. Cohen, 1988; S. Cohen, Kaplan, & Manuck, 1994; Uchino, Cacioppo, & Kiecolt-Glaser, 1996).

Two models that identify the conditions under which different kinds of social support influence health have evolved (S. Cohen & Wills, 1985; House, 1981).

The stress-buffering model proposes that support is related to well-being only (or primarily) for persons under stress. The main (or direct) effect model proposes that social resources have a beneficial effect irrespective of whether persons are under stress. In correlational studies, perceived availability of social resources is most often found to act as a stress buffer, whereas social integration generally does not interact with stress but instead acts independently of stress levels (reviews by S. Cohen & Wills, 1985; Schwarzer & Leppin, 1989). Even so, there are many examples of main effects of perceived support and occasional examples of stress-by-social-integration buffering interactions (e.g., Bolger & Eckenrode, 1991; Falk, Hanson, Isacsson, & Ostergren, 1992). Reports of main effects of perceived support may be wholly or partly attributable to the use of poor or inadequate measures of stressful events. In such cases, even though support was acting as a buffer, only a main effect of support would be found (Cassel, 1976). Conditions under which social integration or other network measures result in stress-buffering still need to be identified (see chapter 3).

Main Effect Model

Figure 1.1 depicts the mechanisms through which social relationships can have main effects on psychological and physical health. Those who participate in a social network are subject to social controls and peer pressures that influence normative health behaviors. For example, their networks might influence whether they exercise, eat low-fat diets, or smoke. Integration in a social network is also presumed to provide a source of generalized positive affect; senses of predictability and stability, of purpose, of belonging and security; and recognition of self-worth because of demonstrated ability to meet normative role expectations (Cassel, 1976; Hammer, 1981; Thoits, 1983; Wills, 1985). These positive psychological states are presumed to be beneficial because they reduce psychological despair (Thoits, 1985), result in greater motivation to care for oneself (e.g., S. Cohen & Syme, 1985), or result in suppressed neuroendocrine response and enhanced immune function (Bovard, 1959; Cassel, 1976; S. Cohen, 1988; Uchino et al., 1996). Having a wide range of network ties also provides multiple sources of information and thereby increases the probability of having access to an appropriate information source. Information could influence health-relevant behaviors or help one to avoid or minimize stressful or other high-risk situations. For example, network members could provide information regarding access to medical services or regarding the benefits of behaviors that positively influence health and well-being. A network may operate to prevent disease by providing tangible and economic services that result in better health and better health care for network members. For example, network members could provide food, clothing, and housing that operate to prevent disease and limit exposure to risk factors. Networks may also provide informal health care that prevents minor illnesses from developing into more serious disease.

It is also possible that isolation causes disease rather than social integration protecting or enhancing health. This approach assumes that isolation increases negative affect and a sense of alienation and decreases feelings of control and

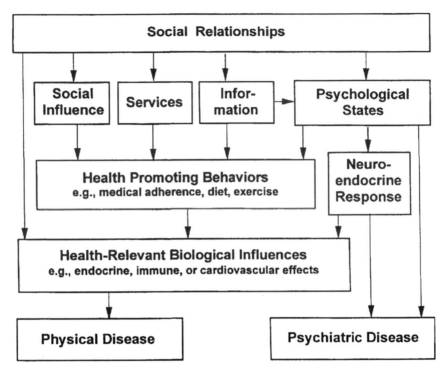

Figure 1.1. Pathways through which social relationships can have direct (main) effects on psychological and physical health. Paths are all drawn in one direction for simplicity but feedback loops are possible.

self-esteem. Alternatively, one can merely view isolation as a stressor. In any case, as noted earlier, these negative psychological states could induce increases in neuroendocrine response, suppress immune function, and interfere with performance of health behaviors.

It is possible that the effects of our social environment on pathways that influence health are not cognitively or behaviorally mediated but instead are "hardwired" responses to our social environment (Bovard, 1959). A hard-wiring hypothesis receiving some recent attention as a basis for intervention derives from work on the synchronization of human biological clocks (Frank et al., 1994). Regularly occurring social interaction is thought to play an important role in entraining and synchronizing our biological clocks (Moore-Ede, Sulzman, & Fuller, 1982). Desynchronization is thought to be harmful to homeostatic and adaptive functioning. Hence, isolated individuals or those who are removed from or lose members of their social network might be at risk for illness because of the loss of social controls over their biological rhythms (Hofer, 1984).

Although we have focused on the main effects associated with an integrated network, perceptions of support availability have also been associated with main (as well as buffering) effects. Such associations may be due to positive affective and cognitive states associated with the knowledge and security provided by the availability of others in times of need. Perceived availability may also buffer minor and daily stressors often not assessed in studies that focus on major stressful life events. Hence, what appears to be a main effect may actually be buffering of unassessed stressful situations. Stress-buffering mechanisms are described next.

Stress-Buffering Model

Figure 1.2 depicts the roles of social support in determining individual responses to potentially stressful events. In this case, support presumably operates by preventing responses to stressful events that are inimical to health. Support may play a role at several different points in the causal chain linking stressors to illness (cf. S. Cohen & McKay, 1984; Gore, 1981; House, 1981; also see the discussion of

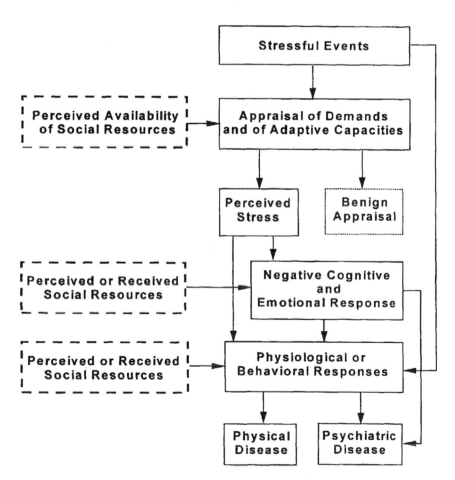

Figure 1.2. Pathways through which social support influences responses to stressful life events. Paths are all drawn in one direction for simplicity but feedback loops are possible.

coping and the appraisal process in Lazarus & Folkman, 1984). First, the belief that others will provide necessary resources may redefine the potential for harm posed by a situation and bolster one's perceived ability to cope with imposed demands, thereby preventing a particular situation from being appraised as highly stressful (Thoits, 1986). Second, support beliefs may reduce or eliminate the affective reaction to a stressful event, dampen physiologic responses to the event, or prevent or alter maladaptive behavioral responses. The availability of persons to talk to about problems has also been found to reduce the intrusive thoughts that act to maintain chronic maladaptive responses to stressful events (Lepore, Silver, Wortman, & Wayment, 1996).

The actual receipt of support could also play a role here. Support may alleviate the impact of stress appraisal by providing a solution to the problem, by reducing the perceived importance of the problem, or by providing a distraction from the problem. It might also tranquilize the neuroendocrine system so that people are less reactive to perceived stress or facilitate healthful behaviors such as exercise, personal hygiene, proper nutrition, and rest (cf. S. Cohen & Wills, 1985; House, 1981).

Threshold or Gradient?

To understand how social support works and how support interventions should be designed, it is necessary to assess the relative effect of increasing amounts of support. Perhaps there is a minimum amount of support required, and after that threshold is reached additional support does not provide greater benefits. It is also conceivable that increasing support is associated in a graded-like (dose-response) relation with increased health benefits. What makes it difficult to resolve this issue is that the answer is probably different for different conceptions (e.g., social integration versus available resources) or types (e.g., emotional versus tangible) of support. Greater progress will be made with the development and use of measurement instruments that have the sensitivity to reliably assess grades of support.

RESEARCH DIRECTIONS

Support Measures

This book underscores the importance of a theoretical perspective and clarity of concepts in research on the role of social relationships in health. There is convincing evidence that social networks and support influence our health. What we need to know now is which network structures and support functions, under what conditions, and for what reasons? This is the level of knowledge that can provide a deeper understanding of how social relationships influence our health and give us the necessary guideposts for the development of successful models of intervention. Taking a theoretical perspective means using a measurement strategy that is tailored to specific research aims and contexts.

In this section of the chapter, we give examples of a number of important questions about the connection between social relationships and health that can be addressed through the creative use of existing measures and the development of new ones. We start with questions about the importance of the structure of social networks. Some of the most provocative evidence in regard to the relations between our social environment and health derives from research on social integration. Those who actively participate in their community and society live longer and are less likely to develop both physical and mental health problems. However, we have little direct evidence for why social participation promotes health. Let us consider three hypotheses: (1) socially integrated people have more diverse self-concepts (parent, friend, worker, and member of a church), and this diversity makes stressful events in any one social domain (e.g., at work) less important; (2) socially integrated people have a more diverse resource pool to call on when under stress; and (3) socially integrated people have a better quality and greater quantity of social interactions, resulting in increased positive affect and decreased negative affect. The relative viability of these competing explanations can be tested by existing measurement techniques. For example, daily diary techniques (chapter 5) can be used to assess the quality and quantity of social interaction, as well as the associated affect, and social integration measures that assess participation in social activities can be compared with those that assess role diversity per se (chapter 3).

There are also many theoretically important questions facing those interested in measurement of support resources (see chapter 4). For example, what is the most useful typology of resources? What are the conditions under which selective resources become effective? Are network members substitutable with respect to the resources they provide? Answering these questions requires further theoretical development of resource typologies and the development of measures to accurately assess resource availability and receipt. This is also an area where the use of daily diary techniques can be helpful in learning about how often support is given and received in day-to-day interactions, the kinds of support that are provided, and their effectiveness.

A critical area of research that has received little attention is the effects of stress on support networks and on perceived and received support. This is a particularly important question for persons with chronic illnesses and their caregivers. Does social participation (integration) deteriorate with illness? Does the quantity, quality, or type of social support change? Do persons under chronic stress stop providing support, thereby creating an imbalance with network members? In this area, simultaneous measurement of network structure (see chapter 3) and function (see chapter 4) may elucidate underlying processes. For example, is support availability more robust among those with diverse (socially integrated) networks? Many of these questions can be addressed with current measurement technology or by tailoring existing measures.

Finally, there is the question of choosing or designing scales to assess the extent to which a support intervention influences the type of support it was intended or designed to generate. The design of these measures depends on the theoretical model on which the intervention is based. For example, some interventions aim to increase both the perception and availability of emotional support, some to augment informational support, and others to mobilize tangible support (see chapters 7, 8, and 9). Although there are increasing numbers of evaluations of the effects of these interventions on specified outcomes, few have also evaluated the hypothesized mediating mechanisms (see chapter 6). Such analyses are essential to understanding why interventions succeed or fail.

Although we have identified some of the important questions facing the field, there are numerous other research questions. The critical issue is that questions are posed and addressed in a manner that adds to our theoretical understanding of the role that social relationships play in health. We especially encourage studies that assess as many levels of these theoretical models as possible, including the social network, interpersonal behaviors, perceptions of support, behavioral and biological concomitants, and health outcomes (e.g., S. Cohen, et al., 1997). In the end, these multifaceted studies will provide the answers to how social relationships influence health and well-being.

Support Interventions

During the two decades that followed the pioneering interventions described earlier, advances in theory and measurement have spurred a new generation of studies involving systematic manipulation of social support on behalf of diverse clinical and community samples. In an effort to translate basic research into practice, demonstration projects and clinical trials have been designed to augment, specialize, intensify, or prolong various types and sources of support for people who are at risk by virtue of particular illnesses, life events, developmental transitions, addictions, or chronic stressors. For example, support groups have been widely implemented in medical settings for persons with such chronic diseases as multiple sclerosis and arthritis, as well as for patients with cancer and heart disease (Devins & Binik, 1996; Fawzy, Fawzy, Arndt, & Pasnau, 1995; Helgeson & Cohen, 1996). In mental health settings, support groups and peer counseling initiatives have been introduced on behalf of people with affective disorders and members of their families. Programs modeled after the Alcoholic Anonymous 12-step recovery strategy have also gained favor, along with those that deploy home visitors to reach underserved community populations such as teenage mothers (Olds et al., 1997) and family caregivers of persons with Alzheimer's disease (Bourgeois, et al., 1996; Lavoie, 1995). In addition, partner support manuals have been developed to assist people who are trying to quit smoking, lose weight, or moderate or control their use of addictive substances (Gottlieb, 1988), and a variety of support initiatives have been launched in workplace health promotion campaigns (R. Y. Cohen, 1988).

Collectively, these group and dyadic interventions are impressive because they reveal the many ways in which it may be possible to engineer support on behalf of people in highly diverse stressful circumstances. However, to date, there is more evidence of the feasibility of marshaling support than of its effectiveness. For example, two reviews of the outcomes of support groups for family caregivers of elderly persons paint a bleak picture with respect to the attainment of desired end states (Lavoie, 1995; Toseland & Rossiter, 1989). The same is true in the context of support groups for cancer patients (Fawzy et al., 1995; Helgeson & Cohen, 1996). Although the authors of these reviews offer their own explanations for the null or mixed findings, such as the facts that the goals of the group were not determined by the intended beneficiaries and that the intervention ended prematurely, the arguments they advance are purely speculative. The program planners did not collect information about the interpersonal dynamics that contributed to and detracted from the desired support process, much less about specific mechanisms that were hypothesized to mediate between stress and well-being. These mediators may involve psychological (e.g., self-efficacy or self-concept), behavioral (e.g., coping efforts or role functioning), emotional (e.g., distress or specific psychiatric symptomatology), or physiologic (e.g., endocrine or immune system functioning or markers of disease progression) processes. In sum, to gain a stronger theoretical grasp of the effects of support and to provide a stronger empirical basis for future interventions, it is necessary to elucidate and test alternative mediating processes that have been proposed to account for the impacts of social support on health and well-being (see chapter 2).

In addition, more concerted efforts should be made to identify the characteristics of those who benefit most and least from the support process. For example, variability in the effects of support may be attributable to differences in the participants' initial risk status, social skills, or network relationships. It is conceivable, for example, that only the most socially isolated individuals reap significant benefits from their contact with new sources of support. Alternatively, perhaps those who suffer from the greatest emotional isolation or from the most conflict with their existing associates benefit most from planned opportunities to exchange support with similar peers. Moreover, as discussed in chapter 7, it may be necessary to screen prospective support group members in terms of their coping and information-seeking styles prior to assigning them to a group to ensure an optimal fit between the individual and the group's structure and social climate. In sum, significant advances in our understanding of the people and conditions that are most and least hospitable to the expression and beneficial effects of support depend on the collection of more detailed information about the participants and about the supportive processes hypothesized to affect their health and well-being.

Another challenge that awaits those planning support interventions is the exquisitely delicate task of creating the conditions that are most hospitable to the formation of relationships that, over time, come to have supportive meaning. As Rutter (1987) observed, social support is not a variable; it is a process that arises through interaction between people. Nor is social support a commodity that can be "delivered" or abstracted from its relational context. Indeed, relationships imbue behavior with supportive meaning, and expressions of support, its withdrawal, and its unexpected absence powerfully affect people's relationships with others. Hence, whether a support group, a home visitor, or a telephone confidant is marshaled to provide support, the program designers have to carefully consider how to make the most auspicious matches from a relationship development standpoint. They will need to consider characteristics of the setting, the kinds of information about the parties to make most and least salient to one another, the kinds of interactions that are most conducive to relationship formation and the expression of support, and how to customize the intervention to each party's particular needs. At the same time, they need to work from a master blueprint that specifies how to enhance coping with the participants' stressful circumstances.

Clues to the important processes involved in relationship development are contained in the literature on close relationships and in some of the better support intervention studies. For example, from the study of the initiation phase of close relationships, we know that attraction and positive affect increase as a function of the parties' perceived similarity, equity in exchanges, and reciprocal disclosure of personal information (Hendrick & Hendrick, 1992). As pointed out in chapter 7, support groups must be carefully composed of people who are likely to view one another as similar with respect to both the nature of their adversity and their demographic characteristics. In addition, group cohesion strongly depends on the expression of mutual aid in response to reciprocal disclosures of experiences and feelings. Hence, as people's supportive requirements begin to be met through these initial perceptions and communications, their interactions begin to take on relationship meaning, setting the stage for greater depth of social penetration and further relationship development. In fact, in their analysis of the outcomes of support groups for the bereaved, Lieberman and Videka-Sherman (1986) found that the greatest benefits accrued to those who formed new friendships characterized by mutual exchanges. For this reason, they state that these groups "are social linkage systems where people form relationships, and in that sense, they provide social support" (p. 442).

Other social psychological factors have also been found to play a critical role in the development of relationships between home visitors and those they visit and between mentors and their protégés. For interactions to take on supportive meaning, the intended support recipient must be reassured about the provider's motives for helping and should not experience ego-relevant costs, feelings of indebtedness, or threats to autonomy from the interactional process (Gottlieb, 1992). Evidence from the literature on recipient reactions to aid underscores these conclusions. It suggests that the intervention will not be seen as supportive if the helper is perceived to be motivated by ulterior motives or acting involuntarily or if the offer of aid carries pejorative implications about the recipient's competence or constrains his or her freedom of action and decision making (Fisher, Nadler, & Whitcher-Alagna, 1982). Equally important, a social psychological context marked by these features does not offer the conditions necessary for relationship development.

In retrospect, it is not surprising that early interventions which concentrated on teaching helping skills to community gatekeepers and to central figures in social networks were abandoned. Our current appreciation of the complex and delicate nature of the support process militates against such a simplistic intervention strategy because it does not take into account the many contingencies that we now recognize govern the expression and acceptance of social support. However, as the chapters in the second half of this book reveal, the two types of interventions that continue to draw great interest—namely, support groups and dyads—along with more focused network-centered initiatives, hold far greater promise. These interventions can be more tightly controlled, in terms of the characteristics of the participants, the key maneuvers, and the dosage of support, which, in turn, facilitates evaluation of their outcomes through the use of conventional research designs, such as randomized controlled trials and assessment of alternative mediating processes.

Although we have tried to pose some of the most important issues involved in designing successful interventions, there are numerous other important questions. The critical issue is that interventions are designed in a manner that adds to a broad theoretical understanding of how support can influence health. By focusing on explicit theories of intervention, we will be able to use existing knowledge to maximize effectiveness while adding to our understanding of how, when, and why interventions are successful.

GOALS AND ORGANIZATION

The fundamental goal of this book is to provide a resource for the selection and development of state-of-the-art techniques for social support assessment and intervention in studies of physical and psychiatric illness in human populations. Subgoals include:

- To provide a broad conceptual framework addressing the role of social relationships in mental and physical health.
- To aid researchers in understanding the conceptual criteria on which measurement and intervention decisions should be made when studying the relations between social support and health.
- To present diverse options for social support measurement, and an analytic framework for decision making in the selection of measures.
- To present diverse options for social support interventions, and an analytic framework for decision making in their selection.

The remainder of the volume is divided into three sections. The first addresses the measurement of social networks and supports. The second addresses support interventions, and the third presents some general comments on the volume and its implications for social support research and intervention.

Outline of Measurement Chapters

Part II of this volume addresses the measurement of social support. The purpose of this section is to aid researchers in making decisions about the appropriate measures to use in specific studies. The overall idea is to provide the conceptual underpinnings of the measure, describe the kinds of studies it is appropriate for, and list the various costs and benefits of using such a measure. We have asked the authors to discuss conceptual or theoretical bases for the measurement techniques they address, questions about the relation between social support and health that can be answered by using the specific measurement technique, the logistical issues that must be considered in using these measures, possible negative effects of our social relationships as measured by this technique, the psychometrics of each measurement instrument, the population sensitivity of the measures, and priorities for future research.

Outline of Intervention Chapters

Part III of this volume addresses different types of interventions to increase social support in the natural environment. The purpose of this section is to aid researchers in making decisions regarding the design of effective interventions. The overall idea is to provide the conceptual underpinnings of these interventions, describe situations for which they would be appropriate, and outline the various costs and benefits of each type of intervention strategy. In this case, authors were instructed to discuss theories underlying the specific type of intervention they address, the crucial considerations in the intervention's design, exemplars of applications to specific populations or stressors, people for whom this intervention is expected to be more or less successful, indicators of support mechanisms and of miscarried support, short-and long-term indicators of impact and potential unintended side effects, the key guiding principles and recommendations, and priorities for future research on this type of intervention.

CONCLUSION

Evidence on the role social relationships play in health is provocative and exciting. However, only by testing and refining theories that account for the associations between social relationships and health can we make substantial strides in understanding these associations and in designing and implementing effective social interventions. It is our hope that this book will help investigators and clinicians to generate theoretical models and measure appropriate aspects of the social context to test and apply them.

REFERENCES

Andersen, B. L. (1992). Psychological interventions for cancer patients to enhance quality of life. *Journal of Consulting and Clinical Psychology, 60,* 552–568.

Barbee, A. P. (1990). Interactive coping: The cheering-up process in close relationships. In S. Duck (Ed.), *Personal relationships and social support* (pp. 46–65). Newbury Park, CA: Sage.

Barrera, M. Jr., Sandler, I. N., & Ramsay, T. B. (1981). Preliminary development of a scale of social support: Studies on college students. *American Journal of Community Psychology, 9,* 435–447.

Bell, R. A., LeRoy, J. B., & Stephenson, J. J. (1982). Evaluating the mediating effects of social supports upon life events and depressive symptoms. *Journal of Community Psychology, 10,* 325–340.

Berkman, L. F., & Syme, S. L. (1979). Social networks, host resistance and mortality: A nine-year follow-up study of Alameda County residents. *American Journal of Epidemiology, 109*, 186–204.

Berkman, L. F., Vaccarino, V., & Seeman, T. (1993). Gender differences in cardiovascular morbidity and mortality: The contribution of social networks and support. *Annals of Behavioral Medicine, 15*, 112–118.

Blazer, D. G. (1982). Social support and mortality in an elderly community population. *American Journal of Epidemiology, 115*, 684–694.

Bolger, N., & Eckenrode, J. (1991). Social relationships, personality, and anxiety during a major stressful event. *Journal of Personality and Social Psychology, 61*, 440–449.

Bourgeois, M. S., Schulz, R., & Burgio, L. (1996). Interventions for caregivers of patients with Alzheimer's disease: A review and analysis of content, process, and outcomes. *International Journal of Aging and Human Development, 43*, 35–92.

Bovard, E. (1959). The effects of social stimuli on the response to stress. *Psychological Reviews, 66*, 267–277.

Broadhead, W. E., Kaplan, B. H., James, S. A., Wagner, E. H., Schoenbach, V. J., Grimson, R., Heyden, S., Tibblin, G., & Gehlbach, S. H. (1983). The epidemiologic evidence for a relationship between social support and health. *American Journal of Epidemiology, 117*, 521–537.

Brownell, A., & Schumaker, S. A. (1984). Social support: An introduction to a complex phenomenon. *Journal of Social Issues, 40*, 1–10.

Caplan, G. (1974). *Support systems and community mental health.* New York: Behavioral Publications.

Cassel, J. (1976). The contribution of the social environment to host resistance. *American Journal of Epidemiology, 104*, 107–123.

Cerhan, J. R., & Wallace, R. B. (1997). Change in social ties and subsequent mortality in rural elders. *Epidemiology, 8*, 475–481.

Coates, D., & Winston, T. (1983). Counteracting the deviance of depression: Peer support groups for victims. *Journal of Social Issues, 39*, 169–194.

Cobb, S. (1976). Social support as a moderator of life stress. *Psychosomatic Medicine, 38*, 300–314.

Cohen, R. Y. (1988). Mobilizing support for weight loss through work-site competitions. In B. H. Gottlieb (Ed.), *Marshaling social support: Formats, processes and effects* (pp. 241–264). Newbury Park, CA: Sage.

Cohen, S. (1988). Psychosocial models of social support in the etiology of physical disease. *Health Psychology, 7*, 269–297.

Cohen, S., Doyle, W. J., Skoner, D. P., Rabin, B. S., & Gwaltney, J. M. Jr. (1997). Social ties and susceptibility to the common cold. *Journal of the American Medical Association, 277*, 1940–1944.

Cohen, S., Kaplan, J. R., & Manuck, S. B. (1994). Social support and coronary heart disease: Underlying psychologic and biologic mechanisms. In S. A. Shumaker & S. M. Czajkowski (Eds.), *Social support and cardiovascular disease.* New York: Plenum.

Cohen, S., & McKay, G. (1984). Social support, stress and the buffering hypothesis: A theoretical analysis. In A. Baum, S. E. Taylor, & J. E. Singer (Eds.), *Handbook of psychology and health* (pp. 253–267). Hillsdale, NJ: Lawrence Erlbaum.

Cohen, S., & Syme, S. L. (1985). Issues in the study and application of social support. In S. Cohen and S. L. Syme (Eds.), *Social support and health* (pp. 3–22). New York: Academic.

Cohen, S., & Wills, T. A. (1985). Stress, social support, and the buffering hypothesis. *Psychological Bulletin, 98*, 310–357.

Cowan, C. P., & Cowan, P. A. (1986). A preventive intervention for couples becoming parents. In C. F. Z. Boukydis (Ed.), *Research on support for parents and infants in the postnatal period*. New York: Ablex.

Cutrona, C. E., & Russell, D. W. (1990). Type of social support and specific stress: Toward a theory of optimal matching. In B. R. Sarason, I. G. Sarason, & G. R. Pierce (Eds.), *Social support: An interactional view*. New York: Wiley.

Cutrona, C. E., Suhr, J. A., & MacFarlane, R. (1990). Interpersonal transactions and the psychological sense of support. In S. Duck (Ed.), *Personal relationships and social support* (pp. 30–45). Newbury Park, CA: Sage.

D'Augelli, A., Vallance, T., Danish, S., Young, P., & Gerdes, J. (1981). The community helpers project: A description of a prevention strategy for rural communities. *Journal of Prevention, 1*, 209–224.

Devins, G. M., & Binik, Y. M. (1996). Facilitation coping with chronic physical illness. In M. Zeidner & N. Endler (Eds.), *Handbook of coping* (pp. 640–696). New York: John Wiley.

Durkheim, E. (1951). *Suicide*. New York: Free Press.

Eckenrode, J. E., & Wethington, E. (1990). The process and outcome of mobilizing social support. In S. Duck (Ed.), *Personal relationships and social support* (pp. 83–103). Newbury Park, CA: Sage.

Falk, A., Hanson, B. S., Isacsson, S. O., & Ostergren, P. O. (1992). Job strain and mortality in elderly men: Social network, support, and influence as buffers. *American Journal of Public Health, 82*, 1136–1139.

Fawzy, F. I., Cousins, N., Fawzy, N. W., Kemeny, M. E., Elashoff, R., & Morton, D. (1990). A structured psychiatric intervention for cancer patients: 1. Changes over time in methods of coping and affective disturbance. *Cancer Intervention, 47*, 720–725.

Fawzy, F. I., Fawzy, N. W., Arndt, L. A., & Pasnau, R. O. (1995). Critical review of psychosocial interventions in cancer care. *Archives of General Psychiatry, 52*, 100–113.

Fisher, J. D., Nadler, A., & Whitcher-Alagna, S. (1982). Recipient reactions to aid. *Psychological Bulletin, 91*, 27–54.

Frank, E., Kupfer, D. J., Ehlers, C. L., Monk, T. H., Cornes, C., Carter, S., & Frankel, D. Interpersonal and social rhythm therapy for bipolar disorder: Integrating interpersonal and behavioral approaches. *The Behavioral Therapist, 17*, 143–149.

Funch, D. P., & Marshall, J. (1983). The role of stress, social support, and age in survival from breast cancer. *Journal of Psychosomatic Research, 27*, 77–83.

Gore, S. (1981). Stress-buffering functions of social supports: An appraisal and clarification of research models. In B. S. Dohrenwend & B. P. Dohrenwend (Eds.), *Stressful life events and their contexts* (pp. 202–222). New York: Prodist.

Gottlieb, B. H. (1978). The development and application of a classification scheme of informal helping behaviors. *Canadian Journal of Behavioural Science, 10*, 105–115.

Gottlieb, B. H. (1988). Support interventions: A typology and agenda for research. In S. Duck (Ed.), *Handbook of personal relationships: Theory, research and interventions* (pp. 519–542). Chichester, England: John Wiley.

Gottlieb, B. H. (1992). Quandaries in translating support concepts to intervention. In H. O. F. Veiel & U. Baumann (Eds.), *The meaning and measurement of social support* (pp. 293–309). Washington, DC: Hemisphere.

Hammer, M. (1981). "Core" and "extended" social networks in relation to health and illness. *Social Science and Medicine, 17*, 405–411.

Helgeson, V., & Cohen, S. (1996). Social support and adjustment to cancer: Reconciling descriptive, correlational, and intervention research. *Health Psychology, 15*, 135–148.

Helgeson, V., Cohen, S., & Fritz, H. L. (1998). Social ties and cancer. In J. C. Holland (Ed.), *Psycho-oncology*, New York: Oxford University Press.

Heller, K. (1979). The effects of social support: Prevention and treatment implications. In A. P. Goldstein & F. H. Kanfer (Eds.), *Maximizing treatment gains: Transfer enhancement in psychotherapy* (pp. 353–382). New York: Academic.

Hendrick, S., & Hendrick, C. (1992). *Liking, loving, and relating*. Belmont, CA: Brooks/Cole.

Hofer, M. A. (1984). Relationships as regulators: A psychobiologic perspective on bereavement. *Psychosomatic Medicine, 46*, 183–197.

House, J. S. (1981). *Work stress and social support*. Reading, MA: Addison-Wesley.

House, J. S., & Kahn, R. L. (1985). Measures and concepts of social support. In S. Cohen & S. L. Syme (Eds.), *Social support and health* (pp. 83–103). New York: Academic.

House, J. S., Landis, K. R., & Umberson, D. (1988). Social relationships and health. *Science, 241*, 540–545.

House, J. S., Robbins, C., & Metzner, H. L. (1982). The association of social relationships and activities with mortality: Prospective evidence form the Tecumseh Community Health Study. *American Journal of Epidemiology, 116*, 123–140.

Hughes, R. J. (1988). Divorce and social support: A review. *Journal of Divorce, 11(3/4)*, 123–145.

Kaplan, G. A., Salonen, J. T., Cohen, R. D., Brand, R. J., Syme, S. L., & Puska, P. (1988). Social connections and mortality from all causes and from cardiovascular disease: Prospective evidence from eastern Finland. *American Journal of Epidemiology, 128*, 370–380.

Lavoie, J. P. (1995). Support groups for informal caregivers don't work! Refocus the groups or the evaluations? *Canadian Journal on Aging, 14*, 580–595.

Lazarus, R. S., & Folkman, S. (1984). *Stress, coping, and adaptation*. New York: Springer.

Lepore, S. J., Silver, R. C., Wortman, C. B., & Wayment, H. A. (1996). Social constraints, intrusive thoughts, and depressive symptoms among bereaved mothers. *Journal of Personality and Social Psychology, 70*, 271–282.

Levy, L. H. (1979). Processes and activities in groups. In M. A. Lieberman & L. D. Borman (Eds.), *Self-help groups for coping with crisis* (pp. 234–271). San Francisco: Jossey-Bass.

Lieberman, M. A., & Videka-Sherman, L. (1986). The impact of self-help groups on the mental health of widows and widowers. *American Journal of Orthopsychiatry, 56*, 435–449.

McGuire, J., & Gottlieb, B. H. (1979). Social support groups among new parents: An experimental study in primary prevention. *Journal of Child Clinical Psychology, 8,* 111–116.

Miller, P. M., & Ingram, J. G. (1979). Reflections on the life events to illness link with some preliminary findings. In I. G. Sarason & C. D. Speilberger (Eds.), *Stress and anxiety* (pp. 313–336). New York: Hemisphere.

Minde K., Shosenberg, N., Marton, P., Thompson, J., Ripley, J., & Burns, S. (1980). Self-help groups in a premature nursery: A controlled evaluation. *Journal of Pediatrics, 96,* 933–940.

Moore-Ede, M. C., Sulzman, F. M., & Fuller, C. A. (1982). *The clocks that time us.* Cambridge, MA: Harvard University Press.

Olds, D. L., Eckenrode, J., Henderson, C. Z. Kitzman, H., Powers, J., Cole, R., Sidora, K. Morris, P. Pettitt, L. M. & Luckey, D. (1997). Long-term effects of home visitation on maternal life course and child abuse and neglect. *Journal of the American Medical Association, 278,* 637–643.

Park, R., & Burgess, E. (Eds.). (1926). *The city.* Chicago: University of Chicago Press.

Reifman, A. (1995). Social relationships, recovery from illness, and survival: A literature review. *Annals of Behavioral Medicine, 17,* 124–131.

Rutter, M. (1987). Psychosocial resilience and protective mechanisms. *American Journal of Orthopsychiatry, 57,* 316–326.

Schoenbach, V. J., Kaplan, B. H., Fredman, L., & Kleinbaum, D. G. (1986). Social ties and mortality in Evans County, Georgia. *American Journal of Epidemiology, 123,* 577–591.

Schwarzer, R., & Leppin, A. (1989). Social support and health: A meta-analysis. *Psychology and Health, 3,* 1–15.

Sosa, R., Kennell, J., Klaus, M., Robertson, M., & Urrutia, J. (1980). The effects of a supportive companion on perinatal problems, length of labor, and mother-infant interaction. *New England Journal of Medicine, 303,* 597–600.

Spiegel, D., Bloom, J. R., & Kraemer, H. C. (1989). Effect of psychosocial treatment on survival of patients with metastatic breast cancer. *Lancet, 2,* 888–891.

Spiegel, D., Bloom, J. R., & Yalom, I. D. (1981). Group support for patients with metastatic breast cancer. *Archives of General Psychiatry, 38,* 527–533.

Steinberg, M., & Gottlieb, B. H. (1994). Appraisals of spousal support among women facing conflicts between work and family. In B. R. Burleson, T. L. Albrecht, & I. G. Sarason (Eds.), *The communication of social support.* Newbury Park, CA: Sage.

Thoits, P. A. (1983). Multiple identities and psychological well-being: A reformation and test of the social isolation hypothesis. *American Sociological Review, 48,* 174–187.

Thoits, P. A. (1985). Social support processes and psychological well-being: Theoretical possibilities. In I. G. Sarason & B. Sarason (Eds.), *Social support: Theory, research and applications* (pp. 51–72). The Hague: Martinus Nijhoff.

Thoits, P. A. (1986). Social support as coping assistance. *Journal of Consulting and Clinical Psychology, 54,* 416–423.

Thomas, W., & Znaniecki, F. (1920). *The Polish peasant in Europe and America.* New York: Alfred A. Knopf.

Toseland, R. W., & Rossiter, C. M. (1989). Group interventions to support family caregivers: A review and analysis. *Gerontologist, 29,* 438–448.

Uchino, B. N., Cacioppo, J. T., & Kiecolt-Glaser, J. K. (1996). The relationship between social support and physiological processes. *Psychological Bulletin, 119,* 488–531.

Vachon, M. S., Lyall, W. A., Rogers, J., Freedman-Letofsky, K., & Freeman, S. (1980). A controlled study of a self-help intervention for widows. *American Journal of Psychiatry, 137,* 1380–1384.

Vogt, T. M., Mullooly, J. P., Ernst, D., Pope, C. R., & Hollis, J. F. (1992). Social networks as predictors of ischemic heart disease, cancer, stroke, and hypertension. *Journal of Clinical Epidemiology, 45,* 659–666.

Weisenfeld, A. R., & Weis, H. M. (1979). A mental health consultation program for beauticians. *Professional Psychology, 10,* 786–792.

Wellman, B. (1985). Domestic work, paid work and net work. In S. Duck & D. Perlman (Eds.), *Understanding personal relationships* (vol. 1). London: Sage.

Wethington, E., & Kessler, R. C. (1986). Perceived support, received support, and adjustment to stressful events. *Journal of Health and Social Behavior, 27,* 78–89.

Wideman, M., & Singer, J. (1984). The role of psychological mechanisms in preparation for childbirth. *American Psychologist, 39,* 1357–1371.

Wills, T. A. (1985). Supportive functions of interpersonal relationships. In S. Cohen & S. L. Syme (Eds.), *Social support and health* (pp. 61–82). New York: Academic.

PART II

Social Support Measures

2

Social Support Theory and Measurement

Brian Lakey
Sheldon Cohen

I. The Stress and Coping Perspective
   A. Supportive Actions
   B. Appraisal
II. The Social Constructionist Perspective
   A. Social Cognition
   B. Symbolic Interactionism
III. The Relationship Perspective
IV. Conclusions

The intent of this chapter is to provide researchers with the background to make informed decisions when selecting measures of social support. Our premise is that these decisions should be informed by theories of how social relationships influence health and well-being. More generally, social support research should have a basis in theories about how social relationships influence our cognitions, emotions, behaviors, and biology.

Our approach is to present brief overviews of three important theoretical perspectives on social support research: (1) the stress and coping perspective, (2) the social constructionist perspective, and (3) the relationship perspective. The stress and coping perspective proposes that support contributes to health by protecting people from the adverse effects of stress. The social constructionist perspective proposes that support directly influences health by promoting self-esteem and self-regulation, regardless of the presence of stress. The relationship perspective predicts that the health effects of social support cannot be separated from relationship processes that often co-occur with support, such as companionship, intimacy, and low social conflict. Brief summaries of these perspectives are presented in Table 2.1.

It is the premise of this chapter that any statement about social support mechanisms must be qualified by the fact that many different interpersonal processes and constructs have been included under the rubric of social support and that each of these has its own unique association with health (Heller & Swindle, 1983).

Table 2.1. Summary of Theoretical Perspectives on Social Support

Perspective	Intellectual Tradition	Aspect of Support Emphasized	Type of Support Measures Emphasized	Support Operates	Emphasizes Stress Buffering or Main Effects of Support
Supportive actions	Stress and coping theory and research	Supportive behaviors provided by others	Reports or observations of supportive behaviors	by promoting coping	Stress buffering
Appraisal	Stress and coping theory and research	Perceived availability of actual support	Perceptions of availability of specific types of support	by promoting less negative appraisals of stress	Stress buffering
Social cognition	Experimental social psychology; Pragmatist Philosophy	Global, evaluative cognitive representation of others	Global evaluations of support quality or availability	by influencing evaluations of self and others	Main effects
Symbolic interactionism	Sociology; Pragmatist Philosophy	Social roles	Social roles	by providing identity	Main effects
Relationships	Research in personal relationships	Companionship, undermining, intimacy	Various	by various mechanisms	Main effects

For example, perceptions of available support, actual help received, seeking support and network characteristics (e.g., size, social integration, and social density) are at best moderately correlated and appear to represent different constructs (Barrera, 1986; Cohen & Wills, 1985; Dunkel-Schetter & Bennett, 1990; Heller & Lakey, 1985; Lakey & Drew, 1997; Sarason, Sarason, & Pierce, 1990). Thus, theories about support's relations to health must consider the diversity of constructs in the literature and how each uniquely influences health.

THE STRESS AND COPING PERSPECTIVE

The most influential theoretical perspective on social support hypothesizes that support reduces the effects of stressful life events on health (i.e., acts as a stress buffer) through either the supportive actions of others (e.g., advice, reassurance) or the belief that support is available. Supportive actions are thought to enhance coping performance (Figure 2.1), while perceptions of available support lead to appraising potentially threatening situations as less stressful (Figure 2.2). This perspective is linked closely with research and theory on stress and coping (Laz-

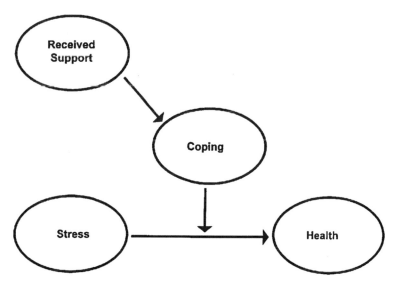

Figure 2.1. The supportive actions approach predicts that received support enhances coping, which buffers the relation between stress and health outcomes.

arus, 1966; Lazarus & Folkman, 1984; Moos & Billings, 1982) and is discussed in most major reviews and theoretical papers on social support (e.g., Barrera, 1986; Caplan, 1974; Cobb, 1976; Cohen & McKay, 1984; Cohen & Wills, 1985; Dean & Lin, 1977; Gottlieb, 1981; Heller, 1979; Heller & Swindle, 1983; Kaplan, Cassel, & Gore, 1977; Thoits, 1986).

Supportive Actions

The stress-support matching hypothesis (Cohen & McKay, 1984; Cutrona & Russell, 1990) is perhaps the most explicit statement of how supportive actions should promote coping. The hypothesis is that social support will be effective in promoting coping and reducing the effects of a stressor, insofar as the form of assistance matches the demands of the stressor. According to this view, each stressful circumstance places specific demands on the affected individual. For example, having someone lend you money may be useful in the face of a temporary job loss but useless in the face of the death of a friend. Similarly, having companions and confidants might be extremely useful when addressing the loss of a friend but less helpful when faced with a sudden economic demand.

Appropriate measures of social support

Because this perspective emphasizes the actual assistance provided by others during stress, studies of these processes focus on measures of received support described in chapters 4 and 5. They include instruments in which respondents report the frequency of the support they received over a given period of time in

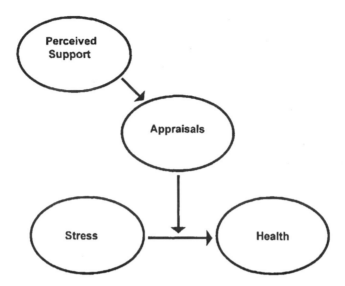

Figure 2.2. The appraisal perspective predicts that beliefs in the availability of support (perceived support) influence appraisals of stressful situations, which buffers the effects of stress on health outcomes.

response to either specified (e.g., Cohen & Lichtenstein, 1990; Coriell & Cohen, 1995) or unspecified stressful events (e.g., Barrera, Sandler, & Ramsey, 1981). Measures have also been developed in which observers count the number of supportive behaviors provided in a given interaction (e.g., Cutrona, Suhr, & MacFarlane, 1990; Heller & Lakey, 1985); or rate the quality of an observed interaction (e.g., DeGarmo & Forgatch, 1997). Inappropriate in this context are measures of perceived support that ask for subjective and global evaluations of social support quality or availability (Sarason, Sarason, & Pierce, 1990).

Hypothesized mediators and analytic issues

Because this perspective predicts that supportive actions promote health and well-being by promoting coping, measures assessing coping efforts and styles should be included in studies of received support. A review of coping measures is beyond the scope of this book. However, a variety of measures of coping are available with extensive data on their reliability and validity (Endler & Parker, 1995; Moos & Schaefer, 1993; Ptacek & Gross, 1997). Some measures ask respondents to report the coping response used in response to a specific stressor (Folkman & Lazarus, 1988). Other measures ask respondents to report what they characteristically do to cope with stress (Carver, Scheier, & Weintraub, 1989). Another type of measure assesses individuals' skill in carrying out a given type of coping. For example, measures of social problem-solving skills have been developed in which respondents indicate how they would solve a social problem and trained judges rate the quality of these responses (e.g., Fisher-Beckfield &

McFall, 1982). The key issue is whether supportive actions alter coping styles or increase coping efforts.

Because this perspective predicts that received support promotes well-being by protecting people from the effects of stress, measures of stress should be included as well. Detailed reviews of the measurement of stress are provided elsewhere (Cohen, Kessler, & Gordon, 1995). However, note that the nature of the stress measure will differ depending on the type of sample under study. Life events checklists or interviews sample a wide range of potential stressors and would be appropriate for general community or college student samples (Turner & Wheaton, 1995; Wethington, Brown, & Kessler, 1995). Measures of stressor severity would be appropriate for samples that are defined by the occurrence of a specific stressor (e.g., caregivers of Alzheimer's patients; Lawton, Moss, Kleban, Glicksman, & Rovine, 1991). People who receive more social support should display a weaker correlation between the amount of stress and health problems than those who receive less social support. The details of appropriate statistical tests of such stress-buffering effects can be found in Cohen and Wills (1985) and Cohen and Edwards (1989).

Because this perspective predicts that enhanced support protects people from stress by improving their coping performance, studies from this perspective should specifically examine such effects. In studies restricted to stressed populations (e.g., chronically ill, unemployed, caregiver for the elderly), analyses designed to test mediation can be used to examine the hypothesis that receipt of support influences health outcomes through its effects on coping (e.g., Baron & Kenny, 1986; Newcomb, 1990). Mediational testing is more complicated in designs that include both stressed and nonstressed control groups to test the stress-buffering hypothesis.

Unresolved research issues

Do measures of supportive actions adequately reflect the amount and quality of the social support received? The most common measures of supportive actions involve self-reports of how much support of various types has been received. However, several scholars have expressed disappointment that such measures have been poor predictors of perceptions of available support and of health (Barrera, 1986; Dunkel-Schetter & Bennett, 1990). This paradox may reflect the fact that receipt of support is often an indirect marker of the magnitude of stress experienced by the receiver (Barrera, 1986; Cohen & Wills, 1985). Although the amount of support received and the need for support are often confounded, some argue that more objective received support measures may reduce the degree of confounding. Measures of received support through behavioral observation have been developed (e.g., Cutrona et al., 1990; chapter 5). One goal of future research should be to compare behavioral observation to self-report measures.

Are support effects stronger if support is matched to the demands of the stressor? The stress-support matching hypothesis (Cohen & McKay, 1984; Cutrona & Russell, 1990) suggests that received support is more likely to predict outcomes when the support is matched optimally to the demands of the stressor. To take this approach, investigators would first need to determine the demands each stressor presents. This determination could be done on theoretical grounds, by measuring study participants' perceptions of demands, or by drawing on other empirical investigations. Measures of received support could then be tailored to reflect these demands. Ideally, one could show that received support that matched stressor demands moderated stressful events, but mismatched received support failed to buffer events (see Cohen & Hoberman, 1983; Tetzloff & Barrera, 1987; for examples of this approach).

How is support related to coping? Important research questions remain on the link between received support and coping. Although this perspective specifically predicts such a link, there have been surprisingly few studies examining the relation between received support and coping (e.g., Frazier, Tix, Klein, & Arikian, in press; Lakey & Heller, 1988; Manne & Zautra, 1989). (There are studies that examine links between perceived support and coping [e.g., Fondacaro & Moos, 1987; Holahan, Moos, & Bonin, 1997; Holahan, Moos, Holahan, & Brennan, 1997]; however, perceived and received support are distinct constructs with only a modest relation to each other.) Additional research on the effects of received support on coping is imperative. For example, does received support promote the initiation and maintenance of coping efforts? Do people change the way they cope in response to received support? What types of received support are most effective in positively influencing coping efforts and styles?

Appraisal

Alternatively, social support might protect persons against the adverse effects of stressors by leading them to interpret stressful situations less negatively (Figure 2.2; Cohen & Hoberman, 1983; Cohen & McKay, 1984). According to Lazarus and colleagues' influential theory of stress and coping, how people interpret situations (i.e., appraisals) is very important in determining an event's stressfulness (Lazarus, 1966; Lazarus & Folkman, 1984). There are two types of appraisals: *primary* and *secondary*. Primary appraisals involve judgments of whether the event is a threat. These judgments involve questions such as "Am I in trouble?" on dimensions such as harm-loss, threat, or challenge. Secondary appraisals involve evaluations of personal and social resources available to cope with the event. Such evaluations involve questions such as "What can I do about it?" More negative appraisals are hypothesized to lead to greater emotional distress (Lazarus & Folkman, 1984).

Cohen and Hoberman (1983; cf. Wethington & Kessler, 1986) hypothesized that the belief that support is available reduces the effects of stress by contributing to less negative appraisals. Consider the recent death of the husband of a frail elderly woman. A threatening primary appraisal might be "Now I am truly alone in the world." A negative secondary appraisal might be "I won't be able to take care of myself." However, if the bereaved believed that she was surrounded by a group of loving, helpful, and committed people, these appraisals might be less threatening. The primary appraisal might be modified to "I have lost my husband, but there are many dear people I am close to" and the secondary appraisal might be changed to "I can count on others to help me with shopping and home maintenance." According to Lazarus's theory, these revised appraisals should lead to less severe emotional reactions to the event. As with received support, perceptions of support availability should be most effective in altering appraisals if they counter the specific needs elicited by the stressful event (Cohen & Hoberman, 1983; Cohen & McKay, 1984).

Appropriate measures of social support

Because this perspective emphasizes beliefs in the availability of support, measures of perceived support are most appropriate for tests of this model (chapter 4). Measures of perceived support ask respondents to make evaluations of the quality or availability of different types of support. Testing the optimal matching hypothesis requires a measure of perceived support that distinguishes between different support functions (see chapter 4). For example, the Interpersonal Support Evaluation List (Cohen & Hoberman, 1983; Cohen, Mermelstein, Kamarck, & Hoberman, 1985) assesses perceptions of the availability of four different types of support: appraisal, belonging, esteem, and tangible support.

Hypothesized mediators and analytic issues

Because this perspective predicts that the beneficial effects of perceived support operate by influencing appraisal, a comprehensive test of this model would include appraisal measures. Unfortunately, there are few well-developed measures of the appraisal process (see review in Monroe & Kelley, 1995). Examples of existing measures include overall ratings of the extent to which life is stressful (Cohen, Kamarck, & Mermelstein, 1983) and ratings of specific life events on dimensions that correspond to primary and secondary appraisal (e.g., Peacock & Wong, 1990).

This perspective also predicts that perceived support operates by reducing the effects of stress. Thus, investigators should test buffering effects, which would require measures of life stressors. Furthermore, because the model hypothesizes that support buffers stress through appraisal processes, measures of appraisals should be included and mediational analyses conducted. This perspective predicts that higher levels of perceived social support should be associated with an attenuated relation between stress and poor health.

Unresolved research issues

How is perceived support related to appraisal? Although some studies have investigated links between perceived support and appraisal (e.g., Cohen & Hoberman, 1983; Dunkel-Schetter, Folkman, & Lazarus, 1987), relatively few have examined how beliefs in the availability of different types of support (e.g., tangible, belonging, or esteem support) are related to primary and secondary appraisals

(Cohen & Hoberman, 1983; Dunkel-Schetter, Folkman, & Lazarus, 1987). Greater understanding of the link between perceived support and appraisal would be an important contribution.

Is perceived support more effective if it matches the demands of the stressor? The appraisal perspective predicts that beliefs about support will influence appraisals insofar as the perceived support matches the demands of the stressor (Cohen & Hoberman, 1983). Because this perspective emphasizes the role of appraisal in determining reactions to stressful events, stressor analyses should focus on appraisals. For example, events might be classified according to the extent to which they involve threats to self-esteem or activate appraisals that tangible resources are needed (Cohen & Hoberman, 1983).

If perceived support influences appraisals, does perceived support then indirectly influence coping? This research question would promote the integration of the supportive actions and appraisal perspectives. The appraisal perspective predicts that perceived support will influence appraisals. Lazarus's stress and coping theory predicts that appraisals directly influence coping. If so, perceived support should influence coping.

THE SOCIAL CONTRUCTIONIST PERSPECTIVE

Social cognition and symbolic interactionism provide an alternative perspective on social support. Although these two views differ in their recent intellectual tradition and methods, they share common origins in pragmatist philosophy and thereby share many core assumptions (Barone, Maddux, & Snyder, 1997). Based upon the pragmatic philosophy and social psychology of James, Dewey, and Mead, the perspective views reality, including social support and the self, as social constructions. *Social constructions* refer to the assumption that people's perceptions about the world do not reflect ultimate reality. Instead, people construct theories and concepts about the world that reflect their social context (Dewey, 1917/1997). However, because there is frequently no clear social consensus, there are important individual and group differences in how people interpret their worlds (Kelly, 1969).

Applying the constructionist perspective to social support suggests new predictions and emphases not found in the stress and coping perspective. First, this perspective suggests that there may be no clear consensus across individuals or groups as to what constitutes supportive behaviors. Second, it predicts that the self and social world (including social support) are inextricably linked. In other words the experience of "self" is largely a reflection of how one is viewed by others (Mead, 1934).

Social Cognition

One modern manifestation of social constructionism is social cognition (Barone et al., 1997), and several authors have applied social-cognitive thought to understanding social support (e.g., Lakey & Cassady, 1990; Lakey & Drew, 1997; Mankowski & Wyer, 1997; T. Pierce, Baldwin, & Lydon, 1997; Sarason, Pierce, & Sarason, 1990). This approach to social support draws heavily from social-cognitive theories of personality and psychopathology (e.g., Beck, Rush, Shaw, & Emery, 1979; Markus, 1977). Social-cognitive views of social support are concerned primarily with the perception of support. A major premise is that once a person develops stable beliefs about the supportiveness of others, day-to-day thoughts about social support are shaded to fit these preexisting beliefs. In comparison to those with low levels of perceived support, those with high levels should interpret the same behaviors as more supportive, have better memory for supportive behaviors, display greater attention to supportive behaviors, and be able to think about support with greater ease and speed (Baldwin, 1992; Lakey & Cassady, 1990; Lakey & Drew, 1997; Mankowski & Wyer, 1997; T. Pierce et al., 1997). Although "objective" characteristics of the social world have an influence on perceived support, perceived support is influenced more strongly by support recipients' impressionistic understanding of supporters' personality characteristics than by the actual support that is provided (Lakey, Ross, Butler, & Bently, 1996).

In explaining the mechanism by which social support is related to health, social-cognitive views of social support draw from cognitive models of emotional disorders (e.g., Beck et al., 1979). Negative thoughts about social relations are thought to overlap with and stimulate negative thoughts about the self, which, in turn, overlap with and stimulate emotional distress (Figure 2.3; Baldwin & Holmes, 1987; Lakey & Cassady, 1990; Sarason, Pierce, & Sarason, 1990). For example, there is evidence that perceived support is associated strongly with self-

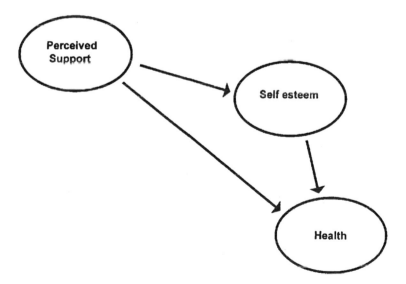

Figure 2.3. The social-cognitive perspective predicts that perceived support promotes self-esteem, which leads to health outcomes. Perceived support also leads directly to health outcomes.

evaluation (Barrera & Li, 1996; Lakey & Cassady, 1990; Maton, 1990; Rowlinson & Felner, 1988) and that priming cognitive representations of different social relations influences self-evaluation and emotion (Baldwin, Carrell, & Lopez, 1990; Baldwin & Holmes, 1987; Baldwin & Sinclair, 1996).

Appropriate measures of social support

Because social-cognitive models emphasize generalized beliefs about the supportiveness of others, general measures of perceived social support are the most appropriate. Chapter 4 discusses measures of perceived social support in detail. General measures of perceived support ask respondents to judge the availability or quality of social support from their social network.

Hypothesized mediators and analytic issues

Although one can derive stress-buffering predictions from the social-cognitive perspective, the most clear prediction is that the relation between perceived support and health does not depend on the level of stress. For example, a component of this approach is that negative thoughts about social relationships are themselves sufficient to elicit negative emotion (Beck et al., 1979). Because the social-cognitive perspective hypothesizes that perceptions of support availability influence thoughts about the self, measures of the self should be included, and mediational analyses should be conducted. A review of measures of self-evaluation is provided in Blascovich and Tomaka (1991).

Unresolved research issues

How do people make support judgments? The link between support perceptions and the actual help that people receive is not as straightforward as support researchers originally believed (Barrera, 1986; Lakey & Drew, 1997). A primary goal for future work in this area is to determine the processes involved in making judgments about the availability of social support. One approach has focused on the role of biases in the perception and memory of supportive people and actions that serve to perpetuate existing beliefs about support (see Lakey & Drew, 1997, for a review). More recent research has focused on how people combine information about supporters to make support judgments (Lutz & Lakey, 1999).

Which personal characteristics of supporters influence judgments of support? Basic research in person memory and judgment suggests that cognitive representations of others typically are dominated by trait concepts and global evaluations, rather than by memories of specific acts (Hastie & Park, 1986; Klein, Loftus, Trafton, & Fuhrman, 1992; Srull & Wyer, 1989). Support judgments may be influenced more strongly by the recipients' global evaluations of targets and views of the targets' personalities than by the memory of specific supportive actions. For example, Lakey, Ross et al. (1996) studied how judgments of target personality and recipient-supporter similarity were related to judging targets' supportiveness. These types of studies require measures of perceived support that refer to the supportiveness of specific persons. Pierce, Sarason, Sarason, Solky-Butzel, & Nagle's (1997) Quality of Relationship Inventory was designed for such a purpose, and the Social Provisions Scale (Cutrona & Russell, 1987) has been adapted to study specific relationships as well.

However, the most important determinants of perceived support probably reflect the unique relation between support recipients and supporters (Kenny, 1994; Lakey, McCabe, Fisicaro, & Drew, 1996). How does supportiveness emerge from the unique pairing of some dyads but not others? Support recipients may use different information about targets in making support judgments (Lakey, Drew, & Sirl, 1999; Lutz & Lakey, 1999). For example, one support recipient may value no-nonsense advice, whereas another recipient may value humor. In addition, different recipients may elicit different supportive behaviors from the same targets. One support recipient may elicit more kindness from one set of targets than would another support recipient; the latter recipient may elicit more kindness from another set of targets. Addressing questions such as these requires a unique set of designs that go beyond the focus of this chapter (see Kenny, 1994; Lakey, McCabe et al., 1996).

How is perceived support related to the self? Another key research issue is the link between thinking about relationships and thinking about the self. Much of this work uses experimental methods whereby thinking about specific relationships activates different self-evaluations (Baldwin & Sinclair, 1996; Baldwin et al., 1990). However, it is possible to investigate links between the self and relationships with correlational methods. For example, Higgins and his colleagues have developed measures of self-discrepancy that assess the extent to which respondents' self-concepts conflict with how they believe others view respondents (Higgins, Klein, & Strauman, 1985). Linville (1987) has used a self-report measure of self-complexity, and Mikulincer (1997) has used questionnaire measures of integration and differentiation of the self.

What categories do people naturally use in thinking about support and social relations? Relationships researchers have elaborated a number of concepts to think about relationships, including supportiveness, companionship, intimacy, and undermining, to name a few (see chapter 5). Support researchers also make fine distinctions between different types of social support (e.g., tangible or emotional support). But do the people we study share our concepts of support? Could the support questions that we ask participants call to their minds a completely different set of concepts than we intended? Social support research has yet to identify the naturally occurring concepts that people use to think about their relationships. Do concepts like supportiveness mean different things to different people (Lutz & Lakey, 1999)? If so, what are the implications for the assessment of social support?

Symbolic Interactionism

Another modern manifestation of social constructionist thought is symbolic interactionism (Stryker, 1980). The major premise of the symbolic interactionist perspective on social support is that the regularization of social interaction, rather than the provision of support per se, is responsible for the maintenance of well-being (Thoits, 1985). Thus, according to the symbolic interactionist perspective, our social environments directly promote health and well-being by providing people with a way of making sense of the self and the world. Social support operates by helping to create and sustain identity and self-esteem (Figure 2.4).

According to Stryker's (1980) version of symbolic interactionism, meaning and identity are derived, in part, from the roles we occupy and create within a social context. People adopt a wide range of different roles, such as father, scholar, musician, son, husband, athlete, and so on. Role concepts that are shared among a group of people help to guide social interaction by providing a common set of expectations about how people should act in different roles. Roles also provide a sense of identity because people use roles as basic conceptual tools in thinking about the self. Evaluations of the self are based on role performance, which is presumed to be rooted in social interactions.

According to Mead (1934), people learn to regulate themselves by applying the standards of the group to their own conduct: "Self-criticism is essentially social criticism, and behavior that is controlled by self-criticism is essentially behavior controlled socially" (p. 255). This aspect of constructionist thought provides a mechanism for facilitating behaviors that could promote health, such as physician visits or increased exercise, and inhibiting behaviors that might be detrimental to

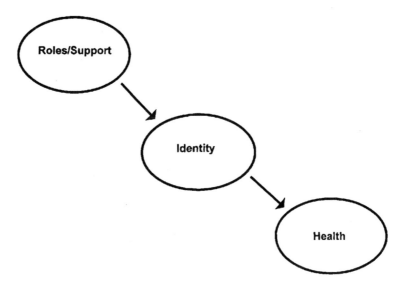

Figure 2.4. The symbolic interactionist persepctive predicts that social roles/support identity, which leads to health outcomes.

health, such as excessive alcohol and tobacco consumption (House, Landis, & Umberson, 1988).

Appropriate measures of social support

Role measures of social integration and social networks (chapter 3) fit with the symbolic interactionist view. These measures are thought to assess the extent to which persons are involved in a broad social network. A core aspect of one type of social integration measure is the number of roles in which individuals participate. Most research within the symbolic interactionist tradition uses these role-based measures. The major question in selecting such a measure is whether the roles that are included represent the range of important social roles in the population that is being studied (chapter 3).

Hypothesized mediators and analytic issues

Because this perspective hypothesizes that social roles promote well-being through building and sustaining identity and self-esteem, studies should include measures of self-esteem and identity. Although there are a large number of measures of self-esteem available, there are fewer nonrole measures of identity (Thoits, 1999). However, measures of self-processes developed by those working from the social-cognitive perspective may be helpful. Examples of measures that might tap pathways linking social roles to psychological well-being include the complexity of self-representations (Linville, 1987), self-discrepancies (Higgins et al., 1985), and differentiation and integration (Mikulincer, 1997).

Although from symbolic interactionism one can derive the hypothesis that diverse social roles protect people from the effects of stress, this perspective most clearly predicts that roles will influence well-being regardless of the presence of stress (chapters 1 and 3; Thoits, 1985). Because multiple roles have their effects through building identity and self-esteem, measures of these constructs should be included, and mediational analyses should be conducted. For example, many roles should be related to greater differentiation of the self-concept, which should be related to greater self-esteem, which, in turn, should be related to greater well-being.

Unresolved research issues

How are roles related to identity? Although symbolic interactionism is clear in predicting that social roles promote a sense of identity and self-esteem, relatively little work has demonstrated links between specific roles or number of roles and identity. This work would be especially worthwhile because it would promote an integration between symbolic interactionism and social cognition. Basic research in social cognition has applied an impressive range of theory and methods for studying information processing about the self. For example, the Stroop Task has been adapted to test hypotheses about the accessibility of various self-concepts (Williams, Mathews, & Macleod, 1996) and the Self-Referent Encoding Task has been developed to probe how aspects of the self are organized in memory (Kihlstrom & Klein, 1994; Rogers, Kuiper, & Kirker, 1977). Priming methodologies have been developed to investigate whether thinking about certain relationships makes specific representations and evaluations of the self more accessible (Baldwin et al., 1990; Baldwin & Sinclair, 1996). Thus, many hypotheses about the relation of roles to the self could be tested in new ways by borrowing concepts and methods from social cognition.

Are subjective evaluations of social roles important? Although most research on roles counts the number of roles in which people participate, an increasing number of studies are including subjective evaluations of roles, especially role importance or commitment (e.g., Brown, Bifulco, & Harris, 1987; Lakey & Edmundson, 1993; Simon, 1992, 1997; Thoits, 1992). Cognitive models of psychopathology (e.g., Beck et al., 1979) have placed great emphasis on how subjective evaluations of important domains of life are related to depression and anxiety. There is also evidence that including subjective evaluations of roles greatly enhances the strength of the relation between roles and emotional distress (Lakey & Edmundson, 1993; Simon, 1997).

Are social roles the most basic naturally occurring constructs in social thought? Symbolic interactionism could benefit social cognition by providing new ideas about the constructs that naturally organize social thought. Mainstream social-cognitive research has been criticized as lacking a true relational quality because many studies primarily involve thinking about trait adjectives (Fiske, 1992; Fiske & Haslam, 1996). A provocative question is whether social-cognitive research is studying cognition about relationships or cognition about trait adjectives. Fiske (1992) has argued that naturally occurring social thought is organized according to relational qualities such as communal sharing and authority ranking rather than in terms of trait adjectives. The concept of roles might provide another valuable way of thinking about the constructs people naturally use in thinking about relationships.

THE RELATIONSHIP PERSPECTIVE

A third perspective on social support conceptualizes support as part of more generic relationship processes (chapter 5). This approach does not represent a coherent perspective linked to a preexisting research literature or intellectual tradition. Instead, it is a group of hypotheses that attribute social support to other relationship qualities or processes. These relationship qualities reflect neither actual help during times of stress nor beliefs about support per se. We believe that this perspective will become increasingly important and provide alternative ways of thinking about social support. One possibility is that our cognitions about our social environment are strongly interrelated and overlapping and that measures of support cannot be discriminated from closely associated concepts such as low conflict, companionship, intimacy, and social skills.

The following definitions of some of these interrelated concepts provide some flavor of their potentially strong associations and overlap with measures of both social networks and social support. Several of these concepts involve descriptions of positive ties between people. For example, companionship involves "shared leisure and other activities that are undertaken primarily for the intrinsic goal of enjoyment" (Rook, 1987; p. 1133; chapter 10). Relationship satisfaction is defined as global, subjective evaluations of relationships (Hendrick & Hendrick, 1997) and intimacy as the "bonded, connected, and close feelings people have toward each other" (Barnes & Sternberg, 1997).

Other concepts describe negative ties. Of particular note is the concept "social conflict," which includes criticism, breaking of promises, or fighting for limited resources. Some studies have found that conflict is a better predictor of health than perceived social support (Fiore, Becker, & Coppel, 1983; Pagel, Erdly, & Becker, 1987; Rook, 1984). Finally, there are dispositional characteristics that influence interpersonal skills. Examples include extraversion and agreeableness. Another notable example is adult attachment styles, which are internal working models of the self and the availability of others. These relatively stable working models are thought to develop in response to the availability of caregivers during childhood (Bowlby, 1969; chapter 5).

There has been little theoretical explication of why relationship qualities such as companionship, intimacy, low conflict, and attachment should lead to emotional and physical well-being. The mechanisms that have been proposed tend to be the same as those hypothesized to link social support concepts to health and include elevating self-esteem (Rook, 1987; Lakey, Tardiff, & Drew, 1994), contributing to positive appraisals, and promoting active coping with stressful events (Bartholomew, Cobb, & Poole, 1997; Sarason, Sarason, & Pierce, 1990).

Another hypothesis drawn from the relationship perspective is that positive, stable, and secure relationships may fulfill a basic, biological need (Baumeister & Leary, 1995; Bowlby, 1969; Leary & Downs, 1995). At one point or another, most of the founding scholars in social support have invoked such a need to explain social support effects (Caplan, 1974; Cobb, 1976; Kaplan et al., 1977; Lowenthal & Haven, 1968). For most of human history, survival has depended upon integration into a social group. Humans in isolation were probably quickly eaten by other animals, killed by other humans, or starved. Thus, the recognition that one was not accepted by the social group or that the social group would not come to one's aid if needed foreshadowed almost certain death. It seems obvious that isolation would become strongly tied to lower self-esteem and control and to heightened levels of negative affect (e.g., Leary & Downs, 1995). Although hypotheses about basic psychological needs are difficult to test empirically (Baumeister & Leary, 1995), the field of evolutionary social psychology is developing strategies for such empirical tests (Buss, 1996).

Appropriate measures of social support

Because of the diversity of the hypotheses that some other aspect of relationships accounts for support effects, it is difficult to say that a given type of social support

measure is most appropriate. Because these hypotheses offer alternative explanations for given social support effects, the choice of a specific social support
measure will usually be determined by the research that originally established
the social support effect to be explained. For example, an investigator who
wanted to test the social conflict hypothesis for an effect originally established
with a social network measure could chose the social network measures used in
the original research. To test a relationship perspective hypothesis, an investigator
will need measures of the relationship processes that are hypothesized to account
for social support. Chapter 5 provides a review of a wide range of such measures
and a discussion of which might be appropriate in specific contexts.

Hypothesized mediators and analytic issues

In contrast to most other perspectives, the relationship perspective hypothesizes
that other relationship qualities lead to both support and health (Figure 2.5). Support is related to health only because it shares a common cause with other relationship processes. Using conflict as an example, this perspective predicts that
people with low support are more likely to have poor health only because low
support is associated with social conflict. However, only conflict has a causal
relation to poor health.

Unresolved research issues

*Do nonsupport relationship processes account for the link between social support
and health?* An important research agenda is to conduct tests of the hypotheses
that relationship processes such as intimacy, companionship, conflict, and attachment style underlie social support effects. For example, Rook (1987) found

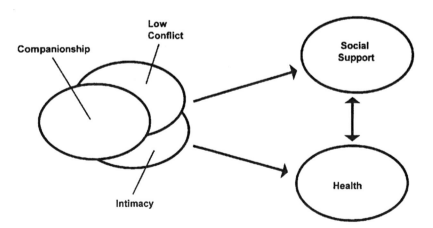

Figure 2.5. Examples of hypotheses from the relationships perspective. Support and
health outcomes both result from companionship, low conflict, and intimacy. The latter
three variables overlap substantially.

that companionship was a stronger predictor of well-being than social support in most analyses. Kaul and Lakey (1999) found that generic relationship satisfaction and perceived support were closely related and that relationship satisfaction could account for perceived support's relation to mental health. In contrast, Reis and Franks (1994) found that social support could account for intimacy's relation to most physical and mental health measures.

A number of studies have shown that adult attachment styles, reports of parental bonding, and perceived support are related (Bartholomew et al., 1997). Anan and Barnett (1999) have shown that attachment style, assessed via the strange situation in preschoolers, predicts perceived support in later childhood. However, there have been fewer studies assessing the extent to which attachment style can account for relations between perceived support and health.

How are relationship processes such as generic quality, intimacy, companionship, and low conflict linked to health? One pathway through which these processes might influence health is by altering the appraisal of stressful events. They might also influence psychological, behavioral, and biological determinants of health, including self-esteem, negative and positive affect, health practices, or endocrine or immune function (see chapter 1). Additional evidence for relations between these concepts and health outcomes, and for the mechanisms responsible for such effects, could provide further insight into their importance in explaining social support processes.

Taking a true relationship approach in research. One challenge in relationships research is developing methods and conceptual tools for studying processes that are a function of relationships rather than individual differences. In both relationships and social support research, research participants typically are assigned a single score that represents their standing on a relationship variable. This score is then analyzed in comparison with other individuals by using statistics such as multiple regression or structural equations. The problem for relationships research is that this way of thinking about and analyzing data is identical to how personality variables are treated. However, relationship processes are a function of neither the support recipient nor the supporter, but reflect their unique relation. Recent developments in social relationship methodology (i.e., the Social Relations Model; Kenny, 1994) and generalizability theory (Cronbach, Gleser, Nanda, & Rajaratnam, 1972; Lakey, McCabe et al., 1996) allow investigators to distinguish between effects due to support recipients, supporters, and relationships, but these methods are underutilized.

CONCLUSIONS

1. Social support research and interventions should be guided by theory so that each study can add to our understanding about how social support influences health and well-being. Too many studies address whether social support is related to health without providing information about how support contributes to health.

2. Investigators must choose social support measures carefully. Measures are not interchangeable. Different measures reflect specific theoretical orientations and are likely to be related to some mechanisms and outcomes but not others. In designing support studies and interventions, it is crucial that the investigators clearly articulate the theoretical perspective that guides their thinking and choose measures that are congruent with that perspective.

3. More research is needed on the determinants of social support. Successful intervention requires an understanding of how social support arises and the determinants of supportive people and supportive actions. Unfortunately, the field has neglected these questions, and interventions have suffered as a result.

In conclusion, we hope we have shown that it is possible and desirable to conduct theoretically based research on social support. In addition, we hope that we have helped investigators see how, by considering theoretical traditions within social support research and by including measures that fit within these traditions, they can help their research make more important contributions to the literature.

REFERENCES

Anan, R. M., & Barnett, D. B. (1999). Perceived social support mediates between prior attachment and subsequent adjustment: A study of urban African American children. *Developmental Psychology, 35* 1210–1122.

Baldwin, M. W. (1992). Relational schemas and the processing of social information. *Psychological Bulletin, 112*, 461–484.

Baldwin, M. W., Carrell, S. E., & Lopez, D. F. (1990). Priming relationship schemas: My advisor and the pope are watching me from the back of my mind. *Journal of Experimental Social Psychology, 26*, 435–454.

Baldwin, M. W., & Holmes, J. G. (1987). Salient private audiences and awareness of the self. *Journal of Personality and Social Psychology, 52*, 1087–1098.

Baldwin, M. W., & Sinclair, L. (1996). Self-esteem and "if . . . then" contingencies of interpersonal acceptance. *Journal of Personality and Social Psychology, 71*, 1130–1141.

Barnes, M. L., & Sternberg, R. J. (1997). A hierarchical model of love and its prediction of satisfaction in close relationships. In R. J. Sternberg & M. Hojjat (Eds.), *Satisfaction in close relationships* (pp. 79–101). New York: Guilford.

Baron, R. M., & Kenny, D. A. (1986). The moderator-mediator variable distinction in social psychological research: Conceptual strategies and statistical considerations. *Journal of Personality and Social Psychology, 51*, 1173–1182.

Barone, D. F., Maddux, J. E., & Snyder, C. R. (1997). *Social-cognitive psychology: History and current domains.* New York: Plenum.

Barrera, M. Jr. (1986). Distinctions between social support concepts, measures, and models. *American Journal of Community Psychology, 14*, 413–445.

Barrera, M. Jr., & Li, S. A. (1996). The relation of family support to adolescents' psychological distress and behavior problems. In G. R. Pierce, B. R. Sarason, & I. G. Sarason (Eds.), *Handbook of social support and the family* (pp. 313–343). New York: Plenum.

Barrera, M. Jr., Sandler, I. N., & Ramsay, T. B. (1981). Preliminary development of a scale of social support: Studies on college students. *American Journal of Community Psychology, 9*, 435–447.

Bartholomew, K., Cobb, R. J., & Poole, J. A. (1997). Adult attachment patterns and social support processes. In G. R. Pierce, B. Lakey, I. G. Sarason & B. R. Sarason (Eds.), *Sourcebook of social support and personality* (pp. 359–378). New York: Plenum.

Baumeister, A. M., & Leary, M. R. (1995). The need to belong: Desire for interpersonal attachments as a fundamental human motivation. *Psychological Bulletin, 117*, 497–529.

Beck, A. T., Rush, A. J., Shaw, B. F., & Emery, G. (1979). *Cognitive therapy of depression.* New York: Guilford.

Blascovich, J., & Tomaka, J. (1991). Measures of self-esteem. In J. P. Robinson, P. R. Shaver, & L. S. Wrightsman (Eds.), *Measures of personality and social psychological attitudes* (pp. 115–160). San Diego, CA: Academic Press.

Bowlby, J. (1969). Attachment and loss: Vol. 1. Attachment. New York: Basic Books.

Brown, G. W., Bifulco, A., & Harris, T. A. (1987). Life events, vulnerability, and onset of depression: Some refinements. *British Journal of Psychiatry, 150*, 30–42.

Buss, D. M. (1996). The evolutionary psychology of human social strategies. In E. T. Higgins & A. W. Kruglanski (Eds.), *Social psychology: Handbook of basic principles* (pp. 3–38). New York: Guilford

Caplan, G. (1974). *Support systems and community mental health: Lectures on concept development.* New York: Behavioral Publications.

Carver, C. S., Scheier, M. F., & Weintraub, J. K. (1989). Assessing coping strategies; A theoretically-based approach. *Journal of Personality and Social Psychology, 56*, 267–283.

Cobb, S. (1976). Social support as a moderator of life stress. *Psychosomatic Medicine, 38*, 300–314.

Cohen, S., & Edwards, J. R. (1989). Personality characteristics as moderators of the relationship between stress and disorder. In R. W. J. Neufeld (Ed.), *Advances in the investigation of psychological stress* (pp. 235–283). New York: Wiley.

Cohen, S., & Hoberman, H. M. (1983). Positive events and social supports as buffers of life change stress. *Journal of Applied Social Psychology, 13*, 99–125.

Cohen, S., Kamarck, T., & Mermelstein, R. (1983). A global measure of perceived stress. *Journal of Health and Social Behavior, 24*, 385–396.

Cohen, S., Kessler, R. C., & Gordon, L. U. (1995). *Measuring stress: A guide for health and social scientists.* New York: Oxford University Press.

Cohen, S., & Lichtenstein, E. (1990). Partner behaviors that support quitting smoking. *Journal of Consulting and Clinical Psychology, 58*, 304–309.

Cohen, S., & McKay, G. (1984). Social support, stress, and the buffering hypothesis: A theoretical analysis. In A. Baum, S. E. Taylor, & J. E. Singer (Eds.), *Handbook of psychology and health* (Vol. 4, pp. 253–267). Hillsdale, NJ: Erlbaum.

Cohen, S., Mermelstein, R., Kamarck, T., & Hoberman, H. (1985). Measuring the functional components of social support. In I. G. Sarason & B. R. Sarason (Eds.), *Social support: Theory, research and application* (pp. 73–94). The Hague: Martinus Nijhoff.

Cohen, S., & Wills, T. A. (1985). Stress, social support, and the buffering hypothesis. *Psychological Bulletin, 98*, 310–357.

Coriell, M., & Cohen, S. (1995). Concordance in the face of a stressful event: When do members of a dyad agree that one person supported the other? *Journal of Personality and Social Psychology, 69,* 289–299.

Cronbach, L. J., Gleser, G. C., Nanda, H., & Rajaratnam, N. (1972). *The dependability of behavioral measurements: Theory of generalizability of scores and profiles.* New York: Wiley.

Cutrona, C. E., & Russell, D. W. (1987). The provision of social relationships and adaptation to stress. In W. H. Jones & D. Perlman (Eds.), *Advances in personal relationships* (Vol. 1, pp. 37–67). Greenwich, CT: JAI Press.

Cutrona, C. E., & Russell, D. W. (1990). Type of social support and specific stress: Toward a theory of optimal matching. In B. R. Sarason, I. G. Sarason, & G. R. Pierce (Eds.), *Social support: An interactional view* (pp. 319–366). New York: Wiley.

Cutrona, C. E., Suhr, J. A., & MacFarlane, R. (1990). Interpersonal transactions and the psychological sense of support. In S. Duck with R. C. Silver (Eds.), *Personal relationships and social support* (pp. 30–45). London: Sage.

Dean, A., & Lin, N. (1977). The stress-buffering role of social support: Problems and prospects for systematic investigation. *Journal of Nervous and Mental Disease, 165,* 403–417.

DeGarmo, D. S., & Forgatch, M. (1997). Confidant support and maternal distress: Predictors of parenting practices for divorced mothers. *Personal Relationships, 4,* 305–317.

Dewey, J. (1917/1997). From "The need for a recovery of philosophy." In L. Menand (Ed.), *Pragmatism: A reader.* New York: Vintage Books.

Dunkel-Schetter, C., & Bennett, T. L. (1990). Differentiating the cognitive and behavioral aspects of social support. In B. R. Sarason, I. G. Sarason, & G. R. Pierce (Eds.), *Social support: an interactional view* (pp. 267–296). New York: Wiley.

Dunkel-Schetter, C., Folkman, S., Lazarus, R. S. (1987). Correlates of social support receipt. *Journal of Personality and Social Psychology, 53,* 71–80.

Endler, N. S., & Parker, J. D. A. (1995). Assessing a patient's ability to cope. In J. N. Butcher (Ed.), *Clinical personality assessment: Practical approaches* (pp. 329–352). New York: Oxford University Press.

Fiore, J., Becker, J., & Coppel, D. B. (1983). Social network interactions: A buffer or a stress? *American Journal of Community Psychology, 11,* 423–439.

Fisher-Beckfield, D., & McFall, R. M. (1982). Development of a competence inventory for college men and evaluation of relations between competence and depression. *Journal of Consulting and Clinical Psychology, 50,* 697–705.

Fiske, A. P. (1992). The four elementary forms of sociality: Framework for a unified theory of social relations. *Psychological Review, 99,* 689–723.

Fiske, A. P., & Haslam, N. (1996). Social cognition is thinking about relationships. *Current Directions in Psychological Science, 5,* 143–148.

Folkman, S., & Lazarus, R. S. (1988). *Manual for the ways of coping questionnaire.* Palo Alto, CA: Consulting Psychologists Press.

Fondacaro, M. R., & Moos, R. H. (1987). Social support and coping: A longitudinal analysis. *American Journal of Community Psychology, 15,* 653–673.

Frazier, P. A., Tix, A. P., Klein, C. D., & Arikian, N. J. (in press). Testing theoretical models of the relation between social support, coping and adjustment to stressful life events. *Journal of Social and Clinical Psychology.*

Gottlieb, B. H. (1981). Preventive interventions involving social networks and social support. In B. H. Gottlieb (Ed.), *Social networks and social support*. Beverly Hills, CA: Sage.

Hastie, R., & Park, B. (1986). The relationship between memory and judgment depends on whether the judgment task is memory-based or on-line. *Psychological Review, 93*, 258–268.

Heller, K. (1979). The effects of social support: Prevention and treatment implications. In A. P. Goldstein & F. H. Kanfer (Eds.), *Maximizing treatment gains: Transfer enhancement in psychotherapy* (pp. 353–382). New York: Academic Press.

Heller, K. & Lakey, B. (1985). Perceived support and social interaction among friends and confidants. In I. G. Sarason & B. R. Sarason (Eds.), *Social support: Theory research and applications* (pp. 287–302). The Hague: Martinus Nijhoff.

Heller, K., & Swindle, R. W. (1983). Social networks, perceived social support, and coping with stress. In R. D. Felner, L. A. Jason, J. N. Moritsugu, & S. S. Farber (Eds.), *Preventive psychology: Theory, research and practice* (pp. 87–103). New York: Pergamon.

Hendrick, S. S., & Hendrick, C. (1997). Love and satisfaction. In R. J. Sternberg & M. Hojjat (Eds.), *Satisfaction in close relationships* (pp. 56–78) New York: Guilford.

Higgins, E. T., Klein, R., & Strauman, T. (1985). Self-concept discrepancy theory: A psychological model for distinguishing among different aspects of depression and anxiety. *Social Cognition, 3*, 51–76.

Holahan, C. J., Moos, R. H., & Bonin, L. (1997). Social support, coping and adjustment: A resources model. In G. R. Pierce, B. Lakey, I. R. Sarason, & B. R. Sarason, (Eds.), *Sourcebook of social support and personality* (pp. 169–186). New York: Plenum.

Holahan, C. J., Moos, R. H., Holahan, C. K., & Brennan, P. L. (1997). Social context, coping strategies, and depressive symptoms: An expanded model with cardiac patients. *Journal of Personality and Social Psychology, 72*, 918–928.

House, J. S., Landis, K. R., & Umberson, D. (1988). Social relationships and health. *Science, 241*, 540–545.

Kaplan, B. H., Cassel, J. C., & Gore, S. (1977) Social support and health. *Medical Care, 15*, 47–58.

Kaul, M., & Lakey, B. (1999). *Where is the support in perceived support? The role of relationship quality, attachment, and enacted support in perceived support's relation to distress.* Manuscript submitted for publication.

Kelly, G. A. (1969). *Clinical psychology and personality: The selected papers of George Kelly* (B. Maher, Ed.). New York: Wiley.

Kenny, D. (1994) *Interpersonal perception: A social relations analysis.* New York: Guilford.

Kihlstrom, J. F., & Klein, S. B. (1994). The self as a knowledge structure. In R. S. Wyer Jr. & T. K. Srull (Eds.), *Handbook of social cognition* (2nd ed.). Hillsdale, NJ: Lawrence Erlbaum.

Klein, S. B., Loftus, J., Trafton, J. G., & Fuhrman, R. W. (1992). Use of exemplars and abstractions in trait judgments: A model of trait knowledge about the self and others. *Journal of Personality and Social Psychology, 63*, 739–753.

Kuhn, T. S. (1970). *The structure of scientific revolutions* (2nd ed.). Chicago: University of Chicago Press.

Lakey, B., & Cassady, P. B. (1990). Cognitive processes in perceived social support. *Journal of Personality and Social Psychology, 59*, 337–343.

Lakey, B., & Drew, J. B. (1997). A social-cognitive perspective on social support. In G. R. Pierce, B. Lakey, I. B. Sarason, & B. R. Sarason (Eds.), *Sourcebook of social support and personality* (pp. 107–140). New York: Plenum.

Lakey, B., Drew, J. B., & Sirl, K. (1999). Clinical depression and perceptions of supportive others: A generalizability analysis. *Cognitive Therapy and Research, 23*, 511–533.

Lakey, B., & Edmundson, D. D. (1993). Role evaluations and stressful events: Aggregate versus role-specific predictors. *Cognitive Therapy and Research, 17*, 249–268.

Lakey, B., & Heller, K. (1988). Social support from a friend, perceived support, and social problem solving. *American Journal of Community Psychology, 16*, 811–824.

Lakey, B., McCabe, K. M., Fisicaro, S., & Drew, J. B. (1996). Environmental and personal determinants of support perceptions: Three generalizability studies. *Journal of Personality and Social Psychology, 70*, 1270–1280.

Lakey, B., Ross, L., Butler, C., & Bentley, K. (1996). Making social support judgments: The role of perceived similarity and conscientiousness. *Journal of Social and Clinical Psychology, 15*, 283–304.

Lakey, B., Tardiff, T. A., & Drew, J. B. (1994). Negative social interactions: Assessment and relations to social support, cognition, and psychological distress. *Journal of Social and Clinical Psychology, 13*, 42–62.

Lawton, P. M., Moss, M., Kleban, M. H., Glicksman, A., & Rovine, M. (1991). A two-factor model of caregiving appraisal and psychological well-being. *Journals of Gerontology, 46*, 181–189.

Lazarus, R. S. (1966). *Psychological stress and the coping process.* New York: McGraw-Hill.

Lazarus, R. S., & Folkman, S. (1984). *Stress, appraisal and coping.* New York: Springer.

Leary, M. R., & Downs, D. L. (1995). Interpersonal functions of the self-esteem motive: The self-esteem system as a sociometer. In M. H. Kernis (Ed.), *Efficacy, agency, and self-esteem* (pp. 123–144). New York: Plenum.

Linville, P. (1987). Self-complexity as a cognitive buffer against stress-related illness and depression. *Journal of Personality and Social Psychology, 52*, 663–676.

Lowenthal, M. F., & Haven, C. (1968) Interaction and adaptation: Intimacy as a critical variable. *American Sociological Review, 33*, 20–29.

Lutz, C. L., & Lakey, B. (1999). *Individual differences in the cognitive representation of social support.* Manuscript submitted for publication.

Mankowski, E. S., & Wyer, R. S. Jr. (1997). Cognitive causes and consequences of perceived social support. In G. R. Pierce, B. Lakey, I. G. Sarason, & B. R. Sarason (Eds.), *Sourcebook of social support and personality* (pp. 141–165). New York: Plenum

Manne, S. L., & Zautra, A. J. (1989). Spouse criticism and support: Their association with coping and psychological adjustment among women with rheumatoid arthritis. *Journal of Personality and Social Psychology, 56*, 608–617.

Markus, H. (1977). Self-schemata and processing information about the self. *Journal of Personality and Social Psychology, 35*, 63–78.

Maton, K. I. (1990). Meaningful involvement in instrumental activity and well-being: Studies of older adolescents and at-risk urban teen-agers. *American Journal of Community Psychology, 18*, 297–320.

Mead, G. H. (1934). *Mind, self, and society.* Chicago: University of Chicago Press.

Mikulincer, M. (1997). Attachment style and mental representation of the self. *Journal of Personality and Social Psychology, 69*, 1203–1215.

Monroe, S. M., & Kelley, J. M. (1995). Measurement of stress appraisal. In S. Cohen, R. C. Kessler, & L. U. Gordon (Eds.), *Measuring stress: a guide for health and social scientists.* (pp. 122–147). New York: Oxford University Press.

Moos, R. H., & Billings, A. G. (1982). Conceptualizing and measuring coping resources and processes. In L. Goldberger & S. Breznitz, (Eds.), *Handbook of stress: Theoretical and clinical aspects* (pp. 212–230). New York: Free Press.

Moos, R. H., & Schaefer, J. A. (1993). Coping resources and processes: current concepts and measures. In L. Goldberger & S. Breznitz (Eds.), *Handbook of stress: Theoretical and clinical aspects* (pp. 234–257). New York: Free Press.

Newcomb, M. D. (1990). What structural equation modeling can tell us about social support. In B. R. Sarason, I. G. Sarason, & G. R. Pierce (Eds.), *Social support: An interactional view* (pp. 26–63). New York: Wiley.

Pagel, M. D., Erdly, W. W., & Becker, J. (1987). Social networks: We get by with (and in spite of) a little help from our friends. *Journal of Personality and Social Psychology, 53*, 793–804.

Peacock, E. J., & Wong, P. T. P. (1990). The Stress Appraisal Measure (SAM): A multidimensional approach to cognitive appraisal. *Stress Medicine, 6*, 227–236.

Pierce, G. R., Sarason, B. R., & Sarason, I. G. (1992). General and specific support expectations and stress as predictors of perceived supportiveness: An experimental study. *Journal of Personality and Social Psychology, 63*, 297–307.

Pierce, G. R., Sarason, I. G., Sarason, B. R., Solky-Butzel, J. A., & Nagle, L. C. (1997). Assessing the quality of personal relationships. *Journal of Personal and Social Relationships, 14*, 339–356.

Pierce, T., Baldwin, M., & Lydon, J. (1997). A relational schema approach to social support. In G. R. Pierce, B. Lakey, I. G. Sarason, & B. R. Sarason (Eds.), *Sourcebook of social support and personality* (pp. 19–48). New York: Plenum

Ptacek, J. T., & Gross, S. (1997). Coping as an individual difference variable. In G. R. Pierce, B. Lakey, I. G. Sarason & B. R. Sarason (Eds.), *Sourcebook of social support and personality* (pp. 69–92). New York: Plenum.

Reis, H. T., & Franks, P. (1994). The role of intimacy and social support in health outcomes: Two processes or one? *Personal Relationships, 1*, 185–197.

Rogers, T. B., Kuiper, N. A., & Kirker, W. S. (1977). Self-reference and the encoding of personal information. *Journal of Personality and Social Psychology, 35*, 677–678.

Rook, K. S. (1984). The negative side of social interaction: Impact on psychological well-being. *Journal of Personality and Social Psychology, 46*, 1097–1108.

Rook, K. S. (1987). Social support versus companionship: Effects on life stress, loneliness, and evaluations by others. *Journal of Personality and Social Psychology, 52*, 1132–1147.

Rowlinson, R. T., & Felner, R. D. (1988). Major life events, hassles, and adaptation in adolescence: Confounding in the conceptualization and measurement of life stress and adjustment revisited. *Journal of Personality and Social Psychology, 55*, 432–444.

Sarason, B. R., Pierce, G. R., & Sarason, I. G. (1990). Social support: The sense of acceptance and the role of relationships. In B. R. Sarason, I. G. Sarason, & G. R. Pierce (Eds.), *Social support: An interactional view* (pp. 9–25). New York: Wiley.

Sarason, B. R., Sarason, I. G., & Pierce, G. R. (1990). Traditional views of social support and their impact on assessment. In B. R. Sarason, I. G. Sarason, & G. R. Pierce (Eds.), *Social support: An interactional view* (pp. 9–25). New York: Wiley.

Simon, R. W. (1992). Parental role strains, salience of parental identity and gender differences in psychological distress. *Journal of Health and Social Behavior, 33*, 25–35.

Simon, R. W. (1997). The meanings individuals attach to role-identities and their implications for mental health. *Journal of Health and Social Behavior, 38*, 256–274.

Srull, T. K., & Wyer, R. S. (1989). Person memory and judgment. *Psychological Review, 96*, 58–83.

Stryker, S. (1980). *Symbolic interactionism: A social structural version.* Menlo Park: CA: Benjamin/Cummings.

Tetzloff, C. E., & Barrera, M. Jr. (1987). Divorcing mothers and social support: Testing the specificity of buffering effects. *American Journal of Community Psychology, 15*, 419–434.

Thoits, P. A. (1985). Social support and psychological well-being: Theoretical possibilities. In I. G. Sarason & B. R. Sarason (Eds.), *Social support: Theory, research and application.* (pp. 51–72). Dordrecht: Martinus Nijhoff.

Thoits, P. A. (1986). Social support as coping assistance. *Journal of Consulting and Clinical Psychology, 54*, 416–423.

Thoits, P. A. (1992). Identity structures and psychological well-being: Gender and marital status comparisons. *Social Psychology Quarterly, 55*, 236–256.

Thoits, P. A. (1999). Self, identity, stress and mental health. In C. S. Aheshensel and J. C. Phelan (Eds.), *Handbook of sociology and mental health* (pp. 345–368). New York: Plenum.

Turner, R. J., & Wheaton, B. (1995). Checklist measurement of stressful life events. In S. Cohen, R. C. Kessler, and L. U. Gordon (Eds.), *Measuring stress: a guide for health and social scientists* (pp. 29–58). New York: Oxford University Press.

Wethington, E., Brown, G. W., & Kessler, R. C. (1995). Interview measurement of stressful life events. In S. Cohen, R. C. Kessler, and L. U. Gordon (Eds.), *Measuring stress: a guide for health and social scientists* (pp. 59–79). New York: Oxford University Press.

Wethington, E., & Kessler, R. C. (1986). Perceived support, received support, and adjustment to stressful life events. *Journal of Health and Social Behavior, 27*, 78–89.

Williams, J. M. G., Mathews, A., & Macleod, C. (1996). The emotional Strop task and psychopathology. *Psychological Bulletin, 120*, 3–24.

3

Measuring Social Integration and Social Networks

Ian Brissette
Sheldon Cohen
Teresa E. Seeman

I. Social Integration
   A. Social Integration Theories
   B. Measuring Social Integration
      1. Role-Based Integration Measures
      2. Social Participation Measures
      3. Perceived Integration Measures
      4. Complex Indicators
   C. Issues in the Measurement of Social Integration
      1. Weighting
      2. Conflict
      3. Scale Components
      4. Social Isolation
   D. Selecting Appropriate Integration Measures
   E. Assessing Pathways Linking Social Integration and Health
   F. Socially Integrated Communities
II. Using Social Network Analysis to Measure Social Integration
   A. An Overview of the Network Perspective
   B. Assessing Structural Properties of Networks
      1. Measures of Network Size and Density
      2. Additional Measures of Network Structure
      3. Representing Network Data
   C. Improving Integration Measures Using Network Concepts
      1. Defining a Tie
      2. Limiting Network Size
III. Future Directions and Conclusions

SOCIAL INTEGRATION

Social integration is the extent to which an individual participates in a broad range of social relationships. Studies conducted across a variety of populations indicate that people who are more socially integrated live longer (reviewed by Berkman, 1995), are more likely to survive myocardial infarction (reviewed by Berkman, 1995; Seeman, 1996), are less likely to report being depressed (reviewed by Cohen, & Wills, 1985), are less likely to suffer a recurrence of cancer (reviewed by Helgeson, Cohen, & Fritz, 1998), and are less susceptible to infectious illness (Cohen, Doyle, Skoner, Rabin, & Gwaltney, 1997) than their less integrated counterparts. The health risks of being isolated are comparable in magnitude to the risks associated with cigarette smoking, blood pressure, and obesity and remain even after controlling for these and other traditional risk factors (House, Landis, & Umberson, 1988; Orth-Gomer & Johnson, 1987).

In this chapter, we illustrate the various ways in which social integration has been measured and provide guidelines for choosing an appropriate measure. We begin by discussing the theoretical underpinnings of the social integration concept and reviewing the various measurement techniques that have been used, including an overview of both individual and community-level social integration measures. We suggest that measurement techniques should be chosen in the context of hypotheses about how the social environment might influence health and with consideration of the characteristics of the population under study. In addition, we discuss pathways through which social integration may affect health and methods for assessing these potential mechanisms. Finally, we present a brief overview of formal social network theory and suggest a number of ways this approach might contribute to our understanding of existing literature on social integration and health and improve how we assess integration.

We are enthusiastic about social integration measures for several reasons. First and foremost, the majority of the evidence regarding social relationships and long-term health outcomes (e.g., all-cause mortality, survival after myocardial infarction, survival with breast cancer, psychiatric disorder) has come from studies using integration measures (cf. Berkman, 1995; Cohen, 1988; House, Landis, & Umberson, 1988). Second, these measures provide promising tools for testing theoretical questions. Third, social integration tends to be stable over time, and thus its influence on health may be easier to assess than the perceptions of social support resources. Fourth, social integration may be more amenable to intervention than perceptions of support.

Social Integration Theories

The concept of social integration is rooted in Durkheim's (1897/1951) seminal work on social conditions and suicide. Durkheim proposed that stable social structure and widely held norms are protective and serve to regulate behavior. Consistent with this reasoning, his analysis of suicide rates indicated that suicide was most prevalent among individuals who were not married and lacked ties with the community and church. Faris's (1934) work on cultural isolation and the development of mental illness also emphasized the importance of social contacts (cf. Jaco, 1954; Ware, 1956). Faris (1934) suggested that socially isolated individuals were at a higher risk for mental disorder. His ideas were grounded in symbolic interactionist tradition and carried the assumption that social interaction was essential to normal personality development and appropriate social conduct.

In contrast to their predecessors, a number of later sociologists suggested that participation in multiple social domains was detrimental to psychological well-being (Coser, 1974; Goode, 1960; Slater, 1963). These theorists viewed people's social environments as a set of interrelated role relationships. The roles prominently discussed included parent, husband or wife, volunteer, church member, and worker. Each role was said to demand different obligations. The more roles, the greater the conflicting obligations and concomitant experience of stress. Goode (1960) used the term *role strain* to illustrate the difficulty of performing multiple roles. Role strain consists of two components, role conflict and role overload. Role conflict occurs when the expectations associated with different roles are discrepant. Role overload occurs when honoring expectations associated with some roles is at the expense of honoring expectations associated with others. As one accumulates more roles, the probability of experiencing role conflict and role overload increases.

Although Goode's ideas have some intuitive appeal, a review by Sieber (1974) noted that empirical data have provided only limited support. In contrast to Goode (1960), Sieber (1974) proposed that possessing multiple roles is beneficial for psychological well-being. He argued that the rewards afforded by multiple roles exceed the burdens associated with role strain. Proposed rewards included accumulating privileges, status security, status enhancement, and self-esteem enhancement. Marks (1977) also suggested that multiple roles were not burdening and added that they could be potential sources of wealth, prestige, sympathy, approval, and favorable self-image. Both Sieber (1974) and Marks (1977) promoted the notion that role accumulation is more gratifying than stressful. This idea is referred to as the *role accumulation* theory. Role accumulation theory resonates with Faris's social isolation hypothesis. Both theoretical views propose that greater levels of social interaction are associated with greater well-being. However, a critical distinction can be made between the two. While Faris (1934) focused on isolation as a stressor, Marks (1977) and Sieber (1974) suggest the greater and more diverse one's social contacts, the better.

A more explicit theory of how social integration benefits health and well-being has been proposed by Thoits (1983). Consistent with symbolic interactionist theorists (Mead, 1934; Stryker, 1980), Thoits argued that people's identities are tied to the social positions or roles they occupy. Social roles are viewed as sets of behavioral expectations that emerge from the social environments in which one interacts. These behavioral expectations instill a sense of predictability in people's lives by providing information about how they ought to act. Also, by meeting role expectations, individuals are given the opportunity to enhance their self-esteem.

Thoits (1983) suggested that role identities provide people information about who they are in an existential sense. Social roles provide a purpose to life. Thus, as people accumulate role-identities, the sense that they possess a meaningful, guided existence strengthens. It is implied that a sense of meaning in life is an integral component of psychological well-being and that failing to have a sense of meaning often leads to improper conduct and deviant self-destructive behavior. This position is called the *identity accumulation* hypothesis (Thoits, 1983).

Cohen (1988) expressed a position similar to Thoits (1983) in his description of identity and esteem models of the psychological influence of social relationships. He has suggested that the ability to meet role expectations may result in cognitive benefits: increased feelings of self-worth and control over one's environment, which may influence health through a variety of pathways. According to Cohen (1988), the cognitive benefits afforded by holding multiple social roles lessen psychological despair, generate positive affect, and facilitate health-promoting behaviors. Cohen (1988) also suggested that social relationships have an impact on health through social and informational influence. Integrated individuals are subject to social controls that may influence the enactment of health behaviors and prevent risky behaviors (cf. Rook, 1990; Umberson, 1987). Social network members may also act as sources of information regarding appropriate medical care. Moreover, the feedback an individual receives from network members may influence symptom reporting and compliance with medical regimens.

Measuring Social Integration

Social integration is a multidimensional construct that is thought to include both the behavioral component of active engagement in a wide range of activities and/ or social relationships and the cognitive component of a sense of communality and an identification with one's social roles. In an attempt to organize our descriptions, we categorized the existing measures according to the components of the social integration construct they assess. Integration measures assessing the number of recognized social positions or social identities are termed *role-based* measures. Measures assessing the extent and frequency of social activities are termed *social participation* measures. Measures assessing individuals' own view of their communality are termed *perceived* integration measures. Finally, measures that blend these various approaches, are termed *complex indicators*. We do not provide a comprehensive review of social integration measures, but rather a sample of the different measurement approaches. Table 3.1 depicts the various approaches to measuring social integration we discuss.

Role-Based Integration Measures

Role-based measures assess participation in different types of social relationships. Typically, social integration is defined as the number of social roles (types of social relationships) for which respondents report active participation. Table 3.2 provides a list of the different types of social roles researchers have assessed, as well as the criteria they used to determine role enactment.

Thoits (1983, 1986) used data from the New Haven community study to construct an index assessing participation in eight different social roles. In this scale,

Table 3.1. Approaches to Measuring Social Integration

Role-Based Measures ▲
Assess the *number of different types of social relationships* in which individuals participate.
Participation-Based Measures
Assess the *frequency* with which individuals engage in various activities.
Perceived Integration Measures
Assess the extent to which *individuals believe they are embedded* in a stable social structure and identify with their fellow community members and social positions.
Complex Indicators
Combine information regarding social ties, community involvement, and frequency of contact with friends and relatives into a single summary index.

respondents are given 1 point for each role in which they indicate active participation for up to a total of 8 points. The roles include spouse, parent, worker, student, group member, church member, neighbor, and friend. Thoits (1986) includes criteria for the possession of each role (see Table 3.2). Her cross-sectional analysis of the New Haven community data indicated possessing more roles was associated with less psychological distress (Thoits, 1983). Thoits (1995) has also developed a role-based measure that includes seven additional roles (lover, son or daughter, son-in-law or daughter-in-law, relative, hobbyist, athlete, and stepparent). This measure allows participants to suggest additional role relationships they view as self-descriptive and contains items assessing role importance. Participants select up to three role identities they consider most important, second most important, and third most important. Thoits (1995) does not report whether the additional roles and prompts concerning role salience provide greater sensitivity in predicting mental health outcomes than the original scale.

Moen, Dempster-McClain, and Williams (1992) employed Thoits's (1986) role accumulation criteria in creating a role-involvement measure to assess the influence of social integration on women over the life course. Moen and colleagues (1989; 1992) examined participation in six roles—worker, church member, friend, relative, neighbor, and club or organization member—in 1956 and once again in 1986. Occupying more roles in 1956 was related to improved functional and perceived health status in 1986, even after controlling for age and previous health. Interestingly, the correlation between the number of roles reported in 1956 and in 1986 was relatively modest ($r = .22$).

Cohen's (1991; Cohen, Doyle, Skoner, Rabin, & Gwaltney, 1997) Social Network Index (SNI) assesses participation in twelve types of social relationships. These include relationships with a spouse, parents, parents-in-law, children, other close relatives, close neighbors, friends, workmates, school mates, fellow volunteers, members of groups without religious affiliations, and members of religious groups. Respondents are said to participate in a relationship if they report talking to a person on the phone or in person at least once every 2 weeks. One point is assigned for each type of relationship in which a person participates, for a total of 12 possible points. (Alternatively, one can assign participants 1 point for *each* of the social and religious groups in which they participate, thereby increasing

Table 3.2. Roles and Enactment Criteria

Role	Enactment Criteria
Parent*	Respondent has children under the age of 18 at home[a,d] ". . . respondents who had minor children living in their households (childrearers) were distinguished from those whose children were 18 or older and/or living out of the household." (Menaghan, 1989, p. 698)
Spouse	Married or living with someone in a marital-like relationship[a,b] Married and living in the same household[c]
Relative*	Has relatives in the area with whom they visit at least occasionally[a] Person had in-person contact with a relative at least once a month[e]
Worker*	Employed either part-time or full-time[a,d,e] Currently working full-time, working part-time, or laid off with a definite date to return[c]
Friend*	Respondent had at least one good friend within an hour's drive[c] Respondent has two or more close friends[a] Respondent had in-person contact with a friend at least once a month[e]
Neighbor*	Visited with a neighbor at least once a month[e] Visits neighbors[a,d]
Student*	Respondent attends classes regularly[a,d] ". . . respondents were considered students if they stated their main reason for not working was that they were in training or school." (Menaghan, 1989, p. 698)
Church Member*	Respondent attends church services at least occasionally[a] Attends religious services on a regular basis[d]
Volunteer*	
Group Member*	"We used membership in groups or clubs rather than attendance. . . ." (Moen et al., 1992, 1619)
Son/Daughter*	
Daughter-in-law/Son-in-law*	

*In Cohen's (1991; Cohen et al., 1997) SNI, a respondent has to report they have contact (either in person or on the phone) with a person from a specific role category at least once every 2 weeks to possess that role.
[a] Thoits, 1986.
[b] Cohen et al., 1997.
[c] Menaghan, 1989.
[d] Moen, Dempster-McClain, & Williams, 1992.
[e] Hong & Seltzer, 1995.

the possible number of roles.) The total number of persons with whom a respondent speaks in person or on the phone at least once every 2 weeks provides an estimate of network size. In a study in which role assessment was followed by inoculation with a common cold virus, Cohen and his colleagues (Cohen et al., 1997) found that increased numbers of roles were associated with a decreased probability of developing a cold. Their data also indicate that possessing a greater number of social roles is related cross-sectionally with increased positive affect, self-esteem, and personal control; less smoking and drinking; better diet and sleep; and more exercise (Cohen, 1991; Cohen et al., 1997). Role accumulation, as measured by the SNI, has also been found to be associated with positive mental health outcomes (reduced anxiety) in response to a stressful exam (Bolger & Eckenrode, 1991).

In addition to assessing the number of social roles occupied, this instrument can also be used to obtain information on the various domains of interaction by collapsing the spouse, parents, parents-in-law, children, and other close relatives items into a single category, kin, and treating the other items as described previously. This results in eight possible domains of interaction. Cohen's SNI is available on-line at: *http://www.psy.cmu.edu/~scohen*.

The challenges facing investigators considering using a role-based integration measure are somewhat different from those considering other types of support measures. Rather than spending time choosing between specific measures, the shrewd researcher is advised to consider which social roles it makes sense to assess and what criteria should be set to indicate role enactment. Table 3.2 summarizes roles commonly assessed and criteria that have been used to indicate role possession. Most of the criteria we list imply that role possession involves both a recognition or acceptance of the social position and an activity component (e.g., frequent interaction within the role). An important question is how many roles to sample. General population studies should consider using a minimum of five or six major roles (spouse, parent, worker, church member, social group member, friend). However, assessing more roles provides greater sensitivity. If you are working with a homogeneous sample you may consider employing some of the roles listed in Table 3.2 or other roles that may be more specific to your sample. The issue of what roles to assess becomes particularly salient in dealing with a sample that may be extreme on some dimension (e.g., cultural or age). In these cases, some of the major roles commonly used will not be applicable and thus may have to be replaced with more relevant ones.

An illustration of a role-based measure catered to a specific population is an index developed by Hong and Seltzer (1995). They constructed a scale to assess the role repertoires of mothers of adult children with mental retardation. Their measure assesses participation in five typical roles (spouse, employee (full-time or part-time), neighbor, friend, and relative) and three roles specific to their population of interest (support group member, parent of a nonhandicapped child, and coresident caregiving mother). Each role was weighted equally and summed to create a role count ranging from 0 to 8. A cross-sectional analysis indicated the greater the number of roles a respondent held, the less likely she was to feel depressed (Hong & Seltzer, 1995).

Social Participation Measures

Social participation measures assess the frequency with which people report engaging in various activities. Single items (e.g., visits with friends) or types of activities (e.g., active leisure) are often used as markers of integration, but they can be combined to create summary participation indices as well (e.g., Robbins, & Metzner, House, 1982). Social participation measures suggest the activities in which integrated people take part confer health benefits. However, the kinds of activities sampled are often engaged in with others and thus also reflect the range of social ties as well. One means of assessing whether it is activities or social activities per se that are important to health would be to assess different kinds of activities separately (e.g., social, going to the movies with a friend, physical-social, playing golf or tennis, solitary-passive, reading) and contrast whether certain categories of activities are especially strong predictors of health.

The Welin Activity Scale (WAS; Welin, Larsson, Svardsudd, Tibblin, & Tibblin, 1992) was originally used in a 12-year prospective study in Gothenbuerg, Sweden. The WAS asks participants to estimate how often they engaged in certain activities over the course of the past year. Activities are divided into three categories: *social activities* (8 items), *home activities* (10 items), and *outside home activities* (14 items). Three response options are provided for each item: never (score = 0), occasionally (score = 1), and often or regularly (score = 2). Ratings for the activities in each category are then summed to create three distinct activities scores. Scores for these three subscales are moderately correlated (.44 to .53) but appear to reflect distinct constructs. Results from the Gothenbuerg study indicate increased social activity was a prospective predictor of less cardiovascular mortality (Welin et al., 1992). In contrast, high levels of home activity were associated with less mortality from causes other than cardiovascular disease and cancer.

The Social Participation Scale (SPS) was created from questions taken from the Tecumseh Community Health Study (House et al., 1982). The SPS assesses participation in four categories of social activity: (1) *intimate social relationships* (e.g., marital status, visits with friends and relatives), (2) *formal organizational involvements outside work* (e.g., going to church meetings), (3) *active and relatively social leisure* (e.g., going to movies, fairs and museums), and (4) *passive and relatively solitary leisure* (e.g., watching television and reading). Parallel items tap respondents' satisfaction with their activities. The items that comprise the "intimate social relationships" section of the SPS resemble those from the role-based measures discussed previously. However, the three remaining sections of the SPS distinguish it from role based measures. Items from these subscales require respondents to estimate the frequency with which they engaged in various types of activities during the past year. Items from the first three participation subscales (excluding items concerning passive activities) can be summed to create a cumulative participation index (see House et al., 1982, for details).

Although House and colleagues (1982) propose scales representing each of four categories of social activity, they fail to report whether these four categories were associated with mortality. However, they did report that among men three specific activities were associated with reduced mortality over a 9- to 12-year follow-up: attending meetings of voluntary associations (formal organizational), going to lectures or classes (active, social leisure), and attending spectator events (active, social leisure). They also found that men reporting higher levels of activities on the cumulative index had lower mortality across the follow-up (House et al., 1982). Among women, only two activities were associated with mortality. The frequency of church attendance (formal organizational) predicted less mortality, and the amount of time spent watching television (passive, solitary leisure) was associated with greater mortality. Although women reporting higher levels of social activities on the cumulative index had lower mortality over the follow-up, this effect was not found when controls for other risk factors were included in the analysis. There were no reliable associations between mortality and satisfaction with activities among both men and women. This suggests that weighting items based on participants' ratings of satisfaction is not always useful.

Perceived Integration Measures

Perceived integration measures assess individuals' feelings of communality and belongingness. Prototypic measures inquire about familiarity with the community and identification with social roles. The perceptions assessed in these measures are thought to reflect characteristics of the social environment, as well as individuals' representations of their environments. Employing both a perceived integration measure and a more structural indicator of social integration (e.g., number of social roles) can allow one to address whether people's perceptions reflect characteristics of their social environment and, more important, whether these perceptions are predictive of health outcomes after controlling for differences in social participation or role engagement.

Heidrich and Ryff (1993) constructed a set of scales to reflect three psychological dimensions of integration in an elderly population: the presence of normative guidelines, the possession of meaningful roles, and the presence of appropriate reference groups. Two of the subscales, the *roles* subscale and the *reference* subscale, are particularly relevant. The *roles* subscale contains 10 items indicating the extent to which individuals perceive themselves as holding important, satisfying, and meaningful roles (e.g., "There are a lot of important things left for people to do after they retire"). The *reference* subscale contains 8 items assessing belongingness—whether individuals view themselves as a member of a social group, sharing values and attitudes with other elderly people (e.g., "I feel a sense of shared values with senior citizens in this country"). Participants are asked to rate the extent to which they agree with each statement on a scale ranging from 1 to 6, with higher scores indicating a higher degree of integration. Each subscale is scored separately. Both subscales were associated with decreased psychological distress and increased life satisfaction in cross-sectional analyses (Heidrich & Ryff, 1993).

Hanson and colleagues (Hanson, Isacsson, Janzon, & Lindell, 1989; Hanson, Isacsson, Janzon, Lindell, & Rastam, 1988) developed the Malmö Influence, Contact, and Anchorage Measure (MICAM) for use in a prospective population study of males in Malmö, Sweden. The measure assesses three markers of social integration: (1) social anchorage, (2) contact frequency, and (3) social participation. The contact frequency and social participation subscales overlap with integration measures previously discussed. However, the social anchorage scale is a novel approach to measuring integration. It contains eight items assessing the degree to which respondents feel integrated into their communities (e.g., "Would you say that you are rooted and have a feeling of familiarity with your neighborhood?"). Unfortunately, there is little evidence to suggest that the MICAM predicts health outcomes. After controlling for a number of variables correlated with mortality,

Hanson and colleagues failed to find an association between any of the three integration markers and all-cause mortality (Hanson et al., 1989).

Complex Indicators

Complex indictors typically combine information about marital status, number of social ties, frequency of contact with friends and relatives, and community involvement into a single summary index. The most recognized complex indicator is Berkman and Syme's (1979) Social Network Index (SNI). This summary measure was created from four distinct components: marital status, a sociability index (based on contact with friends and relatives), church membership, and group membership. The SNI considers both the number and the relative importance of social ties across these four network categories and combines this information into a single summary measure (ranging from 1 to 4). In Berkman's (empirically based) weighting system (1979), an index of intimate contacts (marital status, friends and relatives) is given nearly four times the weight as group membership and twice the weight of church membership.

Higher scores on the SNI were associated with less total mortality in 9-year (Berkman & Syme, 1979) and 17-year follow-ups (Seeman, Kaplan, Knudsen, Cohen, & Guralnik, 1987) of men and women of Alameda County, California. Reynolds and Kaplan's (1990) 17-year follow-up also found that integrated women were less likely to die of cancer. Schoenbach and his colleagues (Schoenbach, Kaplan, Freedman, & Kleinbaum, 1986) used Berkman and Syme's weighting system to create a network index from questions in the Evans County Cardiovascular Epidemiologic Study. The Evans County index predicted mortality but just among white males (Schoenbach et al., 1986). The evidence regarding the SNI's relation to mental health outcomes has been inconsistent (Goodenow, Resine, & Grady, 1990; Schaefer, Coyne, & Lazarus, 1981). Although all of these studies listed employed Berkman & Syme's weighted scoring system, Seeman and her colleagues have also employed a scoring system in which marital status, visits with friends and relatives, and church and group membership contribute equally to the summary index. The index resulting from this unweighted scoring system also predicted mortality during a 5-year follow-up of elderly adults (Seeman, Berkman et al., 1993).

Psychometrics on the SNI and additional evidence for the scale's predictive validity are available in Berkman and Breslow (1983). Instructions for scoring the scale are not published, but can be obtained from Lisa Berkman (*lberkman@hsph.harvard.edu*).

The Social Connections Index (SCI) was developed by Kaplan and colleagues (Kaplan et al., 1988) to investigate mortality rates among males and females in Kuopio and North Karelia, Finland. The SCI contains five questions concerning the extent and frequency of social connections. Items assess social participation: planned visits with friends and relatives, meetings with clubs and societies, number of daily interactions, and marital status. One of the advantages of the SCI is that it is easy to score. Marital status is the only dichotomous variable and is weighted 1 (unmarried) and 4 (married) to equalize its contribution to the summary measure. The remaining questions, all of which yield responses between 1 and 6, are combined with marital status to create a single continuous index. Individuals identified by the SCI as having more social connections had lower mortality from all causes, cardiovascular disease, and ischemic heart disease during the 5-year follow-up (Kaplan et al., 1988). These effects were found among men but not women.

Other complex indicators of social integration have been used in studies of mental health outcomes. Nine items were used to measure social well-being in the Rand Health Insurance Experiment (Donald & Ware, 1982; Donald, Ware, Brook & Davies-Avery, 1978). Social well-being consists of two components: social contacts and activities and social resources. The items in the Rand measure resemble items from other complex indicators, such as frequency of contact with friends and relatives and frequency of church participation. Like complex indicators previously described, these items can be aggregated to create a summary index (scoring is available in Donald & Ware, 1982). Items can also be summed to create distinct measures of social resources and social contacts. Visits with friends and relatives and home visits by friends form the social contacts index. Attendance at religious services, number of neighborhood acquaintances, and number of close friends and relatives form the social resources index. Donald and Ware (1982) report that the social resources and social contacts subscales and their combination, the social well-being scale, all have adequate internal consistencies, alphas ranging from .66 to .88. They also report that these indices are stable over 1-year intervals. In a cross-sectional analysis, the summary index was associated with better mental health regardless of stressful life events. Moreover, in longitudinal analyses, high levels of social well-being were found to predict subsequent improvements in mental health (Williams, Ware, & Donald, 1981). Analyses conducted on the subscales indicated social resources were better predictors of mental health than social contacts (Donald & Ware, 1982).

Issues in the Measurement of Social Integration

Weighting

The issue of whether to employ a weighted scale is particularly germane in considering the use of a role-based measure, a participation measure, or a complex indicator. A number of the complex indicators assign more weight to certain types of relationships (marital status) or contacts (family or friends) to reflect the presumed importance of these ties. We would recommend weighting items only when there is a sound conceptual reason to do so. For example, if a researcher believes that social integration is a marker for emotional support, then it makes sense to weight marital status more than employment status or membership in a social group. However, if the researcher believes that social integration is beneficial because it promotes the development of a diversified self-concept, then there is no reason to weight marital status more than group membership. Although it has yet to be done, one could compare the efficacy of different weighting schemes as a means of testing the various explanations offered for the social integration findings.

Conflict

Social networks can also be inimical to health. Relationships are often accompanied by conflict and stress (Goode, 1960; Rook, 1984; Rook & Pietromonaco, 1987). Interpersonal conflict is associated with increased negative affect (Bolger, DeLongis, Kessler, & Schilling, 1989) and decreased emotional well-being (Abbey, Abramis, & Caplan, 1985) and has been linked to depression and social withdrawal (Evans, Palasano, Lepore & Martin, 1989) and susceptibility to infectious disease (Cohen et al., 1998). Because social integration measures do not explicitly assess the qualitative aspects of social ties, they are relatively insensitive to conflict. Including indicators of conflictual network ties might provide insight regarding the relation between social conflict and social integration and improve existing measures. For example, Rook (1984) found that the number of problematic relationships elderly widowed women reported was cross-sectionally associated with decreased psychological well-being.

Scale Components Another means of better understanding the factors that underlie social integration is to consider separately the different subscales that make up these aggregate measures. Many of these measures have been designed with this intent. For example, the HIE's social well-being scale (Donald & Ware, 1982) contains measures of both social resources and social contacts and activities. The SPS allows investigators to consider the importance of different categories of activity (House et al., 1982). Other scales can be easily adapted to fulfill this purpose as well (e.g., Berkman & Breslow, 1983; Seeman et al., 1987). Role-based measures seem particularly advantageous in this regard. They can be used to discern whether certain types of roles may be particularly important to social integration. However, the low base rate of certain roles would make this option less feasible for studies with small samples.

Social Isolation Social isolation has been implicated as a risk factor in the development of both mental and physical illness (Faris, 1934; Lynch, 1979), which raises the question of whether social integration should be viewed as merely the absence of isolation. The test of social isolation versus social integration is essentially a test of a threshold model versus a more linear model—that is, whether the difference in risk is between isolated and not isolated or whether there is a gradient of protection. Although the conceptualization of social integration we provide suggests integration should be viewed as a gradient of protection, the available empirical evidence has not resolved this issue (Berkman & Breslow, 1983; House, Umberson, & Landis, 1988). This lack of resolution may be because many existing measures include a limited range of social roles and activities in assessing integration and may not be suited for detecting whether there is a gradient of protection.

The question as to whether the social integration effects reflect a threshold effect has implications for those considering intervention. For example, knowing substantial health benefits are gained from active participation in one social role versus none or from having one source of companionship versus none could identify individuals who might benefit most from techniques like grafting a new tie (cf. chapter 8). A word of caution is warranted, though; isolated individuals might possess characteristics (e.g., personality disorders) that may lend them less receptive to intervention (cf. Heller, Thompson, Trueba, Hogg, & Vlachos-Weber, 1991). Moreover, recruiting and retaining isolated participants may prove to be a challenge.

Selecting Appropriate Integration Measures

In deciding what category of measure to use, our advice is to begin by considering your own theories about why social integration is salubrious. Your own hypotheses will dictate which categories of measures may be more appropriate. For example, when testing the hypothesis that health consequences stem from integrated individuals having more social interaction and participating in more gratifying activities, a measure that assesses social participation would be most appropriate. When testing the hypothesis that the belief that one is embedded in a stable social network is sufficient for the observed health benefits, a perceived integration scale would be appropriate. When testing the hypothesis that the benefits of social integration result from having a range of different types of ties that provide information, support, or a diversified self-concept, then a role-based measure would be appropriate. Of the categories of measures we have reviewed, the complex indicators inform us the least about what characteristics of social ties are responsible for the relation between participating in a network and health. This is because they combine different components of social integration into a single index.

Although some measurement techniques may provide better matches to theories, there remains considerable overlap between the various approaches outlined. However, there are techniques that can be used to better understand how social integration affects health. First, using more than one type of integration measure or weighting scales to reflect different theoretical positions can help determine the important underlying processes. Second, measuring potential mediators allows researchers to establish the pathways through which integration operates. We can also gain a better understanding of how integration influences health by taking advantage of the burgeoning intervention tradition (see chapters 6, 7, 8, 9, and 10 in this volume). Because of its robust relation with mental and physical health, integration should be considered a potential component of psychosocial interventions (cf. Arnetz, Theorell, Levi, Kallner, & Eneroth, 1983; Clarke, Clarke, & Jagger, 1992). Moreover, understanding how interventions influence people's existing relationships, patterns of activity, and perceptions of social resource availability may help us to understand why certain interventions are successful and others fail. Successful interventions may have an impact on health by altering patterns of social integration.

Assessing Pathways Linking Social Integration and Health

In planning studies, it is important to include measures that assess the pathways through which social integration may influence health. There is compelling evidence that social integration is important to health but little data regarding the factors that mediate the relation between social integration and health. It is likely that no single process can explain the link between social integration and health. Thus, the goal of the integration researcher should be to identify and understand a range of contributing processes in order to identify which pathways may be most important and most amenable to intervention. It is also important to keep in mind that the effects of social integration on health may be the result of differences in cognitive, behavioral, and biological functioning (see chapter 1). These mediational pathways represent different interdependent levels of analysis. Studies that include measures representing multiple levels will be best able to elucidate the complexities of the pathways that link integration and health.

In the paragraphs that follow, we highlight some of the major psychological and behavioral constructs that have been implicated as potential mediators of the relation between social integration and health (see preceding section on Social Integration Theories). Chapter 1 of this book provides a discussion of the some of the biological—that is, immunological and neuroendocrine—pathways that may link social relationships and health. Measurement of these factors is discussed in Cohen, Kessler, and Underwood-Gordon (1995).

Personal Control Drawing from the symbolic interactionist (most notably Mead, 1934) notion that social roles guide behavioral interactions, Thoits (1983) has suggested that possessing multiple social roles promotes a sense of predictability and controllability in one's life. These positive psychological states are presumed to impact self-care (Cohen, 1988) and mediate the association between role possession and psychological distress (Thoits, 1983). The most often used measure of personal control is Rotter's (1966) locus of control measure. This scale assesses the degree to which people expect that they control their outcomes and the degree to which they expect their outcomes are controlled by others, chance, God, or luck. Rotter's (1966) measure has been criticized on the grounds that it measures only generalized expectations and does not distinguish control over personal outcomes from control over other entities. More recent measures assess perceptions of control over various domains separately. For example, Paulhus's (1983) Spheres of Control (SOC) scale assesses control over personal events (e.g., "When I make plans I am almost certain to make them work"), interpersonal events (e.g., "I have no trouble making friends"), and social and political events (e.g., "The average citizen can have an influence on government decisions"). Other measures distinguish between chance factors and powerful others as external causes of outcomes (Levenson, 1981). (See Leftcourt, 1991, for a review of personal control measures.)

Self-Esteem Several theoretical perspectives suggest that possessing multiple so-cial roles promotes self-esteem and self-worth (Cohen, 1988; Sieber, 1974; Thoits, 1983). Feelings of esteem and self-worth are thought to enhance adaptation to stressful life events, promote positive affect, and prevent depression (Cohen, 1988). There are a substantial number of self-esteem measures available, with the two most widely recognized measures being Rosenberg's Self-Esteem Scale (1965) and Coopersmith's Self-Esteem Inventory (1967, 1981). Both of these measures assess global self-worth and have demonstrated adequate reliability and validity (see Blascovich & Tomaka, 1991). Measures assessing feelings of competence in specific domains are also available. For example, Seeman and her colleagues (See-man, Rodin, & Albert, 1993) have developed a measure to assess competence in interpersonal domains (e.g., interacting with friends and family) and instrumental domains (e.g., ability to handle personal finances). It is worth considering whether feelings of competence in certain domains (e.g., interpersonal, work related) are more important to understanding social integration than global self-esteem.

Meaning and Purpose According to the symbolic interactionist perspective, role identities provide behavioral expectations, meaning, and guidance to life (Mead, 1934; Thoits, 1983). These states are assumed to be prerequisites to psychological health. Meaning or purpose in life has been conceptualized in a variety of ways, with some theorists using the terms to refer to the extent to which individuals identify with their roles (e.g., Simon, 1997; Thoits, 1983) and others using the term to refer to the belief that life provides suitable challenges and rewards and continues to be worth living (Antonovsky, 1979; Burton, 1998). Despite the abun-dance of theoretical work concerning meaning and purpose, this area remains underdeveloped in regard to measurement. The Meaning and Purpose in Life scales on Ryff's (1989) measure of psychological well-being and Antonovsky's (1987) Sense of Coherence scale are among the more established measures. Ryff's (1989) Purpose in Life is particularly noteworthy because it has 20-, 14-, 9-, and 3-item versions and good psychometric qualities. Burton (1998) has developed a 5-item measure of "global integrative meaning." This scale has also demonstrated acceptable psychometric properties and in a cross-sectional analysis has been found to mediate the relation between social integration and psychological dis-tress (Burton, 1998).

Self-Concept A number of theoretical perspectives propose that individuals' self-concepts reflect the social positions they hold (Burke & Tully, 1977; Cooley, 1902; Mead, 1934; Stryker, 1980). This view suggests socially integrated individuals possess more diverse self-concepts. Possessing a diverse self-concept is assumed to influence both how people appraise negative life events and how they respond to negative information about the self (Linville, 1985). Self-concept assessment has a lengthy history. Simple measures such as the Twenty Statements Test (TST) require participants to generate statements in response to the question "Who are you?" Other techniques, such as the Q-sort (e.g., Block, 1961), require participants to sort cards containing self-evaluative statements into different piles according to the extent to which they are deemed self-descriptive. Recent measures of self-concept take into consideration that people can hold multiple self-representations simultaneously (Higgins, Bond, Klein, & Strauman, 1986; Rogers, 1965). For example, Higgins's (1987) measure of self-concept discrepancy requires participants to generate attributes of their actual self, ideal self (their own or others' hopes and goals for them), and ought self (their own or others' beliefs about duties required of them). Other self-concept measures are specific to people in certain age groups (e.g., adult, child, elderly). (See Byrne, 1996, for a review.)

Linville's (1985, 1987) measure of self-complexity comes close to capturing the notion of self-diversity. Based on the Q-sort, in this measure participants are asked to sort cards containing self-descriptive statements into piles that capture different aspects of who the participants think they are. Participants are instructed that they are free to create as many or as few piles as they wish and that they are allowed to use the same descriptive statements in multiple piles. Self-complexity is based on two factors: (1) the number of piles participants generate (more piles mean greater complexity) and (2) the extent to which different self-descriptive statements are used in the piles created (more adjectives mean greater complexity).

Affect Social integration is hypothesized to promote positive affect and prevent negative affect (Cohen, 1988). Depressed affect is hypothesized to alter willingness to enact health behaviors and has been found to be associated with decreased immune competence (Herbert & Cohen, 1993). Taken together, these findings raise the possibility that affect may be one of the pathways through which social integration affects health. Positive and negative affect have been viewed as both stable traitlike characteristics (e.g., Watson, Clark, & Tellegen, 1988) and relatively transitory states (e.g., Nowlis & Green, 1957). The Profile of Mood States (McNair, Lorr, & Droppleman, 1971) and the Nowlis Mood Adjective Checklist (Nowlis & Green, 1965) represent two of the more widely used measures of positive and negative affect. The Trait PANAS (Watson, et al., 1988) represents a widely used trait measure. Stone (1995) provides a comprehensive review of the available measures and a discussion of issues relevant to measuring affect in the context of health research.

Social Controls Several theorists have suggested that the health benefits associated with integration may result from the fact that integrated individuals are subject to additional social controls (House, Landis, & Umberson, 1988; Rook, 1990; Umberson, 1987). In this context, social control is used to refer to two processes: (1) direct efforts others make to influence the health practices of the target and (2) the regulating, stabilizing responsibilities associated with holding social positions (Rook, 1990). These two dimensions are often measured separately. For example, the presence of children in the home has been commonly used as an indicator of role responsibilities (Umberson, 1992), and questions regarding whether respondents perceive that other people deter and promote behaviors relevant to health have been used to assess direct social control efforts (e.g., Rook,

Thuras, & Lewis, 1990). The social control literature is another area in which measurement has not kept pace with theoretical development.

Social Support Social integration is often interpreted as evidence of access to social support resources. However, it is not clear that support has anything to do with the health benefits associated with being socially integrated. In fact, evidence from the mental health literature suggests that integration and social support promote mental health through different pathways and that social integration and perceived support are minimally correlated (Cohen & Wills, 1985). To test the hypothesis that the health benefits associated with social integration stem from the fact that integrated individuals have more support available to them, we recommend measuring support separately. The measurement of received support and perceived support is discussed in chapter 4 of this book.

Socially Integrated Communities

The notion of social capital offers a slightly different perspective on the concept of social integration. Social capital refers to the extent to which communities offer their members opportunities to increase their personal and family resources (Coleman, 1988). Communities that afford increased opportunity for active involvement in formal group activities and better public schooling are said to have increased social capital (Putnam, 1995). This perspective raises the possibility that individual differences in social integration reflect differences in the communities in which people live. Moreover, it also suggests that it is possible for community characteristics to have an independent impact on health and/or interact with an individual's level of social integration.

The primary approach to measuring social capital has been to assess perceptions of individuals and then aggregate responses over neighborhoods or census blocks. Typical measures contain questions regarding group memberships, civic participation, and feelings of communality with one's neighborhood (social cohesion). For example, Sampson Raudenbush, and Earls (1997) developed a five-item trust and cohesion measure. Participants were asked to report whether they agreed with a series of statements about their neighborhoods (e.g., "This is a close-knit neighborhood" and "People in this neighborhood can be trusted"). Cross-sectional data demonstrated neighborhoods higher in social cohesion experienced less violence (e.g., robberies, muggings, gang fights) than those lower in social cohesion (Sampson et al., 1997). Buckner (1988) has also developed a measure of neighborhood cohesion (the Neighborhood Cohesion Instrument [NCI]). This 18-item instrument assesses three proposed dimensions of cohesion: attraction to the neighborhood, neighboring (social interaction), and sense of community. Work by Buckner (1988) has demonstrated that the NCI is positively associated with the length of time people lived in their neighborhood.

Social capital could also be assessed by identifying the extent to which communities afford opportunities for social activities, volunteerism, group membership, leisure, and political activism (Fitzgerald, 1949). For example, one could count the number of parks, golf courses, tennis courts, bars and bowling alleys, churches, social clubs, and community-based volunteer groups per capita. It is also possible to measure the frequency of town meetings and other indicators of civic participation (e.g., PTA meetings, local political party organizations; e.g., Chavis, Hogge, & McMillan, 1986). Such measures identify communities that afford increased opportunity for political activism. Another factor one should consider measuring when conducting community level analyses is the quality of the social services within different communities. For example, communities with more tennis courts, bowling alleys, and parks are also likely to have better hospitals and other social services. In such circumstances, increased accessibility to high-quality health care service may explain why people who live in communities that afford opportunities for integration have better mental and physical health.

Despite their prevalence in community research, social capital has rarely been examined in relation to traditional mental and physical health outcomes. However, in a recent cross-sectional study, Kawachi, Kennedy, Lochner, and Prothrow-Stith (1997) assessed two markers of social capital: the proportion of people in each state who believe others could be trusted and the per capital density of membership in voluntary groups. Both measures were associated with lower all-cause mortality, lower mortality from coronary heart disease and malignant neoplasms, and lower infant mortality. Kawachi and colleagues' (1997) study is the first to show an association between social capital and a traditional health outcome. By including both individual and community-level markers of social integration, future studies will be able to determine whether constructs such as social cohesion and competence account for the social integration effects.

USING SOCIAL NETWORK ANALYSIS TO MEASURE SOCIAL INTEGRATION

In this section, we illustrate how measurement techniques from formal social network theory can be applied to better understand the existing literature on social integration and health and improve social integration measures (see Hall & Wellman, 1985; House & Kahn, 1985). Our discussion of network theory is relatively narrow in focus, and we direct the interested reader to additional resources on network analysis (see also Burt & Minor, 1983; Hall & Wellman, 1985; Mitchell, 1969; Mitchell & Trickett, 1980; Wasserman & Faust, 1994).

An Overview of the Network Perspective

Within formal network theory, the term *network* refers to the ties that connect a specific set of actors or nodes (Mitchell, 1969). Although nodes typically represent individuals, they can just as easily represent other social entities: corporations, groups, or families. Networks can be differentiated by their scope. Personal or ego-centric networks encompass the ties surrounding a single focal individual.

Aggregate or whole networks encompass the total set of ties among members of a population. Because they are most applicable to the measures of social integration we have discussed, we pay exclusive attention to personal networks in which nodes represent individuals and ties represent relationships between individuals.

Network analysis is a quantitative means of describing the relationships that exist between members of an individual's social network. For example, network analysts use the number of nodes contained in a network to provide an estimate of the network's size. For our purposes, network analysis provides a means of measuring properties of networks that may provide a closer match to theories about social integration. We begin our discussion of the network perspective by reviewing measures of network structure that may be relevant to social integration.

Assessing Structural Properties of Networks

Structure is the term used to describe stable patterns that exist among ties. The simplest and most widely used measure of network structure is network size (i.e., the number of people in the network). Network size has been utilized in a number of studies involving health outcomes (e.g., Gallo, 1982; Haines & Hurlburt, 1992; Seeman, Berkman, Blazer, & Rowe, 1994). However, it is a relatively weak predictor of health (see reviews by Cohen & Wills, 1985, and Uchino, Cacioppo, & Kielcolt-Glaser, 1996) and, although correlated with integration, is probably not responsible for the effects of social integration (e.g., Cohen et al., 1997).

Network density is a concept we believe to be more relevant to understanding how social integration operates. Network density refers to the extent to which network members know one another. High-density networks, where network members are acquainted, have been hypothesized as helpful in maintaining one's social identity and promoting the flow of support resources from network members (McKinlay, 1973; Walker, MacBride, & Vachon, 1977; Wellman, 1981). For example, in a cross-sectional study of Korean, Chinese, Japanese, and Filipino immigrants, Kuo and Tsai (1986) found that immigrants who possessed higher-density networks tended to report less depression than those with less dense networks. In contrast, low-density networks are thought to be particularly valuable during life transitions or following changes in one's network, due to, for example, divorce, unemployment, or geographic relocation (Granovetter, 1973; Hirsch, 1980; Hirsch, 1981a; Wilcox, 1981). For example, Hirsch (1980) examined women who were recently widowed and found low-density networks were associated with improved mental health, presumably because these women had portions of their networks which did not overlap with their husbands'. Because integrated individuals are thought to possess a wide range of social relationships, they may possess lower-density networks than their less integrated counterparts, but as of yet there are no data regarding the relation between social integration and network density.

Measures of Network Size and Density

A number of researchers have developed measures to estimate network size and density. These measures may be particularly useful if they are employed in conjunction with standard social integration measures. This would test whether social integration measures remain associated with positive health outcomes after controlling for network characteristics like the density of the participants' personal networks. Systematic analyses of this sort can be used to rule out potential explanations for the social integration effects and also may provide insight about what processes may be operating.

Hirsch's (1979; 1980) Social Network List (SNL) is one of the few measures that has been used to document a relation between a formal network measure (density) and a health outcome (mental health). Hirsch's measure asks respondents to list up to 20 significant others with whom they have contact at least once every 2 weeks and indicate which people are relatives and friends. This provides an estimate of network size. The SNL can also be used to assess density. Participants are asked to list the individuals previously named in a matrix and then indicate individuals they consider to have relationships with each other. One of the easily remedied limitations of this scale is that Hirsch (1980) does not specify the criterion used to judge whether two people have a relationship. Hirsch (1981b; Hirsch & Reischl, 1985) has also used the SNL to obtain density measures for specific portions of respondents' personal networks, boundary density. Boundary density is the proportion of actual to potential ties that exist between network members of any two domains of interaction (e.g., family and work).

Stokes (1985) asks participants to list the initials of people who are "important to their lives" and with whom they have contact at least once a month and indicate which people are their relatives. From these queries, a structural measure (network size) and a measure of network composition (percentage of kin) are obtained. Stokes's SNL (1985) also yields an estimate of network density. Respondents are asked to indicate which network members they believe have contact with each other at least once a month. Density is computed by dividing the number of actual ties among network members by the number of potential ties.

Additional Measures of Network Structure

In addition to network size and density, a number of other measures of network structure may also be of relevance to health (Hall & Wellman, 1985). For example, rather than getting a summary measure of network density, network analysts often distinguish portions of individuals' personal networks that are higher in density than others. These higher-density portions are referred to as *clusters*. This fine-grained network analysis could be useful in determining how the social networks of integrated individuals differ from those of their less integrated counterparts. Moreover, it could be used to examine whether structural network features influence access to social support (Wellman & Wortley, 1990). Table 3.3 lists some network measures that may be relevant to investigators interested in social relationships and health (see Hall & Wellman, 1985; Mitchell & Trickett, 1980). Unfortunately, there are few studies that test the relations between these measures and health outcomes.

Representing Network Data

Network data can be represented graphically in the form of sociograms or in matrices. Simple graphs use nodes to represent actors in a network and lines to represent ties. (For more on graph theory, see Harary, Norman, & Cartwright, 1965, and Hage & Harary, 1983.) A two-way matrix, referred to as a *sociomatrix*, can also be used to represent data. Here, network members are listed in rows and columns, and numeric values reflect the attributes of ties (e.g., strength, intimacy) between two actors. The task of analyzing and managing network data can be formidable, but simple measures of network structure like size and density are relatively simple to estimate. For those interested in engaging in more sophisticated network analyses, we recommend one of the many computer packages designed specifically for network analysis (cf. Wasserman & Faust, 1994). Information about programs that might meet individual specifications can be obtained at the Web page of the International Network for Social Network Analysis (INSNA): *http://www.heinz.cmu.edu/project/INSNA/*.

Table 3.3. Network Features Potentially Relevant to Health

Characteristic	Measure
Range (Size)	The number of network members
Density	The extent to which a network is interconnected; measured by comparing the actual number of direct ties with the number of ties that would exist if all members were directly connected
Degree	The average number of direct ties a network member has with other network members
Reachability	For use with aggregate networks; the maximum number of ties it takes to connect any two nodes
Boundedness	The number of ties that fall within the network's bounds
Cliques	Portions of a network in which all network members are directly tied; has a density of 1.0
Clusters	Portions of the network with high density; defined by less stringent criteria than cliques
Components	For use with aggregate networks; portions of the network where everyone is tied directly or indirectly
Dispersion	The ease with which an individual can make contact with the person; often measured in terms of geographic distance

Improving Integration Measures
Using Network Concepts

In addition to suggesting structural features of social networks with potential implications for health, formal network theorists have addressed a number of issues that might be adopted to improve social integration measurement.

Defining a Tie

Social and health scientists often discuss the relation between participating in a social network and health as if the issue of what is encompassed in the term *social network* was self-evident. However, this is not the case. The definition of what constitutes a tie identifies which individuals are considered nodes in a network. Ties are commonly chosen based on either normative, affective, or interdependence-exchange criteria (Fischer, 1982; McCallister & Fischer, 1978). Normative or formal criteria result in networks that include people who occupy socially recognized roles: mother, daughter, employee, neighbor, friend. Affective criteria encompass individuals respondents feel close to or care about. Finally, interdependence or exchange criteria include people with whom respondents interact regularly, exchange resources, or both (Fischer, 1982). Although there is typically considerable overlap between networks generated by these three techniques, they do tend to elicit different network members (cf. Bernard, et al., 1990). For example, networks based on affective criteria tend to be smaller than networks generated by exchange criteria and contain a higher percentage of kin (Milardo, 1992). Work by Van Groenou, Van Sonderen, and Ormel (1992) has demonstrated the role-based (88% concordance), affective-based (78% concordance), and exchange-based (74% concordance) criteria have all shown adequate test-retest reliability over a 4-week period. Table 3.4 depicts some of the ways these criteria have been operationalized (cf. Laumann, Marsden, & Prensky, 1983; Marsden, 1990).

Social integration measures typically include ties based on normative criteria. For example, in Cohen's SNI (1991; Cohen et al., 1997), a person is judged to be a network member if he or she occupies one of 12 role categories. Although overlooked in the past, affective and exchange-interdependence criteria can also be employed in social integration measures and may be useful for testing ideas about what kinds of processes may underlie the social integration effects. In some instances, a specific definition of a tie may provide a better match to theory. For example, to test the hypothesis that social integration measures reflect the availability of support resources, you should consider employing a definition of a tie that closely reflects this position (e.g., those individuals you feel comfortable turning to for support). Alternatively, the hypothesis that the effects can be attributed solely to intimate ties might be best tested by using an affect-based definition of a tie (e.g., those individuals with whom you feel comfortable sharing personal information and feelings). We also advocate using different types of criteria and comparing the predictive validity of measures based on these different definitions (cf. Bernard et al., 1990; Milardo, 1992).

Table 3.4. Operational Definitions for Network Membership

Source	Criteria
Brugha et al. (1987)	"... those aged at least 14 years living in the household ...; those they considered close relatives or friends." (p. 124)
Henderson, Duncan-Jones, McAuley, & Ritchey (1978)	Links active within the preceding year with a frequency of at least once per month (excluding links developed solely within the context of a formal or institutional relationship.
Stokes (1985)	Up to 20 people who are significant in your life and with whom you have contact at least once a month.
Wellman (1988)	*Intimate network members:* people respondents feel closer to outside their homes. *Significant network members:* people who are in touch with respondents in their daily lives and who are significant in their lives.
Campbell, Marsden, & Hurlburt (1986)	Persons with whom the respondent shares nine kinds of relational contact, adult household members, and other people the respondents deem important.
Burt (1984, 1985)	The people with whom you discussed important matters (over the past 6 months).
Tolsdorf (1976)	Those people to whom respondents feel close and consider they know well.
Hirsch (1980)	Up to 20 significant others with whom the respondents have contact at least once during any 4- to 6-week period.
Sonderen et al. (1992)	"... persons who mean a lot to you and without whom life would be difficult."

The Social Networks in Adult Life questionnaire (SNAL) Antonucci & Akiyama, 1987; Antonucci, Fuhrer, & Dartigues, 1997), also referred to as the *convoy measure*, is an example of a measure that is based on an affective network membership criterion. Respondents begin by naming people to whom they feel so close that it would be difficult for them to imagine life without them and then are prompted to name people with whom they have relationships that are less close (Kahn & Antonucci, 1980). Three concentric circles are used to represent levels of affective attachment. In a cross-sectional study Antonucci et al. (1997) found that increased network size (across all three concentric circles) as measured by the SNAL questionnaire, was inversely associated with depression in an elderly population. The convoy measure provides a straightforward technique to determine network size based on affective closeness, and for this reason it is often used with children (Levitt, Guacci-Franco, & Levitt, 1993). One advantage of the SNAL is that it allows one to compare the relative effectiveness of definitions of ties based on different levels of emotional closeness.

Limiting Network Size

Although researchers often place limits on the number of people an individual can nominate as network members, network size is primarily determined by how you choose to define a tie. As indicated in Table 3.4, definitions of ties vary considerably in inclusiveness. Those investigating social integration have traditionally assessed a very narrow range of network ties (e.g., marital ties, ties with close friends, relatives, and formal churches and social groups) and have experienced a great deal of success in predicting health outcomes from differences in networks typically containing between 5 and 20 members. These measures imply that close ties and ties to established formal organizations (churches and social groups) are critical to health and well-being. However, because few investigators have assessed extended network ties in the study of health, this issue has not been resolved. We currently know little about how properties of people's broader social networks affect health (Haines & Hurlburt, 1992).

FUTURE DIRECTIONS AND CONLUSIONS

Our primary goal in writing this chapter was to provide a resource to aid in the selection and evaluation of social integration measures. Social integration measures have been used across a wide range of scientific disciplines. However, despite their prominence, surprisingly little is known about why they are such powerful predictors of physical and mental health. The association between social integration and health is clear. However, determining whether this relation reflects differences in patterns of social participation, differences in the availability of resources, or differences in cognitive self-concept remains a chief research priority.

We have illustrated that existing categories of integration measures emphasize different components of the social integration construct. For evaluating measurement options, we urge researchers to consider their own hypotheses about how social environment influences health and allow these beliefs to guide measurement selection. We encourage contrasting scales to answer questions about social integration. This includes determining the potential implications that community-level factors may have on health. We also advocate assessing potential mediators of the relation between integration and health. Finally, we have pointed to concepts from formal social network theory as a potential means of exploring how characteristics of the social environment have an impact on health and well-being.

In regard to future directions, one area of interest concerns the development of daily integration measures. One of the principal criticisms of many of the social integration measures and network data more generally is that they are subject to retrospective bias (cf. Bernard, Killworth, Kroenfeld, & Sailer, 1984; Freeman, Romney, & Freeman, 1987). For example, participation-based social integration measures often ask respondents to report about activities and interactions occurring over periods of up to 12 months. Retrospective estimates of this sort are sensitive to recent events and may not adequately reflect what actually occurred months earlier. One way to circumvent these biases is to complement standard integration measures with daily and within-day measures (cf. Eckenrode & Bolger,

1995; Reis & Wheeler, 1991). For example, one might consider assessing individuals' daily social interactions and activities. This information could be used to evaluate the extent to which the daily lives of persons with different levels of social integration differ. For example, one might imagine that socially integrated individuals spend more time interacting with others, engage in more activities, and experience fewer conflicts. Moreover, daily assessments of the number and duration of daily interactions can be used to create behavioral indices of concepts like tie strength and relationship importance. Such techniques would seem to aid in understanding which behavioral and cognitive differences may be responsible for the relation between social integration and health.

Finally, we also believe research in the field of social integration would benefit from a closer alignment with the intervention tradition. Examining intervention programs designed to either alter network structure by grafting a tie (chapter 8) or increase participation by promoting activities (Arnetz et al., 1983; Clarke et al., 1992) in our view is one of the most promising means of elucidating causal mechanisms and influencing health. Natural experiments such as these provide critical opportunities for examining how social integration operates.

REFERENCE

Abbey, A., Abramis, D. J., & Caplan, R. D. (1985). Effects of different sources of social support and social conflict on emotional well-being. *Basic and Applied Psychology, 6,* 111–129.

Antonovsky, A. (1979). *Health, stress and coping: New perspectives on mental and physical well-being.* San Francisco, CA: Jossey-Bass.

Antonovsky, A. (1987). *Unraveling the mystery of health.* San Francisco: Jossey-Bass.

Antonucci, T. C., & Akiyama, H. (1987). Social networks in adult life: A preliminary examination of the convoy model. *Journal of Gerontology: Social Sciences, 42,* 512–527.

Antonucci, T. C., Fuhrer, R., & Dartigues, J. (1997). Social relations and symptomatology in a sample of community-dwelling French older adults. *Psychology and Aging, 12,* 189–195.

Arnetz, B. B., Eyre, M., & Theorell, T. (1982). Social activation of the elderly: A social experiment. *Social Science and Medicine, 16,* 1685–1690.

Arnetz, B. B., & Theorell, T. (1983). Psychological, sociological and health behaviour aspects of a long term activation programme for institutionalized elderly people. *Social Science and Medicine, 17,* 449–456.

Arnetz, B. B., Theorell, T., Levi, L., Kallner, A., & Eneroth, P. (1983). An experimental study of social isolation of elderly people: Psychoendcrine and metabolic effects. *Psychosomatic Medicine, 45,* 395–406.

Berkman, L. F. (1995). The role of social relations in health promotion. *Psychosomatic Medicine, 57,* 245–254.

Berkman, L. F. (1979). Empirically based weighting system. Unpublished manuscript.

Berkman, L. F., & Breslow, L. (1983). *Health and ways of living.* New York: Oxford University Press.

Berkman, L. F., & Syme, S. L. (1979). Social networks, host resistance, and mortality: A nine-year follow-up study of Alameda County residents. *American Journal of Epidemiology, 109*, 186–204.

Bernard, H. R., Johnsen, E. C., Killworth, P. D., McCarthy, C., Shelley, G. A., & Robinson, S. (1990). Comparing four different methods for measuring personal social networks. *Social Networks, 12*, 179–215.

Bernard, H. R., Killworth, P., Kroenfeld, D., & Sailer, L. (1984). The problem of informant accuracy: The validity of retrospective data. *Annual Review of Anthropology, 13*, 495–517.

Blascovich, J., & Tomaka, J. (1991). Measures of self-esteem. In J. P. Robinson, P. R. Shaver, & L. S. Wrightsmith (Eds.). *Measures of personality and social psychology attitudes,* vol.1 (pp. 115–138). San Diego: Academic Press.

Block, J. H. (1961). *The Q-sort method in personality assessment and psychiatric research.* Springfield, IL: Charles C. Thomas.

Bolger, N., DeLongis, A., Kessler, R. C., & Schilling, E. A. (1989). Effects of daily stress on negative mood. *Journal of Personality and Social Psychology, 57*, 808–818.

Bolger, N., & Eckenrode, J. (1991). Social relationships, personality, and anxiety during a major stressful event. *Journal of Personality and Social Psychology, 61*, 440–449.

Brugha, T. S., Sturt, E., MacCarthy, B., Potter, J., Wykes, T., & Bebbington, P. E. (1987). The Interview Measure of Social Relationships: The description and evaluation of a survey instrument for assessing personal social resources. *Social Psychiatry, 22*, 123–128.

Buckner, J. C. (1988). The development of an instrument to measure neighborhood cohesion. *American Journal of Community Psychology, 16*, 771–791.

Burke, P. J., & Tully, J. C. (1977). The measurement of role identity. *Social Forces, 67*, 693–714.

Burt, R. S. (1984). Network items and the general social survey. *Social Networks, 6*, 293–340.

Burt, R. S. (1985). General social survey network items. *Connections, 8*, 119–122.

Burt, R. S., & Minor, M. (Eds.). (1983). *Applied network analysis.* Beverly Hills, CA: Sage.

Burton, R. P. D. (1998). Global integrative meaning as a mediating factor in the relationship between social roles and psychological distress. *Journal of Health and Social Behavior, 39*, 201–215.

Byrne, B. M. (1996). *Measuring self-concept across the life span: Issues and instrumentation.* Washington, DC: American Psychological Association.

Campbell, K. E., Marsden, P. V., & Hurlburt, J. S. (1986). Social resources and socio-economic status. *Social Networks, 8*, 97–117.

Chavis, D. M., Hogge, J. H., & McMillan, D. W. (1986). Sense of community through Brunswick's lens: A first look. *Journal of Community Psychology, 14*, 24–40.

Clarke, M., Clarke, S. J., & Jagger, C. (1992). Social intervention and the elderly: A randomized controlled trial. *American Journal of Epidemiology, 136*, 1517–1523.

Cohen, S. (1988). Psychosocial models of the role of social support in the etiology of physical disease. *Health Psychology, 7*, 269–297.

Cohen, S. (1991). Social supports and physical health: Symptoms, health behaviors, and infectious diseases. In A. L. Greene, E. M. Cummings, & K. H. Karraker (Eds.), *Life-span developmental psychology: Perspectives on stress and coping* (pp. 213–234). Hillsdale, NJ: Erlbaum.

Cohen, S., Doyle, W. J., Skoner, D. P., Rabin, B. S., & Gwaltney, J. M. (1997). Social ties and susceptibility to the common cold. *Journal of the American Medical Association, 277*, 1940–1944.

Cohen, S., Frank, E., Doyle, B. J., Skoner, D. P., Rabin, B. S., & Gwaltney, J. M. (1998). Types of stressors that increase susceptibility to the common cold. *Health Psychology, 17*, 214–223.

Cohen, S., Kessler, R. C., & Underwood-Gordon, L. (1995). *Measuring stress: A guide for health and social scientists.* New York: Oxford University Press.

Cohen, S., & Wills, T. A. (1985). Stress, social support and the buffering hypothesis. *Psychological Bulletin, 98*, 310–357.

Coleman, J. S. (1988). Social capital in the creation of human capital. *American Journal of Sociology, 94*, S95–S120.

Cooley, C. H. (1902). *Human nature and the social order.* New York: Scribner's.

Coopersmith, S. (1967). *The antecendents of self-esteem.* San Francisco: Freeman.

Coopersmith, S. (1981). *The antecedents of self-esteem.* Palo Alto, CA: Consulting Psychologists Press. (Original work published in 1967.)

Coser, L. (1974). *Greedy Institutions.* New York: Free Press.

Donald, C. A., & Ware, J. E. (1982). *The quantification of social contacts and resources.* Santa Monica, CA: Rand.

Donald, C. A., Ware, J. E., Brook, R. H., & Davies-Avery, A. (1978). *Conceptualization and measurement of health for adults in the health insurance study: vol. 4, social health.* Santa Monica, CA: Rand.

Durkheim, E. (1951). *Suicide.* New York: Free Press.

Eckenrode, J., & Bolger, N. (1995). Daily and within-day event measurement. In S. Cohen, R. C. Kessler, & L. Underwood-Gordon (Eds.), *Measuring stress: A guide for health and social scientists* (pp. 80–101). New York: Oxford University Press.

Evans, G. W., Palasano, M. N., Lepore, S. J., & Martin, J. (1989). Residential density and psychological health: The mediating effects of social support. *Journal of Personality and Social Psychology, 57*, 994–999.

Faris, R. E. L. (1934). Cultural isolation and the schizophrenic personality. *American Journal of Sociology, 40*, 155–169.

Fischer, C. S. (1982). *To dwell among friends: Personal networks in town and city.* Chicago: University of Chicago Press.

Fitzgerald, G. B. (1949). *Community organization for recreation.* New York: A. S. Barnes.

Freeman, L. C., Romney, A. K., & Freeman, S. C. (1987). Cognitive structure and informant accuracy. *American Anthropologist, 89*, 310–325.

Gallo, F. (1982). The effects of social support network on the health of the elderly. *Social Work in Health Care, 8*, 65–74.

Goode, W. J. (1960). A theory of role strain. *American Sociological Review, 25*, 483–496.

Goodenow, C., Resine, S. T., & Grady, K. E., (1990). Quality of support and associated psychological functioning in women with rheumatoid arthritis. *Health Psychology, 9*, 266–284.

Granovetter, M. (1973). The strength of weak ties. *American Journal of Sociology, 78*, 1360–1380.

Hage, P., & Harary, F. (1983). *Structural methods in anthropology*. Cambridge: Cambridge University Press.

Haines, V. A., & Hurlburt, J. S. (1992). Network range and health. *Journal of Health and Social Behavior, 33*, 254–266.

Hall, A., & Wellman, B. (1985). Social networks and social support. In S. Cohen & S. L. Syme (Eds.), *Social support and health* (pp. 23–41). New York: Academic.

Hanson, B. S., Isacsson, J. T., Janzon, L., Lindell, S.-E., & Rastam, L. (1988). Social anchorage and blood pressure in elderly men. *Journal of Hypertension, 6*, 503–510.

Hanson, B. S., Isacsson, S. O., Janzon, L., & Lindell, S-E. (1989). Social network and social support influence mortality in elderly men: Prospective population study of men born in Malamo, Sweden. *American Journal of Epidemiology, 130*, 100–111.

Harary, F., Norman, R. Z., & Cartwright, D. (1965). *Structural models: An introduction to the theory of directed graphs*. New York: John Wiley and Sons.

Heidrich, S. M., & Ryff, C. D. (1993). Physical and mental health later in life: The self-system as mediator. *Psychology and Aging, 8*, 327–338.

Helgeson, V. S., Cohen, S., & Fritz, H. L. (1998). Social ties and the onset and progression of cancer. In J. C. Holland & W. Breitbert (Eds.), *Textbook of Psycho-oncology*. New York: Oxford University Press.

Heller, K., Thompson, M. G., Trueba, P. E., Hogg, J. R., & Vlachos-Weber, I. (1991). Peer support telephone dyads for elderly women: Was this the wrong intervention? *American Journal of Community Psychology, 19*, 53–74.

Henderson, S., Duncan-Jones, P., McAuley, H., & Ritchey, K. (1978). The patient's primary group. *British Journal of Psychiatry, 132*, 74–86.

Herbert, T. B., & Cohen, S. (1993). Depression and immunity: A meta-analytic review. *Psychological Bulletin, 113*, 472–486.

Higgins, E. T. (1987). Self-discrepancy: A theory relating self and affect. *Psychological Review, 94*, 319–340.

Higgins, E. T., Bond, R. N., Klein, R., & Strauman, T. (1986). Self-discrepancies and emotional vulnerability: How magnitude accessibility and type of discrepancy influence affect. *Journal of Personality and Social Psychology, 51*, 1–15.

Hirsch, B. J. (1979). Psychological dimensions of social networks: A multimethod analysis. *American Journal of Community Psychology, 7*, 263–276.

Hirsch. B. J. (1980). Natural support systems and coping with major life events. *American Journal of Community Psychology, 8*, 159–172.

Hirsch, B. J. (1981a). Social networks in the coping process. In B. H. Gottlieb (Ed.), *Social networks and social support* (pp. 149–170). Beverly Hills, CA: Sage.

Hirsch, B. J. (1981b). Coping and adaptation in high-risk populations: Toward an integrative model. *Schizophrenia Bulletin, 7*, 164–172.

Hirsch, B. J., & Reischl, T. M. (1985). Social networks and developmental psychopathology: A comparison of adolescent children of a depressed, arthritic or normal parent. *Journal of Abnormal Psychology, 94*, 272–281.

Hong, J., & Seltzer, M. M. (1995). The psychological consequences of multiple roles: The nonnormative case. *Journal of Health and Social Behavior, 36*, 386–398.

House, J. S., & Kahn, R. L. (1985). Measures and concepts of social support. In S. Cohen & S. L. Syme (Eds.), *Social Support and Health* (pp. 83–108). New York: Academic.

House, J. S., Landis, K. R., & Umberson, D. (1988). Social relationships and health. *Science, 241,* 540–545.

House, J. S., Robbins, C., & Metzner, H. L. (1982). The association of social relationships and activities with mortality: Prospective evidence from the Techumseh community health study. *American Journal of Epidemiology, 116,* 123–140.

House, J. S., Umberson, D., & Landis, K. R. (1988). Structures and processes of social support. *Annual Review of Sociology, 14,* 293–318.

Jaco, E. (1954). The social isolation hypothesis and schizophrenia. *American Sociological Review, 19,* 567–577.

Kahn, R. L., & Antonucci, T. C. (1980). Convoys over the life course: Attachment, roles, and social support. In P. Baltes & O. Brim (Eds.), *Life span development and behavior* (vol. 3, pp. 253–286). San Diego: Academic.

Kaplan, G. A., Salonen, J. T., Cohen, R. D., Brand, R. J., Syme, S. L., & Puska, P. (1988). Social connections and mortality from all causes and from cardiovascular disease: Prospective evidence from Easter Finland. *American Journal of Epidemiology, 128,* 370–380.

Kawachi, I., Kennedy, B. P., Lochner, K., & Prothrow-Stith, D. (1997). Social capital, income inequality and mortality. *American Journal of Public Health, 87,* 1491–1498.

Kuo, W. H., & Tsai, Y. (1986). Social networking, hardiness and immigrant's mental health. *Journal of Health and Social Behavior, 27,* 133–149.

Laumann, E. O., Marsden, P. V., & Prensky, D. (1983). The boundary specification problem in network analysis. In R. Burt and M. Minor (Eds.), *Applied network analysis* (pp. 18–34). Beverly Hills, CA: Sage.

Leftcourt, H. M. (1991). Locus of control. In J. P. Robinson, P. R. Shaver, & L. S. Wrightsmith (Eds.), *Measures of personality and social psychology attitudes* (vol. 1, pp. 413–499). San Diego: Academic.

Levenson, H. (1981). Differentiating among internality, powerful others, and chance. In H. M. Leftcourt (Ed.), *Research with the locus of control construct* (vol. 1, pp. 15–63). New York: Academic.

Levitt, M. J., Guacci-Franco, N., & Levitt, J. L. (1993). Convoys of social support in childhood and early adolescence: Structure and function. *Developmental Psychology, 29,* 811–818.

Lin, N., Dean, A. & Ensel, W. (1986). *Social support life events and depression.* Orlando: Academic.

Linville, P. W. (1985). Self-complexity and affect extremity: Don't put all of your eggs in one cognitive basket. *Social Cognition, 3,* 94–120.

Linville, P. W. (1987) Self-complexity as a cognitive buffer against stress related illness and depression. *Journal of Personality and Social Psychology, 52,* 663–676.

Lynch, J. J. (1979). *The broken heart.* New York: Basic Books.

Mardsen, P. V. (1990). Network data and measurement. *Annual Review of Sociology, 16,* 435–463.

Marks, S. (1977). Multiple roles and role strain: Some notes on human energy, time, and commitment. *American Sociological Review, 42,* 921–936.

McCallister, L., & Fischer, C. S. (1978). A procedure for surveying personal networks. *Sociological Methods and Research, 7,* 131–148.

McKinlay, J. B. (1973). Social networks, lay consultation and help seeking behavior. *Social Forces, 51,* 275–292.

McNair, D., Lorr, M., & Droppleman, L. (1971). *Psychiatric outpatient mood scale.* Boston: Psychopharmacology Laboratory, Boston University Medical Center.

Mead, G. H. (1934). *Mind, self, and society.* Chicago: University of Chicago Press.

Menaghan, E. G. (1989). Role changes and psychological well-being: Variations in effects by gender and role repertoire. *Social Forces, 67,* 693–714.

Milardo, R. M. (1992). Comparative methods for delineating social networks. *Journal of Social and Personality Relationships, 9,* 447–461.

Mitchell, J. C. (1969). The concept and use of social networks. In Mitchell, J. C. (Ed.), *Social networks in urban situations* (pp. 1–50). Manchester: Manchester University Press.

Mitchell, R. E., & Trickett, E. J. (1980). Task force report: Social networks as mediators of social support. *Community Mental Health Journal, 16,* 27–44.

Moen, P., Dempster-McClain, D., & Williams Jr., R. M. (1989). Social integration and longevity: An event history analysis of women's roles and resilience. *American Sociological Review, 54,* 635–647.

Moen, P., Dempster-McClain, D., & Williams Jr., R. M. (1992). Successful aging: A life-course perspective on women's multiple roles and health. *American Journal of Sociology, 97,* 1612–1638.

Nowlis, V., & Green, R. (1957). *The experimental analysis of mood.* Technical report of naval research: Contract No. Nonr-668(12).

Orth-Gomer, K., & Johnson, J. V. (1987). Social network interaction and mortality: A six year follow-up study of a random sample of the Swedish population. *Journal of Chronic Disease, 40,* 949–957.

Orth-Gomer, K., Rosengren, A., & Wilhelmsen, L. (1993). Lack of social support and incidence of coronary heart disease in middle-aged Swedish men. *Psychosomatic Medicine, 55,* 37–43.

Paulhus, D. L. (1983). Sphere-specific measures of perceived control. *Journal of Personality and Social Psychology, 44,* 1253–1265.

Putnam, .. D. (1995). Bowling alone: America's declining social capital. *Journal of Democracy, 6,* 65–78.

Reed, D., McGee, D., Yano, K., & Feinlieb, M. (1983). Social networks and coronary heart disease among Japanese men in Hawaii. *American Journal of Epidemiology, 117,* 384–396.

Reis, H. T., & Wheeler, L. (1991). Studying social interaction with the Rochester Interaction Record. In M. P. Zanna (Ed.), *Advances in experimental social psychology* (vol. 24, pp. 269–318). San Diego: Academic.

Reynolds, P., & Kaplan, G. A. (1990). Social connections and risk for cancer: Prospective evidence from the Alameda County study. *Journal of Behavioral Medicine, 16,* 101–110.

Rogers, C. R. (1965). *Client-centered therapy: Its current practice, implications and theory.* Boston: Houghton Mifflin.

Rook, K. S. (1984). The negative side of social interaction. *Journal of Personality and Social Psychology, 46,* 1097–1108.

Rook, K. S. (1990). Social networks as a source of social control in older adults' lives. In H. Giles, N. Coupland, & J. Wiemann (Eds.), *Communication, health and the elderly* (pp. 45–63). Manchester: University of Manchester Press.

Rook, K. S., & Pietromonaco, P. (1987). Close relationships: Ties that heal or ties that bind? *Advances in Personal Relationships, 1,* 1–35.

Rook, K. S., Thuras, P. D., & Lewis, M. A. (1990). Social control, risk taking and psychological distress among the elderly. *Psychology and Aging, 5,* 327–334.

Rosenberg, M. (1965). *Society and the adolescent self-image*. Princeton, NJ: Princeton University Press.

Rotter, J. B. (1966). Generalized expectancies for internal versus external control of reinforcement. *Psychological Monographs: General and Applied, 80*, 1–28.

Ryff, C. D. (1989). Happiness is everything, or is it? Explorations on the meaning of psychological well-being. *Journal of Personality and Social Psychology, 57*, 1069–1081.

Sampson, R. J., Raudenbush, S. W., & Earls, F. (1997). Neighborhoods and violent crime: A multilevel study of collective efficacy. *Science, 277*, 918–924.

Schaefer, C., Coyne, J. C., & Lazarus, R. S. (1981). Health related functions of social support. *Journal of Behavioral Medicine, 4*, 381–406.

Schoenbach, V. J., Kaplan, B. G, Freedman, L., & Kleinbaum, D. G. (1986). Social ties and mortality in Evans County, Georgia. *American Journal of Epidemiology, 123*, 577–591.

Seeman, T. E. (1996). Social ties and health: The benefits of social integration. *Annals of Epidemiology, 6*, 442–451.

Seeman, T. E., & Berkman, L. F. (1988). Structural characteristics of social networks and their relationship with social support in the elderly: Who provides support. *Social Science and Medicine, 26*, 737–749.

Seeman, T. E., Berkman, L. F., Blazer, D., & Rowe, J. W. (1994). Social ties, support and neuroendocrine function: The MacArthur studies of successful aging. *Annals of Behavioral Medicine, 16*, 95–106.

Seeman, T. E., Berkman, L. F., Kohout, L., LaCroix, A., Glynn, R., & Blazer, D. (1993). Intercommunity variations in the association between social ties and mortality in the elderly: A comparative analysis of three communities. *Annals of Epidemiology, 3*, 325–335.

Seeman, T. E., Kaplan, G. A., Knudsen, L., Cohen, R., & Guralnik, J. (1987). Social network ties and mortality among the elderly in the Alameda County study. *American Journal of Epidemiology, 126*, 714–723.

Seeman, T. E., Rodin, J., & Albert, M. A. (1993). Self-efficacy and functional ability: How beliefs relate to cognitive and physical performance. *Journal of Aging and Health. 5*, 455–474.

Sieber, S. D. (1974). Toward a theory of role accumulation. *American Sociological Review, 39*, 567–578.

Simon, R. W. (1997). The meanings individuals attach to role identities and their implications for mental health. *Journal of Health and Social Behavior, 38*, 256–274.

Slater, P. (1963). On social regression. *American Sociological Review, 28*, 339–364.

Sonderen, E. V., Ormel, J., Brilman, E., & Linden van den Heuvell, C. (1992). Personal network delineation: A comparison of the exchange, affective and role-relation approach. In K. Knipscheer & T. C. Antonucci (Eds.), *Social network research: Substantive issues and methodological questions* (pp. 101–120). Amsterdam: Swets & Zeitlinger.

Stokes, J. P. (1985). The relation of social network and individual differences in loneliness. *Journal of Personality and Social Psychology, 48*, 981–990.

Stokes, J. P., & Levine, I. (1986). Gender differences in predicting loneliness from social network characteristics. *Journal of Personality and Social Psychology, 51*, 1069–1074.

Stone, A. A. (1995). Measurement of affective response. In S. Cohen, R. C. Kessler, & L. Underwood-Gordon (Eds.), *Measuring stress: A guide for health and social scientists* (pp. 148–171). New York: Oxford University Press.

Stryker, S. (1980). *Symbolic interactionism: A social structural version.* Menlo Park, CA: Benjamin/Cummings.

Thoits, P. A. (1983). Multiple identities and psychological well-being: A reformulation of the social isolation hypothesis. *American Sociological Review, 48,* 174–187.

Thoits, P. A. (1986). Multiple identities: Examining gender and marital status differences in distress. *American Sociological Review, 51,* 259–272.

Thoits, P. A. (1995). Identity-relevant events and psychological symptoms: A cautionary tale. *Journal of Health and Social Behavior, 36,* 72–82.

Tolsdorf, C. (1976). Social networks, support, and coping. *Family Process, 15,* 407–417.

Uchino, B. N., Cacioppo, J. T., & Kielcolt-Glaser, J. K. (1996). The relationship between social support and physiological processes: A review with emphasis on underlying mechanisms and implications for health. *Psychological Bulletin, 119,* 488–531.

Umberson, D. (1987). Family status and health behaviors: Social control as a dimension of social integration. *Journal of Health and Social Behavior, 28,* 306–319.

Umberson, D. (1992). Gender, marital status and the social control of health behavior. *Social Science and Medicine, 34,* 907–917.

Van Groenou, M. B., Van Sonderen, E., & Ormel, J. (1992). Test-retest reliability of personal network delineation. In K. Knipscheer & T. C. Antonucci (Eds.), *Social network research: Substantive issues and methodological questions* (pp. 121–136). Amsterdam: Swets & Zeitlinger.

Walker, K. N., MacBride, A., & Vachon, M. L. S. (1977). Social support and the crisis of bereavement. *Social Science and Medicine, 11,* 35–41.

Wallston, K. A., Wallston, B. S., & DeVellis, R. (1978). Development of the multidimensional Health Locus of Control scales. *Health Education Monographs, 6,* 161–170.

Ware, E. H. (1956). Mental illness and social conditions in Bristol. *Journal of Mental Science, 102,* 349–357.

Wasserman, S., & Faust, K. (1994). *Social network analysis.* Cambridge: Cambridge University Press.

Watson, D., Clark, L., & Tellegen, A. (1988). Development and validation of brief measure of positive and negative affect: The PANAS scales. *Journal of Personality and Social Psychology, 54,* 1063–1067.

Welin, L., Larsson, B., Svardsudd, K., Tibblin, B., & Tibblin, G. (1992). Social network activities in relation to mortality from cardiovascular diseases, cancer and other causes: A 12-year follow up of the study of men born in 1913 and 1923. *Journal of Epidemiology and Community Health, 46,* 127–132.

Wellman, B. (1981). Applying network analysis to the study of social support. In B. H. Gottlieb (Ed.), *Social networks and social support* (pp. 171–200). Beverly Hills, CA: Sage.

Wellman, B. (1988). The community question re-evaluated. In M. P. Smith (Ed.), *Power, community, and the city.* (pp. 81–107). New Brunswick, NJ: Transaction Books.

Wellman, B., & Wortley, S. (1990). Different strokes from different folks: Community ties and social support. *American Journal of Sociology, 96,* 558–588.

Wilcox, B. L. (1981). Social support in adjusting to marital separation: A network analysis. In B. H. Gottlieb (Ed.), *Social networks and social support* (pp. 97–115). Beverly Hills, CA: Sage.

Williams, A. W., Ware, J. E., & Donald, C. A. (1981). A model of mental health, life events, and social supports applicable to general populations. *Journal of Health and Social Behavior, 22,* 324–336.

4

Measuring Perceived and Received Social Support

Thomas A. Wills
Ori Shinar

I. Conceptual and Theoretical Basis for These Measures
II. Questions and Issues for Using Functional Measures
   A. General Issues for Considering a Measure and Designing a Study
      1. Relevance
      2. Perceived or Received Support
      3. Length
      4. Buffering Effects
      5. Subscale Correlations
      6. Confounders
      7. Negative Interactions
      8. Generality versus Specificity
      9. Structural and Functional Measures
      10. Intervention Research
   B. Measures of Perceived Support
      1. Brief Unidimensional Scales
      2. Broadly-Based Scales of Close and Diffuse Support
      3. Multidimensional Inventories
      4. Network-based Inventories
      5. Measures for Children and Adolescents
   C. Measures of Received Support
   D. Selecting and Using a Support Measure
      1. What Supportive Functions Are Relevant for This Population?
      2. Should I Measure Received Support as Well as Perceived Support?
      3. How Long a Measure Do I Need?
      4. Should I Use a Composite Score or Separate Scale Scores?
      5. Should I Include Measures of Unsupportive Interaction as Well as Support?
      6. Should I Assess Support from Specific Network Members?
      7. Should I Measure Both Availability and Satisfaction with Support?
      8. Will I Need to Adapt the Measure for a Specific Population?
      9. Will I Need to Adapt the Measure for a Particular Stressor?
      10. Will I Need to Adapt the Measure for an Intervention Study?

CONCEPTUAL AND THEORETICAL BASIS
FOR THESE MEASURES

This chapter considers the measurement of supportive functions that are perceived to be *available if needed* (perceived support) or functions that are reported to be *recently provided* (received support). The basic assumption for the choice of such measures is that they tap the availability of resources provided through social relationships that should help persons to cope with acute or chronic stressors.

This approach to support measurement, variously termed the study of *perceived support, available support*, or *functional support*, derives from papers that thoughtfully considered the findings from a generation of social epidemiology research and suggested formulations of the concept of support as a generalized resistance factor (Cassel, 1976; Cobb, 1976; Weiss, 1974). For example, Cobb's (1976) formulation was based on the proposition that supportive functions help persons to deal with crisis and change and posited that the effects of support were based on "information leading the subject to believe that he is cared for and loved . . . esteemed and valued . . . and belongs to a network of communication and mutual obligation" (p. 300). This type of support was posited to be useful to persons confronted with stressors such as unemployment, divorce, or bereavement, enabling individuals with more available support to deal better with esteem threats, emotional distress, loneliness, and practical problems evoked by the stressors.

The original papers on supportive functions influenced the design of a number of new studies. These showed support availability was related to lower levels of physical morbidity and psychological distress, and perceived support measures showed consistent evidence of buffering effects, reducing the impact of life stress on adverse outcomes (Cohen & Wills, 1985; House, 1981). Subsequent research has confirmed these findings, showing functional measures to provide buffering against a variety of life stressors with regard to psychological distress as the outcome (Vaux, 1988; Wills, 1991) and recently showing such effects for some physiological measures (Uchino, Cacioppo, & Kiecolt-Glaser, 1996). Recent epidemiological studies have shown functional measures to be related to lower levels of incident disease and mortality (Hanson, Isacsson, Janzo, & Lindell, 1989; Orth-Gomer, Rosengren, & Wilhelmsen, 1993) and to recovery from life-threatening illness (Berkman, Leo-Summers, & Horwitz, 1992; Williams et al., 1992), as well as showing stress-buffering effects with regard to mortality (Falk, Hanson, Isacsson, & Ostergren, 1992; Rosengren, Orth-Gomer, Wedel, & Wilhelmsen, 1993). Thus, perceived support availability is known to be of considerable significance for health.

The perspective of the functional measurement approach is inherently a multidimensional one. It is assumed that there are different types of supportive functions provided through social relationships, and it is posited that these functions may be differentially useful for various types of problems or stressors (Cohen & McKay, 1984; Cutrona & Russell, 1990; Sandler, Miller, Short, & Wolchik, 1989). Several dimensions of functional support have been delineated (Argyle, 1992;

House, 1981; Wills, 1985). These include *emotional support*, the availability of one or more persons who can listen sympathetically when an individual is having problems and can provide indications of caring and acceptance. *Instrumental support* involves practical help when necessary, such as assisting with transportation, helping with household chores and child care, and providing tangible aid such as bringing tools or lending money. *Informational support* is defined as providing knowledge that is useful for solving problems, such as providing information about community resources and services or providing advice and guidance about alternative courses of action. *Companionship support* involves the availability of persons with whom one can participate in social and leisure activities such as trips and parties, cultural activities (e.g., going to movies or museums), or recreational activities such as sporting events or hiking. A dimension variously termed *feedback, validation*, or *social comparison* is based on the concept that social relationships can provide information about the appropriateness or normativeness of behavior. A summary of supportive functions and their theoretically expected benefits for coping efforts is presented in Table 4.1.

In theory, functional measures should be most relevant to adjustment for persons experiencing a high level of stress. These measures typically show stress-buffering effects; that is, they reduce the relationship between stressors and adverse outcomes. Accordingly, functional measures are most appropriate for studying processes through which social resources contribute to coping with stressors, equally so for the context of epidemiologic research and the context of randomized prevention/intervention research (Lakey & Lutz, 1996; Wills & Filer, 2000). This does not imply that supportive functions will be irrelevant for a generally nonstressed population; many studies show support related to health indices at both lower and higher levels of stress. The buffering model, though, suggests that functional support will have greater effects among persons who are currently confronting stressors and challenges. The nature of stressors in previous research has varied, including indices of stress from negative life events in a number of domains, as well as discrete events that represent either normative transitions (e.g., pregnancy and parenthood) or occurrences such as traumatic accidents and natural disasters. In recent years, functional support measures have been shown also to be protective among children facing stressful normative transitions, such as going from elementary school to junior high school, or nonnormative life events such as death of a parent (Sandler et al., 1989; Wills, Blechman, & McNamara, 1996).

The multidimensional nature of functional measures provides a potentially powerful tool for the researcher because the various functions can be tested with respect to their usefulness for dealing with particular types of problems (e.g., unemployment or bereavement) or their usefulness for individuals with different personality configurations (e.g., inhibited or gregarious persons). The potential gain from this depends on the formulation of specific predictions as to which supportive function will be most effective for a particular type of life stressor (the *matching hypothesis*: Cohen & McKay, 1984; Cutrona, 1990). For example, one could hypothesize that instrumental support is relevant for buffering against fi-

Table 4.1. Description of Supportive Functions

Function	Other Terms	Examples	Theoretical Benefit
Emotional support	Confidant support, esteem support, reassurance of worth, attachment, intimacy	Allow discussion of feelings, expression of concerns/worries; indicate sympathy, approval, caring, acceptance of person	Alters threat appraisal of life events, enhances self-esteem, reduces anxiety/depression, motivates coping
Instrumental support	Tangible support, practical support, behavioral assistance, material aid	Provide money, household goods, tools, transportation, child care, assistance with cooking, cleaning, shopping, repairs	Solves practical problems, allows increased time for rest and relaxation, other coping efforts
Informational support	Advice/guidance, appraisal support, cognitive guidance, problem solving	Provide information about resources, suggest alternative courses of action, provide advice about effectiveness	Increases amount of useful information available to individual, helps obtain needed services, leads to more effective coping
Companionship support	Belonging, socializing, integration[a]	Provide partner for sports, outdoor activities, movies, theater, museums, restaurants, shopping, parties, trips	Produces positive affect, allows for release and recuperation from demands, provides positive distraction from rumination about problems
Validation	Feedback, social comparison	Provide consensus information re prevalence of problems, normativeness of individual's behavior/feelings, individual's relative status in population	Decreases perceived deviancy, allows acceptance of feelings, provides favorable comparisons

[a] Note that this term has a different meaning than applies to structural measures of social integration (chapter 3).

nancial stress but not interpersonal stressors (see Peirce, Frone, Russell, & Cooper, 1996).

Research using functional measures has another potential benefit through contributing to a body of theory on how social support operates (Cohen, 1988; House & Kahn, 1985; Wills & Cleary, 1996). As noted in chapters 1 and 2, theory suggests that available support may be related to adjustment through mechanisms such as altering the cognitive appraisal of events, enhancing self-esteem, improving problem-solving ability, or facilitating important behavioral changes. Through deriving predictions about relevant supportive functions and testing hypothesized mediators of their effects, the researcher can provide a better understanding of how social support operates to affect emotional, behavioral, or physiological outcomes. This benefit accrues equally to intervention studies: A clear specification of how a support-enhancing intervention influences perceived support and hypothesized mediators will provide better understanding of how the intervention operates to produce improved adjustment among the participants (Barrera & Prelow, in press; Lakey & Lutz, 1996; Sandler, Wolchik, MacKinnon, Ayers, & Roosa, 1997).

It should be noted that measures of perceived support and measures of received support are not interchangeable. Empirical studies typically show perceived availability of support to be related to lower levels of symptomatology, but several studies have shown received support measures positively correlated with symptomatology indices (Barrera, 1986; Helgeson, 1993); studies that have included both types of measures show buffering effects for perceived support but not for received support (Dunkel-Schetter & Bennett, 1990; Wethington & Kessler, 1986). Thus it is evident that the processes tapped by perceived and received support measures are not identical. This raises important questions for theory and research design, and understanding the reasons for observed divergence in results is a priority for further research. This issue is discussed subsequently in sections on conceptualizing and choosing support measures.

QUESTIONS AND ISSUES FOR USING FUNCTIONAL MEASURES

A researcher may address several related kinds of questions. The most basic question is: Which dimension(s) of functional support contributes significantly to preventing illness or enhancing adjustment? Does a given dimension show main effects on adjustment, or does it provide evidence of buffering effects? The nature of multidimensional functional measures allows such tests to determine which of several dimensions is most useful for adjustment in a particular population (Cutrona & Russell, 1990; House & Kahn, 1985; Vaux, 1988).

The functional approach may help to sharpen understanding of the support needs of different populations. Previous research has shown emotional support to be a function with surprisingly broad usefulness, even for situations where it does not have obvious utility, and other functions to have unexpected beneficial effects (e.g., Krause, 1987a; Olds, Henderson, Chamberlin, & Tatelbaum, 1986; Rook, 1987); for example, both instrumental support and informational support enhance adjustment to physical illness (Wills & Filer, 2000). Thus researchers should think carefully about what supportive functions are most relevant for the population they are studying. Is there reason to believe that outcomes will be primarily determined by feeling that one is accepted and valued, or are there grounds to expect that participants' functioning will be improved through practical assistance, advice and guidance, or companionship? This decision may be informed by theory on social coping processes (Buunk & Gibbons, 1997; Haggerty, Sherrod, Garmezy, & Rutter, 1994), the demands associated with a particular health condition (Carver, Scheier, & Pozo, 1992; Moos & Schaefer, 1984), and by prior experience with the target population.

Questions about how the effects of social support are mediated can be addressed. This may provide additional yield to the research and involves more thinking at the design stage; that is, researchers consider *how* support is related to the outcome they are studying and whether the effects of supportive relation-ships are mediated through other variables (versus having a direct effect on the outcome). Suggestions about how support operates may come from prior theory, from a researcher's broad knowledge of collateral research on correlates of support and predictors of outcome dimensions, and from experience with the target pop-ulation. Is the effect of support likely attributable to alterations in cognitive ap-praisals of stress? To increased knowledge about disease conditions and appro-priate preventive behaviors? To enhanced self-esteem, efficacy, or mastery? To reduced anxiety or increased optimism about the future? To more effective self-regulation and coping responses? To changes in physiological status such as lower blood pressure or enhanced immune system function? If the answer to any of these questions is yes, then measures of hypothesized mediators may be included in the research, and the investigator can subsequently test specified models of how the effects of support are mediated (cf. chapter 2; Wills & Cleary, 1999). Studies that include even one potential mediator are more informative, and the reliability of brief measures of relevant constructs makes mediational studies fea-sible (see, e.g., Carver, Scheier, & Weintraub, 1989; Wills, 1994). Questions about how the impact of a support intervention is mediated are a particular priority for research (cf. Brand, Lakey, & Berman, 1995, for community-based research; Mal-linckrodt, 1996, for counseling clients; Zhang, 1994, for a school-based interven-tion; Wolchik et al., 1993, for a family sample). Issues for conceptualizing and testing mediation in the context of intervention research are discussed in several sources (Barrera & Prelow, in press; Sandler et al., 1997; West & Aiken, 1997).

The concept of multiple pathways to health outcomes is a natural extension of previous research on supportive functions. Though reducing emotional distress is a plausible mechanism, it is conceivable for some contexts that social relation-ships have direct effects on health status through relatively fixed physiological pathways (Cohen & Herbert, 1996; House, Landis, & Umberson, 1988), that func-tional support plays a significant role in reducing liability to substance abuse (Wills, 1990; Wills & Filer, 2000), and that supportive networks have important effects for facilitating preventive health behaviors (Lewis & Rook, 1999; Potts, Hurwicz, Goldstein, & Berkanovic, 1992; Umberson, 1987). While studies de-signed to address multiple pathways may require more planning and resources, it is likely that they will provide a more complete perspective on support-health relationships.

Another question is how buffering effects occur. It has been generally assumed that buffering occurs through reducing perceived stress, but empirical evidence has provided mixed support for this hypothesis (see Uchino et al., 1996) and suggests that buffering may occur as much through strengthening the effects of protective factors as through reducing the impact of life events (Wills & Cleary, 1996). It is possible that, in some contexts, buffering effects may occur through altering appraisals of negative events, through a direct transfer of resources, or through facilitating change in a health-related behavior. There is opportunity for researchers to add to our understanding of how buffering effects occur.

The effects of different aspects of social relationships may be addressed. For example, chapter 3 delineates how measures of social integration tap the structure of social networks and the number of social connections a person has. Empirical studies show that the correlation between social integration measures and perceived support measures is modest—the availability of supportive functions is not strongly related to the number of social connections a person has. Moreover, literature on social support and mortality has suggested that social integration and functional support may be related to health status through somewhat different mechanisms (Cohen, 1988; Cohen & Wills, 1985). Determining how support availability is related to social connections and roles is a question of continuing interest for the field (House et al., 1988); it is essential to better understand how integration in the community provides access to persons who may become sources of emotional or informational support (cf. Hanson et al., 1989; Rosengren et al., 1993). Where extensive network assessment is feasible, the researcher may be able to study from where in the network the greatest amount of functional support is derived and which individuals provide combinations of different supportive functions (e.g., emotional + instrumental + companionship).

One may ask: What source of support is most effective for enabling participants to achieve better outcomes? Persons potentially could have support from several different sources, including primary relationships, family and relatives, friends, formal helping agents (e.g., physicians, nurses, and other medical personnel), and a more diffuse network that includes coworkers and community contacts. For some research contexts, there may be reason to believe that particular source(s) of support will be more effective, for example, for patients in medical settings (e.g., Dakof & Taylor, 1990; Rose, 1990). This raises questions about the relative value of measuring different sources versus different types of support; hence the research could test for unique contributions of different sources, or combinations of source and type, to adjustment.

It can be informative to study the determinants of perceived support. There may be antecedents in temperament and family relationships that enable some individuals to develop a positive "working model" of social relationships that encourages trust and confiding in others, which is predicted to lead to the development of more supportive relationships (Coble, Gantt, & Mallinckrodt, 1996; Ptacek, 1996; Sarason et al., 1991). The association of perceived support with personality variables from the Big Five system (Goldberg, 1993) or alternative personality systems (Almagor, Tellegen, & Waller, 1995; Zuckerman, Kuhlman, Joireman, Teta, & Kraft, 1993) is of interest both in its own right and for testing contributions of social support that are independent of personality characteristics (Cohen, Sherrod, & Clark, 1986). In some research contexts, it is also theoretically plausible that support mediates the relation between the personality measure and the outcome (e.g., Windle, 1991).

Finally, we would note that studying the relationship between perceived support and received support is an important issue. Previous findings showing generalized measures of received support positively related to symptomatology have been interpreted as indicating that available support is activated in times of high stress, when people most need it; this interpretation also accounts for observed positive correlations of received support measures with current-stress measures (Dunkel-Schetter & Bennett, 1990). While this makes sense from a theoretical standpoint, there is still little understanding of the dynamics of how available support is translated into situations where support is received. This question may be particularly important for intervention research, where investigators need to measure how a support intervention affects actual supportive transactions (Barrera & Prelow, in press; Helgeson, Cohen, Schulz, & Yasko, in press). Research is needed that includes both perceived- and received-support measures, so as to provide more data on the relationship between these two aspects of support systems (see Mermelstein, Cohen, Lichtenstein, Baer, & Kamarck, 1986; Wethington & Kessler, 1986) and help to explicate their relationships to discrete stressors or chronic life strains. In contexts where participants can be assessed before and after a discrete event, one may study the level of support anticipated before the event, support received during the event, and the relation of convergence/divergence of anticipated versus actual support to subsequent outcomes (cf. Cohen & Lichtenstein, 1990; Coriell & Cohen, 1995).

General Issues for Considering a Measure and Designing a Study

In the following section, we discuss several issues that are involved in thinking about a measure of social support. The issues are generally comparable for epidemiologic research and for intervention researchers, though some specialty topics are noted.

Relevance

A primary issue involves the aims of the research and the population the researcher intends to work with. Given the researcher's analysis of stressors and coping demands for this population, are the items relevant to the problems the participants are facing? Are the measured functions likely to be useful to the respondents for dealing with those problems? Does the measure tap support processes that are hypothesized to be important for the types of outcomes considered in the study? This question will help to focus attention on certain measures that seem most promising for the aims of the research.

Perceived or received support

A second issue concerns whether to use a perceived support measure or a received support measure. As noted previously, there are studies in which received support measures were related to lower levels of symptomatology, possibly because they used an extended reporting frame (Krause, 1987b) or concerned coping with natural disasters, where instances of receiving support may be particularly salient (Norris & Kaniasty, 1996). However, there are some opposite findings in the literature (e.g., Helgeson [1993] found received support was positively correlated with symptomatology), and the discrepancies in results have not been resolved at the present time (Dunkel-Schetter & Bennett, 1990). Recent research suggests that dimensional scoring may account for some of the results (Finch et al., 1997), but we suggest that the researcher should tread carefully and study relevant precedents in the literature. Because perceived support measures have an extensive track record of showing inverse correlations with symptomatology, they would be the conservative choice for studies where only one type of measure could be used; preferably, a study would include both perceived and received support measures to gain a better understanding of support perception processes and support enactment processes.

Length

Another issue concerns length. Researchers looking for a measure are usually concerned that the measure is a relatively brief one, and sometimes they incline to the view that the shorter, the better. The position of this chapter is on the side of longer measures. One reason is the psychometric principle that "there's no such thing as a free lunch." Shorter measures inherently have lower reliability, and unless the researcher is able to obtain a sizable sample, then the brevity of a measure is not a necessary virtue (Orth-Gomer & Unden, 1987). (The concept of reliability is discussed in detail in the next section.) Another reason is theoretical: Even seemingly simple stressors or interventions may turn out to be complex (Barrera & Prelow, in press), and for a given population there is usually limited knowledge about the exact nature of supporters and coping demands. Thus the arguments are for measuring a range of supportive functions. Most of the measures discussed here are of moderate length and can be administered in a reasonable time period.

Buffering effects

Evidence that a measure shows stress-buffering effects is a desirable attribute. The basic rationale for perceived support measures is that they tap the availability of functions that help people deal with stressful experiences; hence findings of buffering effects with a given measure strengthen confidence for construct validity. We do note that it is typical in social support research to find underpowered studies, which tried to test for buffering effects with small samples that lacked the ability to detect these effects.[1] Thus in the context of the research to date, findings of significant buffer effects are a good sign, but failures to find buffering effects may be attributable to sample size issues. We hope that this issue may be remedied in the future, but it presents a limiting factor for dealing with previous research.

---

1. The statistical reasons for this are discussed in detail in several places (see Aiken & West, 1991; J. Cohen, 1988; McClelland & Judd, 1993). Becoming acquainted with the statistical issues for detecting interactions is highly recommended for persons planning a study on stress-buffering effects.

Subscale correlations

While several functions have been defined theoretically, in empirical studies it is common to find significant correlations among scales for the perceived availability of emotional, instrumental, and other types of support. This may occur because persons who seek support need (and obtain) several functions, and because persons who provide support are able to do so in several ways. The magnitude of the correlations may be influenced to some extent by the context of the research—for example, one might anticipate higher intercorrelations among functions when studying support from primary relationships than when studying support in medical settings—but is also a property of the measurement instruments. The magnitude of the correlation among subscales in an inventory is an issue to consider because the lower the intercorrelations among subscales, the more likely one is to be able to detect differential effects for various supportive functions.

Confounders

The issue of possible confounders should be considered. This is the case where a third variable (e.g., gender) is correlated with a support measure and also is correlated with a health outcome. In such a case, analyses may be performed to determine whether a relationship between support and health status remains significant when the possible confounder is included in the analyses. It is always desirable to assess a broad range of demographic variables, and the researcher should look for prior evidence of whether a support measure is related to demographic characteristics such as age, ethnicity, or socioeconomic status. There have been suggestions that personality characteristics, such as extraversion or neuroticism, may represent confounders for support effects. There are developmental reasons to expect that temperament dimensions will be related to support relationships (Wills, Cleary, & Shinar, in press), and social support in adulthood is predictable from earlier variables (e.g., Graves, Wang, Mead, Johnson, & Klag, 1998). Therefore, a correlation between social support and some personality measures may be expected. If a given support measure is correlated with one or more personality attributes, then personality measures may be included in new research; the research gain is likely to be enhanced when potential confounders can be tested empirically and shown to be either relevant or irrelevant to the health effects of support.

Negative interactions

Consideration should be given to possible negative aspects of social relationships. Most functional measures primarily assess positive aspects of social relationships, but it is known that interpersonal relationships involve both supportive aspects and potentially conflictual or burdensome aspects and that support and conflict make independent contributions—in opposite directions—to psychological well-being (Abbey, Abramis, & Caplan, 1985; Coyne & Smith, 1991; Rook, 1984; Schulz et al., 1997). Where there is reason to believe that social relationships involve negative aspects as well as supportive aspects, it is advisable to include measures of these dimensions in addition to measures of perceived support, so that both types of effects may be tested (see, e.g., Ruehlman & Karoly, 1991, for general populations; Wills, Sandy & Shinar, 1999, for adolescents; Finch, Okun, Barrera, Zautra, & Reich, 1989, for elderly; Revenson, Schiaffino, Majerovitz, & Gibofsky, 1991, for chronically ill populations).

Generality versus specificity

Another issue concerns the generality versus specificity of the measure. Social support research originally concentrated on buffering with respect to composite indices of life stress, but research in the past few years has increasingly focused on support effects for specific stressors (e.g., unemployment) or specific disease conditions (e.g., arthritis, AIDS). The concern is that a general support measure may not capture all the nuances of stress-support relationships that occur in a particular context (Vaux, 1992). For this reason, it is sensible to use a well-tested functional measure and also to include some new items that are written to capture specific aspects of the stressor characteristics and support needs of the target population. The best case is that the new items will be valid and add predictive validity to the established scales; the worst that can happen is that the new items will not add much new information and the investigator will have the benefit of a known measure with established predictive validity. For reference, an appendix to this chapter provides citations to studies that have studied supportive functions for eight specific health conditions.

Structural and functional measures

When the researcher's primary interest is in how social resources assist people to cope with stressors, a functional measure is the indicated choice. However, we note that selecting a functional measure and including a social integration measure are not mutually exclusive. Major questions in this area concern the relation between social integration and availability of support, and there are few studies that have compared the predictive ability of structural and functional measures (Cohen, 1988). The research gain is likely to be justified by the brevity of typical social integration scales and their record for predicting health outcomes (chapter 3). Intervention researchers also should consider structural measures because several studies have shown increases in network size and/or frequency of contact in the experimental group (Cochran & Henderson, 1990; Krauss, Upshur, Shonkoff, & Hauser-Cram, 1993; McGuire & Gottlieb, 1979).

Intervention research

Several issues may be particularly applicable for researchers measuring change in social support in the context of intervention research. One reason is that measures of perceived support tend to be skewed toward the higher end of the scale (because most people perceive they have a relatively high level of support), and received support measures may also be skewed among stressed populations because these individuals are activating a lot of support resources. Such skewness could reduce the sensitivity of either perceived or received support measures for detecting effects of an intervention (Helgeson, et al., in press). The researcher may wish to study available data on distributions of support measures and should consider adding items to existing measures that tap unique aspects of support that are expected to be affected by the intervention and hence may be less skewed. Assessments of transactions perceived as unsupportive may be more sensitive as outcome measures because the intervention may change the ability of network members to respond effectively to the support needs of a target person, and a successful intervention could decrease the frequency of negative transactions between a supporter and a recipient (Helgeson & Cohen, 1996). Intervention researchers may consider including questionnaire measures of collateral constructs, such as discomfort with seeking support (Hobfoll & Lerman, 1988, 1989), efficacy beliefs about help-seeking (Eckenrode, 1983; Riley & Eckenrode, 1986; Vaux, Burda, & Stewart, 1986), or overprotective buffering by a spouse (Coyne & Smith, 1991). Additional measures of support-giving or support-receiving transactions could be obtained with observational measures (cf. Melamed & Brenner, 1990; see also chapter 5.) Such measures could tap aspects of support processes that are influenced by an intervention but are not directly represented in current measures of perceived support.

Measures of Perceived Support

The following section discusses measures that assess perceived availability of support, typically by describing examples of a supportive function and asking participants to indicate whether they would have these available if needed. The measure is briefly described, psychometric data are summarized, and the record of the measure for predicting health outcomes is noted. Because of the large number of measures that have been published over the past 20 years, our review required some selectivity. Rather than considering every known scale, we discuss measures that have been widely used in support research, and we also discuss several measures that may have interesting properties for some types of research but have not been used as frequently.[2] A summary of the basic characteristics of the measures discussed is presented in Table 4.2.

2. Several types of measures are excluded. Marital status, although probably correlated with the existence of confiding and emotional support, is strictly speaking a structural measure. We excluded studies in which the investigator used some items indicating the existence of a good relationship with one (or more) other persons without indicating what function(s) were provided by those relationships. We also excluded cases where a researcher simply generated a few items that were thought to index social support and used them as such; while this resulted in omission of some interesting studies, the focus of the present chapter is on measures with a clear theoretical background and supporting psychometric information. We do not review measures that specifically index loneliness or lack of support

If a particular support measure taps content that is relevant for the researcher's hypotheses and population, reliability would be a factor to consider for evaluating a measure. The two basic indices of reliability are: (1) internal consistency, the degree to which the items in a scale correlate with each other and hence are measuring a similar construct, and (2) test-retest reliability, the correlation of two scores when the same scale is readministered after a brief interval, which indexes the scale's ability to produce similar values on two occasions. In general, reliability is a prerequisite for validity; a measure with higher reliability is more likely to have predictive validity (for detailed discussion, see Heitzmann & Kaplan, 1988). Internal consistency, the most commonly used index, is typically measured by the Cronbach alpha statistic, which is based on the interitem correlations; test-retest reliability is typically measured by the Pearson r. Values above .80 are considered optimal; values in the range from .70 to .80 indicate adequate reliability for moderate sample sizes (100 to 200 subjects). Measures with reliability values in the .50 to .60 range could be usable in larger samples (above 300 subjects), but caution would be advisable for smaller samples.

Brief Unidimensional Scales

This section discusses scales that are relatively brief in length and aim to assess one function, though some of the measures may assess a mixture of two functions. These are all questionnaire measures.

Some brief questionnaire measures tap one supportive function. At the lower end of the length continuum, Seeman and Berkman (1988) developed an interview with one-item measures for availability of a confidant, indexed by the item "Is there any one special person you know that you feel very close and intimate with"; emotional support, "Can you count on anyone to provide you with emotional support (talking over problems and helping you make a difficult decision)?"; and instrumental support, "Can you count on anyone to help you with daily tasks like grocery shopping, house cleaning, cooking, telephoning, giving you a ride?" The response for the first item is dichotomous (yes or no); the last two items are followed by 11 potential sources who could provide support, and a count is made of the affirmative responses. No psychometric data were reported on the reliability of the measures. A study with 194 elderly subjects found that higher emotional support was related to 6-month survival after myocardial infarction (Berkman, et al., 1992); no significant findings were reported for the confidant or instrumental support scales. A study of 1,965 patients with heart problems by Williams et al. (1992) indicated that persons who were married and had

---

(e.g., Habif & Lahey, 1980; Russell, Peplau, & Cutrona, 1980) because they assess a completely different type of construct (Newcomb & Bentler, 1986), though they may be relevant for some research contexts (cf. Fontana, Kerns, Rosenberg, & Colonese, 1989). We note that there is some theoretical ambiguity about measures that measure participation in a wide range of social and leisure activities (e.g., Welin, Larsson, Svärdsudd, Tibblin, & Tibblin, 1992); these might index companionship support but in form are more like social integration scales; hence they are discussed in chapter 3.

Table 4.2. Measures of Perceived Support

Study	Acronym	Number of Items	Function(s) Measured[a]	Reliability	Notes
Brief Unidimensional Measure					
Seeman & Berkman, 1988	—	1 each	Confidant, emotional, instrumental (count of sources)	n.a.	Confidant item is dichotomous; other scales count number of sources
Williams et al., 1992	—	2	Married/confidant	n.a.	Used as composite score
Hobfoll & Leiberman, 1987	—	10	Emotional (spouse, friends)	.65 full scale); .90 (spouse scale)	Friends' support included as variant version
Brief Compound Measures					
Blazer, 1982	OARS	6	Emotional/instrumental	.82	Developed for elderly population
Hanson & Östergren, 1987	—	4 / 5	Emotional / Instrumental/informational	.93 / n.a.	Used with mixed-age samples
LaRocco, House, & French, 1980	WSS	12	Emotional/instrumental	.73–.83	Worksite support measure; has parallel scales for supervisor, coworkers, home support
Broad Scales of Close and Diffuse Support					
Henderson et al., 1980	ISSI	8 / 16	Emotional (Attachment) / Emotional/instrumental (Integration)[b]	.67 / .71	Developed as interview measure with 52 items in total; adaptations are shorter (12 items total)
Procidano & Heller, 1983	PSS	20 / 20	Emotional/Information (Family) / Emotional/Informationl (Friends)	.90 / .88	Parallel scales for support from family, support from friends
Sarason et al., 1983	SSQ	27	Emotional (mixed sources)	.97	Provides separate scores for amount and satisfaction
Moos & Moos, 1981	FRI, WRI	27	Cohesion, expressiveness, conflict (reversed)[d]	.89 (FRI)	Versions available for family support, worksite support
Brown et al., 1986	SESS	—[c]	Emotional (primary confidant)	n.a.[c]	Interview protocol may be scored for 2–3 additional confidants, emotional, instrumental support

Table 4.2. Measures of Perceived Support (*Continued*)

Study	Acronym	Number of Items	Function(s) Measured[a]	Reliability	Notes
Multidimensional Inventories					
Cohen et al., 1985	ISEL	40	Emotional, instrumental, companionship, validation	.90 for full scale, .70–.80 for subscales	Subscale correlations are moderate. Statistics are for general-population version.
Vaux et al., 1987	SS-B (also SS-A, SS-R)	45	Emotional, instrumental, informational, companionship	.85 (full scale); >.80 for subscales	Subscale correlations are moderate. Scores available for family, friend support. SS-A provides global score for emotional support; SS-R indexes support from listed network members.
Cutrona & Russell, 1987	SPS	24	Attachment, social integration,[b] reassurance of worth, reliable alliance, guidance, nurturance[d]	.91 for full scale, .65–.76 for subscales	High subscale correlations
Network-based Inventories					
Barrera, 1981	ASSIS	—[e]	Emotional, instrumental, informational, companionship, validation	.88 (full scale)	Interview protocol. Score indexes number of persons providing ≥ 1 supportive function. Includes scale for negative interaction.
Dunkel-Schetter, Feinstein, & Call, 1987	UCLA-SSI	70	Emotional, instrumental, informational	n.a.[f]	Interview protocol. Obtains data for at least 3 sources of support. Includes negative-interaction scale.
Measures for Children and Adolescents					
Wills et al., 1992	WPSS	12 (supp) 3 (confl)	Emotional, instrumental, conflict	.85 (emot.), .76 (instr.), .79 (confl.)	Appropriate for 11–16 years. Subscale correlations moderately high. Includes scale for negative interaction.
Reid et al., 1989	MFF	11 (per source)	Emotional, instrumental, informa-	.68 (full scale); .52–	For ages 6–12 years. Interview measure,

Table 4.2. (*Continued*)

Study	Acronym	Number of Items	Function(s) Measured[a]	Reliability	Notes
			tional, companionship	.82 for subscales	uses nonverbal props. Assesses support from parents, sibs, friends, relatives, teachers.
Dubow & Ullman, 1989	SCSS-APP, NET	31 (APP)	Emotional (APP), Emotional, instrumental, informational support from network members (NET)	.88 (APP), .52–.54 test-retest for subscales (NET)	For ages 8–10 years. APP has subscales for parents, peers, teachers. NET has scores for number of network members providing each support function.
Barrera et al., 1993	BSSS	6 (supp) 1 (conf)	Reliable alliance, enhancement of worth, guidance, companionship, affection, intimacy[d]	.82–.90 (full scales, within source)	For ages 12–16 years. Provides global score for overall support from parents, sibs, friends. Includes item on negative interaction.
Newcomb & Bentler, 1986	NLSI	16	Respect, support, inclusion[d]	.54–.82 for subscales	For ages 14–18 years. Provides scores for overall support from parents, family, other adults, peers. Includes measures for loneliness.
Wolchik et al., 1989	CISS	n.a.[e]	Emotional, instrumental, informational, companionship, validation	.52–.85 test-retest for number of supporters	Interview measure, for ages 8–15 years. Provides 4 scores: support from family/nonfamily, adults/peers. Includes section on negative interaction.

Note: n.a. = not applicable.

[a] This section uses the terminology from Table 4.1 for cases where the content of the measure(s) was clearly mapped onto the definitions of support function as in the table. For cases where the content of the measure could not be clearly mapped onto these functions, the original authors' terms are employed.

[b] Note that this scale assesses a different construct than the social integration measures discussed in chapter 3.

[c] This is a lengthy interview protocol with several hundred items involving third-party ratings, so it is difficult to characterize the scale length and the criteria for reliability indices. See authors' reports for more detail.

[d] These are the authors' terms; it was not totally clear how the subscales map onto the definitions in table 4.1. See authors' reports for more detail.

[e] This is an interview protocol with several areas of questioning and multiple sources and ratings, so it is difficult to characterize the number of items.

[f] This interview protocol may be scored for up to 49 different indices, so it is difficult to determine the criteria for reliability.

a confidant showed greater 9-year survival. Williams et al. (1992) used a composite score, so it is unclear whether the confidant item alone or marital status alone predicted mortality. Previous studies have indicated that brief (1 to 3 item) measures of confidant relationships show buffering relationships in samples with 800 to 2,300 subjects (see Cohen & Wills, 1985), so these may have utility for some types of epidemiologic research, but caution would be advisable for research with smaller samples.

A brief scale on emotional support was adapted by Hobfoll and colleagues from an earlier measure by Vanfossen (1981). The scale is termed *intimacy* (Hobfoll & Leiberman, 1987); the items concern the perception that important thoughts and feelings can be shared with others and will be accepted, so it is essentially a measure of emotional support. A basic 6-item scale taps emotional support from spouse; in other versions with 10 and 15 items, scales are included on support from closest friend and from closest family member. Hobfoll and Leiberman (1987) report an alpha of .89 for a 6-item scale on spouse support; Hobfoll and Lerman (1988) report subscale alphas ranging from .72 to .79. This scale has been shown to predict psychological symptomatology in medical settings (Hobfoll & Leiberman, 1987) and to buffer the effect of war-related life events (Hobfoll, London, & Orr, 1988).

A 6-item scale on emotional/instrumental support from the Older Americans and Resources Inventory (OARS; Fillenbaum & Smyer, 1981) was developed for elderly populations but has items with general wording. The OARS items include having a confidant, feeling understood, having someone who would care if something happened, and having someone who would help if one were ill or disabled. The authors reported interrater reliability of $r = .82$. This scale predicted 30-month mortality in a community sample of 331 participants (Blazer, 1982). A similar measure developed in a Swedish study (Hanson & Östergren, 1987) has 4 items on emotional support (test-retest mean item reliability = 93%) and 5 items on instrumental/informational support (reliability not reported). The emotional support scale predicted 5-year mortality in a sample of 621 male participants (Hanson, Isacsson, Janzon, & Lindell, 1989) and there was suggestive evidence of a buffering effect (Falk, Hanson, Isacsson, & Östergren, 1992); here, results for the mixed instrumental support scale were generally nonsignificant. This type of measure has a record of predictive validity, but it has not provided separate findings for emotional and instrumental support.

A brief inventory was developed by LaRocco, House, and French (1980) to provide measures appropriate for worksite settings, based on Cobb's (1987) and Cassel's (1976) models. The 12-item measure has three parallel scales worded to tap support from worksite supervisor, coworkers, and home (spouse and family); each scale indexes a combination of emotional and instrumental support. Alphas for the scales are in the range .73 to .83, and support scores for the three sources are not highly correlated. This measure has shown buffering effects with respect to work-related stress for all three scales in a sample of 636 male workers from a variety of occupational groups (LaRocco et al., 1980) and a sample of 2,800 hourly manufacturing workers (House & Wells, 1978).

Broadly Based Scales of Close and Diffuse Support

Several measures have assessed overall support availability from two types of relationships, variously characterized as attachment versus friendship relationships or strong ties versus weak ties (Granovetter, 1973; Henderson, Byrne, Duncan-Jones, Scott, & Adcock, 1980). The intent is to obtain measures of mixed support functions from a primary relationship with one close person and also from a broader network of alliances with friends and workmates who also provide supportive functions of some kind. The measures include questionnaire scales and interview-based approaches.

The Interview Schedule for Social Interaction (ISSI), developed for epidemiologic research with general-population samples (Henderson, Duncan-Jones, & Byrne, 1980), was based on Bowlby's theory of attachment (e.g., Bowlby, 1969) and Weiss's (1974) model of social relationships. This 52-item interview protocol first makes a determination of the existence of a primary confidant relationship based on an introductory question: "At present, do you have someone you can share your most private feelings with (confide in) or not?" The question is followed by probe items about whether the relationship provides confiding, comfort, and closeness and is likely to endure; this score is termed *attachment*. A score for the existence of friendship or workmate relationships is based on other items asking about persons (aside from the confidant) who provide a sense of reliable alliance and reassurance of worth; this score is termed *integration* (but it assesses a different construct than the social integration scales discussed in chapter 3). After items assessing availability of attachment and integration, further questions explore the perceived adequacy of each type of relationship, that is, whether the respondent wanted more or less of it. Summary scores are constructed for availability of attachment (8 items, alpha = .67), adequacy of attachment (12 items, alpha = .81), availability of integration (16 items, alpha= .71) and adequacy of integration (17 items, alpha = .79). The original reports demonstrated stress-buffering relationships in a community sample of 756 participants, with depression as the outcome (Henderson, Byrne et al., 1980). A briefer questionnaire version has been adapted in subsequent epidemiologic studies. For example, a 12-item version predicted incident heart disease in a sample of 752 male participants (Orth-Gomer, et al., 1993), and stress-buffering relationships with respect to 7-year all-causes mortality were found (Rosengren, et al., 1993); significant results were found for both the attachment scale and the integration scale. Thus the measure has a reasonable track record. The primary drawback is that the inventory does not set out to assess specific support functions. The attachment scale seems to index primarily emotional support, but it and the integration scale may also tap other functions (e.g., instrumental, informational, companionship) in a way that could vary across individuals.

The measure termed Perceived Support from Family and Friends (PSS; Procidano & Heller, 1983) was developed to provide parallel-forms measures of functional support from two sources. A 20-item scale on friend support includes a number of items on availability of closeness, confiding, and emotional support and on getting ideas about how to solve problems, so the functions tapped are primarily emotional and informational support (though there are two items on social companionship). A parallel 20-item scale has the same items, worded for support from family. In each case, a total score for perceived support is computed over the items. In the development studies with college students, the alpha for friend support was .88 and for family support was .90; the two scales were not highly correlated (r's = .21 to .24), and the scales showed correlations with measures of social competence and self-disclosure. The instrument was developed with college students but is suitable for adolescents. The measure has been used with a wide range of symptomatology measures, from anxiety and depression to drug use and suicidal ideation. This measure provides some advantages but assesses primarily emotional and informational support and may be less useful for situations where other functions are highly relevant.

The Social Support Questionnaire (SSQ; I. Sarason, Levine, Basham, & Sarason, 1983) was influenced by Bowlby's (1969) theory of attachment and the authors' theory on sense of acceptance (e.g., I. Sarason, 1990). This instrument consists of 27 items, asking questions such as "Whom can you really count on to listen when you need to talk?" "Who do you feel really appreciates you as a person?" and "Whom can you count on to console you when you are very upset?" For each item, respondents first list the persons they perceive as available for this, with a maximum of nine persons for any given item, and then rate how satisfied they are with those supports. The measure yields a total score for number of supporters and a total score for support satisfaction. Coefficient alpha was .97 for number and .94 for satisfaction. The instrument has been used in several methodological studies involving correlations with other support measures and with personality measures (Sarason et al., 1983; B. Sarason, Shearin, Pierce, & Sarason, 1987) and has been employed in studies with a considerable range of samples. As a global measure of perceived support, this instrument has a reasonable track record. However, it does not provide subscores for any particular supportive function, nor does it distinguish between different sources of support.

The Work Relationships Index (WRI) and Family Relationships Index (FRI) are derived from 100-item inventories, the Work Environment Scales and Family Environment Scales (Moos, 1981; Moos & Moos, 1981). The original inventories were based on theoretical concepts from group research (e.g., Moos & Insel, 1974). The WRI and FRI are 27-item composite measures based on the sum of three subscales that index the concepts of cohesion, the extent to which a person perceives group members are supportive of each other; expressiveness, the extent to which group members are encouraged to express their feelings directly; and conflict (reversed), the extent to which open expression of anger is not characteristic of the group. Wording of the items is adapted for the work environment (WRI) or the family environment (FRI). Psychometric data are reported in the test manuals, for example an alpha of .89 for the FRI (Moos & Moos, 1981). These measures have been extensively used by the authors and by other investigators to index both work-based support and family-based support (e.g., Billings & Moos, 1982, 1984, 1985; Holahan & Moos, 1986, 1987, 1990). It remains unclear what supportive function(s) these scales actually measure, and despite some relatively strong tests they typically do not produce buffer effects (e.g., Burt, Cohen, & Bjorck, 1988; Holahan & Moos, 1986, 1987).

The Self-Evaluation and Social Support Schedule (SESS) is a structured interview schedule designed to assess the availability of confidant relationships. This measure was part of the Life Events and Difficulties Schedule (LEDS, Brown & Harris, 1978), in which detailed reports are elicited from respondents about the nature of stressful events and social relationships; scores are subsequently constructed from third-party ratings of the interview protocol. For the social support component, detailed questioning is conducted about the relationship with a primary confidant (spouse or cohabitee, any lover, friends and relatives), including content about closeness, confiding, intimacy, and dependency. The interview protocol is then dichotomously scored by raters for the existence of a primary confidant relationship, a designation that is reported to be made with perfect interrater agreement (Brown, Andrews, Harris, Adler, & Bridge, 1986). Additional scores may be obtained for availability of two or three other confidants, and the interview information may be used to extract continuous scores for emotional and instrumental support (Parry & Shapiro, 1986). The SESS provides very detailed information about confidant relationships but takes 3 to 4 hours to administer (Brown et al., 1986), and it requires training for both interviewers and raters. It would be most appropriate for a context when lengthy structured interviews are being conducted and ample time is available to assess confidant support.

Multidimensional Inventories

This section covers inventories that assess the perceived availability of more than two supportive functions. They are all questionnaire measures and tap perceived support from a range of sources.

The Interpersonal Support Evaluation List (ISEL; Cohen & Hoberman, 1983) was developed to assess supportive functions as posited by Cobb (1976) and Cassel (1976). This inventory comes in a 40-item general population version and a 18-item college student version. The 40-item inventory provides 10-item subscales for appraisal (emotional) support, instrumental support, companionship support, and self-esteem maintenance through social comparisons. For the full scale, alpha and test-retest reliability are around .90. For the subscales, internal consistency and test-retest reliabilities are in the range from .70 to .80, and the subscales have moderate intercorrelations (Cohen & Hoberman, 1983; Cohen, Mermelstein, Kamarck, & Hoberman, 1985). The ISEL has been widely used in health-related research, has a consistent record for showing stress-buffering effects (see Wills, 1991; Wills & Filer, 2000), and predicts recovery from physical illness (e.g., King, Reis, Porter, & Norsen, 1993). This measure has a good track record and has proven adaptable to a variety of populations. A possible limitation is that it does not include a separate scale that clearly indexes advice and guidance, and supplementation of content might be desirable for settings where this function is believed to be especially important.

The Social Support Behaviors Scale (SS-B: Vaux & Harrison, 1985; Vaux, Riedel, & Stewart, 1987) was developed to measure supportive functions as posited in community research. The 45-item measure has scales termed emotional support, practical assistance, financial assistance, advice-guidance, and socializing; for each item, subjects rate the likelihood that family members and friends would engage in this behavior in a time of need. Separate scores are available for overall support from family and from friends. Internal consistency for the full scale is .85, and alphas for the subscales are reported to be over .80 (Vaux et al., 1987). Subscale correlations are not clearly reported, but it appears from a confirmatory analysis (Vaux et al., 1987, study 5) that the subscales have only moderate intercorrelations. A 23-item variant of this measure provides a global score for appraised emotional support (SS-A: Vaux, et al., 1986). Another variant has availability of the four functions rated for up to 10 specific network members, together with structural indices (SS-R: Vaux & Harrison, 1985). This inventory has received some usage in community psychology. The 45-item inventory may also be administered as a received support measure, with instructions to rate whether each of the items was recently received; this is also discussed in the section on received support.

The Social Provisions Scale (SPS; Cutrona & Russell, 1987) was developed to assess six functions as posited by Weiss (1974). The current 24-item instrument has subscales termed attachment, social integration, reassurance of worth, reliable alliance, guidance, and opportunity for nurturance. Subscale alphas are in the range from .65 to .76, but subscale intercorrelations are rather high, in the range from $r = .55$ to $r = .99$ (Cutrona & Russell, 1987). This measure has been used with a variety of adult populations, from new mothers to elderly community residents, and has been used in intervention research (Mallinckrodt, 1996). The conceptual basis for the scales is mixed, some clearly functional whereas others are more structural; instrumental support is not well represented, so this would be a consideration for situations where this function may be important. The high subscale correlations indicate this measure may be usable to assess a higher-order construct of perceived support, but it would not be likely to detect effects for any individual function.

Network-based Inventories

Several multidimensional inventories are based on a two-stage process, in which the respondent first identifies network members perceived as providing supportive functions and then rates availability and adequacy of the support. The measures described here are both interview schedules.

The Arizona Social Support Interview Schedule (ASSIS; Barrera, 1981) was developed as an interview protocol from much the same theoretical background as the ISEL, with a methodological approach derived from Fischer (1982). It is designed to assess six functions, termed intimate interaction, material aid, physical assistance, guidance, social participation, and positive feedback. In the interview procedure, the respondent is first read a general description of the support function (e.g., "If you wanted to talk to someone about things that are very personal and private, who would you talk to?") and is then asked to give the initials of all the persons who would fit the description as providing that function and to whom the respondent had talked in the last 30 days. There is no limitation on the source of support (defined as "friends, family members, teachers, ministers, doctors, or other people you might know") or on the number of supporters who can be listed. In each section, ratings are also obtained of support satisfaction as in the ISSI. The protocol includes a score for negative interactions, based on the question, "Who are the people that you can expect to have some unpleasant disagreements with, or people that you can expect to make you angry and upset?" The protocol provides a score for total network size, the number of different persons named as providing at least one supportive function, and a score termed conflicted network size, the number of support network members who were also sources of interpersonal conflict. The test-retest reliability for total network score was .88, and the agreement between support persons named in two administrations was 74%. This measure has been used extensively, mainly for predicting psychological symptomatology. It covers a range of supportive functions, though they are defined only briefly in the interview; scores for individual functions are not usually derived for this measure.

The UCLA Social Support Interview (UCLA-SSI; see Dunkel-Schetter, Folkman, & Lazarus, 1987; Dunkel-Schetter & Bennett, 1990) is a 70-item interview protocol usually focused on specific stressors. The respondent is first asked to identify a recent stressful situation and then is asked questions about persons who may provide support relevant to that situation. In the basic instrument, respondents are probed about support from three specific persons (e.g., parent, friend, romantic partner) and asked to rate the extent to which each provides emotional, instrumental, and informational support; in medical settings, the instructions about support sources can be varied (e.g., spouse, family member, physician). In a variant, respondents are given a list of 15 individuals or groups and are asked whether each of them helped in a stressful situation (Dunkel-Schetter, Feinstein & Call, 1987). In addition to obtaining information about types of support functions and sources of support, the instrument is designed to provide ratings about several aspects of support, including quantity, satisfaction, and reciprocation. The interview protocol includes items on negative aspects of social relationships through questions about sources of stress in one's relationships. The inventory may be scored for total number of sources of support or for amounts of emotional, instrumental, and informational support averaged over three sources. The inventory is sometimes administered with wordings to tap perceived availability of support (e.g., "To what extent do you feel you can turn to source X for information and advice regarding your health?") and sometimes with wording to tap received support (e.g., "During the past 3 months, how often did source X give you information and advice about health-related concerns?"); for example, see Helgeson (1993).

Measures for Children and Adolescents

Some measures have been developed specifically for children and adolescents (see Cauce, Reid, Landooman, & Gonzales, 1990; Sandler et al., 1989). The dimensions are similar to those indexed in adult inventories, but the structure and wording are adapted for use with younger populations. Note that some adult measures have also been used to assess family support as perceived by younger populations, particularly the PSS (see, e.g., DuBois, Felner, Meares, & Krier, 1994) and the FRI (see, e.g., Cauce, 1986; Hirsch, 1987).

The Wills Parental Support Scale (WPSS) was developed to provide a brief measure of functional support dimensions appropriate for younger populations. It was based on buffering theory and descriptive studies of supportive functions of parents as perceived by adolescents (Burke & Weir, 1978, 1979; Greenberg, Siegel, & Leitch, 1983). The 15-item questionnaire measure is designed for the age range of 11 to 16 years (Wills, McNamara, & Vaccaro, 1992; Wills, McNamara, Vaccaro, & Hirky, 1996; Wills, Sandy, & Shinar, 1999). It includes subscales for emotional support (e.g., "When I feel bad about something, my parent will listen") and instrumental support (e.g., "If I need help with my school work I can ask my parent about it") and includes a three-item scale for parent-child conflict (e.g., "I have a lot of arguments with my parent"). Internal consistency is .82 to .89 for emotional support, .70 to .81 for instrumental support, and .75 to .82 for parent-child conflict; subscale correlations are in the range from .50 to .60. The support scales predict adolescent problem behavior and show consistent stress-buffering effects with respect to substance use as the outcome (Wills & Cleary, 1996; Wills, et al., 1998, 1999). A possible limitation is that other functional dimensions are not assessed.

The My Family and Friends measure (MFF; Reid, Landesman, Treder, & Jaccard, 1989) was developed based on functional support theory (Cohen & Wills, 1985) to assess functional dimensions in younger children (6 to 12 years of age). The measure is administered with nonverbal props such as names and photographs of network members and a large red thermometer with a moving indicator and key labels to help the child make numerical ratings. The items are administered with dialogue stems (e.g., "When you want to share your feelings, like feeling happy, sad, or mad . . ."), followed by probes to rank availability of network members for an item and a thermometer rating to indicate satisfaction with support. The measure has 5 items to index emotional support; 2 items each to index instrumental, informational, and companionship support; and 1 item on conflict. Psychometric data indicated an overall test-retest correlation of .68 for availability rankings; internal consistency for subscales was in the range of .52 to .82 for parents and was comparable but more variable for other sources (siblings, friends, relatives, and teachers). The psychometric data suggest this may be a useful measure for research with young children if sample size is adequate.

The Survey of Children's Social Support (SCSS; Dubow & Ullman, 1989) is a self-report questionnaire inventory developed for third to fifth graders. The measure was intended to index dimensions of emotional, informational, and instrumental support. A 31-item measure of appraised support (APP) provides a global measure of perceived emotional support and acceptance from various sources. Factor analyses confirmed factors representing appraised support from peers, parents, and teachers, with subscale reliabilities from .78 to .83. A network assessment (NET) ascertains the identity and number of persons who are perceived as providing each of three supportive functions; test-retest data indicated test-retest reliability for total number of supporters was in the range from .52 to .54. Subscale correlations indicated moderate relationships among sources of appraised support (median r = .37) and low relationship of the network scale to the measures of appraised support (Dubow & Ullman, 1989). A study with 361 elementary school children indicated stress-buffering effects for the appraised support measure with respect to independent ratings of behavior problems and academic performance (Dubow & Tisak, 1989; Dubow, Tisak, Causey, Hryshko, & Reid, 1991).

The Barrera Social Support Scale (BSSS; Barrera, Chassin, & Rogosch, 1993) is a six-item measure derived from research by Furman and Buhrmester (1985) that was based on the six social provisions posited by Weiss (1974): reliable alliance, enhancement of worth, guidance, companionship, affection, and intimacy. It provides global scores for overall support from key sources (mother, father, closest sibling, and same-sex best friend). Responses are on a scale from "little or none" to "most possible," so this is more like a perceived adequacy scale. The measure includes a one-item scale for conflict, with the same response scale. Alphas for support, based on ratings within source over the six provisions, ranged from .82 to .90; subscale correlations are not reported but, based on the internal consistencies, must be high. The measure shows main effects with respect to psychological symptomatology, primarily for parental support, but has not shown evidence of buffering effects for risk factors such as parental alcoholism (Barrera et al., 1993).

The Newcomb Loneliness and Support Inventory (NLSI; Newcomb & Bentler, 1986) is a multisource self-report measure designed for adolescents, ages 12 to 18 years. The support section is based on four four-item scales that provide a score indexing respect, support, and inclusion in each of four types of relationships (parents, family members, other adults, and peers). Alphas range from .54 (peers) to .82 (parents). The loneliness section uses a variety of items to index perceived loneliness and lack of inclusion in the same types of relationships. Confirmatory analyses have demonstrated that the support and loneliness scales assess distinct constructs (Newcomb & Bentler, 1986). The support measure is typically used as a global construct in which the four scales are specified as indicators of a latent construct for overall support; this construct essentially represents good relationships with a range of adults, because peer support has a relatively low loading. In longitudinal main-effect tests, this measure predicts a range of outcomes including psychological symptomatology, physical symptomatology, and substance use (Newcomb & Bentler, 1988). A version for young adults has also been developed (Newcomb & Chou, 1989). Buffering effects have not been tested.

The Children's Inventory of Social Support (CISS: Wolchik, Ruehlman, Braver, & Sandler, 1989) is an interview measure based on the ASSIS, adapted for children in the 8- to 15-year age range. The functions indexed are emotional, instrumental, informational, companionship, and feedback. Each dimension of support is defined briefly to the participant, who then lists all the people (from family/nonfamily and adults/peers) who provided this type of support during the past several months. A section on negative interaction is based on a question about people who made them feel "angry, bad, or upset." A measure of support is calculated by summing the number of supportive functions provided by a given source (e.g., nonfamily adults). Subscale alphas within source range from .79 to .90; test-retest corrrelations for number of supporters ranged from .52 to .85. This measure has shown buffering effects in a sample of children from divorced families (Wolchik et al., 1989) and has been used in intervention research (Wolchik et al., 1993).

Measures of Received Support

This section considers measures that tap the receipt of support, typically by asking subjects to indicate how often they have received specific supportive actions within the past 30 days. These include questionnaire measures and interview measures. We note that some measures have been used to index both types of support—through change in the instructions to the participants—hence this section has some overlap with measures from the previous section. There are fewer measures discussed in this section because there is a realistic imbalance in the literature, with a considerable number of reports on the development of perceived support measures but relatively few reports on the development of received support measures. The basic characteristics of the measures are summarized in Table 4.3.

The Inventory of Social Supportive Behaviors (ISSB; Barrera, Sandler, & Ramsay, 1981) is a measure that taps the recent receipt of several types of support. This 40-item inventory includes items concerning recent transactions that involved the receipt of the same kinds of functions assessed by the ASSIS, that is, support domains of emotional, instrumental, informational, and companionship. It is usually administered with instructions to indicate the extent to which each of the 40 items was received (from anyone) during the past 30 days. Internal consistency analyses indicate alphas above .90, and the authors reported a test-retest correlation for a total score of .88. The authors recommended scoring with a single total score for received support; subsequent factor analyses have suggested that the measure has five dimensions similar to those of the ASSIS, but these results have not been totally consistent (see Barrera & Ainlay, 1983; Mc-Cormick, Siegert, & Walkey, 1987; Stokes & Wilson, 1984). The ISSB has been a widely used measure in etiological research, though we were unable to find many instances of its application for intervention studies. This measure has produced some theoretically interesting results (e.g., Norris & Kaniasty, 1996), but findings include some failures to show buffering effects or predicted main effects.

The UCLA-SSI, described previously, is a 70-item interview protocol that has been used as a received support measure, with instructions to describe support recently received from each of three support sources (Dunkel-Schetter, Feinstein, & Call, 1987). There have been fewer usages of this measure in the context of received support. Results from Helgeson's (1993) study showed scores for perceived support and received support were both related to outcomes but in opposite directions; received support was positively correlated with symptomatology (as in Barrera et al., 1981), whereas perceived support was inversely related to symptomatology. As the only interview measure in the literature, the UCLA-

Table 4.3. Measures of Received Support

Study	Acronym	Number of Items	Function(s) Measured	Reliability	Notes
Barrera et al., 1981	ISSB	40	Emotional, instrumental, informational, companionship	>.90 for full scale	Questionnaire measure. Subscale structure not totally consistent over studies.
Dunkel-Schetter et al., 1987	UCLA-SSI[a]	70	Emotional, instrumental, informational	n.a.[b]	Interview protocol, obtains data for at least 3 sources of support. Includes negative-interaction scale.
Vaux et al., 1987	SS-B[a] (SS-A, SS-R)	45	Emotional, informational, instrumental, companionship	>.80 for subscales[c]	Questionnaire measure. SS-A provides global score for emotional support. SS-R indexes support functions from listed network members.
Dubow & Ullman, 1989	SAB	38	Emotional/informational, emotional/esteem enhancement, instrumental.	.61–69 for subscales	Questionnaire measure, for ages 8–10 years. Subscale correlations moderately high. Subscale structure not clear.
Cohen & Lichtenstein, 1990	PIQ	20 (10 pos., 10 neg.)	Mixed[d]	.89 (pos.), .85 (neg.)	Questionnaire measure, keyed to smoking cessation. Includes positive and negative subscales.

Note: n.a. = not applicable; pos. = positive; neg. = negative.

[a] This inventory may be used as a perceived availability measure or a received support measure, depending on the instructional set to the participants.

[b] The interview protocol may be scored for up to 49 different indices, so it is difficult to determine the criteria for reliability. See authors' report for more detail.

[c] These statistics apparently are for administration of the SS-B as an availability measure (see Vaux et al., 1987).

[d] This inventory includes items that might be characterized as emotional and instrumental support, but it is scored for subscales of positive and negative behavior rather than for specific functions.

SSI seems to have potential utility for intervention research; more data on predictive effects would be desirable.

The SS-B, discussed previously, is a 45-item questionnaire measure that may be usable to assess received support by changing the instructional set (Vaux & Harrison, 1985). The psychometrics of this measure for assessing perceived support are favorable, it provides separate scores for family and friend support, and variants provide a network-based assessment and a global score for emotional support, so this measure may have utility for some research contexts. However, beyond the original development studies, we could not readily find usages of this scale as a received support measure, so the psychometric characteristics for such applications remain unclear.

The SCSS (Dubow & Ullman, 1989, described previously) includes a scale for assessing received support for younger children. The Scale of Available Behaviors (SAB) is a 38-item measure in which children rate how frequently they are the recipient of a given supportive behavior. Though the measure was hypothesized to have a three-dimensional structure based on specified functions, factor analyses did not confirm the hypothesized structure; instead, they were suggestive of factors termed emotional/informational support, emotional/esteem enhancement, and instrumental support, which had subscale reliabilities from .61 to .69. Subscale correlations indicated substantial relationships among the received-support dimensions (median $r = .64$). Construct validity correlations were similar to those for the perceived support measure (Dubow & Ullman, 1989), but this measure has not yet received wide usage and more data are needed.

The Partner Interaction Questionnaire (PIQ, Cohen & Lichtenstein, 1990) is an inventory designed to index receipt of specific behaviors relevant to smoking cessation. The current version is a 20-item inventory that includes 10 positive behaviors (i.e., supportive of cessation) and 10 negative behaviors (i.e., detrimental to cessation) that a partner might perform during the course of a smoking cessation attempt. It is scored for positive and negative subscales rather than for receipt of specific functional dimensions. This instrument has a good track record for predicting smoking cessation (see Mermelstein, et al., 1986; Mermelstein, Lichtenstein, & McIntyre, 1983) and provides a paradigm for studying how a received support measure may be adapted to the coping needs of a specific health-related issue. Note also that the PIQ is not highly correlated with either social integration scales or perceived availability measures (see Mermelstein et al., 1986); hence it assesses a unique aspect of supportive processes.

Selecting and Using a Support Measure

In light of the previous discussion about issues for research and properties of the measures, what guidelines may be laid out for selecting a measure? Here we suggest some decision points and heuristics that may be useful with reference to the population that the researcher is going to work with.

What Supportive Functions Are Relevant
for This Population?

The primary theoretical question is what supportive functions would be most relevant for these participants. This is the crucial decision for the researcher, to be made on the basis of prior theory and research and on focused pilot studies where possible. All the measures discussed here index emotional support, the most broadly useful function (Cohen & Wills, 1985; Wills, 1991), but other functions may be relevant for specific populations. The selection of a measure including certain supportive functions should be guided by the researcher's theory about what functions are relevant.

If emotional support is hypothesized to be the only relevant function, then a unidimensional measure may be sufficient. However, it is entirely possible that this approach could miss important relationships that were not countenanced by the researcher's working theory. Thus the conservative decision is to use a multidimensional measure. A researcher conducting an intervention study should give special consideration to this issue, so as to have support measures that are well mapped onto the kinds of supportive transactions that are expected to be influenced by the intervention, and may wish to develop items tapping specific aspects of supportive transactions, so that they may be added to existing measures.

Should I Measure Received Support as Well as
Perceived Support?

It is clear from the research discussed here that measures of perceived and received support are not identical; in some contexts, they may not even be highly correlated (Mermelstein et al., 1986). There are studies showing that received support measures produce significant findings over extended time frames (Krause, 1987b), in the context of coping with natural disasters (Norris & Kaniasty, 1996), and in the context of smoking cessation (Cohen & Lichtenstein, 1990), so it is evident that they have potential utility. However, the existing discrepancies in results for perceived and received support measures have not been resolved at the present time (e.g., Dunkel-Schetter & Bennett, 1990). Thus, the researcher considering a received-support measure should study this issue thoroughly and read previous literature.

We think there is an argument for including both perceived and received support measures in a study. In epidemiologic research, there is a lack of data on how the two aspects of support are related, and studies that include both types of measures are likely to be informative. For intervention research, global appraisals of perceived support might be relatively stable over time, whereas measures of receipt of supportive behavior could be able to reflect recent changes brought about by an intervention. The balanced potential of the measures may be enhanced through keying perceived support measures to specific support sources that are likely to be affected by the intervention, and through focusing received support measures on the kinds of supportive transactions that participants need (see Barrera & Prelow, in press; Lakey & Lutz, 1996).

How Long a Measure Do I Need?

In this review, we have discussed measures with a considerable range of lengths. The record of research with sizable samples has shown replicable results for dimensional measures in the vicinity of 10 items per scale, so there are grounds for recommending this as a minimum guideline. Since unidimensional scales take only 1 or 2 minutes to administer, they represent a feasible procedure, and a multidimensional inventory with 30 to 40 items will take only a few minutes to complete. Interview measures, of course, have more items and take longer to complete but may be appropriate for research contexts where more assessment time is available. We note that significant findings have been obtained for single-item measures but only with very large samples, so we suggest caution about this approach.

The researcher should recognize that this guideline applies for sizable samples. When working with skewed outcome measures (e.g., depression), interaction hypotheses, and/or small samples (< 100 subjects), statistical power should be a serious concern, anticipated by the researcher before the study is initiated (see J. Cohen, 1988; McClelland & Judd, 1993). All reasonable attempts should be made to address this issue through using some combination of longer measures, multiple indicators, repeated measurements, and intensive assessment procedures.

Should I Use a Composite Score or Separate Scale Scores?

The functional approach to support measurement hypothesizes different supportive functions, and most measures have indexed two or more functions, some as many as six. In practice, however, some studies have then combined the subscales into a single score for support because the subscale correlations were high. If the researcher's aim is simply to study whether support has beneficial effects, using a composite score may be a reasonable decision. However, this practice limits the potential for the researcher to detect unique effects for particular functions and to test for theoretically interesting questions about the matching of support functions with properties of stressors (chapters 1 and 2; Cutrona, 1990).

The desirability of testing effects for specific functions suggests that in selecting a measure the researcher should carefully consider the subscale correlations. Of the multidimensional inventories discussed here, only two (the ISEL and the SS-B) have provided evidence of subscale correlations in the low to moderate range. This may be a relevant consideration for many applications.

Should I Include Measures of Unsupportive Interaction as Well as Support?

In the research discussed here, measures of negative interaction with network members (either overt conflict or transactions that are perceived as unsupportive) often have an independent effect on outcomes, and the measures are brief. Thus including a measure for this dimension is clearly recommended if theoretically warranted. Researchers may consider extending existing measures to provide more information about the issues around which negative or unsupportive interactions occur and the frequency with which they occur (cf. Cohen & Lichtenstein, 1990; Coriell & Cohen, 1995; Ruehlman & Wolchik, 1988).

Intervention researchers should consider such measures because they provide an additional domain for detecting outcome effects. The researcher planning an intervention study should consult theoretical work on social strain and "unsuccessful helping attempts" (e.g., Coyne, Ellard, & Smith, 1990; Coyne, Wortman, & Lehman, 1988; Rook, 1990) and consider developing some items to tap the frequency of transactions in which someone tried in good faith to be supportive but was perceived by the recipient as being either unsupportive or critical (Lehman, Ellard, & Wortman, 1986; Manne & Zautra, 1989; Ruehlman & Wolchik, 1988). These kinds of transactions may become less frequent over the course of an intervention and hence provide an additional means for detecting significant intervention effects (see Helgeson et al., in press).

Should I Assess Support from Specific Network Members?

It is difficult to formulate a clear general guideline on this issue. The decision will be determined by the particular context of the researcher's sample and interests. The inventories that tap overall functional support from a variety of sources (ISEL, SPS, and SS-B) have a good track record for predicting important outcomes in both general populations and specific samples (e.g., elderly), so there is no reason to believe that one must necessarily use a network-based measure. At the same time, health research may involve hypotheses about differential effects for support from family, friends, and health care professionals, and such research may consider using network-based measures such as the ASSIS or UCLA-SSI.

The researcher should recognize that in such research there is a trade-off between precision and breadth of measurement. The functional inventories assess in detail what aspects of supportive functions are available across sources, whereas the network-based measures, in assessing which network members provide various types of support, provide fairly general definitions of supportive functions to the subjects; in the latter case, there is more room for subjective interpretations of what, for example, "emotional support" really is. The decision to emphasize precision of the constructs measured versus ability to obtain information about contributions of particular network members will be guided by the researcher's theoretical goals and their perspective on coping and adaptation. Ideally, the researcher using a network-based measure will decide in advance whether data from different sources will be lumped together, as has been done in some previous research, or, if not, how data from separate sources will be analyzed.

For researchers working with young children, there is a clear recommendation: Include assessments of several sources. A substantial difference from adult scales is that the source of support (e.g., parents vs. peers) may be as important as the function (e.g., emotional vs. informational) (Dubow & Ullman, 1989). Hence the ideal study would include assessments of supportive functions from parents, peers, teachers, and other adults. Some trade-off again is involved between obtaining precise measures of several supportive functions and obtaining assessments about several different sources of support.

Should I Measure Both Availability and Satisfaction with Support?

Several functional inventories have provided procedures for assessing both the perceived availability of support and the respondent's perceived satisfaction with (or perceived adequacy of) that support. This raises a question about the incremental status of satisfaction measures. The epidemiologic research is clear that availability indices have a consistent track record for showing predicted effects, so our recommendation would be to measure availability as the primary index. Studies with mortality as the outcome have generally shown predictive effects for availability but not for adequacy (cf. Hanson et al., 1989; House, Robbins, & Metzner, 1982; Orth-Gomer et al., 1993; Rosengren et al., 1993). There may be cases where perceived adequacy of support is of particular interest, but if assessment time is limited in an epidemiologic study, a decision to focus on availability would be reasonable.

For intervention research, a different set of priorities may be warranted. A substantial part of the support deficiency for some populations may be dissatisfaction with the effectiveness of helping efforts or, alternatively, a negative perceptual tendency such that the actual supportiveness of network members is underestimated (Helgeson et al., in press; Lakey & Lutz, 1996). In this context, it may be important to assess satisfaction as well as availability, and intervention studies have, in fact, shown significant changes in satisfaction with support (Barrera & Prelow, in press; Helgeson et al., in press). Thus there is a clear rationale for including both availability and satisfaction measures in intervention research.

Will I Need to Adapt the Measure for a Specific Population?

Previous research has shown that findings on supportive functions are quite robust across different parts of the life span from childhood to old age, and findings on functional measures have generally not shown large differences in effects for men and women (Wills, 1998; Wills & Filer, 2000). In this sense, the research is reassuring. One could conclude that the theory of supportive functions is broadly applicable and predict with some confidence that existing measures of emotional and informational support will have significant effects in new populations.

At the same time, for further research we have emphasized the desirability of pilot studies to sharpen the understanding and assessment of perceived support, so that new items can be used to supplement standardized measures. Such formative research can be guided by questions such as: What aspects of support should be particularly salient for this group? Are stressor-support matching requirements more or less relevant for this population? Such questions may help to shed more light on unique aspects of supportive processes.

We do note that research on social support and ethnicity is less developed. While evidence of cross-cultural validity is available (Tate, 1996), some studies have suggested caution about using current measures of social integration or social support in other cultures (see, e.g., Ho, 1991; Reed, McGee, Yano, & Feinlieb, 1983; Sugisawa, Liang, & Liu, 1994). Researchers working in other cultures may need to do more pilot studies to test the relevance of developed scales and extend understanding of how supportive relationships are conceptualized in a given cultural population; for a progammatic example, see Dressler (1991, 1994); Dressler, Balieiro, and Dos Santos (1997); Dressler, Grell, Gallagher, and Viteri (1992); and Dressler, Mata, Chavez, Viteri, and Gallagher (1986).

Will I Need to Adapt the Measure for a Particular Stressor?

As was the case with population issues, previous research has demonstrated that current measures of functional support have a reasonable record for showing buffering effects with respect to stress measured by typical life events checklists, which assess individuals' total exposure to a range of life stressors. This record is reassuring, as it indicates that a new study has a good chance of replicating previous findings by using a current off-the-shelf support measure. For some research, this may be a satisfactory goal because the support measure is embedded in a context of other measures and hypotheses that will help to advance knowledge about how social support contributes to adjustment.

Some researchers, however, may have the aim of sharpening understanding of what aspects of social support are relevant for dealing with particular stressors, for example, examination stress (Bolger & Eckenrode, 1991; Coriell & Cohen, 1995) or being HIV positive (Demas, Schoenbaum, Wills, Doll, & Klein, 1995). Descriptive research may help to provide more detailed knowledge about exactly what kinds of problems the participants are dealing with, how they perceive the nature of their problems, and the potential avenues to resolution of these problems. Pilot studies could produce suggestions about aspects of support that are relevant to the particular stressors the participants face, and these could be used to write items that can be included to supplement existing measures. The appendix provides citations to literature on specific health conditions, which might be useful in this respect.

Will I Need to Adapt the Measure for an Intervention Study?

It is difficult to provide firm guidelines on this issue because research on support group interventions is a new and rapidly developing field, and few precedents are available to guide the selection of measures for the context of research that aims to change levels of social support. Intervention researchers have discussed this issue from different perspectives (see Barrera & Prelow, in press; Lakey & Lutz, 1996; Sandler et al., 1997) but a technology of support measurement for intervention contexts is currently not well developed. Perhaps the only clear methodological guideline we can suggest is that researchers not just make up their own measure; there is sufficient literature available to provide a basis for choosing measures that provide a reasonable starting point for evaluating the effects of an intervention study (Helgeson & Cohen, 1996). The track record of these measures for predicting psychological and physical outcomes indicates that relevant dimensions of supportive functions have been successfully defined and measured, so it would seem imprudent for an intervention researcher to ignore this evidence and simply make up an untested measure.

At the same time, it should be recognized that the issues relevant for intervention studies are not necessarily the same as those involved in predictive and etiological research. We have tried to outline issues and questions that are relevant for selecting a measure for an intervention study, and these are summarized in Table 4.4.

At the most general level (termed A-level questions), consider the stressors impinging on the target population, the supportive functions that would be most relevant for countering those stressors, and the persons who would be most appropriate for providing those functions. At the next (B) level, consider what is the mapping between the desired outcomes of the intervention and the type of support measured (structural, functional, or both). Assuming that a functional measure is relevant for the intervention goals, then C-level questions ask about the precise aims of the intervention: What dimensions of supportive functions does the intervention wish to influence, what sources of support does the intervention aim to involve (e.g., spouse, family, friends, helping professionals, neighbors, workmates), and is the researcher really interesting in changing perceived support or in trying to change rates of received-support transactions? From the previous questions and decisions, the researcher then may focus on potential measures and ask relevance and matching questions: To what extent are the items in the measure directly relevant to the goals of the intervention? Is the level of generality versus specificity of the measure well matched to the intent of the intervention; for example, if instrumental support is the target, does one wish to increase perceived availability of material aid of all types, or does the intervention aim to increase specific support such as assistance with daily activities or providing transportation to a hospital? Will I need to add items that are closely tailored to the support needs of the target population? Given the expected impact of the intervention, will I need to measure additional constructs such as satisfaction with support, discomfort with help seeking, or unsuccessful helping attempts; and will I need to use additional assessment methods such as observational coding or recording of daily interactions? The reader's course in the decision tree and the answers to the questions will vary considerably, but considering these questions may help researchers select appropriate measures and build an assessment technology for intervention research. We think that thought-

Table 4.4. Decision Questions for Intervention Researchers

The first part of the decision process (A-level) is three interrelated questions:

A1: What exactly are the demands and stressors impinging on, and most troublesome for, this population?

A2: What are the resources, provided through social relationships, that would help to reduce or eliminate the impact of the stressors?

A3: From a relationship perspective, who is best suited (would be most appropriate) to provide those resources?

There follows a second type of decision (B-level), whose answers are not mutually exclusive:

B: Does the intervention aim (1) to increase network size and/or frequency of contact with network members, or (2) to increase certain types of support (available supportive functions) and/or satisfaction with the delivery of those supportive functions?

If B1 only: use social integration measure.
If B2 only: use functional measure.
If B1 + B2: use both types of measures.

Assuming a functional measure is desirable, then the following questions about the aims and impact of the intervention (C-level) should be considered:

C1: What supportive function(s) does the intervention try to change?

C2: What source(s) of support, indigenous or grafted, does the intervention aim to influence so as to change levels of available support?

C3: Does the intervention aim to influence perceived support, received support, or both?

Then for a potential support measure {X}:

D1: To what extent is the content of {Measure X} directly relevant to the intervention goals and targeted sources?

D2: Is the level of generality vs. specificity of the measure well suited to the types of supportive perceptions or interactions that the intervention aims to influence?

D3: Is the content of {Measure X} exactly suited to this purpose, or should I create or add items that are tailored to the demands and support needs of the target population?

D4: Given the expected impact of the intervention, will I need to measure additional constructs (e.g., satisfaction with support, unsuccessful helping attempts) or use additional methods (e.g., behavioral observation of support transactions)?

---

fully designed intervention studies can add to knowledge both on the process of intervention effects and on the evaluation of these effects.

Acknowledgments—This work was facilitated by Research Scientist Development Award K02 DA00252 from the National Institute on Drug Abuse. The authors thank Sheldon Cohen, Ben Gottlieb, James House, Brian Lakey, Karen Rook, and Alan Vaux for comments on a draft of the chapter.

REFERENCES

Abbey, A., Abramis, D. J., & Caplan, R. D. (1985). Effects of different sources of social support and social conflict on emotional well-being. *Basic and Applied Social Psychology, 6*, 111–129.

Aiken, L. S., & West, S. G. (1991). *Multiple regression: Testing and interpreting interactions*. Newbury Park, CA: Sage.

Almagor, M., Tellegen, A., & Waller, N. G. (1995). The Big Seven Model: A cross-cultural replication and further exploration of the basic dimensions of natural language trait descriptors. *Journal of Personality and Social Psychology, 69*, 300–307.

Argyle, M. (1992). Benefits produced by supportive social relationships. In H. O. F. Veiel & U. Baumann (Eds.), *The meaning and measurement of social support* (pp. 13–32). New York: Hemisphere.

Barrera, M. (1981). Social support in the adjustment of pregnant adolescents. In B. H. Gottlieb (Ed.), *Social networks and social support* (pp. 69–96). Beverly Hills, CA: Sage.

Barrera, M. (1986). Distinctions between social support concepts, measures, and models. *American Journal of Community Psychology, 14*, 413–445.

Barrera, M., & Ainlay, S. L. (1983). The structure of social support: A conceptual and empirical analysis. *Journal of Community Psychology, 11*, 133–143.

Barerra, M. Jr., Chassin, L., & Rogosch, F. (1993). Effects of social support and conflict on adolescent children. *Journal of Personality and Social Psychology, 64*, 602–612.

Barrera, M., & Prelow, H. (in press). Interventions to promote social support in children and adolescents. In D. Cicchetti, J. Rappaport, I. Sandler, & R. Weissberg (Eds.), *The promotion of wellness in children and adolescents*. Washington, DC: Child Welfare League of America.

Barrera, M., Sandler, I. N., & Ramsay, T. B. (1981). Preliminary development of a scale of social support. *American Journal of Community Psychology, 9*, 435–447.

Berkman, L. F., Leo-Summers, L., & Horwitz, R. I. (1992). Emotional support and survival after myocardial infarction: A prospective, population-based study of the elderly. *Annals of Internal Medicine, 117*, 1003–1009.

Billings, A. G., & Moos, R. H. (1982). Social support and functioning among community and clinical group: A panel model. *Journal of Behavioral Medicine, 5*, 295–31.

Billings, A. G., & Moos, R. H. (1984). Coping, stress, and social resources among adults with unipolar depression. *Journal of Personality and Social Psychology, 46*, 877–891.

Billings, A. G., & Moos, R. H. (1985). Life stressors and social resources affect posttreatment outcomes among depressed patients. *Journal of Abnormal Psychology, 94*, 140–153.

Blazer, D. G. (1982). Social support and mortality in an elderly community population. *American Journal of Epidemiology, 115*, 684–694.

Bogat, G. A., Sullivan, L. A., & Grober, J. (1993). Applications of social support to preventive interventions. In D. S. Glenwick & L. A. Jason (Eds.), *Promoting health and mental health in children, youth, and families* (pp. 205–232). New York: Springer.

Bolger, N., & Eckenrode, J. (1991). Social relationships, personality, and anxiety during a major stressful event. *Journal of Personality and Social Psychology, 61*, 440–449.

Bowlby, J. (1969). *Attachment and loss: vol. 1. Attachment*. London: Hogarth Press.

Brand, E., Lakey, B., & Berman, S. (1995). Preventive psychoeducational approach to increase perceived social support. *American Journal of Community Psychology, 23*, 117–135.

Brown, G. W., Andrews, B., Harris, T., Adler, Z., & Bridge, L. (1986). Social support, self-esteem and depression. *Psychological Medicine, 16*, 813–831.

Brown, G. W., & Harris, T. (1978). *Social origins of depression.* New York: Free Press.

Burke, R. J., & Weir, T. (1978). Benefits to adolescents of informal helping relationships with their parents and peers. *Psychological Reports, 42*, 1175–1184.

Burke, R. J., & Weir, T. (1979). Helping responses of parents and peers and adolescent well-being. *Journal of Psychology, 102*, 49–62.

Burt, C. E., Cohen, L. H., & Bjorck, J. P. (1988). Perceived family environment as a moderator of young adolescents' life stress adjustment. *American Journal of Community Psychology, 16*, 101–122.

Buunk, B., & Gibbons F. X. (Eds.). (1997). *Health, coping, and social comparison.* Mahwah, NJ: Erlbaum.

Carver, C. S., Scheier, M. F., & Pozo, C. (1992). Conceptualizing the process of coping with health problems. In H. S. Friedman (Ed.), *Hostility, coping and health* (pp. 167–187). Washington, DC: American Psychological Association.

Carver, C. S., Scheier, M. F., & Weintraub, J. K. (1989). Assessing coping strategies: A theoretically-based approach. *Journal of Personality and Social Psychology, 56*, 267–283.

Cassel, J. (1976). The contribution of the social environment to host resistance. *American Journal of Epidemiology, 104*, 107–123.

Cauce, A. M. (1986). Social networks and social competence: Exploring the effects of early adolescent friendships. *American Journal of Community Psychology, 14*, 607–628.

Cauce, A. M., Reid, M., Landesman, S., & Gonzales, N. (1990). Social support in young children: Measurement, description, and behavioral impact. In I. G. Sarason, B. R. Sarason, & G. Pierce (Eds.), *Social support: An interactional perspective.* New York: Wiley.

Clark, M. S., & Reis, H. T. (1988). Interpersonal processs in close relationships. *Annual Review of Psychology, 39*, 609–672.

Cobb, S. (1976). Social support as a moderator of life stress. *Psychosomatic Medicine, 38*, 300–314.

Coble, H. M., Gantt, D. L., & Mallinckrodt, B. (1996). Attachment, social competency, and the capacity to use social support. In G. R. Pierce, B. R. Sarason, & I. G. Sarason (Eds.), *Handbook of social support and the family* (pp. 141–172). New York: Plenum.

Cochran, M., & Henderson, C. R. (1990). Formal supports and informal social ties: A case study. In M. Cochran, M. Larner, D. Riley, L. Gunnarsson, & C. Henderson (Eds.), *Extending families: The social networks of parents and their children* (pp. 230–261). New York: Cambridge University Press.

Cohen, J. (1988). *Statistical power analysis for the behavioral sciences* (2nd ed.). New York: Academic Press.

Cohen, S. (1988). Psychosocial models of the role of social support in the etiology of physical disease. *Health Psychology, 7*, 269–297.

Cohen, S., & Herbert, T. B. (1996). Health psychology: Psychological factors and physical disease from the perspective of human psychoneuroimmunology. *Annual Review of Psychology, 47*, 113–142.

Cohen, S., & Hoberman, H. (1983). Positive events and social supports as buffers of life change stress. *Journal of Applied Social Psychology, 13*, 99–125.

Cohen, S., & Lichtenstein, E. (1990). Partner behaviors that support quitting smoking. *Journal of Consulting and Clinical Psychology, 58*, 304–309.

Cohen, S., & McKay, G. (1984). Social support, stress, and the buffering hypothesis: A theoretical analysis. In A. Baum, J. E. Singer, & S. E. Taylor (Eds.), *Handbook of psychology and health* (vol. 4, pp. 253–267). Hillsdale, NJ: Erlbaum.

Cohen, S., Mermelstein, R., Kamarck, T., & Hoberman, H. M. (1985). Measuring the functional components of social support. In I. G. Sarason & B. R. Sarason (Eds.), *Social support: Theory, research and applications* (pp. 73–94). The Hague: Martinus Nijhoff.

Cohen, S., Sherrod, D. R., & Clark, M. S. (1986). Social skills and the stress-protective role of social support. *Journal of Personality and Social Psychology, 50*, 963–973.

Cohen, S., & Wills, T. A. (1985). Stress, social support, and the buffering hypothesis. *Psychological Bulletin, 98*, 310–357.

Coriell, M., & Cohen, S. (1995). Concordance in the face of a stressful event: When do members agree that one supported the other? *Journal of Personality and Social Psychology, 69*, 289–299.

Coyne, J. C., Ellard, J. H., & Smith, D. A. F. (1990). Unsupportive relationships, interdependence, and unhelpful exchanges. In I. G. Sarason, B. R. Sarason, & G. Pierce (Eds.), *Social support: An interactional view* (pp. 129–149). New York: Wiley.

Coyne, J. C., & Smith, D. A. F. (1991). Couples coping with a myocardial infarction: A contextual perspective on wives' distress. *Journal of Personality and Social Psychology, 61*, 404–412.

Coyne, J., Wortman, C., & Lehman, D. (1988). The other side of support: Emotional overinvolvement and miscarried helping. In B. Gottlieb (Ed.), *Marshaling social support* (pp. 305–330). Beverly Hills, CA: Sage.

Cutrona, C. E. (1990). Stress and social support: In search of optimal matching. *Journal of Social and Clinical Psychology, 9*, 3–14.

Cutrona, C. E., & Russell, D. W. (1987). The provisions of social relationships and adaptation to stress. In W. H. Jones & D. Perlman (Eds.), *Advances in personal relationships* (vol. 1, pp. 37–67). Greenwich, CT: JAI.

Cutrona, C. E., & Russell, D. (1990). Type of social support and specific stress: Toward a theory of optimal matching. In B. R. Sarason, I. G. Sarason, & G. R. Pierce (Eds.), *Social support: An interactional view* (pp. 319–366). New York: Wiley.

Dakof, G. A., & Taylor, S. E. (1990). Victims' perceptions of social support: What is helpful from whom? *Journal of Personality and Social Psychology, 58*, 80–89.

Demas, P., Schoenbaum, E. E., Wills, T. A., Doll, L. S., & Klein, R. S. (1995). Stress, coping and attitudes toward HIV treatment in injecting drug users: A qualitative study. *AIDS Education and Prevention, 7*, 428–442.

Dressler, W. W. (1991). Social support, lifestyle incongruity, and arterial blood pressure in a Southern Black community. *Psychosomatic Medicine, 53*, 608–620.

Dressler, W. W. (1994). Cross-cultural differences and social influences in social support and cardiovascular disease. In S. A. Shumaker & S. M. Czajkowski

(Eds.), *Social support and cardiovascular disease* (pp 167–192). New York: Plenum.

Dressler, W. W., Balieiro, M. C., & Dos Santos, J. E. (1997). The cultural construction of social support in Brazil: Associations with health outcomes. *Culture, Medicine, and Psychiatry, 21*, 303–335.

Dressler, W. W., Grell, G. A., Gallagher, P. N., & Viteri, F. E. (1992). Social factors affecting social class differences in blood pressure in a Jamaican community. *Social Science and Medicine, 35*, 1233–1244.

Dressler, W. W., Mata, A., Chavez, A., Viteri, F. E., & Gallagher, P. N. (1986). Social support and arterial blood pressure in a central Mexican community. *Psychosomatic Medicine, 48*, 338–350.

DuBois, D. L., Felner, R. D., Meares, H., & Krier, M. (1994). Prospective investigation of the effects of socioeconomic disadvantage, life stress, and social support on early adolescent adjustment. *Journal of Abnormal Psychology, 103*, 511–522.

Dubow, E. F., & Tisak, J. (1989). The relation between stressful life events and adjustment in elementary school children: The role of social support and problem-solving skills. *Child Development, 60*, 1412–1423.

Dubow, E. F., Tisak, J., Causey, D., Hryshko, A., & Reid, G. (1991). A two-year longitudinal study of stressful life events, social support, and problem-solving skills: Contributions to children's adjustment. *Child Development, 62*, 583–599.

Dubow, E. F., & Ullman, D. G. (1989). Assessing social support in elementary school children: The survey of children's social support. *Journal of Clinical Child Psychology, 18*, 52–64.

Dunkel-Schetter, C., & Bennett, T. L. (1990). Differentiating the cognitive and behavioral aspects of social support. In I. G. Sarason, B. R. Sarason, & G. R. Pierce (Eds.), *Social support: An interactional view* (pp. 267–296). New York: Wiley.

Dunkel-Schetter, C., Feinstein, L., & Call, J. (1987). UCLA Social Support Inventory. Unpublished manuscript, University of California, Los Angeles.

Dunkel-Schetter, C., Folkman, S., & Lazarus, R. (1987). Correlates of social support receipt. *Journal of Personality and Social Psychology, 53*, 71–80.

Eckenrodo, J. (1983). The mobilization of social supports: Some individual constraints. *American Journal of Community Psychology, 11*, 509–520.

Falk, A., Hanson, B. S., Isacsson, S.-O., & Östergren, P-O. (1992). Job strain and mortality in elderly men: Social network, support, and influence as buffers. *American Journal of Public Health, 82*, 1136–1139.

Fillenbaum, G. G., & Smyer, M. A. (1981). The development, validity, and reliability of the OARS Multidimensional Functional Assessment Questionnaire. *Journal of Gerontology, 36*, 428–434.

Finch, J. F., Barrera, M., Okun, M. A., Bryant, W. H. M., Pool, G. J., & Snow-Turek, A. L. (1997). The factor structure of received social support: Dimensionality and the prediction of depression and life satisfaction. *Journal of Social and Clinical Psychology, 16*, 323–342.

Finch, J. F., Okun, M. A., Barrera, M., Zautra, A. J., & Reich, J. W. (1989). Positive and negative social ties among older adults: Measurement models and prediction of psychological well-being. *American Journal of Community Psychology, 17*, 585–605.

Fischer, C. S. (1982). *To dwell among friends: Personal networks in town and city.* Chicago: University of Chicago Press.

Fontana, A. F., Kerns, R. D., Rosenberg, R. L., & Colonese, K. L. (1989). Support, stress, and recovery from coronary heart disease: A longitudinal causal model. *Health Psychology, 8,* 175–193.

Furman, W., & Buhrmester, D. (1985). Children's perceptions of the personal relationships in their social networks. *Developmental Psychology, 21,* 1014–1024.

Goldberg, L. R. (1993). The structure of phenotypic personality traits. *American Psychologist, 48,* 26–34.

Granovetter, M. (1973). The strength of weak ties. *American Journal of Sociology, 78,* 1360–1380.

Graves, P. L., Wang, N.-Y., Mead, L., Johnson, J. V., & Klag, M. J. (1998). Youthful precursors of midlife social support. *Journal of Personality and Social Psychology, 74,* 1329–1336.

Greenberg, M. T., Siegel, J. M., & Leitch, C. J. (1983). The nature and importance of attachment relationships to parents and peers during adolescence. *Journal of Youth and Adolescence, 12,* 373–386.

Habif, V. L., & Lahey, B. B. (1980). The life-stress depression relationship: Use of social support as a moderator variable. *Journal of Behavioral Assessment, 2,* 167–173.

Haggerty, R. A., Sherrod, L. R., Garmezy, N., & Rutter, M. (1994). *Stress, risk, and resilience in children and adolescents.* Cambridge: Cambridge University Press.

Hanson, B. S., Isacsson, J. T., Janzon, L., & Lindell, S.-E. (1989). Social network and social support influence mortality in elderly men: Prospective population study of men born in 1914 in Malmö, Sweden. *American Journal of Epidemiology, 130,* 100–111.

Hanson, B. S., & Östergren, P.-O. (1987). Different social network and social support characteristics: Theoretical and methodological aspects. *Social Science and Medicine, 25,* 849–859.

Heitzmann, C. A., & Kaplan, R. M. (1988). Assessment of methods for measuring social support. *Health Psychology, 7,* 75–109.

Helgeson, V. S. (1993). Two important distinctions in social support: Kind of support and perceived versus received. *Journal of Applied Social Psychology, 23,* 825–845.

Helgeson, V. S., & Cohen, S. (1996). Social support and adjustment to cancer: Reconciling descriptive, correlational, and intervention research. *Health Psychology, 15,* 135–148.

Helgeson, V. S., Cohen, S., Schulz, R., & Yasko, J. (in press). Group support interventions for people with cancer: Benefits and hazards. In A. Baum & B. Andersen (Eds.), *Psychosocial interventions and cancer.* Washington, DC: American Psychological Association.

Henderson, S., Byrne, D. G., Duncan-Jones, P., Scott, R., & Adcock, S. (1980). Social relationships, adversity and neurosis: A study of associations in a general population sample. *British Journal of Psychiatry, 136,* 354–383.

Henderson, S., Duncan-Jones, P., & Byrne, D. (1980). Measuring social relationships: The Interview Schedule for Social Interaction. *Psychological Medicine, 10,* 723–734.

Hirsch, B. J. (1987). Adolescent coping and support across multiple social environments. *American Journal of Community Psychology, 13,* 381–392.

Ho, S. C. (1991). Health and social predictors of mortality in an elderly Chinese cohort. *American Journal of Epidemiology, 133,* 907–921.

Hobfoll, S. E., & Leiberman, J. R. (1987). Personality and social resources in immediate and continued stress resistance among women. *Journal of Personality and Social Psychology, 52*, 18–26.

Hobfoll, S. E., & Lerman, M. (1988). Personal relationships, personal attributes, and stress resistance: Mothers' reactions to their child's illness. *American Journal of Community Psychology, 16*, 565–589.

Hobfoll, S. E., & Lerman, M. (1989). Predicting receipt of social support: A longitudinal study of parents' reactions to their child's illness. *Health Psychology, 8*, 61–77.

Hobfoll, S. E., London, P., & Orr, E. (1988). Mastery, intimacy, and stress resistance during war. *Journal of Community Psychology, 16*, 317–331.

Holahan, C. J., & Moos, R. H. (1986). Personality, coping, and family resources in stress resistance. *Journal of Personality and Social Psychology, 51*, 389–395.

Holahan, C. J., & Moos, R. H. (1987). Risk, resistance, and psychological distress: A longitudinal analysis with adults and children. *Journal of Abnormal Psychology, 96*, 3–13.

Holahan, C. J., & Moos, R. H. (1990). Life stressors, resistance factors, and improved psychological functioning. *Journal of Personality and Social Psychology, 58*, 909–917.

House, J. S. (1981). *Work stress and social support.* Reading, MA: Addison-Wesley.

House, J. S., & Kahn, R. L. (1985). Measures and concepts of social support. In S. Cohen & S. L. Syme (Eds.), *Social support and health* (pp. 83–108). Orlando: Academic Press.

House, J. S., Landis, K. R., & Umberson, D. (1988). Social relationships and health. *Science, 241*, 540–545.

House, J. S., Robbins, C., & Metzner, H. L. (1982). The association of social relationships and activities with mortality. *American Journal of Epidemiology, 116*, 123–140.

House, J. S., & Wells, J. A. (1978). Occupational stress, social support and health. In A. McLean, G. Black, & M. Colligan (Eds.), *Reducing occupational stress: Proceedings of a conference* (pp. 8–29). Washington, DC: U.S. Government Printing Office (HEW Publication 78–140).

King, K. B., Reis, H. T., Porter, L. A., & Norsen, L. H. (1993). Social support and long-term recovery from coronary artery surgery: Effects on patients and spouses. *Health Psychology, 12*, 56–63.

Krause, N. (1987a). Chronic financial strain, social support, and depressive symptoms among older adults. *Psychology and Aging, 2*, 185–192.

Krause, N. (1987b). Life stress, social support, and self-esteem in elderly populations. *Psychology and Aging, 2*, 349–356.

Krauss, M. W., Upshur, C. C., Shonkoff, J. P., & Hauser-Cram, P. (1993). The impact of parent groups on mothers of infants with disabilities. *Journal of Early Intervention, 17*, 8–20.

Lakey, B., & Lutz, C. J. (1996). Social support and preventive and therapeutic interventions. In G. R. Pierce, B. R. Sarason, & I. G. Sarason (Eds.), *Handbook of social support and the family* (pp. 435–465). New York: Plenum.

LaRocco, J. M., House, J. S., & French, J. R. P. (1980). Co-worker and leader support as moderators of stress-strain relationships in work situations. *Journal of Applied Psychology, 63*, 629–634.

Lehman, D., Ellard, J., & Wortman, C. (1986). Social support for the bereaved:

Recipients' and providers' perspectives on what is helpful. *Journal of Consulting and Clinical Psychology, 54,* 438–446.

Lewis, M. A., & Rook, K. S. (1999). Social control in personal relationships: Impact on health behaviors and psychological distress. *Health Psychology, 18,* 63–71.

MacKinnon, D. P., Johnson, C. A., Pentz, M. A., Dwyer, J. H., Hansen, W. B., Flay, B. R., & Wang, E. Y.-I. (1991). Mediating mechanisms in a school-based drug prevention program. *Health Psychology, 10,* 164–172.

Mallinckrodt, B. (1996). Change in working alliance, social support, and psychological symptoms in brief therapy. *Journal of Counseling Psychology, 43,* 448–455.

Manne, S. L., & Zautra, A. J. (1989). Spouse criticism and support: Their association with coping and psychological adjustment among women with rheumatoid arthritis. *Journal of Personality and Social Psychology, 56,* 608–617.

McClelland, G. H., & Judd, C. M. (1993). Statistical difficulties of detecting interactions and moderator effects. *Psychological Bulletin, 114,* 376–390.

McCormick, I. A., Siegert, R. J., & Walkey, F. H. (1987). Dimensions of social support: A factorial confirmation. *American Journal of Community Psychology, 15,* 73–82.

McGuire, J. C., & Gottlieb, B. H. (1979). Social support groups among new parents: An experimental study in primary prevention. *Journal of Clinical Child Psychology, 8,* 111–116.

Melamed, B. G., & Brenner, G. F. (1990). Social support and chronic medical illness: An interaction-based approach. *Journal of Social and Clinical Psychology, 9,* 104–117.

Mermelstein, R., Cohen, S., Lichtenstein, E., Baer, J. S., & Kamarck, T. (1986). Social support and smoking cessation and maintenance. *Journal of Consulting and Clinical Psychology, 54,* 447–453.

Mermelstein, R., Lichtenstein, E., & McIntyre, K. (1983). Partner support and relapse in smoking cessation programs. *Journal of Consulting and Clinical Psychology, 51,* 465–466.

Moos, R. H. (1981). *Work Environment Scale manual.* Palo Alto, CA: Consulting Psychologists Press.

Moos, R. H., & Insel, P. (1974). *Work Environment Scale preliminary manual.* Palo Alto, CA: Consulting Psychologists Press.

Moos, R. H., & Moos, B. S. (1981). *Family Environment Scale manual.* Palo Alto, CA: Consulting Psychologists Press.

Moos, R. H., & Schaefer, J. A. (1984). The crisis of physical illness: An overview. In R. H. Moos (Ed.), *Coping with physical illness* (vol. 2, pp. 3–26). New York: Plenum.

Newcomb, M. D. (1990). What structural equation modeling can tell us about social support. In B. R. Sarason, I. G. Sarason, & G. R. Pierce (Eds.), *Social support: An interactional view* (pp. 64–94). New York: Wiley.

Newcomb, M. D., & Bentler, P. M. (1986). Loneliness and social support: A confirmatory hierarchical analysis. *Personality and Social Psychology Bulletin, 12,* 520–535.

Newcomb, M. D., & Bentler, P. M. (1988). Impact of adolescent drug use and social support on problems of young adults: A longitudinal study. *Journal of Abnormal Psychology, 97,* 64–75.

Newcomb, M. D., & Chou, C.-P. (1989). Social support among young adults: Latent variable models of quantity and satisfaction within six life areas. *Multivariate Behavioral Research, 24,* 233–256.

Norris, F. H., & Kaniasty, K. (1996). Received and perceived social support in times of stress. *Journal of Personality and Social Psychology, 71,* 498–511.

Olds, D. L., Henderson, C. R., Chamberlin, R., & Tatelbaum, R. (1986). Preventing child abuse and neglect: A randomized trial of nurse home visitations. *Pediatrics, 78,* 65–78.

Orth-Gomer, K., Rosengren, A., & Wilhelmsen, L. (1993). Lack of social support and incidence of coronary heart disease in middle-aged Swedish men. *Psychosomatic Medicine, 55,* 37–43.

Orth-Gomer, K., & Unden, A.-L. (1987). The measurement of social support in population surveys. *Social Science and Medicine, 24,* 83–94.

Parry, G., & Shapiro, D. A. (1986). Social support and life events in working class women. *Archives of General Psychiatry, 43,* 315–323.

Peirce, R. S., Frone, M. R., Russell, M., & Cooper, M. L. (1996). Financial stress, social support, and alcohol involvement: A longitudinal test of the buffering hypothesis in a general population survey. *Health Psychology, 15,* 38–47.

Potts, M. K., Hurwicz, M., Goldstein, M. S., & Berkanovic, E. (1992). Social support, health-promotive beliefs, and preventive health behaviors among the elderly. *The Journal of Applied Gerontology, 11,* 425–440.

Procidano, M. E., & Heller, K. (1983). Measures of perceived social support from friends and from family: Three validation studies. *American Journal of Community Psychology, 11,* 1–24.

Ptacek, J. T. (1996). The role of attachment in perceived support and the stress and coping process. In G. R. Pierce, B. R. Sarason, & I. G. Sarason (Eds.), *Handbook of social support and the family* (pp. 495–520). New York: Plenum.

Reed, D., McGee, D., Yano, K., & Feinlieb, M. (1983). Social networks and coronary heart disease among Japanese man in Hawaii. *American Journal of Epidemiology, 117,* 384–396.

Reid, M., Landesman, S., Treder, R., & Jaccard, J. (1989). "My family and friends": Six- to twelve-year-old children's perceptions of social support. *Child Development, 60,* 896–910.

Revenson, T. A., Schiaffino, K. M., Majerovitz, S. D., & Gibofsky, A. (1991). The relation of positive and problematic support to depression among rheumatoid arthritis patients. *Social Science and Medicine, 33,* 807–813.

Riley, D., & Eckenrode, J. (1986). Social ties: Subgroup differences in costs and benefits. *Journal of Personality and Social Psychology, 51,* 770–778.

Rook, K. S. (1984). The negative side of social interaction: Impact on psychological well-being. *Journal of Personality and Social Psychology, 46,* 1097–1108.

Rook, K. S. (1987). Social support versus companionship: Effects on life stress, loneliness, and evaluations by others. *Journal of Personality and Social Psychology, 52,* 1132–1147.

Rook, K. S. (1990). Parallels in the study of social support and social strain. *Journal of Social and Clinical Psychology, 12,* 118–132.

Rose, J. H. (1990). Social support and cancer: Adult patients' desire for support from family, friends, and health professionals. *American Journal of Community Psychology, 18,* 439–464.

Rosengren, A., Orth-Gomer, K., Wedel, H., & Wilhelmsen, L. (1993). Stressful life events, social support, and mortality in men born in 1933. *British Medical Journal, 307,* 102–105.

Ruehlman, L. S., & Karoly, P. (1991). Development and preliminary validation of the Test of Negative Social Exchange (TENSE). *Psychological Assessment, 3,* 97–104.

Ruehlman, L. S., & Wolchik, S. A. (1988). Personal goals and interpersonal support and hindrance as factors in psychological distress and well-being. *Journal of Personality and Social Psychology, 55,* 293–301.

Russell, D., Peplau, L., & Cutrona, C. (1980). The UCLA Loneliness scale: Concurrent and discriminant validity. *Journal of Personality and Social Psychology, 39,* 472–480.

Sandler, I. N., Miller, P., Short, J., & Wolchik, S. A. (1989). Social support as a protective factor for children in stress. In D. Belle (Ed.), *Children's social networks and social supports* (pp. 277–307). New York: Wiley.

Sandler, I. N., Wolchik, S. A., MacKinnon, D., Ayers, T. S., & Roosa, J. W. (1997). Developing linkages between theory and intervention in stress and coping processes. In S. A. Wolchik & I. N. Sandler (Eds.), *Handbook of children's coping: Linking theory and intervention* (pp. 3–40). New York: Plenum.

Sarason, B. R., Pierce, G. R., Shearin, G. R., Sarason, I. G., Waltz, J. A., & Poppe, L. (1991). Perceived support and working models of self and others. *Journal of Personality and Social Psychology, 60,* 273–287.

Sarason, B. R., Shearin, E. N., Pierce, G. R., & Sarason, I. G. (1987). Interrelations of social support measures: Theoretical and practical implications. *Journal of Personality and Social Psychology, 52,* 813–832.

Sarason, I. G. (1990). Social support: The sense of acceptance and the role of relationships. In B. R. Sarason, I. G. Saraon, & G. R. Pierce (Eds.), *Social support: An interactional view* (pp. 97–128). New York: Wiley.

Sarason, I. G., Levine, H. M., Basham, R. B., & Sarason, B. R. (1983). Assessing social support: The Social Support Questionnaire. *Journal of Personality and Social Psychology, 44,* 127–139.

Schulz, R., Newsom, J. T., Mittelmark, M., Burton, L., Hirsch, C., & Jackson, S. (1997). Health effects of caregiving: The cardiovascular health study. *Annals of Behavioral Medicine, 19,* 110–116.

Seeman, T. E., & Berkman, L. F. (1988). Structural characteristics of social networks and their relationship with support in the elderly. *Social Science and Medicine, 7,* 737–749.

Stokes, J. P., & Wilson, D. G. (1984). The Inventory of Socially Supportive Behaviors: Dimensionality, prediction, and gender differences. *American Journal of Community Psychology, 12,* 53–70.

Sugisawa, H., Liang, J., & Liu, X. (1994). Social networks, social support, and mortality among older people in Japan. *Journal of Gerontology: Social Sciences, 49,* S3–S13.

Tate, U. (1996). Cross-cultural validation of measures of social support. *Psychological Reports, 79,* 271–274.

Uchino, B. N., Cacioppo, J. T., & Kiecolt-Glaser, J. K. (1996). The relationship between social support and physiological processes: A review with emphasis on underlying mechanisms and implications for health. *Psychological Bulletin, 119,* 488–531.

Umberson, D. (1987). Family status and health behaviors: Social control as a dimension of social intergration. *Journal of Health and Social Behavior, 28,* 306–319.

Vanfossen, B. L. (1981). Sex differences in the mental health effects of spouse support and equity. *Journal of Health and Social Behavior, 22*, 130–143.

Vaux, A. (1988). *Social support: Theory, research, and intervention.* New York: Praeger.

Vaux, A. (1992). Assessment of social support. In H. O. F. Veiel & U. Baumann (Eds.), *The meaning and measurement of social support* (pp. 193–216). New York: Hemisphere.

Vaux, A., Burda, P., & Stewart, D. (1986). Orientation towards utilizing support resources. *Journal of Community Psychology, 14*, 159–170.

Vaux, A., & Harrison, D. (1985). Support network characteristics associated with support satisfaction and perceived support. *American Journal of Community Psychology, 13*, 245–268.

Vaux, A., Philips, J., Holly, L., Thomson, B., Williams, D., & Stewart, D. (1986). The Social Support Appraisals (SS-A) Scale: Studies of reliability and validity. *American Journal of Community Psychology, 14*, 195–220.

Vaux, A., Riedel, S., & Stewart, D. (1987). Modes of social support: The Social Support Behaviors (SS-B) Scale. *American Journal of Community Psychology, 15*, 209–237.

Weiss, R. S. (1974). The provisions of social relationships. In Z. Rubin (Ed.), *Doing unto others* (pp. 17–26). Englewood Cliffs, NJ: Prentice-Hall.

Welin, L., Larsson, B., Svärdsudd, K., Tibblin, B., & Tibblin, G. (1992). Social network and activities in relation to mortality from cardiovascular disease, cancer and other causes: A 12-year follow-up of the Study of Men Born in 1913 and 1923. *Journal of Epidemiology and Community Health, 46*, 127–132.

West, S., & Aiken, L. (1997). Toward understanding individual effects in multiple component prevention programs: Design and analysis strategies. In K. Bryant, M. Windle, & S. West (Eds.), *New methodological approaches for prevention research* (pp. 167–209). Washington, DC: American Psychological Association.

Wethington, E., & Kessler, R. C. (1986). Perceived support, received support, and adjustment to stressful life events. *Journal of Health and Social Behavior, 27*, 78–89.

Williams, R. B., Barefoot, J. C., Califf, R. M., Haney, T. L., Saunders, W. B., Pryor, D. B., Hlatky, M. A., Siegler, I. C., & Mark, D. B. (1992). Prognostic importance of social resources among patients with CAD. *Journal of the American Medical Association, 267*, 520–524.

Wills, T. A. (1985). Supportive functions of interpersonal relationships. In S. Cohen & S. L. Syme (Eds.), *Social support and health* (pp. 61–82). Orlando: Academic Press.

Wills, T. A. (1990). Multiple networks and substance use. *Journal of Social and Clinical Psychology, 9*, 78–90.

Wills, T. A. (1991). Social support and interpersonal relationships. In M. Clark (Ed.), *Review of personality and social psychology* (vol. 12, pp. 265–289). Newbury Park, CA: Sage.

Wills, T. A. (1994). Self-esteem and perceived control in adolescent substance use. *Psychology of Addictive Behaviors, 8*, 223–234.

Wills, T. A. (1998). Social support and health in women. In E. Blechman & K. Brownell (Eds.), *Behavioral medicine and women: A comprehensive handbook* (pp. 118–123). New York: Guilford.

Wills, T. A., Blechman, E. A., & McNamara, G. (1996). Family support, coping and competence. In E. M. Hetherington & E. A. Blechman (Eds.), *Stress, coping, and resiliency in children and the family* (pp. 107–133). Hillsdale, NJ: Erlbaum.

Wills, T. A., & Cleary, S. D. (1996). How are social support effects mediated: A test for parental support and adolescent substance use. *Journal of Personality and Social Psychology, 71,* 937–952.

Wills, T. A., & Cleary, S. D. (1999). Theoretical models and frameworks for child health research. In D. Drotar (Ed.), *Handbook of research in pediatric and clinical child psychology* (pp. 21–49). New York: Kluwer Academic.

Wills, T. A., Cleary, S. D., Shinar, O., (in press). Temperament dimensions and health behavior. In L. Hayman, J. R. Turner, & M. Mahon (Eds.), *Health and behavior in childhood and adolescence.* Mahwah, NJ: Erlbaum.

Wills, T. A., & Filer, M. (2000). Social networks and social support. In A. Baum & T. Revenson (Eds.), *Handbook of health psychology.* (pp. 209–234) Mahwah, NJ: Erlbaum.

Wills, T. A., Mariani, J., & Filer, M. (1996). The role of family and peer relationships in adolescent substance use. In G. R. Pierce, B. R. Sarason, & I. G. Sarason (Eds.), *Handbook of social support and the family* (pp. 521–549). New York: Plenum.

Wills, T. A., McNamara, G., Vaccaro, D., & Hirky, A. E. (1996). Escalated substance use: A longitudinal grouping analysis from early to middle adolescence. *Journal of Abnormal Psychology, 105,* 166–180.

Wills, T., Sandy, J., & Shinar, O. (1999). Cloninger's constructs related to substance use level and problems in late adolescence. *Experimental and Clinical Psychopharmacology 7,* 122–134.

Wills, T. A., Vaccaro, D., & McNamara, G. (1992). The role of life events, family support, and competence in adolescent substance use. *American Journal of Community Psychology, 20,* 349–374.

Wills, T. A., Windle, M., & Cleary, S. D. (1998). Temperament and novelty seeking in adolescent substance use: Convergence of dimensions of temperament with constructs from Cloninger's theory. *Journal of Personality and Social Psychology, 74,* 387–406.

Windle, M. (1991). The difficult temperament in adolescence: Associations with family support and problem behaviors. *Journal of Clinical Psychology, 47,* 310–315.

Zhang, Q. (1994). An intervention model of constructive conflict resolution and cooperative learning. *Journal of Social Issues, 50,* 99–116.

Zuckerman, M., Kuhlman, D. M., Joireman, J., Teta, P., & Kraft, M. (1993). A comparison of three structural models of personality: The Big Three, the Big Five, and the Alternative Five. *Journal of Personality and Social Psychology, 65,* 757–768.

Wolchik, S. E., Ruehlman, L. S., Braver, S. L., & Sandler, I. N. (1989). Social support of children of divorce: Direct and stress buffering effects. *American Journal of Community Psychology, 17,* 485–510

Wolchik, S. E., West, S. G., Westover, S., Sandler, I. N., Martin, A., Lustig, J., Tein, J.-Y., & Fisher, J. (1993). The children of divorce parenting intervention: Outcome evaluation of an empirically based program. *American Journal of Community Psychology, 21,* 293–311.

APPENDIX 1: STUDIES OF SUPPORT EFFECTS FOR SPECIFIC HEALTH CONDITIONS

ARTHRITIS

Affleck, G., Pfeiffer, C., Tennen, H., & Fifield, H. (1988). Social support and psychosocial adjustment to rheumatoid arthritis. *Arthritis Care and Research, 1*, 71–77.

Affleck, G., Tennen, H., Urrows, S., & Higgins, P. (1994). Person and contextual features of daily stress reactivity. *Journal of Personality and Social Psychology, 66*, 329–340.

Brown, G. K., Wallston, K. A., & Nicassio, P. M. (1989). Social support and depression in rheumatoid arthritis: A one-year prospective study. *Journal of Applied Social Psychology, 19*, 1164–1181.

Fitzpatrick, R., Newman, S., Archer, R., & Shipley, M. (1991). Social support, disability and depression: A longitudinal study of rheumatoid arthritis. *Social Science and Medicine, 33*, 605–611.

Fitzpatrick, R., Newman, S., Lamb, R., & Shipley, M. (1988). Social relationships and psychological well-being in rheumatoid arthritis. *Social Science and Medicine, 27*, 399–403.

Goodenow, C., Reisine, S. T., & Grady, K. E. (1990). Quality of social support and associated social and psychological functioning in women with rheumatoid arthritis. *Health Psychology, 9*, 266–284.

Lanza, A. F., Cameron, A. E., & Revenson, T. A. (1995). Perceptions of helpful and unhelpful support among married individuals with rheumatic diseases. *Psychology and Health, 10*, 449–462.

Penninx, B. W. J. H., Van Tilburg, T., Deeg, D. J. H., Kriegsman, D. M. W. (1997). Direct and buffer effects of social support and personal coping resources in individuals with arthritis. *Social Science and Medicine, 44*, 393–402.

Revenson, T. A., & Majerovitz, S. D. (1991). The effects of chronic illness on the spouse: Social resources as stress buffers. *Arthritis Care and Research, 4*, 63–72.

Revenson, T. A., Schiaffino, K. M., Majerovitz, S. D., & Gibofsky, A. (1991). The relation of positive and problematic support to depression among rheumatoid arthritis patients. *Social Science and Medicine, 33*, 807–813.

Smith, C. A., & Wallston, K. A. (1992). Adaptation in patients with chronic rheumatoid arthritis: Application of a general model. *Health Psychology, 11*, 151–162.

Suurmeijer, T. P. B. M., Doeglas, D. M., Briancon, S., Krijnen, W. P. (1995). The measurement of social support in the "European Research on Incapacitating Disease and Social Support" study. *Social Science and Medicine, 40*, 1221–1229.

Taal, E., Rasker, J. J., Seydel, E. R., & Wiegman, O. (1993). Health status, adherence with health recommendations, self-efficacy and social support in patients with rheumatoid arthritis. *Patient Education and Counseling, 20*, 63–76.

Weinberger, M., Tierney, W. M., Booher, P., & Hiner, S. L. (1990). Social support, stress, and functional status in patients with osteoarthritis. *Social Science and Medicine, 30*, 503–508.

CANCER

Ell, K., Nishimoto, R., Mediansky, L., Mantell, J., & Hamovitch, M. (1992). Social relationships, social support and survival among patients with cancer. *Journal of Psychosomatic Research, 36*, 531–541.

Helgeson, V. S., Cohen, S., & Fritz, H. L. (1998). Social ties and the onset and progression of cancer. In J. C. Holland (Ed.), *Psycho-oncology New York: Oxford University Press.* (pp. 99–109).

Lackner, S. L., Goldenberg, S., Arizza, G., & Tjosvold, I. (1994). The contingency of social support. *Qualitative Health Research, 4*, 224–243.

Ma, J. L. C. (1996). Desired and perceived social support from family, friends, and health proessionals: A panel study in Hong Kong of patients with nasopharyngeal carcinoma. *Journal of Psychosocial Oncology, 14*, 47–68.

Northouse, A. L. (1988). Social support in patients' and husbands' adjustment to breast cancer. *Nursing Research, 37*, 91–95.

Primomo, J., Yates, B. C., & Woods, N. F. (1990). Social support for women during chronic illness: The relationships among sources and types of adjustment. *Research in Nursing and Health, 13*, 153–161.

Rose, J. H. (1990). Social support and cancer: Patients' desire for support from family, friends, and health professionals. *American Journal of Community Psychology, 18*, 439–464.

Rose, J. H. (1993). Interactions between patients and providers: An exploratory study of age differences in emotional support. *Journal of Psychosocial Oncology, 11*, 43–67.

Veiel, H. O., Crisand, M., Stroszeck-Somschor, H., & Herrle, J. (1991). Social support of chronically strained couples. *Journal of Social and Personal Relationships, 8*, 279–292.

Waxler-Morrison, N., Hislop, T. G., Mears, B., & Kan, L. (1991). Effects of social relationships on survival for women with breast cancer: A prospective study. *Social Science and Medicine, 33*, 177–183.

CARDIOVASCULAR DISEASE

Bastone, E. C., & Kerns, R. D. (1995). Effects of self-efficacy and perceived social support on recovery-related behaviors after coronary artery bypass graft surgery. *Annals of Behavioral Medicine, 17*, 324–330.

Brownley, K. A., Light, K. C, & Anderson, N. B. (1996). Social support and hostility interact to influence clinic, work, and home blood pressure in black and white men and women. *Psychophysiology, 33*, 434–445.

Cohen, S., Kaplan, J. R., & Manuck, S. B. (1994). Social support and heart disease: Underlying psychological and biological mechanisms. In S. Shumaker & S. M. Czajkowski (Eds.), *Social support and cardiovascular disease* (p. 195–221). New York: Plenum.

Ell, K., & Dunkel-Schetter, C. (1994). Social support and adjustment to myocardial infarction and coronary artery bypass survery. In S. A. Shumaker & S. M. Czajkowski (Eds.), *Social support and cardiovascular disease* (pp. 301–332). New York: Plenum.

Fontana, A. F., Kerns, R. D., Rosenberg, R. L., & Colonese, K. L. (1989). Support, stress, and recovery from coronary heart disease: A longitudinal causal model. *Health Psychology, 8*, 175–193.

Frasure-Smith, N., Lesperance, F., & Talajic, M. (1995). The impact of negative emotions on prognosis following myocardial infarction. *Health Psychology, 14,* 388–398.

Holahan, C. J., Moos, R. H., Holahan, C. K., & Brennan, P. L. (1995). Social support, coping, and depressive symptoms in a late-middle-aged sample of patients reporting cardiac illness. *Health Psychology, 14,* 152–163.

Kulik, J. A., & Mahler, H. I. (1993). Emotional support as a moderator of adjustment and compliance after coronary artery bypass surgery: A longitudinal study. *Journal of Behavioral Medicine, 16,* 45–63.

Wilcox, V. L., Kasl, S. V., & Berkman, L. F. (1994). Social support and physical disability in older people after hospitalization. *Health Psychology, 13,* 170–179.

Yates, B. C. (1995). Relationships among social support and short- and long-term outcomes in men with coronary heart disease. *Research in Nursing and Health, 18,* 193–203.

DIABETES

Connell, C. M., Davis, W. K., Gallant, M. P., & Sharpe, P. (1994). Impact of social support, social cognitive variables, and perceived threat on depression among adults with diabetes. *Health Psychology, 13,* 263–273.

Griffith, L. S., Field, B. J., & Lustman, P. J. (1990). Life stress and social support in diabetes: Association with glycemic control. *International Journal of Psychiatry in Medicine, 20,* 365–372.

Hanson, C. L., Henggeler, S. W., & Burghen, G. A. (1987). Social competence and parental support as mediators of the link between stress and metabolic control in adolescents with diabetes mellitus. *Journal of Consulting and Clinical Psychology, 55,* 529–533.

Krause, N. (1995). Stress and diabetes mellitus in later life. *International Journal of Aging and Human Development, 40,* 125–143.

Littlefield, C. H., Rodin, G. M., Murray, M. A., & Craven, J. L. (1990). Influence of functional impairment and social support on depressive symptoms in persons with diabetes. *Health Psychology, 9,* 737–749.

Wallander, J. L., & Varni, J. W. (1989). Social support and adjustment in chronically ill and handicapped children. *American Journal of Community Psychology, 17,* 185–201.

HIV/AIDS

Blaney, N. T., Goodkin, K., Morgan, R. O., & Feaster, D. (1991). A stress-moderator model of distress in early HIV-1 infection: Concurrent analysis of life events, hardiness and social support. *Journal of Psychosomatic Research, 35,* 297–305.

Collins, R. L. (1994). Social support provision to HIV-infected gay men. *Journal of Applied Social Psychology, 24,* 1848–1869.

Hays, R. B., Turner, H., & Coates, T. J. (1992). Social support, AIDS-related symptoms, and depression among gay men. *Journal of Consulting and Clinical Psychology, 60,* 463–469.

Lackner, J. B., Joseph, J. G., Ostrow, D. G., & Eshleman, S. (1993). The effects of social support on HSCL-assessed depression and distress in a cohort of HIV-positive and negative gay men: A longitudinal study of six time points. *Journal of Nervous and Mental Disease, 181*, 632–638.

Nott, K. H., & Power, M. J. (1995). The role of social support in HIV infection. *Psychological Medicine, 25*, 971–983.

Pakenham, K. I., Dadds, M. R., & Terry, D. J. (1994). Relationships between adjustment to HIV and both social support and coping. *Journal of Consulting and Clinical Psychology, 62*, 1194–1203.

Persson, L., Gullberg, B., Hanson, B. S., Moestrup, T., & Ostergren, P. O. (1994). Social network, social support, and CD4 lymphocyte values in HIV-infected homosexual men in Malmö, Sweden. *Journal of Epidemiology and Community Health, 48*, 580–585.

Theorell, T., Blomkvist, V., Jonsson, H., Schulman, S., Berntorp, E., & Stigendel, L. (1995). Social support and the development of immune function in human immunodeficiency virus infection. *Psychosomatic Medicine, 57*, 32–36.

KIDNEY DISEASE

Burton, H. J., Kline, S. A., Lindsay, R. M., & Heidenheim, P. (1988). Social support and outcome in end-stage renal disease. *General Hospital Psychiatry, 10*, 260–266.

Christensen, A. J., Smith, T. W., Turner, C. W., Holman, J. M., Gregory, M. C., & Rich, M. A. (1992). Social support and adherence in dialysis: An examination of main and buffering effects. *Journal of Behavioral Medicine, 15*, 313–325.

Christensen, A. J., Wiebe, J. S., Smith, T. W., & Turner, C. W. (1994). Predictors of survival among hemodialysis patients: Effect of perceived family support. *Health Psychology, 13*, 521–525.

Devins, G. M., Mann, J., Mandin, H., Paul, L. C., Hons, R. B., Burgess, E. D., Taub, K., Schorr, S., Letourneau, P. K., & Buckle, S. (1990). Psychosocial predictors of survival in end-stage renal disease. *Journal of Nervous and Mental Disease, 178*, 127–133.

MULTIPLE SCLEROSIS

Gulick, E. E. (1994). Social support among persons with multiple sclerosis. *Research in Nursing and Health, 17*, 195–206.

Lehman, D. R., & Hemphill, K. J. (1990). Recipients' perceptions of support attempts and attributions for support attempts that fail. *Journal of Social and Personal Relationships, 7*, 563–574.

Wineman, N. M. (1990). Adaptation to multiple sclerosis: The role of social support, functional disability, and perceived uncertainty. *Nursing Research, 39*, 294–299.

PREGNANCY

Collins, N. L., Dunkel-Schetter, C., Loebel, M., & Scrimshaw, S. C. M. (1993). Social support correlates of birth outcomes and postpartum depression. *Journal of Personality and Social Psychology, 65*, 1243–1258.

Dunkel-Schetter, C., Sagrestano, L. M., Feldman, P., & Killingsworth, C. (1996). Social support and pregnancy: A comprehensive review focusing on ethnicity and culture. In G. R. Pierce, B. R. Sarason, & I. G. Sarason (Eds.), *Handbook of social support and the family* (pp. 375–412). New York: Plenum.

Gottlieb, L. N., & Mendelson, M. J. (1995). Mothers' moods and social support when a second child is born. *Maternal-Child Nursing Journal, 23*, 3–14.

McWilliams, E. (1994). The association of perceived support with birthweights and obstetric complications. *Journal of Reproductive and Infant Psychology, 12*, 115–122.

Norbeck, J. S., DeJoseph, J. F., & Smith, R. T. (1996). A randomized trial of an empirically-derived social support intervention to prevent low birthweight among African American women. *Social Science and Medicine, 43*, 947–954.

Pollak, K. I., & Mullen, P. D. (1997). An exploration of the effects of partner smoking, type of social support, and stress on postpartum smoking in married women who stopped smoking during pregnancy. *Psychology of Addictive Behaviors, 11*, 182–189.

Turner, R. J., Grindstaff, C. F., & Phillips, N. (1990). Social support and outcome in teenage pregnancy. *Journal of Health and Social Behavior, 31*, 43–57.

5

Measuring Relationship Properties and Interactions Relevant to Social Support

Harry T. Reis
Nancy Collins

I. The Relationship Processes Perspective
   A. Relationship Processes and Social Support
   B. Perceived Partner Responsiveness
   C. Nature and Extent of Interdependence
   D. Sentiment
   E. A Functional Perspective
   F. Differentiating Relationship Processes From Social Support
II. Measures of Relationship Properties Relevant to Perceiving and Providing Social Support in Particular Relationships
   A. Perceived Partner Responsiveness
      1. Intimacy
      2. Trust
      3. Perceived Acceptance
   B. Nature and Extent of Interdependence
      1. Closeness
      2. Interdependence Orientation
   C. Commitment
   D. Sentiment
      1. Satisfaction
      2. Love
      3. Conflict
   E. Family Environment
III. Measures of Relationship Properties Relevant to Perceiving and Providing Social Support Assessed in Dispositional Terms
   A. Empathy
   B. Emotional Expressiveness
   C. Attachment
   D. Perceived Acceptance
   E. Social Competence
   F. Commentary on Self-Report Measures

Preparation of this chapter was supported by National Science Foundation grant SBR-9870524 to Nancy Collins

IV. Measures of Support Interaction
   A. Microanalytic Behavioral Observations of Supportive Interaction
      1. Social Support Behavior Code
      2. Interactive Coping Behavior Coding System and Support Activation Behavioral Coding System
      3. Social Support Interaction Coding System
      4. Hierarchical Coding System for Sensitivity of Comforting Messages
   B. Observation of Marital Interaction
      1. Marital Interaction Coding System
      2. Rapid Couples Interaction Scoring System
      3. Specific Affect Coding System
   C. Observation of Family Interaction
      1. Defensive and Supportive Communication Interaction System
      2. Parent-Adolescent Interaction Coding System
      3. Commentary on Observational Methods
   D. Daily Experience Reports of Social Support
      1. Interval-contingent
      2. Signal-contingent
      3. Event-contingent
      4. Commentary on Diary Measures
V. Concluding Comments

One of the more engaging ideas behind the concept of social support is the notion that interpersonal interactions may in some way influence health and well-being. Nearly all of the early papers that served as a rallying point for this once-emergent and now-established area of research describe social support as a process involving transactions with significant others that facilitate coping with stress and other life burdens and tasks. It therefore seems reasonable, in studying social support, to put as much stress on the first word, *social*, as on the second word, *support*. Unfortunately, the literature has tended to emphasize the latter, with considerably less attention directed to interactional and relationship processes that foster or inhibit the expression and reception of support.

Conceptualized in social terms, support is the natural product of relationships exhibiting certain properties or involving certain types of interaction. In other words, both supportive interaction and the perception that support would be available if needed (cf. chapters 2 and 4) should be more common to the extent that relationships possess relevant properties. Similarly, it is assumed that perceptions of support availability can be traced to actual interpersonal events.

In this chapter, we describe measures of several relationship processes that contribute to social support. Our approach is directed at identifying interpersonal processes that underlie one or more types of perceived social support. We do so by examining manifestations of these processes in three general classes of phenomena: relationship properties, partner characteristics, and interpersonal events. We do not address associations between social support and health or well-being;

rather, we intend to extend backward a causal model of these phenomena by identifying interpersonal determinants of social support, as well as by describing the role of relationships as a context for the development of social support.

In the first section of the chapter, for orientation purposes, we briefly discuss the component processes perspective we adopt, showing how it conceptualizes the social support process. Our subsequent review of specific measures has two major sections. We first describe relationship properties relevant to social support phenomena. Some of these properties describe relationships with particular partners, whereas others are measured across relationships, as general social predispositions. We then review two kinds of studies of supportive interaction: laboratory-based behavioral observation and naturalistic diary studies. Owing to the availability of many relevant, well-constructed measures, our coverage is necessarily selective. We emphasize constructs and measures with the greatest potential for social support research.

Each major section highlights one of three general methods: self-report questionnaires, behavioral observation in controlled settings, and naturalistic diaries (Reis, 1994). Unfortunately, most researchers tend to rely on only one of these methods, thereby giving credence to the criticism of potentially method-bound findings. For this reason, we feel it necessary to set the stage by invoking Webb, Campbell, Schwartz, and Sechrest's (1966) arguments in favor of "multiple operationalism." Every research method has unique advantages and limitations and therefore can at best illuminate only aspects of the overall picture. Moreover, because all methods to some extent capture methodological as opposed to substantive variance, findings from a single paradigm or instrument tend to have limited generalizability. Definitive evidence about validity is therefore unlikely to be obtained from a single study or method; instead, as Brewer (2000) argues, validity is best defined as a feature of research programs having many studies with diverse methods, samples, and contexts that triangulate around a core set of principles. The diverse methods and measures described in our review offer excellent possibilities for researchers to apply a multimethod approach in their own investigations.

THE RELATIONSHIP PROCESSES PERSPECTIVE

Adopting a "process" approach refers to the goal of understanding mechanisms by which particular phenomena occur. Applied to social support, the relationship processes approach begins with the assumption that social support reflects the operation of basic mechanisms central to close relationships. There is good reason to make this assumption. For example, "volunteer help in time of need," "show emotional support," and "ask for personal advice" are primary rules, or expectations, about friendship (Argyle & Henderson, 1985), and most marital vows incorporate explicit statements about support availability and provision. Collectivism, a dominant motive in many cultures and groups, stipulates that individuals will respond to the needs of others within their group as if they were their own (Markus & Kitayama, 1991). Even more generally, the evolutionary significance of relationships is rooted in the adaptive value of cooperative action and emotional bonding, factors central to supportive interaction (Baumeister & Leary, 1995; Hazan & Zeifman, 1999). It is therefore reasonable to propose that expectations of support from significant others, as well as motivation to provide support to them, are shaped by the selfsame processes that establish and maintain close relationships. Of course, some processes are more relevant than others; in this chapter, we review several of the more central processes.

Figure 5.1 illustrates the model we use. To understand social support as an interpersonal process, three types of phenomena need to be investigated: (1) properties of relationships in which supportive interactions occur, (2) interpersonal predispositions that influence interaction and relationships, and (3) features of supportive interactions that take place. We explicitly differentiate relationship properties and supportive interactions (both of which may involve similar processes) for several reasons. First, they represent different levels of analysis. Interaction refers to a single interpersonal encounter, whereas relationships involve synthesis of the details of past, present, and imagined future interactions into generalized expectations, attributions, identities, and patterns of communication (Hinde, 1997). These two levels of analysis are not always differentiated clearly; in our view, the failure to do so may obscure understanding of processes by which a sense of relationship is abstracted from single episodes, as well as processes by which interaction is shaped by preexisting beliefs and expectations. Second, studies of relationships tend to focus on relatively abstract qualities of the interchange between partners that may lose meaning if interpreted out of context—that is, without understanding the participants' personal and historical points of view— whereas interactions tend to describe relatively more concrete behaviors.

Figure 5.1 indicates that relationships may influence social support in two ways: directly, whereby certain relationship properties engender the belief that a partner would provide support, if needed, and indirectly, whereby these properties make supportive interactions more likely. These two paths correspond roughly to the "other relationship quality" and "supportive actions" perspectives described by Lakey and Cohen in chapter 2. As discussed later, these paths may involve functionally similar behaviors and feelings and, because they tend to occur in the same relationships, may be difficult to untangle.

The model assumes that processes operating within relationships matter most, as opposed to the existence of a relationship per se or to generalized interpersonal predispositions. Although relevant to relationship-based support, it is conceptually clearest to treat interpersonal predispositions, such as social self-esteem, extraversion, or sensitivity to rejection, as personal characteristics (i.e., as traits and traitlike tendencies) residing within individuals rather than within relationships. Relationship properties, including perceptions of a relationship, are thereby determined by the interaction of interpersonal events with these predispositions. Several of the processes reviewed have both dispositional and relational aspects (e.g., trust, attachment).

This focus dictates that we primarily describe instruments tailored to assessment of specific relationships and partners. After all, people do not have relationships with generalized others, they have relationships with particular people

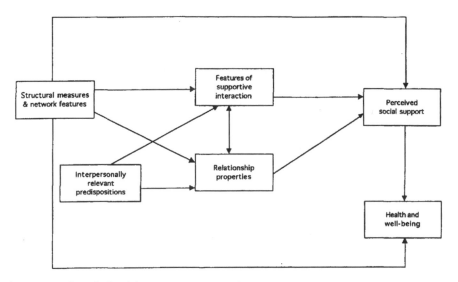

Figure 5.1. The relationship processes perspective.

who interact with them in particular ways. Existing, albeit limited, research affirms the value of differentiating global and relationship-specific properties in the area of social support. For example, Pierce, Sarason, and Sarason (1992) found that after the effects of global support had been controlled, relationship-specific support, especially from friends, still significantly predicted loneliness. Similar results were obtained by Davis, Morris, and Kraus's (1998) comparison of the Social Provisions Scale with a checklist assessing availability of 30 supportive resources from family, friends, and romantic partners (e.g., a feeling of being needed, unbiased opinions). Still other studies demonstrate that perceptions of available or desired support may vary widely from one target to another, for example, among romantic partners, family, and peers (Cutrona, Cole, Colangelo & Assouline, 1994; Newcomb & Bentler, 1986) or among spouses, family, friends, health care providers, and other cancer patients (Dakof & Taylor, 1990). Indeed, the potential gain from assessing support in relationship-specific terms led Sarason, Sarason, and Gurung (1997) to suggest that global perceptions of support, which are far more prevalent in the literature, may substantially underestimate the impact of relationships on health and adjustment.

We do not subscribe to the notion that relationship properties arise from nonspecific feelings about a partner, independent of actual transactions that an outside observer might verify. Rather, the two-headed arrow in Figure 5.1 indicates reciprocal influence: Interactions are affected by the underlying relationship (as well as more ephemeral contextual factors), and relationship properties emerge out of experiences in repeated interaction (broadly construed to include partners' reactions to, and construals of, those interactions).

Conceptualizing interactions and relationships at different levels of analysis does not imply that different processes are involved. In fact, these perspectives may complement each other to illuminate the interpersonal determinants of social support. Often the best understandings of a given process arise from simultaneously considering the interplay of discrete events and global relationship properties, although, to be sure, the precise nature of this interplay has received inadequate attention. For example, how do perceptions of support availability relate to actual supportive interactions? Under what circumstances do intimate interactions lead to the development of intimate relationships? How are general feelings about a partner like love and trust reflected in specific interpersonal acts? Keeping levels of analysis distinct makes possible investigation of these fundamental questions.

For this reason, and also because in most instances research paradigms investigating these two levels of analysis have evolved independently, our review of measures examines separately self-reported descriptions of global relationship properties and observational studies of supportive social interactions.[1] Nevertheless, readers may wish to keep their interplay in mind, especially in those instances in which similar concepts are implicated and in which the same conceptual process can be understood better by considering its operation at both levels of analysis.

Relationship Processes and Social Support

It would be naive to assume that relationships influence social support nonspecifically, that is, that "good" or "close" relationships maximize all types of social support. The field's catalogue of distinct, highly specific processes describing different aspects of relational behavior, emotion, and thought (see Berscheid & Reis, 1998, or Hinde, 1997, for overviews) is copious. Although many processes undoubtedly co-occur in actual relationships, years of research and theory have documented distinctive and separable causal antecedents, mechanisms, and consequences. Just as social support is multifaceted, therefore requiring meticulous differentiation among related constructs, so, too, are fine-grained analyses of the differential relevance of various interpersonal constructs warranted. In other words, the component process approach we adopt argues not that good or close relationships are necessarily supportive but rather that specific processes are likely to be linked to specific kinds of social support. Unfortunately, to date, relatively few studies have investigated this type of discriminative hypothesis, and we hope that our review facilitates such research.

If social support is obtained in relationships, it makes good sense to begin by examining variations in relationships, on the assumption that differences in the nature of social support provision will relate to functional differences among

---

1. Current practice often confounds methods of assessment with level of analysis; that is, relationship properties are usually assessed by self-reports (inasmuch as these properties are usually based on the participant's perspective and synthesize many interactions over time), whereas supportive interactions are usually assessed observationally. In principle, there is no reason why this confound is necessary.

relationships. This task would be simplified by a conceptual model for classifying the many processes that characterize relationships. Although no consensually accepted scheme currently exists, drawing on several investigations and theoretical analyses of this issue (e.g., Hinde, 1997; McClintock, 1983; Wiggins, 1982; Wish, Deutsch, & Kaplan, 1976) leads us to propose three basic dimensions: perceived partner responsiveness, interdependence, and sentiment. Figure 5.2 groups the various processes reviewed in this chapter according to their central theoretical focus. To be sure, some of the relationship properties, interpersonal predispositions, and interaction features discussed in this chapter are at least somewhat relevant to more than one of the three-dimensions; the relationship field is sufficiently eclectic that its major constructs and research programs are cross-cutting and do not map easily onto each other. Nevertheless, these groupings may help to distinguish the processes reviewed in terms of typical behaviors, underlying mechanisms, and relevance to social support.

Perceived Partner Responsiveness

Perceived partner responsiveness reflects the psychological "core" self—that is, the "aggregate of bits of information, motivations, interpersonal patterns, and control processes" (Baumeister, 1995, p. 500) that define who one is—and how partners are perceived to respond to the many public manifestations of self. Thus, intimacy is a cardinal process, defined as feeling understood, validated, and cared for by partners who are aware of facts and feelings central to one's self-conception

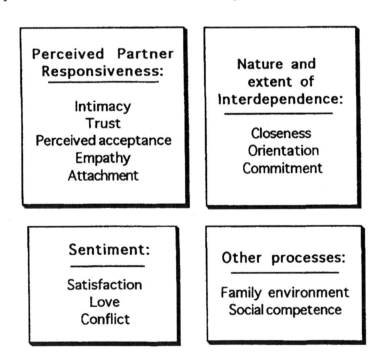

Figure 5.2. Dimensions of relationships.

(Reis & Shaver, 1988). Contributing to this perception is trust (the expectation that partners can be counted on to respect and fulfill important needs) and acceptance (the belief that partners accept one for who one is). Empathy is also relevant because it signals awareness of, and appreciation for, a partner's core self. Attachment also contributes to perceived partner responsiveness, notwithstanding its link to interdependence and sentiment, because of the fundamental role of perceiving that one is worthy of, and can expect to receive, love and care from significant others.

Nature and Extent of Interdependence

The nature and extent of interdependence refers to an important structural feature of relationships, namely, the degree and type of causal influence each partner has on the other (Kelley, 1983). Although defined diversely, closeness is a prototypical construct, embodying the commonsense notions that relationships differ in the extent to which partners are involved with each other and that the closer a relationship is, the more each partner's behavior affects the other's. Relationships also vary in the nature of interdependence, however, that is, norms that govern the exchange of benefits (including help and support). Commitment is another feature of interdependence, imbuing the relationship bond with future orientation. We distinguish interdependence from perceived responsiveness in Figure 5.2 to denote that partners can be interdependent without being responsive to the self (e.g., coworkers) and can be responsive without interdependence (e.g., psychotherapy).

Sentiment

Sentiment subsumes various manifestations of partners' affect toward each other, usually expressed in terms of positivity and negativity, the major dimensions underlying interpersonal perception. Satisfaction is an important indicator of relationship sentiment, as are criticism and conflict. Love, which differs from satisfaction in several respects, also represents relationship sentiment. We include emotional expressivity in this dimension because of its relevance to the communication of sentiment between partners.

A Functional Perspective

How do these dimensions relate to social support? That is, what kinds of questions about social support are each best suited for addressing? Although simple answers to this broad issue are not feasible, we recommend that researchers begin with a functional analysis of the transactions likely to engender different types of support. Just as it is often suggested that, to be effective, social support should correspond in nature to the stressor and resources needed, so, too, should support be functionally similar to the properties and interactions that characterize a relationship. Therefore, particular types of social support are most likely to develop in relationships entailing repeated interactions that provide appropriate experiences, thoughts, and feelings for that type of support to develop. For example, deeply intimate conversation seems likely to foster the belief that partners are emotionally supportive and that their informational support is insightful, because intimacy involves a perceived emotional connection between a partner and one's inner self. Furthermore, it is not just the type of support that depends on the relationship context; it is also the domain of problems to which that support may be applied. For example, spousal support is more likely to be helpful when dealing with personal matters than with technical work problems about which the spouse is unfamiliar.

We propose that researchers consider the *functional congruence* between relationship processes and the types of support under investigation. Relationship processes can be highlighted either by examining properties of relationships or by observing specific interactions (which, we assume, as discussed earlier, reciprocally derive from and generate the former). In other words, we have noted that social support is embedded in relationships, but clearly, not all relationships are supportive, and not all supportive relationships are supportive in the same way. What relationship properties foster or inhibit the expression and receipt of particular types of social support? We suggest that exchange and perceived availability of particular types of support are most likely within a relationship context characterized by functionally congruent interpersonal transactions. Relationship characteristics are important, therefore, because they shape actual support transactions, as well as partners' perceptions of, and expectations about, those transactions.

In this light, perceived partner responsiveness and related components might be hypothesized to pertain most directly to social support involving the self and personally important motives, goals, and activities. Trust and intimacy, for example, may be particularly germane to appraisal or esteem support, especially regarding stressors relevant to self-defining contexts and experiences. By contrast, perceived partner responsiveness may be less critical around issues peripheral to the self or for supportive acts that do not implicate the self (e.g., babysitting, driving a neighbor to work). We do not imply that intimate partners would be uninterested in providing self-irrelevant support; rather, we propose that the degree of perceived partner responsiveness in a relationship plays a less determining role for such support than for self-relevant concerns.

Interdependence processes might be expected to relate most clearly to support activities that reflect structural connections between partners' lives, both in the present and anticipated in the future. In other words, the more interwoven partners' lives are, the more they may be expected to offer direct assistance when needed. This might be evident not just in a single support episode but more so in the level of supportiveness across situations and time, because committed long-term relationships provide multiple opportunities for reversing the roles of support seeker and provider. Because interdependence does not necessarily imply emotional ties, the correlation with emotional and esteem types of support would be weaker than with tangible, belonging, and appraisal support. Interdependence processes may also influence certain support activities indirectly, to the extent that interdependent partners share in each other's outcomes.

Finally, although broad feelings such as liking and disliking probably influence most interpersonal behaviors, relationship affect is most directly relevant to support types that involve expression or experience of affect. For example, displaying sympathy and support for a partner's transgression or setback might be most common when partners possess strong positive feelings about each other and least likely when they feel hostile or critical. To be sure, people in love would probably help each other move to a new residence or figure out how to juggle work and family activities; however, less affectively intense processes may also generate such assistance. Because affective positivity does not always imply knowledge of, and responsiveness to, the self, sentiment would be somewhat less central to forms of support involving shared personal knowledge than would perceived partner responsiveness.

Whether or not these predictions are verified in research should not obscure the more general point: that the distinguishing features of different types of social support should have their roots in functionally congruent types of interaction and relationship properties. We also would make a similar point about supportive interventions: Effective interventions should target the particular relationship processes thought to underlie the desired type of social support.

Differentiating Relationship Processes from Social Support

The functional congruence hypothesis raises an important question about the degree to which relationship processes can be differentiated from social support itself. After all, to the extent that social support is intrinsic, to take a hypothetical example, to intimacy, as opposed to being a product of interactions in intimate relationships, the concepts would be theoretically and methodologically indistinguishable. There are several reasons why it is sensible to differentiate relationship processes from social support, however. First, in nearly all cases, support pertains to a narrower set of situations and behaviors than the corresponding relationship properties do; that is, defined interpersonally, supportive interactions involve attempts to provide coping assistance in response to expressed or perceived distress (Thoits, 1986). Intimacy encompasses behaviors other than helping and usually is not conditioned on distress. Similarly, relationships are defined as interdependent because partners influence each other greatly or as affectively positive because partners experience positive affect in each other's actual or imagined presence. Neither definition represents the essential nature of support very well. A second reason is that supportive resources are often exchanged in nonintimate relationships. For example, tangible assistance or informational guidance may occur absent of intimacy, as with coworkers, teammates, or counselors.

To be sure, support is more likely to the extent that relationships are responsive, interdependent, and affectively positive. This is why our model embeds social support in an interpersonal context, shaped by the particular strengths and weaknesses of an existing relationship. At this stage of theoretical development, if we are to move beyond unidimensional global characterizations, it is important to clearly articulate and differentiate the various theoretical processes that contribute to a relationship (Heller & Rook, 1997). This is why Figure 5.1 separates the components of actual interaction, personal predisposition, and relationship properties.

Our review is limited to existing, validated measures. Because no measures currently exist for several important constructs, some processes theorized to be relevant to social support are not discussed. Under the first major heading, we describe measures that apply to a particular relationship. These instruments generally adopt one of two foci: perceptions of a partner's feelings about oneself or perceptions of a relationship. The second major heading summarizes related constructs measured from a more general perspective, that is, feelings or behavior about relationships in general. In nearly all cases, many more measures exist than can be reviewed within a single chapter. We therefore highlight only a small number of representative, psychometrically satisfactory, and well-known or particularly promising measures. We regret the invidious comparisons that our choices may invite.

MEASURES OF RELATIONSHIP PROPERTIES RELEVANT TO PERCEIVING AND PROVIDING SOCIAL SUPPORT IN PARTICULAR RELATIONSHIPS

This section reviews measures (listed for convenience in Table 5.1) of properties contributing to the perception that a partner has provided, or can be expected to provide, support when needed. In most instances, these properties also predict greater likelihood of giving support, for two reasons. First, certain properties assume that partners provide supportive resources similar to those they expect to receive. For example, a communal orientation involves attention to a partner's needs as well as perceiving a favorable response to one's own needs. Second, mutuality is central to processes such as intimacy and trust (Reis & Shaver, 1988), in the sense that perceiving partners to be responsive typically enhances the desire to reciprocate.

Perceived Partner Responsiveness

Measures that appraise relationships from the standpoint of perceptions of a partner's feelings about, and responsiveness to, the self are included under this heading. This dimension is theorized to underlie expectations that a partner will provide support if needed, presumably because responsive partners are attentive to, and concerned about, each other's personal welfare.

Intimacy

Intimacy, one of the more commonly studied relationship properties, has been defined diversely, both in terms of specific interaction features (notably, personalistic self-disclosure and responsive, empathic listening) and general relationship qualities. Most definitions emphasize notions about emotional openness and interdependence, expressions of mutual support and understanding, and trust

Table 5.1. Self-Report Measures of Support-Relevant Processes in Particular Relationships

Perceived Partner Responsiveness
Intimacy
  Personal Assessment of Intimacy in Relationships (Schaefer & Olson, 1981)
  Waring Intimacy Interview (Waring & Reddn, 1983)
  Intimate Friendship Scale (Sharabany, 1994)
  Miller Social Intimacy Scale (Miller & Lefcourt, 1983)
Trust
  Trust Scale (Rempel, Holmes, & Zanna, 1985)
  Willingness to Sacrifice (Van Lange et al., 1997)
Perceived Acceptance
  Perceived Acceptance Scale (Brock, Sarason, Sanghvi, & Gurung, 1998)

Nature and Extent of Interdependence
Closeness
  Relationship Closeness Inventory (Berscheid, Snyder, & Omoto, 1989b)
  Inclusion of Other in the Self Scale (Aron, Aron, & Smollan, 1992)
Interdependence Orientation
  Communal Orientation Scale (Clark, Ouellette, Powell, & Milburg, 1987)
  Exhcange Orientation Scale (Murstein, Wadlin, & Bond, 1987)
  Exchange Orientation Scale (Mills & Clark, 1994)
Commitment
  Commitment Level Scale (Rusbult et al., 1998)

Sentiment
Satisfaction
  Marital Adjustment Test (Locke & Wallace, 1959)
  Dyadic Adjustment Scale (Spanier, 1976)
  Relationship Assessment Scale (Hendrick, 1988)
  Satisfaction Level Scale (Rusbult et al., in press)
  Positive and Negative Marital Qualities Scale (Fincham & Linfield, 1997)
  Spouse Observation Checklist (Weiss et al., 1973)
  Areas of Change Questionnaire (Weiss et al., 1973)
Love
  Passionate Love Scale (Hatfield & Sprecher, 1986)
  Triangular Love Scale (Sternberg, 1997)
  Love Attitudes Scale (Hendrick & Hendrick, 1986)
Conflict
  Conflicts and Problem-Solving Scales (Kerig, 1996)
  Quality of Relationships Index (Pierce et al., 1991)
  Family Emotional Involvement and Conflict Scale (Shields et al., 1992)
  Willingness to Accommodate (Rusbult et al., 1991)
  Communications Patterns Questionnaire (Christensen, 1988)

Other processes
  Family Environment Scale (Moos & Moos, 1986)
  Family Adaptability and Cohesion Scale (Olson et al., 1983; Olson, 1991)
  Family Assessment Measure (Skinner et al., 1983)
  Sibling Relationship Questionnaire (Furman & Buhrmester, 1985)

(Prager, 1995; Reis & Patrick, 1996). Key to these conceptualizations is the perception that a partner is aware of highly personal self-relevant information and can be expected to be respectful, accepting, and responsive when this information is expressed or when relevant circumstances arise. Thus, although the particular properties thought to compose intimacy sometimes vary, most models relate intimacy to social support functions that involve emotional openness, interpersonal acceptance, and shared personal knowledge.

The mediational pathway depicted in Figure 5.1. has been supported by several studies. For example, Reis and Franks (1994) found that predictive effects of intimacy on subjective health in an adult community sample were mediated by perceived social support; the reverse path (i.e., support leads to intimacy) was not supported. Johnson, Hobfoll, and Zalcberg-Linetzy (1993) found that intimacy underlies perceptions of social support, probably because intimate partners are motivated to behave supportively (Hobfoll, Nadler & Leiberman, 1986).

A popular measure of intimacy, the Personal Assessment of Intimacy in Relationships (PAIR; Schaefer & Olson, 1981), has subscales representing emotional (e.g., "My partner listens to me when I need someone to talk to"), social (e.g., "My partner disapproves of my friends"), intellectual (e.g., "My partner helps me clarify my thoughts"), sexual (e.g., "Sexual expression is an essential part of our relationship"), and recreational (e.g., "I share in very few of my partner's interests") intimacy, which may be used concurrently or independently. There is also a conventionality subscale, which can be used to assess self-presentational biases. Each subscale has six items, and reliability coefficients tend to be high. Developed, validated, and used extensively with both dating and married couples of diverse ages, the PAIR is applicable across varied circumstances or relationship types and is easy to complete.

Other instruments tend to slice the same general notions somewhat differently. Some cast a wider, conceptually more differentiated net. For example, the Waring Intimacy Interview (Waring & Reddon, 1983), developed from lay conceptions of intimacy and used with married couples, has subscales for conflict resolution, sexuality, affection, identity, compatibility, expressiveness, autonomy, and cohesion; Sharabany's (1994) Intimate Friendship Scale, applicable to children's and adolescents' friendships, has subscales for frankness and spontaneity, sensitivity and knowing, exclusiveness, helping, taking and giving, common activities, trust, and loyalty. Other measures conceptualize intimacy in a less differentiated, more global way, such as the 17-item Miller Social Intimacy Scale (Miller & Lefcourt, 1983), although item content covers much the same territory as more multidimensional measures.

Prager (1995) provides an extensive review of intimacy measures, including information about reliability, validity, and empirical effectiveness.

Trust

Although trust is often discussed in dispositional terms, Holmes (1991) has argued that trust is better conceptualized in relationship-specific terms. Trust, which involves "people's abstract positive expectations that they can count on partners to care for them and be responsive to their needs, now and in the future" (Holmes & Rempel, 1989, p. 188), is based on the conviction that partners will put aside immediate self-interest to be caring and responsive in addressing one's needs. Trust therefore reflects perceptions of a partner's attachment to the relationship and faith in his or her dependability and concern. Circumstances in which help and support are needed or desired seem particularly likely to influence development of trust within this definition, in that such situations maximize one's ability to infer whether a partner has one's welfare or selfish interests at heart. Once established, trust in a specific partner is likely to foster perceptions of support availability across most dimensions of support, but especially those involving emotional closeness and appraisals of the ability to cope with stressful or threatening circumstances.

The 16-item Trust Scale (Rempel, Holmes & Zanna, 1985), one of a small number of trust scales cued to specific relationships rather than general attitudes about human nature, provides an overall score as well as subscores on three dimensions: predictability ("My partner is very unpredictable. I never know how he/she is going to act from one day to the next"), dependability ("I can rely on my partner to keep the promises he/she makes to me"), and faith ("Though times may change and the future is uncertain, I know my partner will always be ready and willing to offer me strength and support"). The last of these factors, anticipation of support that goes beyond actual available evidence, is particularly important to their model. Reliability coefficients for the subscales and overall measure tend to be > .70. Good evidence for construct validity with dating and marital couples has been demonstrated correlationally and in laboratory experiments (Holmes, 1991).

Also promising is a new measure of the willingness to sacrifice short-term self-interest to promote the well-being of a partner or relationship (Van Lange, Rusbult, Drigotas, Arriaga, & Witcher, 1997). This brief scale begins by asking respondents to list their four most important life activities, other than their romantic relationship. Respondents are then asked to imagine that it was no longer possible to engage in each activity while maintaining their relationship and to rate on a nine-point scale the degree to which they would consider giving up each activity to preserve the relationship. Van Lange et al. (1997) report internal consistency (alphas) across six studies ranging from .69 to .83. They also state that test-retest correlations were significant in two studies. The measure is correlated significantly with observed behavior in a laboratory task and with partner reports in dating and married samples.

Perceived Acceptance

Researchers became interested in the concept of perceived acceptance in response to the suggestion that social inclusion and exclusion may have played a critical role during evolution (Baumeister & Leary, 1995). The Perceived Acceptance Scale (Brock, Sarason, Sanghvi, & Gurung, 1998) is designed to assess the perception that specific others care for and value oneself (e.g., "My family is sensitive to my personal needs"). The overall 44-item measure includes four role-defined subscales (mother, father, family, and friends) with alpha coefficients of .80 or higher; presumably, the scale content might be modified to describe other partners (e.g., a best friend or spouse). The subscales have discriminant validity in that target-specific acceptance differentially predicts support ratings from that target.

Nature and Extent of Interdependence

Under this heading, we group measures that consider the nature or strength of a relationship from a structural point of view, independent of whatever sentiments the partners may have for each other.

Closeness

Insofar as many of the more interesting products of interpersonal relations, including social support, arise in close relationships, defining the construct *closeness* would seem to be of paramount importance. There is little consensus in this regard, however (Berscheid, Snyder, & Omoto, 1989a). Some uses of the term refer to particular relationship types (e.g., marriage, confidants), whereas other uses conflate closeness with properties such as love, nurturance, or commitment. As a result, there is often conceptual ambiguity about how this construct relates to relationship qualities such as social support. Clearly, for the construct to be useful, relationships considered to be "close" ought to differ systematically from those that are "not close" along theoretically definable and psychometrically assessable dimensions. Furthermore, the association between social support functions and closeness is likely to depend on the particular definition of closeness that is chosen. For example, measures that focus on the subjective sense of closeness probably relate best to emotional and esteem support, whereas behavioral closeness might be expected to relate better to tangible support and network involvement.

The Relationship Closeness Inventory (RCI; Berscheid, Snyder & Omoto, 1989b) operationalizes closeness in terms of the day-to-day impact that partners have on each other's activities along three dimensions: frequency of interaction (three items estimating time spent together per day), diversity of activities (number of different activities performed with the partner during the week, chosen from a checklist of 38 relatively mundane activities; e.g., did laundry, visited friends, went to a concert), and strength of impact (34 items assessing the extent to which the partner is perceived to influence thoughts, feelings, behavior, and future plans; e.g., "X influences how I spend my free time"). Subscale totals can be used as raw scores or transformed to 1-to-10 scales with skew-corrected norms. Internal consistency of the strength and diversity scales is high (.90, .87); the frequency subscale is lower (.56), although, as the authors note, there is no good reason to expect high consistency on this dimension. As for validity, the RCI discriminates between relationships described as close and not and predicts breakup in college student romantic relationships over 3 months (Berscheid et al., 1989b).

A more subjective sense of connection is captured by the Inclusion of Other in the Self Scale (IOS; Aron, Aron, & Smollan, 1992), a single-item pictorial measure.

Respondents select among seven pairs of intersecting circles, one each representing self and partner, that range from nonoverlapping to near-total intersection. By eschewing numbers and words, the IOS is presumed to better capture the subjective sense of interconnection inherent in this and other conceptions of closeness. Aron et al. propose a two-factor model—feeling close and behaving close—and argue that the IOS is the only existing measure that taps both. Test-retest reliability over 2 weeks in a sample of college students is high ($r = .83$). Validity has been established by predicting breakups of dating relationships over 3 months and with implicit non–self-report measures (e.g., reaction time tasks; Aron & Fraley, 1999).

Interdependence Orientation

Interdependence is qualified not only by the degree of connection but also by the nature of that interdependence. A popular typology is that of Clark and Mills (1979; Mills & Clark, 1994), who differentiate communal and exchange relationships along several dimensions (see also Fiske, 1992). Of particular relevance to social support is a qualitative distinction in the basis for support provision. In communal relationships, people feel responsible for each other's welfare, and they offer and expect help according to need. In exchange relationships, in contrast, help and support are not linked to needs but rather are given in proportion to past benefits received or anticipated future benefits. Communal and exchange relationships therefore do not differ in terms of the type or amount of support but rather in the reasons that support is given. It should be noted that, like most theorizing in this area, Clark and Mills explicitly assume that people participate in both types of relationships in different contexts or with different partners. Thus, although these measures are global rather than specific, they seem readily modifiable to characterize particular relationships.

The Communal Orientation Scale (Clark, Ouellette, Powell, & Milberg, 1987) has 14 items reflecting perceptions of available help (e.g., "I expect people I know to be responsive to my needs and feelings") and willingness to assist others (e.g., "I often go out of my way to help another person"). In one study of 561 college students, Cronbach's alpha was .78 and test-retest (intraclass) reliability over 11 weeks was .68. The measure has predicted behavioral helpfulness in several laboratory studies. Associations with subtypes of social support within ongoing relationships have not been investigated, and item content does not imply a differentiated pattern. The Exchange Orientation Scale (Murstein, Wadlin, & Bond, 1987) assesses this tendency with items addressing both perceived overbenefit (e.g., "It bothers me if people I like do more for me than I do for them") and underbenefit (e.g., "It bothers me if people I like do less for me than I do for them"). The 9-item Exchange Orientation Scale (Mills & Clark, 1994) is similar.

Commitment

Commitment, the tendency to maintain a relationship and feel psychologically dependent (in the sense of connected) on it, depends on three factors: satisfaction, perceived unavailability of desirable alternatives, and investments in the relationship (Rusbult & Buunk, 1993). Because commitment implies motivation to preserve an existing relationship and thereby promotes pro-relationship behavior, commitment should relate broadly to supportive activities during a partner's distress. For example, commitment enhances the willingness to forgo immediate self-gratification to promote the well-being of a partner or relationship (Van Lange, et al., 1997), although research has not examined differences among various types of support.

Rusbult, Martz, and Agnew's (1998) seven-item Commitment Level Scale is both face-valid and effective. A representative item is "I am committed to maintaining my relationship with my partner," rated on 0-to-9 (do not agree at all–agree completely) scales. The measure has been applied to dating, married, gay, and lesbian couples and has high internal consistency (alphas range between .91 and .95). In one study, test-retest reliability was .80 over 4 weeks in dating couples and .75 over 1 year for married persons. Construct validity has been established both behaviorally (e.g., decisions to stay or leave a relationship, tendencies to derogate alternatives) and with self-reported pro-relationship behaviors (e.g., constructive responses to conflict; Rusbult & Van Lange, 1996). Incremental validity in predicting breakups over and above popular constructs such as satisfaction, adjustment, and closeness has also been reported (Rusbult et al., 1998).

Sentiment

Perhaps more than any single dimension, researchers have studied the affective tone of relationships. This is no less true for social support, in which it is commonly hypothesized that affective qualities of a relationship predict support availability and provision, especially for those types of support that involve affect (e.g., emotional and self-esteem support). Debate exists, however, as to whether supportive effects are best explained by the beneficial impact of positivity or by the harmful effects of negativity (Rook, 1998). For example, in a 1-year prospective study of depressive symptoms, Monroe, Bromet, Connell, and Steiner (1986) concluded that the health benefits of social support were less attributable to positive consequences of support than to shared variance between lack of support and the negative consequences of marital conflict. Implicit in this debate is the question of whether relationship sentiment should be conceptualized as bivariate or bipolar—in other words, whether positive and negative affect represent independent qualities or whether they are opposing ends of a single unhappy-to-happy continuum (as typically assumed). The bivariate position, for which evidence is beginning to accumulate, is consistent with studies of affect (e.g., Watson, Clark, & Tellegen, 1988) and attitudes (e.g., Cacioppo, & Gardner, & Berntson, 1997), in which bivariate models have been well supported. For this reason, we discuss satisfaction and conflict separately, although with few exceptions existing measures are not well suited for differentiating positivity and negativity in relationships.

Affective qualities are important for another reason. Sentiments provide powerful heuristics that may influence other judgments; thus, the "sentiment override" hypothesis proposes that ratings of specific relational properties (such as intimacy or trust) may in actuality represent feelings along a more basic negative-positive dimension (Weiss, 1980). Sentiment override should not be confused with social desirability, a largely methodological problem; instead, it refers to confounding of processes that people may find difficult to differentiate in their minds and in their ratings. To the extent that the sentiment override hypothesis is correct, findings based on self-report measures of complex processes (including social support) may be misspecified, leading some researchers to advocate that relationship measures be required to demonstrate incremental validity over and above measures of sentiment. This step is rare in practice but compelling when successful.

Satisfaction

By far the two most popular measures of marital adjustment are the 15-item Marital Adjustment Scale (MAT; Locke & Wallace, 1959) and 32-item Dyadic Adjustment Scale (DAS; Spanier, 1976; Busby, Christensen, Crane, & Larson [1995] present a revised 14-item version). Both measures have excellent psychometric properties; predict divorce well beyond chance in longitudinal studies; have demonstrated validity in diverse samples varying in age, ethnicity, social class, and sexual orientation; and have produced an extensive list of known correlates. Item content is diverse on both measures. The MAT taps general satisfaction, disagreement, joint activities and responsibilities, and feelings about the decision to marry, whereas the DAS assesses consensus about dyadic matters (e.g., religion, leisure), satisfaction, cohesion, and affective expression. The MAT and DAS tend to be highly correlated with each other, suggesting little practical distinction between them.

There is substantial debate about whether these scales are better construed as multidimensional measures of adjustment and adaptation (although designed to be multidimensional, factor analyses have yielded inconsistent results) or as unidimensional scales of marital quality (which in practice is the typical usage). As Fincham, Beach, and Kemp-Fincham (1997) note, these and other similar measures: "consist of a polyglot of items . . . ranging from reports of specific behaviors that occur between spouses to evaluative inferences regarding the marriage as a whole. Typically, an overall score is computed by summing over the items, but it is not clear how such a score should be interpreted" (p. 277). They propose, instead, that marital quality be defined by subjective, relatively undifferentiated evaluations (Fincham & Bradbury, 1987). In fact, this is how most researchers use the MAT and DAS—as a continuous scale running from distressed to satisfied—although this practice seems appropriate only for a small subset of items. Other measures are explicitly designed to meet Fincham and Bradbury's criterion: for example, the seven-item Relationship Assessment Scale (RAS; Hendrick, 1988), which includes face-valid items such as "In general, how satisfied are you with your relationship?" or the similar five-item Satisfaction Level Scale (SLS; Rusbult et al., 1998). The RAS, which was developed with college student dating couples, has an alpha of .86 and correlates .83 with the satisfaction subscale of the DAS.

Alpha for the SLS is reported to vary from .92 to .95. Satisfaction is also assessed sometimes with a single global item, the psychometric disadvantages of single items notwithstanding. A major advantage of subjective evaluation measures such as the RAS or SLS is flexibility for comparing across different relationship types. Scales developed for the marital context generally include content (e.g., shared decision making) inappropriate for other close relationships.

Global satisfaction scales do not distinguish positive and negative dimensions, however, as noted previously. A new measure offered by Fincham and Linfield (1997) has three items, each assessing general subjective evaluations of positive and negative features of a marriage. In a sample of 123 couples married at least 3 years, alpha coefficients for each subset were high (.87 to .91), but their intercorrelation was modest, as hypothesized ($r = -.37$). More important, the positive and negative scales discriminatively predict several independent measures, over and above a unidimensional measures (the MAT).

More behaviorally oriented measures of marital satisfaction are also popular, for example, checklists of behaviors and activities in which spouses may engage daily (Spouse Observation Checklist; Weiss, Hops, & Patterson, 1973) and of changes desired in the partner across various domains (Areas of Change Questionnaire; Weiss et al., 1973). Finally, marital satisfaction is often assessed from observational studies of spousal interaction that use structured interaction tasks and detailed coding of observed behaviors (discussed later in this chapter). A good overview of these tools is provided by Follette and Jacobson (1985).

Love

Although complexly differentiated models of love are popular, a more basic distinction, between passionate and companionate love, receives the most widespread support. The former is characterized by strong emotions and a desire for union with the other, whereas the latter concerns affection and respect felt for someone with whom one's life is intertwined. Although studies directly linking love to social support are rare, the well-established impact of companionate love on pro-relationship behavior leads us to predict a strong and multifaceted effect. Passionate love, in contrast, seems more relevant in the early stages of romantic relationships, although it, too, would be expected to relate broadly to social support.

Hatfield and Sprecher's (1986) Passionate Love Scale, the short form of which has 15 items and an alpha coefficient of .91, includes items such as "I possess a powerful attraction for_____" and "I feel happy when I am doing something to make_____happy." A 1 (not at all) to 9 (definitely true) scale is used for each item. The revised Triangular Love Scale (TLS; Sternberg, 1997) has subscales for passion (e.g., "My relationships with_____is very romantic"), intimacy (e.g., "I have a relationship of mutual understanding with_____"), and commitment (e.g., "I am committed to maintaining my relationship with_____"). Some researchers use the latter two scales as a measure of companionate love, although in our view this construct is better represented by intimacy alone. The TLS uses a 1 (not at all) to 9 (extremely) scale. Each subscale has 15 items, with reported alpha coefficients above .90.

Construct validity for these measures is established primarily from correlations with other self-report measures and relationship longevity. At first glance, discriminant validity appears problematic in that passion and companionship (as well as commitment) tend to be highly correlated. However, factor analyses generally confirm their independence, and when scores are residualized against each other, their distinct character and unique correlates are clear (Aron & Westbay, 1996). Researchers wishing to differentiate these constructs should rely on residualized scores.

The attachment and IOS scales discussed earlier are sometimes used to index romantic love. The Love Attitudes Scale (Hendrick & Hendrick, 1986) is also popular, but focuses on general attitudes about love rather than feelings about a specific partner.

Conflict

Conflict, including both arguments and expression of negative sentiments toward a partner, is widely believed to impair relationships; for example, Christensen and Walczynski argue that "once a relationship has been well established, conflict is the most important proximal factor affecting satisfaction in the relationship and ultimately its course" (1997, p. 250). We expect conflict to contribute not only to the willingness to provide support to a partner but also to the perception that support is available from that partner, if needed. Conflict is so intrinsic to perceived nonsupport that in some studies it is defined as such, designating a hostile reaction to interactions in which support was sought or possible (e.g., Bradbury & Pasch, 1994). We nevertheless view conflict as a relational predictor of support because these two qualities are empirically and conceptually distinguishable.

In marital relationships, conflict is often assessed by behavioral observation of discussions of problems (reviewed later). The degree or frequency of self-reported conflict can also be gauged with single-item self-reports of the frequency, intensity, or impact of conflict (for example, "How often do you and your spouse have an unpleasant disagreement?" rated on a five-point scale ranging from "once a week or more" to "never"; McGonagle, Kessler, & Gotlib, 1993), although such items are clearly subjective and likely to be less effective than multiple-item measures. They are better suited to multiday assessments (such as in diary studies, discussed later), in which the sequence or accumulation of day-to-day conflict is of interest.

The Conflicts and Problem-Solving Scales (CPS; Kerig, 1996) assesses four dimensions of couple conflict (frequency, severity, resolution aftermath, and problem-solving efficacy). It can also be scored for six strategies of dealing with conflict (collaboration, avoidance, stalemate, verbal aggression, physical aggression, child involvement). Internal consistency coefficients are high ($\geq. 75$). Although the measure is relatively new, correlations between spouses are mostly in the moderate range (median $r = .59$), and validity with several self-report measures of marital distress and functioning appears promising. The CPS has been used with relatively diverse community samples.

Multiple-item self-report scales of conflict and negativity are sometimes created by selecting items from the marital satisfaction and adjustment measures described earlier. It is unclear how well these measures would generalize to other types of relationships. The 14-item conflict subscale of the Quality of Relationships Index (QRI; Pierce, Sarason, & Sarason, 1991) was designed to apply to any type of relationship (a sample item is "How angry does this person make you feel?"). For each target, internal consistency is reported to be high (.88 or higher), but supporting the measure's discriminant validity, correlations among targets are nonsignificant. As expected, rated conflict correlates negatively with the perceived supportiveness of that same person.

The Family Emotional Involvement and Conflict Scale (FEICS; Shields, Franks, Harp, McDaniel, & Campbell, 1992) is specialized to family conflict. It has two subscales, each with seven items rated on 1 (almost never) to 5 (almost always) scales, concerning perceived criticism (e.g., "My family is always trying to get me to change") and emotion involvement (e.g., "If I am upset, people in my family get upset too"). Of particular relevance to support researchers is that the scale was developed in a lower- to middle-class family medicine center with respondents aged 40 and older. Both scales have good internal consistency (alphas = .82, .74) and correlated between .25 and .39 with the tangible, appraisal, and belonging subscales of the ISEL.

The belief that conflict per se may be less important than how a couple deals with it has engendered measures for assessing methods of coping with conflict. These measures seem especially pertinent to support within committed interdependent relationships like marriage, inasmuch as conflict is inevitable; support may then be a highly constructive response to disagreement, whereas nonsupport is likely to exacerbate conflict. One promising measure concerns accommodation, the willingness to respond constructively to a partner's potentially destructive behavior (Rusbult, Verette, Whitney, Slovik, & Lipkus, 1991). This 16-item scale presents respondents with a stem describing a partner's destructive action, followed by possible reactions: for example, "When my partner says or does things I don't like, I talk to him/her about what's upsetting me," rated on a 0 (never) to 8 (constantly) scale. Responses are sorted along two dimensions: constructive-destructive and active-passive, resulting in four categories labeled *voice, loyalty, exit,* and *neglect.* The subscales show reasonable internal consistency (.60 and higher) and good convergent validity with observer-coded open-ended accounts and with behavior in simulation games and laboratory interaction tasks.

Another measure of coping with relationship conflict is the Communication Patterns Questionnaire (CPQ; Christensen, 1988), which contains 35 items describing communicative strategies such as support, coercion, manipulation, mutuality, avoidance, and the "demand/withdraw" pattern, in which criticisms, complaints, or emotional requests are met with defensiveness and passivity. The scales have moderate internal consistency (mostly above .70), predict behavior in laboratory interaction (Christensen & Heavey, 1990), changes in marital satisfaction over the first 2 years of marriage, and marital adjustment (Noller & White, 1990). Neither the CPQ nor the accommodation measure has been adapted for nonromantic relationships, and it is unclear how well these constructs apply to less interdependent relationships.

Family Environment

Many and diverse self-report measures have been developed to assess characteristics of the family environment. These measures, too numerous to review presently (see Grotevant & Carlson, 1989, for a comprehensive compilation) differ in several respects. Some feature one or two apriori theoretically chosen dimensions, whereas others are more descriptively exhaustive; also, some focus on dyadic relationships within the family, whereas others emphasize a family's overall climate. These measures are relevant to social support for several reasons, the most important of which is that the nuclear family is for most people, more often than other relationships, the primary source of social support (and also bothersome perceptions of nonsupport). Consequently, studies of social support within the family, especially relevant in developmental and family-system approaches, may benefit from inclusion of multidimensional assessments of family climate. Two popular measures are summarized next (see also Skinner, 1987).

The Family Environment Scale (FES; Moos & Moos, 1986) is composed of 10 subscales reflecting an individual's perceptions of the family environment. Three address relationship functions (cohesion, emotional expressiveness, and conflict), five concern personal growth in a family context (independence, moral-religious emphasis, orientations toward achievement, intellectual-cultural activities, and active recreation), and two deal with system maintenance (clarity of organization, control). These dimensions seem likely to pertain differentially to social support, with some more pertinent to emotional support (e.g., expressiveness) and others more relevant to belonging and network functions. The cohesion dimension is sometimes used as an indicator of support, in part because it predicts ratings of received social support from family members (Sandler & Barrera, 1984).

The FES, a commercially distributed measure, has 90 items, each rated as either true/mostly true or false/mostly false. A sample item is "We think things out for ourselves in our family." The FES has been used extensively in families varying across ethnic, social class, age, family composition, and clinical or health status. Coefficient alphas and test-retest reliabilities over periods as long as 1 year range between .61 and .91. Validity has been established both by discriminating normal from disturbed families on various dimensions and through construct validity in a wide variety of studies (Moos & Moos, 1986).

The Family Adaptability and Cohesion Scale (FACES; Olson, 1991; Olson et al., 1991) is a self-report inventory that assesses two dimensions defining a circumplex model: cohesion and adaptability. Whereas the FACES was originally designed to be curvilinear (i.e., extremely low or high levels were thought to be less desirable than moderate levels), newer versions acknowledge that these effects are more likely to be linear (i.e., higher levels of cohesion and adaptability are optimal). Both dimensions predict social support in that greater connectedness and flexibility in families relate to support availability and receipt.

The FACES uses a 5-point rating scale. A 30-item version (FACES II) yielded alpha coefficients for cohesion and adaptability of .87 and .78, respectively; a 20-item version (III) fared somewhat worse: .77 and .62, respectively. Perhaps more important, the two subscales are highly correlated in the latter ($r = .65$) but essentially uncorrelated in the former ($r = .03$; Olson, 1991). Both versions have been used extensively with diverse samples and have established validity similar to the FES. Correlations between family members are modest, suggesting that perceptions of the family environment depend to a considerable extent on the individual's perspective (Olson et al., 1983).

Other family environment measures of potential interest to social support researchers include the Family Assessment Measure (Skinner, Steinhauer, & Santa-Barbara, 1983), which has subscales for affective expression, affective involvement, and control, and the Sibling Relationship Questionnaire (Furman & Buhrmester, 1985), which assesses warmth/closeness, relative status, conflict, and rivalry among siblings during childhood.

MEASURES OF RELATIONSHIP PROPERTIES RELEVANT TO PERCEIVING AND PROVIDING SOCIAL SUPPORT ASSESSED IN DISPOSITIONAL TERMS

In this section, we review relationship properties that are assessed from the perspective of personal predispositions to behave toward others in particular ways. In all cases, we conceptualize these properties in a manner similar to the prior section, that is, that a given relationship possesses these qualities to varying extents and that individuals vary in the degree to which they exhibit these qualities in one or another relationship. However, from an operational standpoint, these measures ask about the individual's tendency to approach relationships (or certain types of relationships) in one or another fashion. As such, they are clearly relevant to understanding the interpersonal origins of support, although the degree to which general dispositional measures can explain variability across different relationships remains to be established. Table 5.2 lists the measures reviewed in this section.

Empathy

Empathy, a multifaceted construct whose precise definition still generates lively debate, is important because of its strong theoretical link to helpfulness. Meta-analyses of this extensive literature reveals positive, moderate-sized links between empathy and diverse prosocial and cooperative behaviors (Eisenberg & Miller, 1987), ranging from tangible actions (e.g., sharing candy or volunteering assistance) to emotional support (e.g., comforting a distressed other). Although empathy is usually assessed as a global disposition and the target of help is most

Table 5.2. Measures of Relationship Processes Assessed in Dispositional Terms

Perceived partner responsiveness
Attachment Style
   Adult Romantic Attachment Measure (Brennan, Clark, & Shaver, 1998)
   Adult Attachment Interview (George, Kaplan, & Main, 1985)
   Bartholomew's Adult Attachment Interview (Bartholomew & Horowitz, 1991)
   Inventory of Parent and Peer Attachment (Armsden & Greenberg, 1987)
Perceived Acceptance
   Rejection Sensitivity Questionnaire (Downey & Feldman, 1996)

Sentiment
Empathy
   Interpersonal Reactivity Index (Davis, 1980; Davis & Kraus, 1991)
Emotional Expressiveness
   Emotional Expressiveness Questionnaire (King & Emmons, 1990)
   Ambivalence over Emotional Expressiveness Questionnaire (King & Emmons, 1990)
   Berkeley Expressivity Questionnaire (Gross & John, 1997)
   Self-Expressiveness in the Family Questionnaire (Halberstadt et al., 1995)

Other processes
Social Competence
   Interpersonal Competence Questionnaire (Buhrmester et al., 1988)
   Social Skills Inventory (Riggio, 1986)
   Simulated Social Interaction Test (Curran, 1982)

often a stranger, the potential relevance of empathic arousal to support within ongoing relationships is clear. To Batson (1991), for example, concern with the well-being of another is the primary motive underlying most helpful activity.

Among many measures of self-reported empathy, the Interpersonal Reactivity Index (IRI; Davis, 1980; Davis & Kraus, 1991) best differentiates three components commonly acknowledged as distinct: perspective taking (the cognitive capacity to understand another person's point of view), empathic concern (feelings of warmth, compassion, and concern for a distressed other, sometimes termed *sympathy*); and personal distress (personal anxiety about another's misfortune). Empathic concern differs from personal distress in being other-oriented rather than self-oriented and in motivating helpful behavior rather than other distress-reducing behaviors, such as escape. The IRI also includes a fantasy subscale that seems less relevant to social support.

The IRI subscales have seven items each, rated on 1 (does not describe me well) to 5 (describes me well) scales. Sample items are as follows: perspective taking, "I try to look at everybody's side of a disagreement before I make a decision"; empathic concern, "I am often quite touched by things that I see happen"; and personal distress, "In emergency situations, I feel apprehensive and ill-at-ease." Davis and Kraus (1991) reports internal consistency coefficients in the .7 to .8 range across several studies, and 2 to 3-month test-retest reliabilities ranging from .61 to .76, primarily in studies of college students.

The question of construct validity regarding the IRI and other measures of empathy is more complex. The IRI subscales, and similar measures, are generally correlated with appropriate self-report measures (e.g., social competence, relationship affect) and with partner perceptions of an individual's social behavior (e.g., good communication, warmth; Davis & Kraus, 1991). Nevertheless, across several laboratory interaction studies in which subjects' estimates of a partner's thoughts and feelings are compared to what those partners report having thought or felt at the same moment, self-reported dispositional empathy tends to be unrelated to actual empathic accuracy (Davis & Kraus, 1997). The impact of empathy on relational support may therefore be more a function of general warmth, concern, or openness than of the ability to discern a partner's state of mind. If so, empathy and, in particular, the empathic concern subdimension may reflect emotional support more than other forms of support (Trobst, Collins, & Embree, 1994).

To our knowledge, empathic accuracy has not been related to social support, although the construct appears to have considerable relevance. Accuracy does increase as a function of acquaintance (Colvin, Vogt, & Ickes, 1997) and presumably contributes to more effective relationship functioning, although in certain circumstances, such as when awareness of a partner's specific thoughts and feelings might threaten relationship security, empathic accuracy may be reduced (Ickes & Simpson, 1997; Simpson, Ickes, & Blackstone, 1995). Because empathic accuracy requires verification against an objective standard (i.e., the partner's actual thoughts and feelings or consensus ratings), assessment procedures tend to more labor intensive than self-reports. Two respected and effective approaches are Ickes's Unstructured Interaction Paradigm, in which, following a 5-minute laboratory conversation, each partner's thoughts and feelings are compared, thought by thought, to the other's deduction (Ickes, Stinson, Bissonnette, & Garcia, 1990), and the Social Relations Model (Kenny, 1994), in which multiple persons' ratings of one another are statistically decomposed into variance components, using self-descriptions or consensus ratings as criteria for accuracy.

Emotional Expressiveness

Emotional expressiveness refers to the tendency to display emotions outwardly, usually, but not exclusively, through nonverbal channels. Most measures focus on perceived availability of emotions to observers, primarily in terms of the willingness and capacity to reveal or conceal emotions rather than the degree of emotion felt. Although some measures are unidimensional, others distinguish expression of positive and negative feelings. Both apply to emotional support for several reasons. First, communication in close relationships is greatly influenced by nonverbal displays of emotion. Second, it seems likely that interactive qualities such as affirmation and responsiveness, key to the perception of emotional support, depend on visible expressions of warmth, understanding, and sympathy, whereas feeling unsupported is more likely following nonverbal displays of negative affects such as anger, disapproval, and criticism.

King and Emmons (1990) developed parallel measures, the Emotional Expressiveness Questionnaire (EEQ) and the Ambivalence over Emotional Expressiveness Questionnaire (AEQ), the latter of which assesses doubts and conflict about revealing one's feelings to others. The rationale for the AEQ stems from the hypothesis that emotional suppression is detrimental only if one is conflicted about it. The EEQ has 16 items and three subscales: positive expression (7 items, "Watching television or reading a book can make me laugh out loud"), negative expression (4 items, "When I am angry people around me usually know"), and intimacy expression (5 items, "When I really like someone they know it"). The 28-item AEQ has two subscales: ambivalence over expressing positive emotions (16 items, "Often I find that I am not able to tell others how much they really mean to me") and ambivalence about expressing various negative emotions (12 items, "I feel guilty after I have expressed anger to someone"). All items are rated on 5-point never-to-frequently scales. Used primarily with college student samples, the various subscales have alpha coefficients ranging from .63 to .87, moderate correlations with each other and with comparable self-report measures, and moderate correlations with reports averaged across several well-acquainted peers.

The Berkeley Expressivity Questionnaire (Gross & John, 1997) has three subscales: positive expressivity (4 items, "When I'm happy, my feelings show"), negative expressivity (6 items, "No matter how nervous or upset I am, I tend to keep a calm exterior"), and impulse strength (6 items, "I experience my emotions very strongly"). Response format is 1 (strongly disagree) to 7 (strongly agree). Despite the shorter format, reported internal consistencies are .70 or higher, and confirmatory factor analyses support a hierarchical three-factor solution; that is, although the BEQ can be used as a single score, the data are better accounted for by a three-factor solution with a correlation of .52 between the positive and negative subscales. Most relevant to social support research are validity correlations with peer reports (rs = .41, .43, and .48 for the three subscales, respectively) and with observer ratings of emotional expressions while watching sad or amusing videotapes. Discriminant validity among the positive and negative subscales is especially good, despite the correlation between scales.

A final measure targeted specifically at emotional expressiveness within the family context is the Self-Expressiveness in the Family Questionnaire (SEFQ; Halberstadt, Cassidy, Stifter, Parke, & Fox, 1995). This 40-item measure (and a 24-item short form) has subscales for positive expression (e.g., "telling someone how nice they look") and negative expression (e.g., "expressing momentary anger over a trivial irritation"). Item content reflects a broad definition of emotional expression and balances dominant and submissive status. A 1-to-9 frequency of expression scales is used. Internal consistency coefficients of both the long and short forms tend to be above .80, and test-retest reliability is high. The measure has been used effectively with community samples, and construct validity with other self-report measures is good.

Attachment

Attachment theory describes how mental models of self-in-relation-to-others derive from the affective quality of infant-caregiver relations. Although Bowlby's original theory focused on child development, Hazan and Shaver's (1987) suggestion that adult romantic relationships may serve many of the same functions as infant-caregiver attachments opened the door to studies of adult romantic relationships in attachment terms. Several conceptual models have been proposed, some emphasizing dispositional qualities of attachment security and insecurity (commonly called *attachment styles*) and others stressing normative processes (see Cassidy & Shaver, 1999, for an overview). Although the range of constructs covered by existing models diverges, Collins and Read's (1990) description of three main components—perceived dependability of partners, comfort with closeness, and anxiety about relationships—is prototypical.

Not surprisingly, attachment relates to the perception of support availability. For example, among women having an abortion, attachment style predicted perceived support from male partners (Cozzarelli, Sumer, & Major, 1998), and secure individuals perceive greater support from friends and family and report better use of support resources in coping with stress (Ognibene & Collins, 1998). Attachment style also predicts better emotional coping in families with a hospitalized intensive care patient (Eldredge, 1999). As for supportive interaction, independent observers rate avoidant men as less emotionally supportive of their female partners during discussions of conflictual issues (Simpson, Rholes, & Phillips, 1996). Also, insecure attachment predicts poor utilization of available support resources during stressful circumstances (Mikulincer, Florian, & Weller, 1993). Clear differential associations between attachment and dimensions of support have not yet been identified, although theoretical models have been offered (e.g., Bartholomew, Cobb, & Poole, 1997).

Three major distinctions divide the many existing measures of attachment (see Crowell, Fraley & Shaver, 1999, for a review). First, some scales refer to specific relationships, whereas others describe relationships or partners in general. Few studies have explicitly compared one to the other, and it is not clear how well existing measures capture this important difference. Second, some measures assess relationships with parents, whereas others concern adult romantic relationships (or, less commonly, close friendships). Third, there are self-report questionnaires and interview procedures, in which trained coders evaluate qualities of information processing (e.g., emotional openness and coherence). Unfortunately, the important conceptual and methodological ramifications of these distinctions have yet to be delineated empirically.

Hazan and Shaver's (1987) seminal measure for studying adult romantic attachment was admittedly crude; respondents classified themselves into one of three categories: secure, avoidant, or anxious-ambivalent. More recent work suggests that continuous scales of the dimensions underlying attachment styles may be both psychometrically and conceptually superior. Brennan, Clark, and Shaver (1998) conducted a series of integrative analyses using all 323 unique items contained in 14 of the best-known measures. The resulting Adult Romantic Attachment Measure has two 18-item scales, one assessing avoidance (e.g., "I am very comfortable being close to romantic partners") and the other anxiety (e.g., "I worry about being abandoned"). Respondents evaluate each item on 7-point "strongly disagree" to "strongly agree" rating scales. Both subscales have alpha coefficients above .90, and together they account for impressive levels of variance in the original measures (many of which displayed good evidence of construct validity). This measure can also classify respondents according to a predominant style, and although further evaluation is needed, it seems likely to emerge as a consensus choice among self-report scales.

Armsden and Greenberg's (1987) 28-item Inventory of Parent and Peer Attachment is a good example of self-report measures of parent-child attachment. Suitable for use with adolescents, it has three subscales—mutual trust, communication quality, and alienation—and high levels of internal consistency (alphas above .80) and construct validity.

Interview measures tend to be justified in terms of biases inherent in self-observation and self-report, which may be potent in the domain of attachment-related defenses and anxieties. Most popular is the Adult Attachment Interview (AAI; George, Kaplan, & Main, 1985), a lengthy and deeply probing interview in which adults are asked to provide memories and impressions of attachment-related experiences in two forms: overall evaluations and specific biographical episodes. Trained coders analyze these interviews for coherence and consistency in representing attachment-relevant issues—for example, the availability and coherence of specific memories that support or contradict general impressions and emotions. Access to the AAI is limited because of the extensive (and somewhat secretive) training required to become proficient and because the interview and coding protocol is quite labor-intensive. Nevertheless but in part because of the rigor these procedures entail, the AAI is considered by some researchers to be the gold standard for assessing attachment to parents.

Using many of the same principles and procedures, Bartholomew and Horowitz (1991) developed a semistructured interview for attachment to close friends and romantic partners. (They also describe a similar interview for family attachment.) In their protocol, which requires significantly less (but still substantial) training but taps many of the same outside-of-awareness processes as does the AAI, each interview is coded on 1-to-9 scales for the extent of resemblance to prototypes of the four major attachment styles (secure, preoccupied, dismissing, fearful), as well as 15 dimensions relevant to attachment (e.g., emotional expressiveness, coherence). Interrater reliability ranges from moderate to high (.55 to .96). Construct validity is demonstrated by modest correlations with various self-report and friend-report measures, highlighting a common conceptual core but indicating that method variance is substantial.

Finally, based on the assumption that the process of caregiving in adult intimate relationships involves many of the processes central to attachment, Kunce and Shaver (1994) developed a Caregiving scale that assesses the way in which individuals habitually note and respond to a partner's needs. Caregiving, which may or may not be recognized by the recipient as intended, overlaps substantially with the concept of social support, although this measure has not yet been used in this manner. The scale's four major dimensions are proximity versus distance; sensitivity versus insensitivity to a partner's needs, feelings, and nonverbal signals; cooperation versus control in supporting a partner's efforts to solve problems; and compulsive caregiving, the tendency to become overinvolved with, or overburdened by, a partner's problems.

Perceived Acceptance

The Rejection Sensitivity Questionnaire (RSQ; Downey & Feldman, 1996) describes chronic tendencies to expect, readily perceive, and overreact to cues of possible social rejection. Although the RSQ itself refers to dispositional rather than relationship-specific qualities, it predicts responses to perceived rejection from intimate partners (Downey, Freitas, Michaelis, & Khouri, 1998). The RSQ asks respondents to indicate the extent to which they would anticipate an accepting or rejecting response to each of 18 hypothetical situations (e.g., "You ask your boyfriend/girlfriend if he/she really loves you"). The RSQ has good internal consistency and test-retest reliability (both coefficients = .83). Inherent in the construct is the perception of lack of support, spanning both instrumental and emotional dimensions. Rejection sensitivity also triggers hostile and nonsupportive behavior to partners, particularly by women.

Social Competence

Substantial evidence links social competence to well-being and relational success (Spitzberg & Cupach, 1989). Effectiveness in providing social support to others is undoubtedly influenced by social competence, but as yet it is not clear just which competencies are most critical.[2] That social skills do pertain is demonstrated by Cohen, Sherrod, and Clark (1986), who showed that three social skills (assertiveness, self-disclosure, and lack of self-consciousness) prospectively predicted development of friendship and perceived support (and presumably support provision as well).

In part, this gap may be traced to heterogeneity in how social competence is defined and assessed. Whereas some definitions feature relatively concrete, conceptually delimited competencies (e.g., initiation skills, shyness), others are broad and diffuse (e.g., popularity). Skills may be dispositional or relationship-specific (although rarely studied as such). Operationally, social competence can be assessed via self-report, partner report, or third-party coding of observed interaction. Because these methods tend to correlate in the low-to-moderate range, at best, some commentators feel that they reflect different perspectives and perhaps even different constructs.

Comprehensive reviews of existing measures are available (e.g., Bellack & Hersen, 1998; Spitzberg & Cupach, 1989). Self-report methods, considerably more prevalent than partner reports or direct observations, take one of two forms: unidimensional measures of specific qualities relevant to skilled interpersonal behavior (e.g., anxiety [Leary, 1983], shyness [Jones, Briggs, & Smith, 1986], assertiveness [Levenson & Gottman, 1978], or empathy [reviewed previously,]), or multidimensional inventories. For example, the Interpersonal Competence Questionnaire (ICQ; Buhrmester, Furman, Wittenberg, & Reis, 1988) has eight items for each of five tasks fundamental to relating effectively: initiation, assertion about

---

2. Some measures work around this issue by considering support provision itself a skill.

negative feelings, self-disclosure, emotional support, and conflict management. Self-ratings are correlated with reports by roommates and by friends and new acquaintances who evaluated respondents' behavior after a laboratory conversation. The ICQ indicates that different skills are relevant in different types of relationships (e.g., same-sex friendship vs. romance) and interactions (e.g., becoming acquainted vs. supporting an intimate), implicating the need to differentiate skills according to the type of support needed and the nature of the stressor, as our functional congruence hypothesis proposed. Another self-report measure with demonstrated validity (i.e., correlations with behavioral ratings) is the Social Skills Inventory (SSI; Riggio, 1986), which has 15 items on each of seven subscales: emotional expressivity, emotional sensitivity, emotional control, social expressivity, social sensitivity, social control, and social manipulation.

A good example of an observation-based assessment is the Simulated Social Interaction Test (SSIT; Curran, 1982), in which participants are videotaped as they respond to eight hypothetical situations introduced by a narrator and enacted with a confederate. Some of these situations are germane to social support (e.g., heterosexual conflict, interpersonal warmth). Third parties rate the videotapes on 11-point Likert scales for two major dimensions: social anxiety and general social skill.

Commentary on Self-Report Measures

The seemingly ubiquitous appeal of self-report measures has several roots: They are convenient for both participants and researchers, standards for establishing the rudiments of reliability and construct validity are not overly burdensome, and measures can be tailored to reflect the fine points of a conceptual position. Most important, they permit assessment of relationship qualities from the individual's perspective. Most variables in this area show no better than moderate levels of agreement between partners or between interactants and outside observers. Sometimes this is interpreted as a methodological failing; more likely, it reflects the importance of personal perspectives on matters that are inherently subjective and idiosyncratic. For this reason, self-report measures are irreplaceable tools for assessing relationship properties.

Our review highlights several important methodological considerations that have received insufficient attention, prominent among which is the issue of discriminant validity. Four decades ago, Campbell and Fiske (1959) argued that establishing the validity of a construct and measure requires confirmation not only by correlation with related variables but also by noncorrelation with conceptually unrelated variables. Discriminant validity helps rule out method-related artifacts (e.g., response bias) and delineates conceptual boundaries among measures. Although some of the instruments described previously have demonstrated discriminant validity, more typically evidence is missing or minimal.

The issue of discriminant validity suggests three additional points warranting attention. First, as discussed earlier, in some cases it is not clear how the variable in question can or should be differentiated from social support itself. For example, to what extent is perceived criticism a relationship process independent of social support or perceived nonsupportiveness when help is desired? Second, Weiss's (1980) "sentiment override" hypothesis, noted previously, proposes that relationship measures may predict outcomes not necessarily because of the fine points of a hypothesis but rather because of variance shared with overall positivity. The centrality of positivity-negativity as a basic dimension of interpersonal evaluation suggests that careful controls for this more parsimonious variable are needed. Third, we sometimes wondered whether these measures were at times casting ever-finer theoretical distinctions with diminishing practical impact, similar to Sechrest's (1963) suggestion that incremental validity be a fundamental requirement of scale construction—that is, that new measures should explain (both conceptually and regression-wise) variance over and above existing instruments. To be sure, many of the scales reviewed herein reflect researcher attention to these issues. We believe, however, that further consideration is needed.

MEASURES OF SUPPORTIVE INTERACTION

At the beginning of this chapter, Figure 5.1 proposed that supportive interactions are embedded in ongoing relationships and shaped by their properties. Supportive interaction is often investigated directly, rather than by self-report, using either of two methods: observational studies of a single controlled interaction and diary studies of ongoing everyday interaction. The impact of relationship properties on social support may be highlighted and explained by determining the degree to which specific supportive behaviors depend on relevant relationship properties.

The observational approach is founded on two premises: that the most appropriate level of analysis is the interaction (rather than the individual) and that self-reports are potentially misleading. Regarding the former, it is commonly assumed that because social support necessarily depends on the behavior of two persons (i.e., a donor and a recipient), interaction, rather than perceptions by solitary individuals, should serve as the focus of investigation. As for self-report bias, many studies demonstrate that retrospective, global ratings are substantially and systematically biased by cognitive and motivational processes intrinsic to the task of recollecting, summarizing, and interpreting past experience into current impressions (e.g., Schwarz, Groves, & Schuman, 1998). Furthermore, people may not be fully aware of specific details that are nevertheless important; even if aware, they may have difficulty translating their experiences into the more abstract constructs that questionnaires typically assess (Weick, 1968). Observational methods, in contrast, provide an objective account of interaction, to the extent that behavior can be recorded and correctly characterized by independent observers.

Observational studies are never undertaken lightly; they are labor-intensive (often exceptionally so), costly, and time-consuming. Nevertheless, observational methods have great appeal because they provide detailed, objective data about interaction. A typical study of supportive interaction has three major components: a support-relevant context is experimentally created (for example, by asking a dyad to discuss a problem one of them is having); participants are allowed to interact freely for a standard, usually brief interval; and trained coders analyze videotapes of the interaction according to highly structured criteria. Implicit in this strategy is the assumption, more often taken as an article of faith than as a hypothesis to be tested, that participants under observation act in a manner representative of their behavior in more natural, private settings. The fact that observational studies often demonstrate considerable validity and predictive power suggests that this assumption may be reasonable. Another important assumption is that independent observers, who do not have access to the participants' interpretations or to the history or private meaning systems of a given dyad, are capable of properly comprehending the meaning of a given verbal or nonverbal message. Some observational systems have examined this issue by comparing observer codes and participant ratings; in other cases, the fact that observer codes effectively predict some outside criterion is taken as prima facie evidence of validity.

In a somewhat different vein, daily experience studies (sometimes called *diary studies*) share the assumption that the details of real interaction matter but emphasize the importance of natural contexts (Reis & Gable, 2000). These methods collect repeated reports from participants using structured item formats and time-sampling procedures. Although not considered as objective reports, because they necessarily describe behavior from the participant's vantage point, the focus on detailed, repeated, contemporaneous reports minimizes many of the biases present in global questionnaires. Also, the sheer volume of data collected allows researchers to examine sensitively natural variations in the processes under investigation, as well as the impact of contextual, relational, and temporal factors.

In the sections that follow, we first review several observational coding systems for assessing supportive interaction. Subsequently, we describe a few prominent and representative coding systems for studying marital and family interaction along dimensions relevant to social support. We conclude with an overview of daily experience methods, a much newer but potentially valuable approach to studying supportive interaction. Testifying to the appeal of all these methods despite their cost is the fact that far too many protocols exist than can be covered here. We therefore focus on measures that are, or seem likely to be, useful for determining how relationship processes contribute to social support. Bakeman (2000) and Weick (1968, 1985) provide excellent introductions to observational methodology; Reis and Gable (2000) review event sampling. An informative overview of observational coding systems for marriage and family research is presented by Markman and Notarius (1987).

Microanalytic Behavioral Observations of Supportive Interaction

Social Support Behavior Code

The SSBC was developed by Cutrona and Suhr (Cutrona & Suhr, 1992; Cutrona, Suhr, & MacFarlane, 1990). In the typical study, participants take turns disclosing a current source of personal distress. Each problem is discussed for 10 minutes and, after each segment, partners complete a questionnaire to assess perceived supportiveness of their partner's behavior. Videotaped behavioral interactions are then coded by trained observers who focus on the support-provider's behavior.

The SSBC assesses the frequency of 23 individual behaviors along the five broad categories of support listed in Table 5.3: information, tangible, emotional, esteem, and social network support. The SSBC also tallies negative behaviors, but because the interaction task is designed to elicit cooperation, negative behavior occurs infrequently. The coding system (Cutrona & Suhr, 1994), which mostly concerns verbal behavior, grew out of existing support literature and surveys of

Table 5.3. Microanalytic Behavioral Observation Coding Schemes for Supportive Interactions

---

A. Social Support Behavior Code (SSBC; Cutrona & Suhr, 1992)
   Information support (advice, factual input)
   Tangible support (offers of assistance or resources)
   Emotional support (expressions of caring or empathy)
   Esteem support (expressions of respect or confidence in the person's competence)
   Social network support (communicating similarity or belonging to a group of similar others)
   Negative behaviors (sarcasm, criticism, disagreements, interruptions, complaints, refusals)
B. Interactive Coping Behavior Coding System (ICBCS; Barbee & Cunningham, 1995)
   Solve (problem-focused/approach; e.g., help, advice)
   Solace (emotion-focused/approach; e.g., reassurance, affection)
   Dismiss (problem-focused/avoidance; e.g., minimizing the problem)
   Escape (emotion-focused/avoidance; e.g., distraction, discouraging emotional expression)
C. Support Activation Behavior Coding System (SABCS; Barbee & Cunningham, 1995)
   Ask (direct/verbal; e.g., giving details, asking for help or advice)
   Cry/pout (direct/nonverbal; e.g., appearing sad, seeking closeness)
   Hint/complain (indirect/verbal; complaining without asking for help, whining)
   Sigh/sulk/fidget (indirect/nonverbal; e.g., expressing irritation or distraction)
D. Social Support Interaction Coding System (SSICS; Bradbury & Pasch, 1994)
   Helper codes:
      Positive Instrumental (e.g., suggestion, questions)
      Positive Emotional (e.g., reassurance, encouragement)
      Positive Other
      Negative (e.g., criticism, blame)
      Neutral
      Off-task
   Help-seeker codes:
      Positive (e.g., reacts positively to suggestions)
      Negative (e.g., whines, criticizes)
      Neutral
      Off-task
E. Hierarchical Coding System for Sensitivity of Comforting Messages (Applegate, 1978; Burleson, 1985)
   Levels of increasing sensitivity:
      1. Denial of support-seeker's perspective
      2. Implicit recognition of support-seeker's perspective
      3. Explicit recognition and elaboration of support-seeker's perspective

married couples, in which spouses were asked to describe specific behaviors that they would like partners to enact in response to stressful events.

Applied primarily to married couples, the SSBC has also been used with friendship dyads. Mean interrater reliability (intraclass correlations) across the six major categories is .77 (Cutrona & Suhr, 1992). Evidence for predictive validity is provided in a series of studies (e.g., Cutrona, 1996a, 1996b; Cutrona, Hessling, & Suhr, 1997; Cutrona & Suhr, 1992, 1994; Cutrona, Suhr, & MacFarlane, 1990). Construct validity is demonstrated by correlations between the total number of support behaviors coded and observer ratings of global interaction supportiveness (rs = .71 to .79), and participant ratings of global supportiveness (r = .32 for support-provider, r = .20 for support-recipient; Cutrona, Suhr, & MacFarlane, 1990).

Interactive Coping Behavior Coding System and Support Activation Behavioral Coding System

The ICBCS and SABCS coding systems concern a typology of specific communicative behaviors expected to arise during "interactive coping" (Barbee, 1990; Barbee & Cunningham, 1995; Gully, 1993). The SABCS focuses on the help seeker, whereas the ICBCS focuses on the potential help provider. *Interactive coping* is defined as a dynamic behavioral process in which one individual responds verbally and nonverbally, in helpful or unhelpful ways, to another person's problem or expression of emotion. (The authors refer to the process as interactive coping rather than social support because helpers' behaviors are not always positive, and the outcome of the interaction may not be beneficial.) Codes are based on Barbee and Cunningham's (1995) sensitive interactions systems theory, which seeks to explain help-seeking and help-giving transactions in dyads and how this process is influenced by a broad range of factors pertaining to the help seeker, the help giver, their relationship, and the context in which support seeking occurs. The theory provides a detailed description of the interactive coping process and predicts whether an interaction will reduce or exacerbate the help seeker's distress.

These two coding systems have been used primarily with friends but in addition with dating couples and in experimental studies of unacquainted dyads. The ICBCS focuses on 28 specific verbal and nonverbal behaviors that help providers may display in response to another's problem or emotion, based on two underlying dimensions: (1) problem-focused versus emotion-focused strategies and (2) problem approach versus avoidance. Crossing these two dimensions yields the four strategies of interactive coping noted in Table 5.3. Each complete thought is classified as one of the four coping strategies. Thus, a complex sentence that contains several different coping strategies would receive more than one code. Each behavioral act (e.g., hugging the speaker) is also coded. Verbal behaviors can be coded from videotapes or from transcripts that minimize knowledge about gender or other characteristics that may affect observer ratings. Interrater reliability ranges from .91 to .95 (Barbee, 1990; Gulley, 1993, as cited in Barbee & Cunningham, 1995).

The SABCS focuses on the person in need and is designed to identify 33 specific behaviors that help or hinder obtaining support. Crossing two dimensions of support activation—verbal versus nonverbal behaviors and direct versus indirect strategies—yields the four general strategies shown in Table 5.3. Interrater reliability is reported as .95 (Barbee & Cunningham, 1995). Evidence for construct and predictive validity is provided by studies using diverse methods, including behavioral observation, role-playing, experimentation, diary and event-sampling, and qualitative methods (Barbee & Cunningham, 1995).

Social Support Interaction Coding System

The SSICS was developed for behavioral observations in which married spouses are asked to discuss a personal issue that is not a marital problem (something about themselves that they would like to change; Bradbury & Pasch, 1994; Pasch, Bradbury, & Davila, 1997; Pasch, Bradbury, & Sullivan, 1997). Partners alternate in the help-seeking and help-providing roles in two 10-minute interactions. These two roles are distinguished in the behaviorally based coding system.

The SSICS is rooted in the support literature and social learning theories of marriage, and it features positive and negative behaviors enacted during interaction. As Table 5.3 indicates, each speech turn by helpers receives one of the six codes, whereas each helpee's speech turn is given one of four codes. To date, the coding scheme has been used only with married couples. Pasch, Bradbury, and Sullivan (1997) report adequate reliabilities (kappa = .69; 79% agreement for helper behavior; kappa = .76, 87% agreement for helpee behaviors). Construct and predictive validity is reported with two samples of newlywed couples (Bradbury & Pasch, 1994; Pasch, Bradbury, & Davila, 1997; Pasch, Bradbury, & Sullivan, 1997).

Hierarchical Coding System for Sensitivity of Comforting Messages

Developed by Applegate (1978) and Burleson (1985) to study verbal comforting messages, this protocol uses a role-playing paradigm whereby participants are presented with a series of hypothetical scenarios in which another person experiences an emotionally stressful event. The comforting quality of verbal responses is then coded. Comforting messages are defined as messages intended to lessen emotional distress arising from everyday hurts and disappointments. This definition has several implications. First, the coding system is limited primarily to provision of emotional support. Second, it examines comforting in response to everyday occurrences rather than to severe or chronic life events. Third, the coding scheme focuses exclusively on verbal behavior.

The coding system is based on hierarchical scaling of the extent to which the distressed person's feelings and perspective are explicitly acknowledged and elaborated. Messages are categorized along three major levels of increasing sensitivity or "sophistication" (and presumably effectiveness): (1) denial of perspective, in which speakers explicitly or implicitly condemn, ignore, or discredit the distressed other's feelings; (2) implicit recognition, in which speakers provide implicit acceptance or otherwise positive responses without explicitly mentioning, elaborating, or legitimizing the other's feelings; and (3) explicit recognition and elaboration, in which speakers acknowledge, legitimize, and attempt to clarify the other's feelings. Within each major level are three sublevels, yielding a score from 1 to 9 for each message (or message component).

In one format, an entire comfort message (or speech sample) is assigned a code that describes the highest level displayed in the communication. In this case, raters evaluate the predominant focus of a message. Alternatively, each individual element of a message can be coded. Coder reliability in both formats tends to be high. Two role-playing studies that used audiotaped messages, one with children and adolescents (Burleson, 1984) and another with mothers of school-age children (Applegate, Burleson, Burke, Delia, & Kline, 1985), reported interrater correlations of .94 and .90, respectively. An observational study of subject-confederate interaction found interrater reliability (alpha) of .78 (Tamborini, Salomonson, & Bahk, 1993).

To date, this procedure has been used in observational studies of support interactions and in laboratory studies pairing individuals with peers or confederates, with samples of mothers, teachers, day-care workers, children and adolescents, college students, and dating partners. Evidence for construct and predictive validity is summarized by Burleson (1994). For example, individuals who employ relatively sophisticated strategies in the role-playing procedure tend to employ similarly sophisticated strategies in the "real world" (Applegate, 1980). Also, children and adults who offer more sensitive messages are perceived more positively than are children and adults who employ less sensitive strategies (Burleson et al., 1986; Burleson & Samter, 1985; Samter, Burleson, & Basden, 1989). Finally, in a laboratory study of problem disclosure, the distressed subject's evaluations of a partner's response was correlated with ratings by independent observers (Burleson & Samter, 1985).

Observation of Marital Interaction

The special importance of marriage within the study of relationships is reflected in the popularity of observational studies for characterizing marital interaction. Evolved from the tradition of behavior analysis and aimed explicitly at identifying specific behaviors that distinguish distressed and nondistressed couples, these coding systems generally focus on couple communication about relationship problems (Weiss & Heyman, 1990). Social support tends not to be an explicit focus of these systems, both because most relationship problems are dyadic rather than individual (and therefore would not necessarily be expected to elicit a supportive response from one partner to the other) and because these systems were devised to characterize interaction broadly. Nevertheless, the sorts of processes that these coding systems typically articulate are highly relevant to the support process in marriage. Their widespread familiarity and extensive psychometric development should also enhance appeal to support researchers.

The two coding systems described next are the two most widely used marital observation coding systems. More details about these protocols, as well as several others, are provided by Markman and Notarius (1987).

Marital Interaction Coding System

One of the earliest and most enduringly popular methods, the MICS was designed to identify counterproductive behaviors employed by distressed couples and thereby help improve their conflict resolution skills (Weiss, Hops, & Patterson, 1973; Weiss & Summers, 1983). The MICS is a microanalytic coding system that tallies the frequency of specific communicative behaviors as couples discuss for 10 minutes a problematic issue in their relationship. The most recent revision (MICS-4; Heyman, Weiss, & Eddy, 1995) somewhat broadens the traditional focus on overt behavior that requires no observer inference by increasing attention to affective nuance and by combining cues necessary to define behaviors that have no definitive single marker (e.g., withdrawal). Trained observers code interactions divided into "dyadic behavior units," defined by several criteria to represent each change of behavior, thought, or speaker turn in conversation.

There is no standard method for combining the 33 MICS-4 codes into categories, although several a priori grouping schemes have been proposed. Particularly relevant to social support research are four patterns listed in Table 5.4: validation, invalidation, blame, and facilitation. Heyman, Eddy, Weiss, and Vivian (1995) attempted to derive a consensual grouping scheme from factor analyses of 994 couple interactions. Four factors emerged: hostility, humor, responsibility discussion, and constructive problem engagement. A major benefit of the MICS-4 is its flexibility to permit analysis of particular microcodes or user-generated theoretically derived groupings. In either case, data can be analyzed according to the relative frequency of a behavior or in sequential analyses (i.e., whether a given behavior by one spouse increases or decreases the probability of certain responses by the other; for example, in distressed couples, expressions of blame often increase the likelihood of reciprocal blame.

Interrater reliability of the MICS codes is high, reflecting extensive training of coders; reliance on concrete, well-defined coding criteria; and extensive development and revision of the protocols. (Heyman, Weiss, & Eddy, 1995 set a criterion of .70 agreement with a master coder.) Validity has been established by demonstrating that various MICS codes effectively distinguish chronically distressed and nondistressed couples and are associated with changes in the marital relationship, such as from therapy (Weiss & Summers, 1983).

Rapid Couples Interaction Scoring System

A modification of the earlier Couples Interaction Coding System (Gottman, 1979), the RCISS was devised to provide a relatively fast and economical means of coding overt interaction behaviors that at a purely descriptive level distinguish distressed and nondistressed couples (Gottman, 1994; Krokoff, Gottman, & Haas, 1989). The RCISS concentrates on the positive-negative dimension of interaction

Table 5.4. Coding Systems for Observation of Marital and Family Interaction

---

Marital Interaction Coding Systems

A. Marital Interaction Coding System IV (MICS-IV; Heyman, Weiss, & Eddy, 1995)

    33 behavior codes that may be combined in various ways, such as:

        Validation (agree, approve, accept responsibility, comply)

        Invalidation (disagree, disapprove, deny responsibility, excuse, noncomply)

        Blame (criticize, mindread negative, putdown, turnoff)

        Facilitation (assent, disengage, humor, mindread positive, positive touch, question, paraphrase, reflect, smile/laugh)

B. Rapid Couples Interaction Scoring System (RCISS; Gottman, 1994)

    Speaker codes:

        Positive (problem description, task-oriented information, assent, humor, other positive)

        Negative (complain, criticize, negative relationship-issue talk, "yes-but" responses, defensiveness, put-downs, escalate negative affect, other negative)

    Listener codes:

        Positive (back-channels present, facial movement present, positive facial expression, gaze pattern, responsive facial movement)

        Negative (no back-channels, no facial movement, negative facial expession, look away)

C. Specific Affect Coding System (SPAFF; Gottman & Krokoff, 1989)

    Neutral

    Positive (affection/caring, humor, interest/curiosity, joy/enthusiasm)

    Negative (anger, disgust/contempt, sadness, fear, whining)

Family Interaction Coding Systems

A. Defensive and Supportive Communication Interaction System (Alexander, 1973)

    Defensiveness (judgmental, control, indifference, superiority)

    Supportiveness (information seeking/giving, problem-solving, empathic understanding, equality)

B. Parent-Adolescent Interaction Coding System (PAICS; Robin & Weiss, 1980)

    Positive behavior (agree, appraisal, consequential thinking, facilitation, humor, probelm-solving, problem-specification)

    Negative behavior (command, complain, defensive, interrupt, put-down)

    Neutral behavior

---

more than the CISS (or MICS) does, while providing somewhat less detail about specific behaviors and sequences. Considering the ample research that demonstrates the impact of affect and affect reciprocity on marital interaction, whether this emphasis entails conceptual loss is not yet evident. Ratings are based on a 15-minute "snapshot" of interaction as spouses attempt to resolve a major problem area in their marriage. Each speaker turn (i.e., all utterances until one speaker yields the floor to the other) is coded for objectively verifiable overt behaviors by speakers and by listeners; criteria are intended to require little or no inference by coders.

The RCISS codes encompass both affect displays and verbal content along dimensions of valence and communication style. Coding categories were retained from the prior, more comprehensive system if they were consistent and not infrequent across entire interactions. As shown in Table 5.4, speaker codes include five positive behaviors and eight negative behaviors, whereas listener codes include five positive and four negative responses. Codes are used primarily in two ways: a continuous score subtracting the number of negative codes from the number of positive codes for the entire interaction (separately for speakers and listeners) and probabilities of positive-negative sequences across speaker turns. "Point graphs," representing the slope over time of accumulated positivity and negativity, have also been developed.

The RCISS has been used widely with couples of diverse education, age, and socioeconomic status. Gottman (1994) reports interobserver correlations of .62 for speaker scores and .75 for listener scores. Validity is established by comparison with other coding systems (primarily the MICS and CISS), distinctions between distressed and nondistressed couples, and predictions of separation and divorce (Gottman, 1994). Also, correlations have been reported between videotaped laboratory interactions and audiotaped conversations at home (Krokoff et al., 1989).

Specific Affect Coding System

To provide greater detail about affect during marital problem solving, Gottman and Krokoff (1989) developed an adjunct measure, the SPAFF, which codes affect at each speech turn from global impressions of verbal, voice tone, facial, gestural, contextual, and body movement cues relevant to emotional expression and control. Subcodes are combined to arrive at scores for neutral, positive, and negative affect (see Table 5.4). Reliabilities (kappas) reported for the SPAFF range around .70 (Gottman, 1994). Validity is similar to the RCISS.

Observation of Family Interaction

The behavioral observation tradition is well represented in family research. Grotevant and Carlson (1989) describe 13 different coding schemes for family interaction, focusing on the family as a context for psychopathology (e.g., adolescent delinquency) or for child development (e.g., moral development). Most of these schemes are rooted either in social learning theory or in family systems theory and utilize verbal interaction in at least triadic situations (two parents and one school-age or adolescent child). Much like marital interaction coding systems, these schemes focus on conflict or problem-related interaction, and none is designed specifically to assess supportive interactions. However, several include behavior codes relevant to support processes. Furthermore, as with marital interaction, studies of family interaction are potentially important to social support research because, for most people, the family is the primary relational context in which support is sought, provided, and hoped for.

Some coding schemes were designed for observing unstructured interactions in the home, although most were designed for the lab. In the typical laboratory study, family members are asked to engage in one or more structured tasks, including problem-area discussions or cooperative activities (e.g., playing a game or planning a family vacation). Next we describe two coding systems of particular relevance for investigating support processes in the family.

Defensive and Supportive Communication Interaction System

This system, developed by Alexander (1973; Alexander & Parsons, 1973), was derived from small-groups research and is rooted in family systems theory. Family interaction data are obtained from two videotaped family discussions: (1) responses to an open-ended question (e.g., "What are good parents?") and (2) a resolution of differences task. The coding scheme includes eight behavior codes used to create composites representing defensiveness and supportiveness (specified in Table 5.4). Coding can be done for time sampling (e.g., behavior is coded every 12 seconds), naturally occurring speech units (e.g., each talk turn), or thought units. Interrater reliability is high (percent agreement ranges from 81% to 94%). The coding scheme has discriminated families with and without delinquent adolescents, between experimentally induced conditions of conflict and cooperation, and between more or less successful therapeutic interventions.

Parent-Adolescent Interaction Coding System

The PAICS was designed as a counterpart to the MICS, discussed previously (Robin & Weiss, 1980). Like the MICS, the PAICS is rooted in social learning theory and utilizes a family problem-solving task. In the typical study, parents and adolescents complete a questionnaire recalling disagreements about 44 specific issues (e.g., curfew, smoking). Families are then audiotaped for 10 minutes while they attempt to resolve each of the two issues with the greatest frequency and anger intensity. Interactions are divided into behavior units, each of which is coded into one of 15 mutually exclusive categories and then aggregated into positive, negative, and neutral composites (see Table 5.4). Frequencies across the two 10-minute interactions can be summed for the 15 individual codes or for the three higher-level categories. Scores can be computed for the family as a whole or for each family member. Interrater agreement tends to be good (average correlations for six pairings of four coders ranged from .73 to .92 for the higher order categories. Average percent agreement on the 15 specific categories ranged from 51% to 81%. Construct validity has been established by differentiating families who participated in communication training or family therapy from no-treatment controls, as well as families with distressed and nondistressed mother–adolescent son relationships.

Commentary on Observational Methods

Observational methods are prized for their objectivity and specificity. Because the presence or absence of certain behaviors is determined by independent observers, subjectivity and other forms of self-report bias are eliminated: One can be sure that the data accurately portray actual interaction. Also, observational codes tend to be concrete and detailed, affording considerable range in the types of variables that can be derived—for example, counts of specific behaviors (e.g., smiles, criticisms, interruptions), relatively more abstract constructs (e.g., validation, proximity seeking), and sequential patterns (e.g., negative affect reciprocity). In other words, accurate, detailed descriptions of interaction between relationship partners can be obtained from a relatively brief encounter. To many researchers, these advantages outweigh the great costs of observational research in terms of time and effort.

Observational studies require controlled settings, a potential liability whose impact has received little empirical scrutiny. Experimental contexts may influence the range of behaviors elicited by making some options more salient and others inadvisable; for example, a psychological laboratory may evoke self-reflection or compliance to a greater extent than one's living room. Moreover, when participants are aware of being monitored, social desirability and politeness norms may minimize displays of distasteful behavior before researchers' knowing eyes, yielding data that reflect optimal more than typical performance (Ickes & Tooke, 1988). Even the simple fact of being committed to completing a 15-minute interaction to receive a substantial payment may diminish reliance on a common real-life strategy for coping with spousal criticism: leaving the room. In short, the breadth of generalizability of observational findings should not be assumed without empirical demonstration.

An important issue for aspiring observational researchers concerns the level of coding. Some schemes rely on discrete, molecular categories—whether an utterance was critical, for example—about which coders need make little or no inferences. Other schemes focus on more global meanings, requiring that coders make informed judgments about a speaker's intent or motivation. Which sort of system is used depends on conceptual analysis. For example, one might conceptualize social support in terms of the number and timing of positive statements and nonverbal signals expressed as a partner discusses a problem. However, social support may depend less on specific acts and more on the assumed intent of a response—whether a listener's comments facilitate problem appraisal or whether they tend to interfere, for example. Given the time and effort that observational research entails, adoption of a particular method and coding scheme requires caution, forethought, and pilot testing.

Daily Experience Reports of Social Support

Another strategy for obtaining interaction-based reports of social support relies on event-sampling, or daily experience, methodology. This method involves repeated assessment via structured diaries of thoughts, feelings, and behavior that occur during spontaneous everyday activity. Several methodological premises guide this approach: (1) that because context is an important determinant of behavior, to maximize ecological validity, behavior should be studied in its natural context; (2) that common distortions in self-report data may be minimized by detailed reports collected with little time delay; and (3) that everyday support, as opposed to support for major life events, warrants attention.

Diary studies provide flexible tools adaptable to diverse research questions. For one, diary methods may render rich descriptive accounts of behavior patterns, such as of support seeking and support provision. Descriptive data are often over-looked in the behavioral sciences, despite their importance, especially in the early stages of research, for documenting the nature and breadth of a phenomenon (Kelley, 1997). For example, diary methods may address such critical basic questions as: When do people desire or seek social support, and when is it offered? To whom do people turn for which types of support, and does this depend on their relationship status? To what extent, and under what conditions, do the perspectives of help seekers and potential help givers differ?

Daily experience data are also valuable for theory testing, especially when research questions concern the determinants of variations in existing support. Typical diary data are used in one of two ways. First, they may be aggregated across many observations to produce reliable, detailed indexes of experience, usually the frequency, distribution, or average ratings of subjective variables, which may then be related to hypothesized contextual or dispositional factors (e.g., personality, stress, relationship qualities, marital status, involvement in social networks). Second, diary studies enable researchers to explore patterns of variation and co-variation as behavior fluctuates across normal ongoing activity. For example, one might examine associations between end-of-day assessments of social support and the nature of that day's activity (to study correlates of variation over time) or that day's symptoms or physiological function (to study the health consequences of support). Studies of variability across time are rapidly gaining in popularity with the advent and growing accessibility of powerful statistical methods, such as multilevel modeling (also called *hierarchical linear modeling*), for specifying within-person covariation, and sequential analysis, for detecting the impact of prior circumstances on subsequent circumstances. Gable and Reis (1999) review these methods.

Finally, event sampling may also be used to evaluate outcomes of support interventions. Differences in diary reports of social support or involvement before and after an intervention would provide compelling evidence of its effectiveness.

In a typical event-sampling study, participants complete structured reports according to a prearranged schedule. Wheeler and Reis (1991) distinguished three sampling strategies: interval-contingent, signal-contingent, and event-contingent. The relative benefits and limitations of each scheme is discussed in more detail by Reis and Gable (2000).

Interval-contingent

This strategy requires recording at regularly scheduled intervals, most commonly the end of each day. Interval-contingent methods are useful when the behavior in question occurs irregularly and when little distortion is expected from delayed reports. Aggregated data across the record-keeping period are useful for identifying dispositional correlates of support. For example, Emmons and Colby (1995) obtained daily reports of problems and support seeking (instrumental, emotional, and advice) for 21 days. Ambivalence about emotional expression (this measure is discussed earlier in this chapter) was related to lesser support seeking in response to stress. A noteworthy feature of this study is that diary reports of support seeking were validated by peer reports (friends and family) collected at the conclusion of the study.

Interval-contingent, end-of-day diaries are ideally suited for analyzing temporal sequences and their covariates. For example, Repetti (1989) explored the impact of work stress among air traffic controllers on family interaction. Objective measures of workload were obtained for 3 days, along with daily descriptions of social interaction by both spouses. Social withdrawal from spouses was greater on higher stress days, but spousal support lessened the destructive impact of stress. In a study conducted by Caspi, Bolger, and Eckenrode (1987), an urban community sample of 96 women provided daily ratings of stressful events and mood for 28 days. Stress was associated with poorer same-day mood regardless of support. However, social support (measured prior to the study and defined as the number of persons one could rely on when needed) moderated the effect of stress on next-day mood. Under low support, stressful events were associated with poorer mood on the following day. However, this spillover effect was much weaker for women with moderate levels of support, and even reversed for women with high levels of support (i.e., high levels of support increased the likelihood of positive mood on the day following a stressful event). These are the sorts of patterns that single-instance assessments cannot identify.

Signal-contingent

This method, exemplified by the Experience Sampling Method (ESM; Csikszent-mihalyi & Larson, 1984) and the Ecological Momentary Assessment (EMA; Stone, Shiffman, & DeVries, 1999), asks for an immediate report whenever a prompt is received, usually from pagers, preprogrammed wristwatches, or palmtop computers. Signals (usually from 6 to 10 per day) may follow a fixed or random schedule or may be randomized within fixed blocks of time. Signal-contingent recording has two main rationales: First, by eliminating delay between event and report, most distortions in retrospective self-reports are eliminated. Second, randomness in the signaling schedule permits accurate estimation of experience and activity across the entire day. Signal-contingent reports may be less helpful when signals are likely to bypass infrequent events (as is possible for certain types of supportive interactions).

For example, Harlow and Cantor (1995) used a combination of signal-contingent and interval-contingent recording over 15 days. Participants reported their mood and current activity at five random signals per day; that evening, they described those activities along several dimensions, including the presence or absence of an "emotional supporter." Results revealed that the presence of emotional supporters, but not other persons, reduced the impact of stress on long-term well-being. Their study also incorporated several trait-level predictors of emotional support seeking, illustrating how daily event studies can be used in conjunction with dispositional (or relationship quality) measures.

Event-contingent

Event-contingent reports are obtained whenever relevant events, such as a socially supportive interaction or a stressful event, occur. The Rochester Interaction Record (RIR; Reis & Wheeler, 1991), which requires a report whenever a social interaction lasting 10 minutes or longer has occurred, is representative. Like ESM and EMA, the RIR seeks to minimize distortion by obtaining reports immediately after an event; unlike them, the RIR permits delay when recording would be substantially impractical or inconvenient. The prime justification for event-contingent recording is to obtain data about all events that occur, affording detailed, highly specific descriptions of social activity, both generally and subdivided into categories (e.g., same-sex, opposite-sex, best friends, romantic partners; other methods are less likely to provide a sufficient number of reports for less frequent partners). For example, RIR studies have examined variables likely to be central to social support processes (as described earlier) such as amount of interaction, intimacy, satisfaction, emotional tone, help giving, and help receipt. The possibility of differentiating relationships as a function of these variables is particularly relevant for questions about the role of relationship processes in social support (cf., Figure 5.1).

Cutrona (1986) used an interval-contingent protocol similar to the RIR to examine the prevalence of supportive interpersonal behaviors in the presence or absence of stressful life events. A sample of college undergraduates completed a global measure of perceived support (the Social Provisions Scale; SPS) and then, for 2 weeks, kept social contact and end-of-day records describing their five most significant interactions of the day. Four domains of support were assessed: emotional support (expressed caring or concern, listened to confidences); informational support (gave advice, expressed point of view on a problem you were having); self-esteem support (complimented you); and tangible/instrumental support (did something to help solve a problem). An open-ended measure of stressful events (any event that left participants upset for 2 hours or more) was also used.

Informational, self-esteem, and tangible support were significantly more frequent on stressful than nonstressful days; esteem support was equally prevalent. Supportive acts reported on stressful days were expressed concern (95%), listened (81%), gave advice (72%), expressed point of view (63%), gave esteem support (50%), and gave tangible support (12%). Most relevant to the model shown in Figure 5.1 is the obtained link between supportive interaction and general perceptions of social support. On days with at least one stressor, individuals high in perceived support reported receiving more support of all types except tangible assistance and rated their interactions as more helpful; there was no link on nonstress days.

Support provision may also be examined in the context of general socializing. Tidwell, Reis, and Shaver (1996) included two support items in the RIR: I helped/supported other, and Other helped/supported me. Each item was rated on a 7-point scale (1 = not at all, 7 = a great deal). A factor combining these items with two items assessing self-disclosure and other-disclosure was labeled *promotive interaction.* A sample of 125 undergraduate students completed these records for 1 week. Among participants involved in a romantic relationship, interactions with romantic partners were more supportive than interactions with others. Also, attachment style predicted variability in perceived support across interactions. Preoccupied individuals reported the most variability (suggesting hyperreactivity to others), secure individuals described moderate variability, and avoidant individuals experienced the least variability (suggesting avoidance of close relationships).

Commentary on Diary Measures

The primary advantage of event-sampling approaches is their ability to provide detailed, contemporaneous records of ongoing behavior, thoughts, and feelings that maximize ecological validity. With them, support processes can be assessed in natural, spontaneous, and often diverse contexts. Data can be analyzed by temporal sequence, in aggregate or subdivided according to time, situation, or relationships, or in response to specific events and circumstances (Reis & Gable, 2000; Schwartz & Stone, 1998). If both members of a dyad participate, support provision and receipt can be assessed simultaneously and compared, an important but virtually unstudied question.[3] Also, moment-by-moment (or day-by-day) reports of supportive events can be related to more generalized measures to gauge the relative roles of specific interactions and personality predispositions as sources of perceptions of support availability.[4] Diary data also have the major advantage of minimizing distortion due to bias in recollecting, selecting, and summarizing across many events.

Diary methods have disadvantages, too. They are very labor-intensive for researchers and participants, and it is generally difficult to use more than a relatively small number of fixed items. (The rapid development of powerful palmtop computers capable of providing varied item content contingent on prior or current activity minimizes this limitation, however.) Attrition may be high if a protocol is cumbersome or if the data collection period is too long, and participant compliance with scheduling and recording instructions must be explicitly maintained and carefully monitored to ensure validity. (Recent studies [Gable & Reis, 1999; Litt, Cooney, & Morse, 1998] suggest that timeliness cannot be assumed.) Sampling schemes must be designed to capture both a sufficient number and variety of events or time units; diary studies are unlikely to tap rare but important events (e.g., death of a spouse, loss of a job) unless those events are specifically targeted.

These protocols have great potential for addressing questions about the roots of social support in ongoing relational activity, a necessary complement to be-

3. Some researchers have suggested that "visible support"—support about which recipients and providers agree—may actually be less beneficial than "invisible support," which is provided but recipients are unaware of receiving it.

4. For example, this approach was taken by Emmons and Colby (1995), who found a small but significant correlation ($r=.20$) between a five-item composite of daily support over 1 month and global ratings of perceived social support (ISEL).

havioral observation, which, as previously described, is limited to a single, constrained setting (i.e., the observational laboratory) and which does not examine variation across time, contexts, and partners. If it is reasonable to imagine a continuum ranging from global self-reports (subjective evaluations of relatively broad categories or phenomena) to behavioral observation (objective coding of discrete behaviors), event sampling occupies the middle ground.

CONCLUDING COMMENTS

This chapter has reviewed many different measures for assessing social support from the perspective of relationship properties and specific interactions. We have hopscotched our way around this extraordinarily rich and extensive literature to highlight the barest bones of some of the more promising resources available to researchers interested in the interpersonal, transactional roots of social support. For the constructs reviewed, other useful measures exist, some of which will undoubtedly prove to be valuable in particular settings or with particular samples. By necessity, we focused on a relatively selective group of constructs, most of which await further research to clarify their role in the support process. Undoubtedly, many other constructs, variables, and specific interactive behaviors contribute to people's belief that a particular partner is providing, or would provide, social support. All of them can and should be investigated.

Relationship measures not only are useful for studies of social support but also can be invaluable in the design and conduct of interventions. For example, intervention researchers might want to screen participants in terms of predispositional properties (e.g., attachment, rejection sensitivity, emotional expressiveness) that predict who is likely to respond most and least to an intervention (see chapters 6 and 7). Similarly, researchers interested in changing health behaviors such as smoking, nutrition, or diabetes regulation might assess relationship properties (e.g., marital or family adaptation) to help account for the differential impact of interventions, or interventions might be tailored to existing interpersonal circumstances, for example, to provide resources that complement those available in ongoing relationships or to enhance naturally supportive interaction between partners. In other words, interventions (which, after all, are themselves a source of supportive interactions and potential relationships) may be designed to fit an individual's existing interpersonal predispositions and circumstances.

We hope that our review makes plain the remarkable depth and breadth of methods for studying relationships and interactions. We are convinced that their application to the topic of social support offers tremendous potential for enhancing the field's knowledge base. When the construct of social support was first introduced in the 1970s, researchers waxed enthusiastic about the twofold prospects of first identifying and then intervening in social circumstances affecting the onset and course of disease. Nowadays that initial rush of excitement has abated somewhat, although the construct remains as viable as ever. That social support is related to health is no longer questioned; literature reviews unequivocally show that the phenomenon is real and important. Nevertheless, when all is said and done, social support today remains more a promising concept than an established, fleshed-out fact, in large part because of the two great questions that continue to be debated: By what mechanisms does social support influence physical function? And what exactly is social support? The high probability that answers to these questions are more likely to be multifaceted rather than unidimensional does not diminish their fundamental importance to the field's further progress.

This chapter has been dedicated primarily to the second question. In many respects, we see it as the more important, or at least sequentially prior, question, in that mechanisms for a phenomenon cannot be identified and authenticated before its putative causal variable is clearly defined, both conceptually and operationally. We therefore hope this chapter invigorates researchers seeking the interpersonal roots of social support. Indeed, if social support is to deserve the leading adjective "social" in its name—as hypothesized by philosophers from the biblical era to the existentialists, by scientists from Durkheim and James to the many researchers working today, and by popular artists from Irving Berlin and George Eliot to the Indigo Girls and Anne Tyler—its essential character must emerge from something that transpires in the context of interaction between persons engaged in ongoing relationships with each other. Identifying that something—or, as seems more likely, those somethings—depends on sensitive and comprehensive assessments of the qualities of interactions and relationships. No more—but no less either.

REFERENCES

Alexander, J. F. (1973). Defensive and supportive communications in normal and deviant families. *Journal of Consulting and Clinical Psychology, 40*, 223–231.

Alexander, J. F., & Parsons, B.V. (1973). Short-term behavioral intervention with delinquent families: Impact on family process and recidivism. *Journal of Abnormal Psychology, 81*, 219–225.

Applegate, J. L. (1978). *Four investigations of the relationship between social cognitive development and person-centered regulative and interpersonal communication.* Unpublished doctoral dissertation, University of Illinois at Urbana-Champaign.

Applegate, J. L. (1980). Person- and position-centered teacher communication in a day-care center. In N. K. Denzin (Ed.), *Studies in symbolic interaction*, vol. 3 (pp. 59–96). Greenwich, CT: JAI Press.

Applegate, J. L., Burleson, B. R., Burke, J. A., Delia, J. G., & Kline, S. L. (1985). Reflection-enhancing parental communication. In I. E. Sigel (Ed.), *Parental belief systems: The psychological consequences for children.* Hillsdale, NJ: Lawrence Erlbaum.

Argyle, M., & Henderson, M. (1985). *The anatomy of relationships.* London: Penguin.

Armsden, G. C., & Greenberg, M. T. (1987). The Inventory of Parent and Peer Attachment: Relationships to well-being in adolescence. *Journal of Youth and Adolescence, 16*, 427–454.

Aron, A., Aron, E. N., & Smollan, D. (1992). Inclusion of other in the self scale and the structure of interpersonal closeness. *Journal of Personality and Social Psychology, 63,* 596–612.

Aron, A., & Fraley, B. (1999). Relationship closeness as including others in the self: Cognitive underpinnings and measures. *Social Cognition, 17,* 140–160.

Aron, A., & Westbay, L. (1996). Dimensions of the prototype of love. *Journal of Personality and Social Psychology, 98,* 409–429.

Bakeman, R. (2000). Behavioral observation and coding. In H. T. Reis & C. Judd (Eds.), *Handbook of research methods in social and personality psychology* (pp. 138–159). New York: Cambridge University Press.

Barbee, A. P. (1990). Interactive coping: The cheering-up process in close relationships. In S. Duck & R. Silver (Eds.), *Personal relationships and social support* (pp. 46–65). London: Sage.

Barbee, A. P., & Cunningham, M. R. (1995). An experimental approach to social support communications: Interactive coping in close relationships. In B. R. Burleson (Ed.), *Communication Yearbook,* vol. 18 (pp. 381–413). Thousand Oaks, CA: Sage.

Bartholomew, K., Cobb, R. J., & Poole, J. A. (1997). Adult attachment patterns and social support processes. In G. R. Pierce, B. Lakey, I. G. Sarason & B. R. Sarason (Eds.), *Sourcebook of social support and personality* (pp. 359–378). New York: Plenum.

Bartholomew, K., & Horowitz, L. M. (1991). Attachment styles among young adults: A test of a four-category model. *Journal of Personality and Social Psychology, 61,* 226–244.

Batson, C. D. (1991). *The altruism question: Toward a social-psychological answer.* Hillsdale, NJ: Lawrence Erlbaum.

Baumeister, R. F. (1995). Self. In A. S. R. Manstead and M. Hewstone (Eds.), *The Blackwell Encyclopedia of Social Psychology* (pp. 496–500). Cambridge, MA: Basil Blackwell.

Baumeister, R. F., & Leary, M. R. (1995). The need to belong: Desire for interpersonal attachment as a fundamental human motivation. *Psychological Bulletin, 117,* 497–529.

Bellack, A. S., & Hersen, M. (1998). *Behavioral assessment: A practical handbook,* 4th ed. Boston: Allyn and Bacon.

Berscheid, E., & Reis, H. T. (1998). Attraction and close relationships. In D. T. Gilbert, S. Fiske, & G. Lindzey (Eds.), *The handbook of social psychology,* 4th ed., vol. 2 (pp. 193–281). Boston: McGraw-Hill.

Berscheid, E., Snyder, M., & Omoto, A. M. (1989a). Issues in studying close relationships: Conceptualizing and measuring closeness. In C. Hendrick (Ed.), *Close relationships: Review of personality and social psychology,* vol. 10 (pp. 63–91). Newbury Park, CA: Sage.

Berscheid, E., Snyder, M., & Omoto, A. M. (1989b). The Relationship Closeness Inventory: Assessing the closeness of interpersonal relationships. *Journal of Personality and Social Psychology, 57,* 792–807.

Bradbury, T. N., & Pasch, L. A. (1994). *The social support interaction coding system.* Unpublished coding manual, University of California, Los Angeles.

Brennan, K. A., Clark, C. L., & Shaver, P. R. (1998). Self-report measurement of adult attachment: An integrative overview. In J. A. Simpson & W. S. Rholes (Eds.), *Attachment theory and close relationships* (pp. 46–76). New York: Guilford.

Brewer, M. B. (2000). Research design and issues of validity. In H. T. Reis & C. Judd (Eds.), *Handbook of research methods in social and personality psychology* (pp. 3–16). New York: Cambridge University Press.

Brock, D. M., Sarason, I. G., Sanghvi, H., & Gurung, R. A. R. (1998). The perceived acceptance scale: Development and validation. *Journal of Social and Personal Relationships, 15*, 5–21.

Buhrmester, D., Furman, W., Wittenberg, M. T., & Reis, H. T. (1988). Five domains of interpersonal competence in peer relationships. *Journal of Personality and Social Psychology, 55*, 991–1008.

Burleson, B. R. (1984). Age, social-cognitive development, and the use of comforting strategies. *Communication Monographs, 51*, 140–153.

Burleson, B. R. (1985). The production of comforting messages: Social-cognitive foundations. *Journal of Language and Social Psychology, 4*, 253–273.

Burleson, B. R. (1994). Comforting messages: Significance, approaches, and effects. In B. R. Burleson, T. L. Albrecht, & I. G. Sarason (Eds.), *Communication of social support: Messages, interactions, relationships, and community* (pp. 3–28). Thousand Oaks, CA: Sage.

Burleson, B. R., Applegate, J. L., Burke, J. A., Clark, R. A., Delia, J. G., & Kline, S. L. (1986). Communication correlates of peer acceptance in childhood. *Communication Education, 35*, 349–361.

Burleson, B. R., & Samter, W. (1985). Consistencies in theoretical and naive evaluations of comforting messages. *Communication Monographs, 52*, 103–123.

Busby, D. M., Christensen, C., Crane, D. R., & Larson, J. H. (1995). A revision of the dyadic adjustment scale for use with distressed and nondistressed couples: Construct hierarchy and multidimensional scales. *Journal of Marital and Family Therapy, 21*, 289–308.

Cacioppo, J. T., Gardner, W. L., & Berntson, G. G. (1997). Beyond bipolar conceptualizations and measures: The case of attitudes and evaluative space. *Personality and Social Psychology Review, 1*, 3–25.

Campbell, D. T., & Fiske, D. W. (1959). Convergent and discriminant validation by the multitrait-multimethod matrix. *Psychological Bulletin, 56*, 81–105.

Caspi, A., Bolger, N., & Eckenrode, J. (1987). Linking person and context in the daily stress process. *Journal of Personality and Social Psychology, 52*, 184–195.

Cassidy, J., & Shaver, P. R. (1999). *Handbook of attachment: Theory, research, and clinical applications.* New York: Guilford.

Christensen, A. (1988). Dysfunctional interaction patterns in couples. In P. Noller & M. A. Fitzpatrick (Eds.), *Perspectives on marital interaction* (pp. 31–52). Philadelphia: Multilingual Matters.

Christensen, A., & Heavey, C. L. (1990). Gender and social structure in the demand/withdraw pattern of marital conflict. *Journal of Personality and Social Psychology, 59*, 73–81.

Christensen, A., & Walczynski, P. T. (1997). Conflict and satisfaction in couples. In R. J. Sternberg & M. Hojjat (Eds.), *Satisfaction in close relationships* (pp. 249–274). New York: Guilford.

Clark, M. S., & Mills, J. (1979). Interpersonal attraction in exchange and communal relationships. *Journal of Personality and Social Psychology, 37*, 12–24.

Clark, M. S., Ouellette, R., Powell, M. C., & Milberg, S. (1987). Recipient's mood, relationship type, & helping. *Journal of Personality and Social Psychology, 53*, 94–103.

Cohen, S., Sherrod, D. R., & Clark, M. S. (1986). Social skills and the stress-protective role of social support. *Journal of Personality and Social Psychology, 50*, 963–973.

Collins, N. L., & Read, S. J. (1990). Adult attachment, working models, and relationship quality in dating couples. *Journal of Personality and Social Psychology, 58*, 644–663.

Colvin, C. R., Vogt, D. S., & Ickes, W. (1997). Why do friends understand each other better than strangers do? In W. Ickes (Ed.), *Empathy accuracy* (pp. 169–93). New York: Guilford.

Cozzarelli, C., Sumer, N., & Major, B. (1998). Mental models of attachment and coping with abortion. *Journal of Personality and Social Psychology, 74*, 453–467.

Crowell, J. A., Fraley, R. C., & Shaver, P. R. (1999). Measurement of individual differences in adolescent and adult attachment. In J. Cassidy & P. R. Shaver (Eds.), *Handbook of attachment: Theory, research, and clinical applications* (pp. 434–465). New York: Guilford.

Csikszentmihalyi, M., & Larson, R. (1984). *Being adolescent.* New York: Basic Books.

Curran, J. P. (1982) A procedure for the assessment of social skills: The simulated social interaction test. In J. P. Curran & P. M. (Eds.), *Social skills training* (pp. 348–398). New York: Guilford.

Cutrona, C. E. (1986). Behavioral manifestations of social support: A microanalytic investigation. *Journal of Personality and Social Psychology, 51*, 201–208.

Cutrona, C. E. (1996a). Social support as a determinant of marital quality: The interplay of negative and supportive behaviors. In G. R. Pierce, B. R. Sarason & I. G. Sarason (Eds.), *Handbook of social support and the family* (pp. 173–194). New York: Plenum.

Cutrona, C. E. (1996b). *Social support in couples: Marriage as a resource in times of stress.* Thousand Oaks, CA: Sage.

Cutrona, C. E., Cole, V., Colangelo, N., & Assouline, S. G. (1994). Perceived parental social support and academic achievement: An attachment theory perspective. *Journal of Personality and Social Psychology, 66*, 369–378.

Cutrona, C. E., Hessling, R. M., & Suhr, J. A. (1997). The influence of husband and wife personality on marital social support interactions. *Personal Relationships, 4*, 379–393.

Cutrona, C. E., & Suhr, J. A. (1992). Controllability of stressful events and satisfaction with spouse support behaviors. *Communication Research, 19*, 154–174.

Cutrona, C. E., & Suhr, J. A. (1994). Social support communication in the context of marriage: An analysis of couples' supportive interactions. In B. R. Burleson (Ed.), *Communication of social support: Messages, interactions, relationships, and community* (pp. 113–135). Thousand Oaks, CA: Sage.

Cutrona, C. E., Suhr, J. A., & MacFarlane, R. (1990). Interpersonal transaction and the psychological sense of support. In S. Duck & R. Silver (Eds.), *Personal relationships and social support* (pp. 30–45). London: Sage.

Dakof, G. A., & Taylor, S. E. (1990). Victims' perceptions of social support: What is helpful from whom? *Journal of Personality and Social Psychology, 58*, 80–89.

Davis, M. H. (1980). A multidimensional approach to individual differences in empathy. *JSAS: Catalog of Selected Documents in Psychology, 10*, 85.

Davis, M. H., & Kraus, L. A. (1991). Dispositional empathy and social relationships. In W. H. Jones & D. Perlman (Eds.), *Advances in personal relationships* (pp. 75–115). London: Jessica Kingsley.

Davis, M. H., & Kraus, L. A. (1997). Personality and empathic accuracy. In W. Ickes (Ed.), *Empathy accuracy* (pp. 144–168). New York: Guilford.

Davis, M. H., Morris, M. M., & Kraus, L. A. (1998). Relationship-specific and global perceptions of social support: Association with well-being and attachment. *Journal of Personality and Social Psychology, 74,* 468–481.

Downey, G., & Feldman, S. I. (1996) Implications of rejection sensitivity for intimate relationships. *Journal of Personality and Social Psychology, 70,* 1327–1341.

Downey, G., Freitas, A. L., Michaelis, B., & Khouri, H. (1998). The self-fulfilling prophecy in close relationships: Rejection sensitivity and rejection by romantic partners. *Journal of Personality and Social Psychology, 75,* 545–560.

Eisenberg, N., & Miller, P. A. (1987). The relation of empathy to prosocial and related behaviors. *Psychological Bulletin, 101,* 91–119.

Eldredge, D. H. (1999). *Spouses' distress in intensive care units: Influences from attachment theory.* Unpublished doctoral dissertation, University of Rochester.

Emmons, R. A., & Colby, P. M. (1995). Emotional conflict and well-being: Relation to perceived availability, daily utilization, and observer reports of social support. *Journal of Personality and Social Psychology, 68,* 947–959.

Fincham, F., Beach, S., & Kemp-Fincham, S. (1997). Marital quality: A new theoretical perspective. In R. Sternberg & M. Hojjat (Eds.), *Satisfaction in close relationships* (pp. 275–304). New York: Guilford.

Fincham, F. D., & Bradbury, T. N. (1987). The impact of attributions in marriage: A longitudinal analysis. *Journal of Personality and Social Psychology, 53,* 510–517.

Fincham, F. D., & Linfield, K. J. (1997). A new look at marital quality: Can spouses feel positive and negative about their marriage? *Journal of Family Psychology, 4,* 489–502.

Fiske, A. P. (1992). The four elementary forms of sociality: Framework for a unified theory of social relations. *Psychological Review, 99,* 689–723.

Follette, W. C., & Jacobson, N. S. (1985). Assessment and treatment of incompatible marital relationships. In W. Ickes (Ed.), *Compatible and incompatible relationships* (pp. 333–361). New York: Springer Verlag.

Furman, W., & Buhrmester, D. (1985). Children's perceptions of the qualities of sibling relationships. *Child Development, 56,* 448–461.

Gable, S. L., & Reis, H. T. (1999). Now and then, them and us, this and that: Studying relationships across time, partner, context, and person. *Personal Relationships 6,* 415–432.

George, C., Kaplan, N., & Main, M. (1985). *The Berkeley Adult Attachment Interview.* Unpublished protocol, Department of Psychology, University of California, Berkeley.

Gottman, J. M. (1979). *Marital interaction: Experimental investigations.* New York: Academic Press.

Gottman, J. M. (1994). *What predicts divorce? The relationship between marital processes and marital outcomes.* Hillsdale, NJ: Erlbaum.

Gottman, J. M., & Krokoff, L. J. (1989). Marital interaction and satisfaction: A longitudinal view. *Journal of Consulting and Clinical Psychology, 57,* 47–52.

Gross, J. J., & John, O. P. (1997). Revealing feelings: Facets of emotional expressivity in self-reports, peer ratings, and behavior. *Journal of Personality and Social Psychology, 72,* 435–448.

Grotevant, H. D., & Carlson, C. I. (1989). *Family assessment: A guide to methods and measures.* New York: Guilford.

Gully, M. R. (1993). *Sequential analysis of social support elicitation and provision behaviors.* Unpublished doctoral dissertation, University of Louisville.

Halberstadt, A. G., Cassidy, J., Stifter, C. A., Parke, R. D., & Fox, N. A. (1995). Self-expressiveness within the family context: Psychometric support for a new measure. *Psychological Assessment, 7,* 93–103.

Harlow, R. E., & Cantor, N. (1995). To whom do people turn when things go poorly? Task orientation and functional social contacts. *Journal of Personality and Social Psychology, 69,* 329–340.

Hatfield, E., & Sprecher, S. (1986). Measuring passionate love in intimate relations. *Journal of Adolescence, 9,* 383–410.

Hazan, C., & Shaver, P. (1987). Romantic love conceptualized as an attachment process. *Journal of Personality and Social Psychology, 52,* 511–524.

Hazan, C., & Zeifman, D. (1999). Pair bonds as attachments. In J. Cassidy & P. R. Shaver, P. (Eds.), *Handbook of attachment: Theory, research, and clinical applications* (pp. 336–354). New York: Guilford.

Heller, K., & Rook, K. S. (1997). Distinguishing the theoretical functions of social ties: Implications for support interventions. In S. W. Duck (Ed.), *Handbook of personal relationships* (pp. 649–670). New York: Wiley

Hendrick, C., & Hendrick, S. S. (1986). A theory and method of love. *Journal of Personality and Social Psychology, 50,* 392–402

Hendrick, S. (1988). A generic measure of relationship satisfaction. *Journal of Marriage and the Family 50,* 93–98.

Heyman, R. E., Eddy, J. M., Weiss, R. L., & Vivian, D. (1995). Factor analysis of the marital interaction coding system (MICS). *Journal of Family Psychology, 9,* 209–215.

Heyman, R. E., Weiss, R. L., & Eddy, J. M. (1995). Marital interaction coding system: Revision and empirical evaluation. *Behavioral Research Therapy, 33,* 737–746.

Hinde, R. (1997). *Relationships: A dialectical perspective.* East Sussex, England: Psychology Press.

Hobfoll, S. E., Nadler, A., & Leiberman, J. (1986). Satisfaction with social support during crisis: Intimacy and self-esteem as critical determinants. *Journal of Personality and Social Psychology, 51,* 296–304.

Holmes, J. G. (1991). Trust and the appraisal process in close relationships. In W. H. Jones & D. Perlman (Eds.), *Advances in Personal Relationships,* vol. 3 (pp. 57–104). London: Kingsley.

Holmes, J. G., & Rempel, J. K. (1989). Trust in close relationships. In C. Hendrick (Ed.), *Review of Personality and Social Psychology,* vol. 10: *Close Relationships* (pp. 187–220). London: Sage.

Ickes, W., Stinson, L., Bissonnette, V., & Garcia, S. (1990). Naturalistic social cognition: Empathic accuracy in mixed-sex dyads. *Journal of Personality and Social Psychology, 59,* 730–742.

Ickes, W., & Simpson, J. A. (1997). Managing empathic accuracy in close relationships. In W. Ickes (Ed.), *Empathy accuracy.* New York: Guilford.

Ickes, W., & Tooke, W. (1988). The observational method: Studying the interactions of minds and bodies. In S. Duck, D. Hay, S. Hobfoll, W. Ickes, & B. Montgomery (Eds.), *The Handbook of Personal Relationships: Theory, research, and interventions* (pp. 79–97). Chichester, England: Wiley.

Johnson, R. J., Hobfoll, S. E., & Zalcberg-Linetzy, A. (1993). Social support knowledge and behavior and relational intimacy: A dyadic study. *Journal of Family Psychology, 6,* 266–277.

Jones, W. H., Briggs, S. R., & Smith, T. G. (1986). Shyness: Conceptualization and measurement. *Journal of Personality and Social Psychology, 51,* 629–639.

Kelley, H. H. (1983). Analyzing close relationships. In H. H. Kelley, E. Berscheid, A. Christensen, J. H. Harvey, T. L. Huston, G. Levinger, E. McClintock, L. A. Peplau, & D. L. Peterson (Eds.), *Close relationships* (pp. 20–67). New York: Freeman.

Kelley, H. H. (1997). The "stimulus field" for interpersonal phenomena: The source of language and thought about interpersonal events. *Personality and Social Psychology Review, 1,* 140–169.

Kenny, D. A. (1994). *Interpersonal perception.* New York: Guilford.

Kerig, P. K. (1996). Assessing the links between interparental conflict and child adjustment: The conflicts and problem-solving scales. *Journal of Family Psychology, 10,* 454–473.

King, L. A., & Emmons, R. A. (1990). Conflict over emotional expression: Psychological and physical correlates. *Journal of Personality and Social Psychology, 58,* 864–877.

Krokoff, L. J., Gottman, J. M., & Haas, S. D. (1989). Validation of a global rapid couples interaction scoring system. *Behavioral Assessment, 11,* 65–79.

Kunce, L. J., & Shaver, P. R. (1994). An attachment-theoretical approach to caregiving in romantic relationships. In K. Bartholomew & D. Perlman (Eds.), *Advances in personal relationships,* vol. 5: *Attachment processes in adulthood* (pp. 205–237). London: Jessica Kingsley.

Leary, M. R. (1983). Social anxiousness: The construct and its measurement. *Journal of Personality Assessment, 47,* 66–75.

Levenson, R. W., & Gottman, J. M. (1978). Toward the assessment of social competence. *Journal of Consulting and Clinical Psychology, 46,* 453–462.

Litt, M. D., Cooney, N. L., & Morse, P. (1998). Ecological momentary assessment (EMA) with treated alcoholics: Methodological problems and potential solutions. *Health Psychology, 17,* 48–52.

Locke, H. J., & Wallace, K. M. (1959). Short marital adjustment and prediction tests: Their reliability and validity. *Marriage and Family Living, 21,* 251–255.

Markman, H. J., & Notarius, C. I. (1987). Coding marital and family interaction: Current status. In T. Jacob (Ed.), *Family interaction and psychopathology: Theories, methods, and findings* (pp. 329–390). New York: Plenum.

Markus, H. M., & Kitayama, S. (1991). Culture and the self: Implications for cognition, emotion, and motivation. *Psychological Review, 98,* 224–253.

McClintock, E. (1983). Interaction. In H. H. Kelley, E. Berscheid, A. Christensen, J. H. Harvey, T. L. Huston, G. Levinger, E. McClintock, L. A. Peplav & D. R. Peterson (Eds.), *Close relationships* (pp. 68–109). New York: Freeman.

McGonagle, K. A., Kessler, R. C., & Gotlib, I. H. (1993). The effects of marital disagreement style, frequency and outcome on marital disruption. *Journal of Social and Personal Relationships, 10,* 385–404.

Mikulincer, M., Florian, V., & Weller, A. (1993). Attachment styles, coping strategies, and posttraumatic psychological distress: The impact of the Gulf War in Israel. *Journal of Personality and Social Psychology, 64,* 817–826.

Miller, R. S., & Lefcourt, H. (1983). Social intimacy: An important moderator of stressful life events. *American Journal of Community Psychology, 11,* 127–139.

Mills, J., & Clark, M. S. (1994). Communal and exchange relationships: Controversies and research. In R. Erber & R. Gilmour (Eds.), *Theoretical frameworks for personal relationships* (pp. 29–42). Hillsdale, NJ: Erlbaum.

Monroe, S. M., Bromet, E. J., Connell, M. M., & Steiner, S. C. (1986). Social support, life events, and depressive symptoms: A 1-year prospective study. *Journal of Consulting and Clinical Psychology, 54,* 424–431.

Moos, R., & Moos, B. (1986). *Family environment scale manual.* Palo Alto, CA: Consulting Psychologists Press.

Murstein, B. I., Wadlin, R., & Bond, C. F. Jr. (1987). The revised exchange-orientation scale. *Small Group Behavior, 18,* 212–223.

Newcomb, M. D., & Bentler, P. M. (1986). Loneliness and social support: A confirmatory hierarchical analysis. *Personality and Social Psychology Bulletin, 12,* 520–535.

Noller, P., & White, A. (1990). The validity of the Communication Patterns Questionnaire. *Journal of Consulting and Clinical Psychology, 4,* 478–482.

Ognibene, T. C., & Collins, N. L. (1998). Adult attachment styles, perceived social support and coping strategies. *Journal of Social and Personal Relationships, 15,* 323–345.

Olson, D. H. (1991). Commentary: Three-dimensional (3-D) circumplex model and revised scoring of FACES III. *Family Process, 30,* 74–79.

Olson, D. H., McCubbin, H. I., Barnes, H., Larsen, A., Muxen, M., & Wilson, M. (1983). *Families: What makes them work.* Beverly Hills, CA: Sage.

Pasch, L. A., Bradbury, T. N., & Davila, J. (1997). Gender, negative affectivity, and observed social support behavior in marital interaction. *Personal Relationships, 4,* 361–378.

Pasch, L. A., Bradbury, T. N., & Sullivan, K. T. (1997). Social support in marriage: An analysis of intraindividual and interpersonal components. In G. R. Pierce, B. Lakey, I. G. Sarason, & B. R. Sarason (Eds.), *Sourcebook of social support and personality* (pp. 229–256). New York: Plenum.

Pierce, G. R., Sarason, B. R., & Sarason, I. G. (1992). General and specific support expectations and stress as predictors of perceived supportiveness: An experimental study. *Journal of Personality and Social Psychology, 63,* 297–307.

Pierce, G. R., Sarason, I. G., & Sarason, B. R. (1991). General and relationship-based perceptions of social support: Are two constructs better than one? *Journal of Personality and Social Psychology, 61,* 1028–1039.

Prager, K. J. (1995). *The psychology of intimacy.* New York: Guilford.

Reis, H. T. (1994). Domains of experience: Investigating relationship processes from three perspectives. In R. Erber & R. Gilmour (Eds.), *Theoretical frameworks for personal relationships* (pp. 87–110). Hillsdale, NJ: Erlbaum.

Reis, H. T., & Franks, P. (1994). The role of intimacy and social support in health outcomes: Two processes or one? *Personal Relationships, 1,* 185–197.

Reis, H. T., & Gable, S. (2000). Event sampling and other methods for studying daily experience. In H. T. Reis & C. Judd (Eds.), *Handbook of research methods in social and personality psychology* (pp. 190–222). New York: Cambridge University Press.

Reis, H. T., & Patrick, B. C. (1996). Attachment and intimacy: Component processes. In A. Kruglanski & E. T. Higgins (Eds.), *Social psychology: Handbook of basic principles* (pp. 523–563). New York: Guilford.

Reis, H. T., & Shaver, P. (1988). Intimacy as an interpersonal process. In S. W. Duck (Ed.), *Handbook of personal relationships* (pp. 367–389). Chichester, England: Wiley.

Reis, H. T., & Wheeler, L. (1991). Studying social interaction with the Rochester Interaction Record. *Advances in Experimental Social Psychology, 24,* 269–318.

Rempel, J. K., Holmes, J. G., & Zanna, M. P. (1985). Trust in close relationships. *Journal of Personality and Social Psychology, 49,* 95–112.

Repetti, R. L. (1989). Effects of daily workload on subsequent behavior during marital interaction: The roles of social withdrawal and spouse support. *Journal of Personality and Social Psychology, 57,* 651–659.

Riggio, R. E. (1986). Assessment of basic social skills. *Journal of Personality and Social Psychology, 51,* 649–660.

Robin, A. L., & Weiss, J. G. (1980). Criterion-related validity of behavioral and self-reported measures of problem-solving communication skills in distressed and non-distressed parent-adolescent dyads. *Behavioral Assessment, 2,* 339–352.

Rook, K. S. (1998). Investigating the positive and negative sides of personal relationships: Through a lens darkly? In B. H. Spitzberg & W. R. Cupach (Eds.), *The dark side of close relationships* (pp. 369–393). Mahwah, NJ: Erlbaum.

Rusbult, C. E., & Buunk, B. P. (1993). Commitment processes in close relationships: An interdependence analysis. *Journal of Social and Personal Relationships, 10,* 175–204.

Rusbult, C. E., Martz, J. M., & Agnew, C. R. (1998). The investment model scale: Measuring commitment level, satisfaction level, quality of alternatives, and investment size. *Personal Relationships, 5,* 357–392.

Rusbult, C. E. & Van Lange, P. A. M. (1996). Interdependence processes. In E. T. Higgins & A. Kruglanski (Eds.), *Social psychology: Handbook of basic principles* (pp. 564–596). New York: Guilford.

Rusbult, C. E., Verette, J., Whitney, G. A., Slovik, L. F., & Lipkus, I. (1991). Accommodation processes in close relationships: Theory and preliminary empirical evidence. *Journal of Personality and Social Psychology, 60,* 53–78.

Samter, W., Burleson, B. R., & Basden, L. (1989). Behavioral complexity is in the eye of the beholder: Effects of cognitive complexity and message complexity on impressions of the source of comforting messages. *Human Communication Research, 15,* 612–629.

Sandler, I. N., & Barrera, M. (1984). Toward a multidimensional approach to assessing the effects of social support. *American Journal of Community Psychology, 12,* 37–52.

Sarason, B. R., Sarason, I. G., & Gurung, R. (1997). Close personal relationships and health outcomes: A key to the role of social support. In S. Duck (Ed.), *Handbook of personal relationships: Theory, research and interventions,* 2nd ed. (pp. 547–573). Chichester, England: Wiley.

Schaefer, M. T., & Olson, D. H. (1981). Assessing intimacy: The PAIR inventory. *Journal of Marriage and Family Therapy, 7,* 47–60.

Schwartz, J. E., & Stone, A. A. (1998). Strategies for analyzing ecological momentary assessment data. *Health Psychology, 17,* 6–16.

Schwarz, N., Groves, R. M., & Schuman, H. (1998). Survey methods. In D. T. Gilbert, S. Fiske, & G. Lindzey (Eds.), *The handbook of social psychology*, 4th ed., vol. 2 (pp. 143–179). Boston: McGraw-Hill.

Sechrest, L. (1963). Incremental validity: A recommendation. *Educational and Psychological Measurement, 23*, 153–158.

Sharabany, R. (1994). Intimate friendship scale: Conceptual underpinnings, psychometric properties and construct validity. *Journal of Social and Personal Relationships, 11*, 449–469.

Shields, C. G., Franks, P., Harp, J., McDaniel, S., & Campbell, T. L. (1992). Development of the family emotional involvement and criticism scale (FEICS): A self-report scale to measure expressed emotion. *Journal of Marital and Family Therapy, 18*, 395–407.

Simpson, J. A., Ickes, W., & Blackstone, T. (1995). When the head protects the heart: Empathic accuracy in dating relationships. *Journal of Personality and Social Psychology, 69*, 629–641.

Simpson, J. A., Rholes, W. S., & Phillips, D. (1996). Conflict in close relationships: An attachment perspective. *Journal of Personality and Social Psychology, 71*, 899–914.

Skinner, H. A. (1987). Self-report instruments for family assessment. In T. Jacob (Ed.), *Family interaction and psychopathology: Theories, methods, and findings* (pp. 427–452). New York: Plenum.

Skinner, H. A., Steinhauer, P. D., & Santa-Barbara, J. (1983). The family assessment measure. *Canadian Journal of Community Mental Health, 2*, 91–105.

Spanier, G. B. (1976). Measuring dyadic adjustment: New scales for assessing the quality of marriage and similar dyads. *Journal of Marriage and the Family, 38*, 15–28.

Spitzberg, B. H., & Cupach, W. R. (1989). *Handbook of interpersonal competence research*. New York: Springer-Verlag.

Sternberg, R. J. (1997). Construct validation of a triangular love scale. *European Journal of Social Psychology, 27*, 313–335.

Stone, A. A., Shiffman, S. S., & DeVries, M. (1999). Ecological momentary assessment. In D. Kahneman, E. Diener, & N. Schwarz, (Eds.), *Well-being: The foundations of hedonic psychology* (pp. 26–39). New York: Russell Sage.

Tamborini, R., Salomonson, K., & Bahk, C. (1993). The relationship of empathy to comforting behavior following film exposure. *Communication Research, 20*, 723–738.

Thoits, P. A. (1986). Social support as coping assistance. *Journal of Consulting and Clinical Psychology, 54*, 416–423.

Tidwell, M. O., Reis, H. T., & Shaver, P. R. (1996). Attachment, attractiveness, and social interaction: A diary study. *Journal of Personality and Social Psychology, 71*, 729–745.

Trobst, K. K., Collins, R. L., & Embree, J. M. (1994). The role of emotion in social support provision: Gender, empathy and expressions of distress. *Journal of Social and Personal Relationships, 11*, 45–62.

Van Lange, P. A., Rusbult, C. E., Drigotas, S. M., Arriaga, X. B., & Witcher, B. S. (1997). Willingness to sacrifice in close relationships. *Journal of Personality and Social Psychology, 72*, 1373–1395.

Waring, E. M., & Reddon, J. R. (1983). The measurement of intimacy in marriage: The Waring Intimacy Questionnaire. *Journal of Clinical Psychology, 39*, 53–57.

Watson, D., Clark, L. A., & Tellegen, A. (1988). Development and validation of brief measures of positive and negative affect: The PANAS Scales. *Journal of Personality and Social Psychology, 54*, 1063–1070.

Webb, E. J., Campbell, D. T., Schwartz, R. D., & Sechrest, L. (1966). *Unobtrusive measures.* Skokie, IL: Rand McNally.

Weick, K. E. (1968). Systematic observational methods. In G. Lindzey and E. Aronson (Eds.), *The handbook of social psychology,* 2nd ed. (pp. 357–451). Reading, MA: Addison-Wesley.

Weick, K. E. (1985). Systematic observational methods. In G. Lindzey and E. Aronson (Eds.), *The handbook of social psychology,* 3rd ed. (pp. 567–634). New York: Random House.

Weiss, R. L. (1980). Strategic behavioral marital therapy: Toward a model for assessment and intervention. In J. P. Vincent (Ed.), *Advances in family intervention, assessment and theory,* vol. 1 (pp. 229–271). Greenwich, CT: JAI Press.

Weiss, R. L., & Heyman, R. E. (1990). Observation of marital interaction. In F. D. Fincham & T. N. Bradbury (Eds.), *The psychology of marriage: Basic issues and applications* (pp. 87–117). New York: Guilford.

Weiss, R. L., Hops, H., & Patterson, G. R. (1973). A framework for conceptualizing marital conflict: A technology for altering it, some data for evaluating it. In L. D. Handy & E. L. Mash (Eds.), *Behavior change: Methodology concepts and practice* (pp. 309–342). Champaign, IL: Research Press.

Weiss, R. L., & Summers, K. J. (1983). Marital interaction coding system-III. In E. E. Filsinger (Ed.), *A sourcebook of marriage and family assessment* (pp. 85–115). Beverly Hills, CA: Sage.

Wheeler, L., & Reis, H. T. (1991). Self-recording of events in everyday life. *Journal of Personality, 59*, 339–354.

Wiggins, J. S. (1982). Circumplex models of interpersonal behavior in clinical psychology. In P. C. Kendall & J. N. Butcher (Eds.), *Handbook of research methods in clinical* psychology (pp. 183–221). New York: Wiley.

Wish, M., Deutsch, M., & Kaplan, S. J. (1976). Perceived dimensions of interpersonal relations. *Journal of Personality and Social Psychology, 33*, 409–420.

PART III

Social Support Interventions

6

Selecting and Planning
Support Interventions

Benjamin H. Gottlieb

I. Selecting Appropriate Support Strategies
II. Conditions Hospitable to the Introduction of New Ties
   A. When the Existing Social Network Is Impoverished, Drained or Conflictual
   B. When the Existing Social Network Reinforces Undesirable Behaviors or Identities
   C. When the Existing Network Lacks Experiential Knowledge
   D. When Specialized Knowledge and Expert Opinion Are Required
III. Conditions Warranting Intervention within the Natural Network
   A. When the Attainment of Health Goals Strongly Depends on the Behavior of One or More Network Members
   B. When the Existing Network Needs Strengthening to Meet Long-Term, Continuing Support Needs
   C. When the Presenting Problem or Outside Intervention Is Highly Stigmatizing
   D. When There Is a Cultural Gap between the Support Recipient and External Providers
IV. Network and Support Assessment
   A. Identifying and Changing Processes That Mediate Support's Effects
   B. A Framework for Planning Support Interventions: Critical Issue
      1. Characteristics of Support: Dosage
      2. Scope of Support
   C. Characteristics of the Support Recepient
   D. Creating a Hospitable Social Psychological Context
   E. A Final Caution: Do No Harm!
V. Conclusion

Home visitors, mentors, lay telephone counselors, support groups, labor coaches, friendly companions, network restructuring, and therapeutic allies—these represent a sampling of the varied avenues that have been taken by health and human services personnel, as well as intervention researchers, who wish to improve the quantity, quality, durability, or suitability of the support people receive or believe they can gain from others. One scheme for classifying these support strategies organizes them on the basis of two dimensions related to the providers of support: (1) the nature of the provider's relationship to the recipient of support, the primary distinction being between naturally existing and new social ties; and (2) the unit of support, with the distinction being between a dyadic relationship and a larger set of social ties (Gottlieb, 1988). Accordingly, when a nurse-educator is enlisted to make a series of telephone calls to cancer patients for the purpose of providing continuing support and information, the intervention involves the development of support in a dyadic, new relationship context. When a group of family members, relatives, neighbors, and friends is brought together by a social worker to plan ways they can support a family that is struggling with the demands of raising a young child who has a serious developmental disorder, the intervention involves changes in a set of natural social ties.

As different as these initiatives may be in the specific activities they entail and in the outcomes they aim to attain, they are predicated on a corpus of theory and evidence linking social relationships to health and morale. Hence, the challenge facing those planning support interventions is to determine which strategy of altering the social environment or the exchanges that occur among its members is most likely to achieve specific health-related ends, taking into consideration the circumstances, needs, and preferences of the intended beneficiaries. It is by virtue of their emphasis on mobilizing the social environment to meet people's psychosocial needs that support interventions differ from other clinical and community interventions. Unlike traditional psychotherapy, the beneficial effects conferred by support interventions arise from direct interaction with existing or newly introduced primary group members, not from the training, insights, or social learning gained through interaction with a professional practitioner. Instead, professionals who design support interventions assume an indirect role, carefully matching the resources of the social environment to the psychosocial needs of the individual or target group at risk. As revealed in this chapter and the three succeeding chapters, these matches can be effected by planned changes in the structure or composition of the social field, changes in the individuals' attitudes or behavior toward it, or changes in the quality and frequency of interaction between the individual and one or more members of the social network.

This chapter's principal objective is to provide guidance to those planning support interventions regarding the grounds for selecting the appropriate type of intervention strategy and regarding the main elements that should be taken into consideration in designing such interventions. Following on the heels of earlier discussions of support interventions (Gottlieb, 1988; Rook & Dooley, 1985; Vaux, 1988), the chapter addresses the conditions and contexts that call for and preclude particular support strategies and provides a generic framework for designing initiatives that marshal or augment social support. The chapter concentrates on person-centered rather than system-centered initiatives, mainly because so little work has been done on ways of altering the structure and policies of organizations and institutions in order to enhance their occupants' access to or actual receipt of support (see, for examples, Adelman & Frey, 1994; Felner, Ginter, & Primavera, 1982). The chapter is neither a review of the literature on the effects of specific support interventions nor a critical appraisal of the particular maneuvers that have been used in prior interventions. Each of the following three chapters deals with those details. Here, a template is provided for planning ways of optimizing the supportive dimension of people's social worlds to accomplish particular health-related goals, when presented with candidates who have differing needs, participate in different social ecologies, and rely on different ways of handling adversity.

SELECTING APPROPRIATE SUPPORT STRATEGIES

Judicious decisions about appropriate support strategies can be informed by careful assessment of selected features of the social environment in which the target population is embedded, certain personal characteristics of members of that population, and consideration of that population's unmet needs for certain types of support that are hypothesized to promote its health or particular health behaviors. Although such an evidence-based planning approach may seem obvious, it is rarely adopted by those who design support programs. This is because agencies tend to offer only a limited number of service modalities and therefore fit their clients to these services rather than offering the services that suit their clients. For example, most local chapters of the Alzheimer Society offer support groups for family caregivers, despite the fact that some clients already gain support through their contact with other caregivers in their personal networks, while others have no means of transportation to the group meetings or feel uneasy about the prospect of disclosing their personal problems to strangers or listening to strangers talk about their distress. Moreover, because most agencies do not keep records of the number and characteristics of clients who did not accept an invitation to join a support group and of those who dropped out, they do not get feedback about their market penetration and retention; that is, they do not learn how the program refusers and drop-outs differ from the users with respect to their personal characteristics and social networks. In addition, positive evaluations by the relatively small proportion of clients who complete the support group program are likely to encourage the agency to continue to offer this service without recognizing that it is not an acceptable or optimal means of serving many other clients who have unmet needs for support.

A second reason that practitioners do not conduct baseline support network assessments is because they tend to adopt such a singular focus on individual clients or patients that they ignore the wider social ecology's influence on them. Health professionals who have not been trained in family practice often neglect to take into consideration the varied ways in which household members may interfere with the patient's treatment regimen or contradict the physician's advice regarding lifestyle changes in nutrition, exercise, and involvement in employment. Similarly, professionals miss opportunities to boost the effects of their own interventions by enlisting the aid of key associates in the patient's social orbit. For these reasons, and others yet to be addressed, clinicians do not investigate potential network-based sources of or impediments to support but tend to introduce a new social tie—an occupational therapist or nurse-practitioner—as the agent of support.

Yet a third reason that practice is not founded on an initial network and support assessment is that the tools needed to do so have not been widely available. Many of these tools are presented in the first section of this volume. In this chapter, key assessment issues that bear on the planning of support interventions are highlighted, commencing with a consideration of conditions that tip the scale toward either a network-centered support intervention or a strategy of marshaling support from one or more new social ties (Table 6.1). These conditions, summarized in Table 1, are derived from both the basic and intervention research, as well as from discussion with the authors of the three chapters that follow.

CONDITIONS HOSPITABLE TO THE INTRODUCTION OF NEW TIES

Each of the following points suggests the advisability of planning a program in which one or more new social ties are introduced as sources of support.

When the Existing Social Network Is Impoverished, Drained, or Conflictual

Individuals who are lonely or socially isolated because they inhabit a sparsely populated network or a network in which the members compete for scarce resources rather than cooperating and supporting one another would not be appropriate candidates for an intervention involving the mobilization of support from their social field unless a great deal of effort is expended on initial network development. For example, friendly visitors are routinely deployed in nursing homes because the residents are usually too needy or impaired to meet one another's supportive needs. Similarly, people who live in chronically stressful circumstances or suffer from relatively enduring health problems may be unable to

Table 6.1. Conditions Warranting Two Types of Support Interventions

Conditions Warranting the Introduction of New Ties
When the existing social network is impoverished, drained, or conflictual
When the existing social network reinforces undesirable behaviors or identities
When the existing network lacks experiential knowledge
When specialized knowledge and expert opinion are required
Conditions Warranting Intervention within the Natural Network
When the attainment of health goals strongly depends on the behavior of one or more network members
When the existing network needs strengthening to meet long-term, continuing support needs
When the presenting problem or outside intervention is highly stigmatizing
When there is a cultural gap between the support recipient and external providers

enlist the practical help and emotional support of their associates if the latter are preoccupied with their own stressors, suffer from chronic resource impoverishment, or feel overtaxed and drained by their past efforts to provide such aid.

There are also circumstances in which people cannot maintain their social ties because of the constraints imposed by a stressful event or life difficulty. For example, efforts to weave supportive personal networks among individuals who have chronic psychiatric problems are stymied by frequent rehospitalizations and housing changes that disrupt patterns of interaction. In addition, some life events have radiating effects on network members that undermine their ability to render needed support, either because they are preoccupied with their own problems or because they have determined that their associate is to blame for the event's occurrence and therefore undeserving of their support. For example, people often make harsh judgments of individuals who are involved in a divorce, those who have been accused of a criminal offense, or those who have worked so hard and long on their jobs as to incur a serious health crisis and then withhold or withdraw support to convey their disapproval. In short, when network members make derogatory attributions for stressful events, it is unlikely that they can summon the compassion needed to contribute to a support intervention.

When the Existing Social Network Reinforces Undesirable Behaviors or Identities

When people undergo stressful life events and role transitions, they typically orient themselves to and seek out similar peers who are able to help them integrate their new identities. This is clearly illustrated among couples who are anticipating or actually undergoing the transition to first-time parenthood. Gradually, their point of social reference changes from network members who do not share their life change to couples and family members who do (Gottlieb & Pancer, 1988). Through parent education and birth preparation classes, they recruit other couples who are launching their families, while also selectively intensifying their interactions with couples they already know through employment, voluntary associations, and neighborhood affiliations. Couples who do not have these contacts within their networks or whose associates do not demonstrate desirable or effective role performance are suitable candidates for interventions that import support from the wider community.

Other examples of people who may wish to shed or deemphasize former identities but cannot do so because of their network's reinforcement of those identities are young widows whose networks continue to reinforce their former marital and domestic roles long after the death of their spouses (Hirsch, 1980), and individuals who are returning to their network after lengthy periods of incarceration in prison or institutionalization in a mental hospital. Similarly, recent retirees who are among the first in their social network to leave the workforce are likely to have more trouble integrating their new identity without access to new associates who are also retired, as is the case for people who are returning to school or higher education in midlife (Suitor, 1987). For people experiencing these and other "off-time" life changes, such as delayed marriage or childbearing and early involvement in caregiving to elderly relatives, the prospects for identifying natural network members who can provide identity-relevant support (Thoits, 1985) are dim. Hence, it is more appropriate to graft one or more new ties onto their network.

The same logic applies to individuals who wish to make certain kinds of behavioral changes but participate in social networks that block or undermine these goals. The most familiar illustrations come from the addictions and health behavior fields, where it has been found that key network members reinforce self-injurious, unhealthful, or deviant behaviors. For example, there is strong and consistent evidence that alcoholics need to repudiate their drinking buddies if they wish to maintain their resolve to moderate their drinking or abstain altogether (Humphreys & Noke, 1997). This is why Alcoholics Anonymous serves as a substitute personal community, encouraging its members to develop personal relationships with one another and offering separate self-help groups, such as Alateen, for the alcoholic's family members. The smoking cessation and weight loss literatures also highlight the importance of efforts to keep people from exposure to social contacts who provide subtle cues for the undesirable habits or from network members who model, encourage, or reinforce these habits (Cohen et al., 1988).

When the Existing Network Lacks Experiential Knowledge

Related to the previous point, when there are few or no network members who have ever experienced the same life event, transition, or stressful circumstances as the intended support recipient, then it is much harder for that individual to gain needed emotional support and information about ways of coping. For example, it is appropriate to introduce one or more new ties when people experience nonnormative events that leave them with few associates with whom they can compare and share the experience. This point is substantiated by Suitor, Pillemer, and Keeton (1995), who examined sources of support reported by women who had recently returned to school after many years of absence and women who had recently become the primary caregivers of an elderly parent. Their findings revealed that experiential similarity was more important than structural similarity in the women's choice of sources of support. Specifically, they found that both immediately after the role transition and 1 year later, both groups of women were significantly more likely to name people in their network who had experienced the same transition as sources of emotional support than to name people who were similar to them on such structural variables as age, gender, and marital status. In addition, people with the same life experiences were less likely to be named as sources of stress than demographically similar network members. The authors conclude that the basis for these patterns of preference is the superiority of the empathy and understanding communicated by those who have walked in the same shoes, along with their superior ability to accept the distress accompanying these life changes.

It follows that program planners should opt for the introduction of new ties when there are no experientially similar peers in the intended beneficiaries' social networks, or at least none who is accessible and acceptable as a source of support from the recipient's perspective. Workplace mentoring programs, such as those described in chapter 8, in which a new recruit or an employee who is being groomed for a senior position is put under the wing of a seasoned veteran, are based on the recognition that there is no one in the protégé's social network who can provide the guidance and support needed to learn the ropes. Similarly, the assignment of home visitors to low-income, teenage mothers is predicated on the assumption, if not the verification through network assessment, that no one in the young mother's life has the experiential knowledge to share with her, much less the knowledge of health issues and resources, needed to serve as an effective source of support. Moreover, for many personal reasons, including their tendency to be judgmental, overbearing, or critical, network members may be unacceptable sources of support to the mother. In addition, the program planners may find these network members unacceptable if they model or encourage maternal practices that are unsafe, unhealthy, or downright neglectful or abusive. A vast literature in the field of child maltreatment testifies to the elevated risk of harm to children whose parents are embedded in such a social milieu (Garbarino & Stocking, 1980).

When Specialized Knowledge and Expert Opinion Are Required

Program planners are also likely to introduce a supporter who comes from outside the natural network when a component of the intervention involves the dissemination and interpretation of highly specialized or technical information that is not likely to be known or well understood by the general public, and when they anticipate that the support recipients will raise many thorny questions and concerns that call for well-informed and judicious responses on the part of the support provider. This is the case in such illness contexts as cancer, heart disease, arthritis, and multiple sclerosis, diseases that are marked by inherent heterogeneity in the patient population, rapid changes in treatment practices, and attendant ambiguity and uncertainty about diagnoses, prognoses, and complications. In fact, in addition to emotional support, health-related interventions typically provide informational support, and although not explicitly articulated, it is likely that information is most effectively learned and used when it is delivered in an emotionally supportive context. For example, based on their review of different types of support interventions for cancer patients, Helgeson and Cohen (1996) conclude that educational interventions produce outcomes superior to interventions that are strictly based on peer group discussions "because patients receive both informational support and informal emotional support" (p. 146). Similarly, as Eckenrode and Hamilton observe in chapter 8, there is increasing recognition of the fact that the instruction offered by home visitors, involving both their coaching and modeling activities, has the strongest effects when the visitor communicates empathic understanding to the intended beneficiary.

Moreover, many interventions have the goal of linking people to community resources that are either unknown to members of their social networks or deemed to be too difficult to access because of logistical or daunting bureaucratic factors. Hence, a home visitor, health educator, or similar individual can serve bridging and service brokerage functions that are not supplied by natural network members (see, for example, Olds et al., 1997). It has also been suggested that the information and personalized counseling provided by an expert supporter can reduce inappropriate and excessive use of costly health services by reducing anxiety and distress, improving cooperation with health care professionals, and promoting adherence to prescribed medical regimens (Devins & Binik, 1996a). More generally, it has been shown that it is the weak or second-order ties in people's networks that afford access to new information, social contacts, and job opportunities (Granovetter, 1973). This suggests that, when the network is small and densely knit, a new tie could be introduced as a strategy of importing novel resources.

CONDITIONS WARRANTING INTERVENTION WITHIN THE NATURAL NETWORK

A second set of conditions warrant initiatives that enlist one or more network members as key support providers. These initiatives either restructure the social field, improve its support-related transactions, or supplement the support provided by a key associate or primary caregiver.

When the Attainment of Health Goals Strongly Depends on the Behavior of One or More Network Members

Recognizing that people in the immediate social environment play a pivotal role in the process of behavior change, undermining, sabotaging, or assisting their associates, those planning interventions have tried different ways of enlisting their support. For example, Cohen et al. (1988) have shown that smoking cessation and its maintenance depend on the expression of a variety of types of support on the part of network members. To this effect, they developed the Partner Interaction Questionnaire, which identifies 61 positive and negative behaviors of the spouses of people who are trying to restrict or quit smoking, and used this classification scheme to train spouses to increase their supportive behaviors. Similarly, in the addictions field, Sobell (1986) has drawn on data concerning the natural resolution of drinking problems and the maintenance of recovery to write a partner support manual that prescribes the ways in which a spouse or another key household member can help an alcoholic associate moderate or kick the habit and avoid relapse. In addition, health professionals have enlisted key network members to act as surrogate therapists with respect to the control of hypertension (Earp & Ory, 1979; Levine et al., 1979), compliance with pediatric anticonvulsive therapy (Shope, 1980), and in-home hemodialysis (Chowanek & Binik, 1982; Lowry & Atcherson, 1984).

When the Existing Network Needs Strengthening
to Meet Long-Term, Continuing Support Needs

With the aging of the population, social policies that favor community care, and the greater prevalence of chronic illnesses and diseases, increased attention has been devoted to shoring up the coping skills and emotional well-being of family members who render around-the-clock care to a loved one. The field of gerontology has seen an explosion of research on the vicissitudes of family care, particularly the care of relatives with probable dementia, along with numerous interventions designed to "support the supporters." These interventions include one or more of the following components: individual counseling, support groups, respite programs, educational information, skills training, and crisis intervention (for a review of initiatives on behalf of caregivers of persons with Alzheimer's disease, see Bourgeois, Schulz, & Burgio, 1996). Similarly, parents of children with severe physical or emotional disabilities and serious medical conditions tend to be encapsulated within the caregiving role, calling for family-and network-centered supportive initiatives that shore up their coping skills and quality of life. One recently created program, Support Clusters, serves families with a child who has a dual diagnosis of both a developmental disability and a mental health condition (Center for Research and Education in the Human Services, 1993). Rather than taking an enhanced service system approach, which was deemed unlikely to result in more durable or robust support for the labeled persons and their families or in meaningful influence and control by the families themselves, the program designers assisted the families to identify significant figures in their existing support network, including both informal sources and professional helpers, invited the latter to an initial orientation meeting to explain the project's general goals and processes and to allow the invitees to decide whether they wished to join the support cluster, and then facilitated a series of cluster meetings devoted to strategies of meeting cluster members' support needs. In its design, this intervention was more responsive to the family's support needs than past initiatives, which placed the onus of identifying, recruiting, and soliciting help from network members on the already burdened families themselves (Schilling, Gilchrist, & Schinke, 1984).

When the Presenting Problem or Outside
Intervention Is Highly Stigmatizing

When people feel disgraced by a stressor, condition, or status and cannot countenance its disclosure to outsiders, efforts should first be made to mobilize support from those in the natural network who are privy to this information. In fact, in most instances, when people are concerned about stigma, they are correct in assuming that other people will avoid or reject them, and so the probability of mobilizing support from sources beyond the network is strongly attenuated. Witness the negative reactions received by people with disfigurements and the disapprobation of individuals who suffer from depression (Coyne, 1976; Notarius & Herrick, 1988).

It is also noteworthy that extra-network intervention can be perceived as stigmatizing if it publicly identifies an individual on the basis of a deficiency, risk status, or disability of some sort. Children who are "red-tagged" on the basis of their risk of school failure; adolescents who are identified as being at risk of early school leaving, unwanted pregnancy, or problems with anger management; and persons who are HIV positive or have AIDS or a sexually transmitted disease are all likely to be highly sensitive to the possibility that their existing problems will be compounded by public revelation. For this reason, if there is no possibility of intervention within their natural networks, then outside intervention may at least minimize potential stigma by adopting a universal approach to program delivery or by delivering support in a social context composed of fellow sufferers. But even the latter tactic may fail to recruit participants if they do not wish their identities to be known to others. For example, in smaller communities, survivors of childhood sexual assault may be reluctant to join a support group because of fear that they will be recognized by someone they know, even though that person is also a survivor.

When There Is a Cultural Gap between the Support Recipient and External Providers

Because the forms and meanings of social support have been found to vary according to gender, ethnicity, and age (Neighbors & Jackson, 1984; Valle & Vega, 1980; Vaux, 1985), it stands to reason that interventions need to be culturally sensitive. They must take into account the influence of cultural blueprints on the structural properties of social networks, their norms about helping, patterns of help seeking, and the very meanings that support takes on. Indeed, from a policy perspective, one of the most appealing aspects of support interventions is their ecological sensitivity and validity, illustrated by the use of informal gatekeepers and voluntary associations among populations that are unserved or underserved by the mainstream institutions of the community. Cultural insiders know that a weight loss program that precludes participation in the Sunday church dinner because the fried chicken is strictly prohibited by the dietitian is destined to fail, and that Friday afternoon workout sessions will be poorly attended by the Jewish stroke survivors because the sessions overlap with the start of the sabbath.

When culture is defined with a small c, it can refer to the mores and norms that are shared by the inhabitants of a particular organization, association, profession, or other social entity. Glidewell, Tucker, Todt, and Cox (1983) investigated the ways in which support was expressed among public school teachers and found that the norms of autonomy, individuality, and equality that are inculcated during the process of their professional socialization made teachers reluctant to exchange support openly and explicitly. Doing so would suggest that one party—the supporter—was superior to the other, thereby violating the rules of the game. Glidewell et al. (1983) found that support was expressed in much more covert and subtle ways, largely through the casual exchange of anecdotes about ways of dealing with troublesome students and parents, lunchroom conversations about curriculum materials that were particularly useful or poorly developed, and the like. In these ways, no one transgressed the unwritten professional norms dictating that teachers should not seek or receive help to meet job-related demands. Anyone planning initiatives designed to strengthen the support in such a milieu would need to appreciate and operate in accordance with these cultural norms and patterns of giving and receiving help.

NETWORK AND SUPPORT ASSESSMENT

Considered together, the preceding factors spotlight those aspects of the social network's structure, internal relationships, and supportive provisions that deserve careful examination to plan appropriate interventions. Logically, this assessment should be conducted in relation to the goals of the intervention so as to make the resulting knowledge as pertinent as possible to the health objectives at hand. Minimally, the ingredients of the assessment should include information about: (1) the respondent's close associates, including household members; (2) the extent to which these associates provide the types of support needed to meet the demands of the stressor or to achieve certain kinds of health-related behavioral change; (3) the extent to which interactions with these associates is marked by conflict, criticism, or other tensions; and (4) the possibility of enlisting the aid of one or more network members for the purpose of intensifying or specializing their support, especially members with similar experience. As the chapters in the measurement section of this book reveal, there are many different tools for obtaining such information. In addition, different formats can be used to collect the information. One approach is to represent the network graphically by placing the respondent in the center of a circle and asking him or her to arrange associates at surrounding distances that signify the closeness of the relationships. Once the network's composition is obtained, the respondent can then provide the interactional and functional information listed previously, along with information about the contexts in which interaction takes place, the extent of experiential similarity, and any other information relevant to the goals of the intervention.

A more penetrating assessment would include collecting baseline data regarding the respondents' current health status or level of functioning and then relating these data to selected social support or social integration measures that are applied at the same time. This approach was adopted in a telephone support intervention developed by Heller, Thompson, Trueba, Hogg, & Vlachos-Weber (1991) on behalf of a sample of isolated elderly women. Prior to the intervention, measures of perceived family and friend support were taken and correlated with measures of loneliness, depression, and morale, revealing that family support had a stronger bearing on mental health than friendship support. Unfortunately, the intervention focused on the introduction of a new friendship tie, partly because a pilot study had spotlighted the importance of friends in moderating loneliness but mainly because the extant literature underscored the unique contribution that friends make to the morale of elderly persons. As the authors observe: "A lesson to be learned from this study is that intervention programs should not be designed relying only on what is known in the extant literature. Data on the role of social ties for the specific intervention sample also are crucial" (Heller et al., 1991, p. 70).

As previously discussed, there are situations in which the aims of the intervention preclude enlisting the support of existing network members and other circumstances in which the goals warrant the mobilization of support from natural associates. For example, there are medical conditions and diseases that require knowledge of complex diagnostic and treatment information, as well as medical services, and that call for judicious consultation with patients about how they wish to proceed. In these instances, emotional support is best rendered in conjunction with highly specialized knowledge that is unavailable to the lay public. Moreover, as chapter 8 point out, a review of home visitation programs revealed that credentialed professionals tend to be more effective as sources of support because of their authoritative knowledge and wide experience, even though a lay person from the beneficiary's network could be trained to provide the necessary information. In contrast, when the behavior of one or more network members is directly implicated in the genesis or maintenance of adverse health or disability or when it serves as a barrier to adaptation or recovery, then it is essential to work with and through the natural network.

Identifying and Changing Processes That Mediate Support's Effects

Implicit in the preceding discussion is the idea that program planners must carefully consider the kinds of support that are needed from particular sources to promote particular health-related ends. This proposition has two interrelated components, each of which has a critical bearing on the design of support interventions. The first component concerns what has been called the matching hypothesis, and the second refers to the mechanisms through which social support affects health outcomes. The matching hypothesis suggests that, by virtue of their relationship to the support recipient, their life experience, and their own resources, different network members specialize in providing different types of support (Cohen & McKay, 1984; Cutrona & Russell, 1990), some making a greater contribution to meeting emotional needs, some satisfying informational needs, and some fulfilling needs for practical aid, including financial assistance and personal services. In their detailed exposition of the matching hypothesis, Cutrona and Russell (1990) divide social support into five basic functions or dimensions: emotional support, social integration, esteem support, tangible aid, and informational support. They also identify several dimensions that underlie stressful life events, such as their controllability, desirability, and duration of consequences. On the basis of their review of a large number of social support studies, they articulate a theory in which certain dimensions of stress arouse particular supportive needs whose satisfaction results in improved health outcomes. For example, they find substantial evidence that uncontrollable events call for increases in emotional support, whereas controllable events arouse needs for instrumental support.

These ideas can be traced onto the preceding guidelines for deciding whether intervention should focus on actors within or outside the natural network. For instance, when the existing network lacks experiential knowledge, it cannot offer the empathic understanding that is needed; therefore, the situation calls for the introduction of new sources of emotional support. Similarly, when the network lacks the specialized knowledge needed to provide an individually tailored expert opinion, an external agent is needed to provide such informational support. Moreover, because some types of support can be provided only by certain categories of network members because of normative patterns of relationship specialization, intervention options are limited to the social network. For example, there is a vast body of evidence revealing that older adults' friends and family members fulfill distinctive support functions; the closest family members (e.g., a parent or romantic partner) provide emotional attachment, and other kin provide personal care, financial aid, and other forms of practical help, whereas friends provide opportunities for socializing and companionship, instilling a sense of belonging (Crohan & Antonucci, 1989; Rook & Schuster, 1996; Weiss, 1974). A corollary finding is that kin make a unique contribution to the maintenance and promotion of physical health, particularly through providing long-term personal care, whereas friends increase the enjoyment and boost the morale of elderly persons through the companionship, social integration, and sense of inclusion they offer. It follows that one category of associate may complement and even supplement the other's functions but cannot substitute for those functions, at least not on a long-term basis. To do so would violate both broadly held norms about family obligations and long-established patterns of interaction and resource exchange within the network.

This overview of the matching hypothesis should help to place in perspective and refine the guideline stating that network-centered intervention is warranted when the existing network needs strengthening to meet long-term, continuing support needs. Specifically, intervention aimed to shore up the physical health of community-dwelling elderly persons should center on enhancing the quality, quantity, or duration of the instrumental aid provided by kin, whereas initiatives devoted to optimizing the morale of older adults should concentrate on promoting the companionate and socially integrative functions of their kith.

Whereas considerations arising from the matching hypothesis call for program planners to assess the kinds of support that are needed and who can best supply them, considerations related to the issue of support's mechanisms involve questions about how support accomplishes its much heralded beneficial effects on health outcomes. Of course, these two issues are inseparable because the beneficial health effects of social support are predicated on changes in particular mediating processes that are largely governed by the unique supportive functions of different network members. This point is clearly illustrated by two nonintervention studies that examined the ways in which the effects of the social support provided by different categories of network members were mediated. Drawing on attachment theory, Stroebe, Stroebe, Abakoumkin, & Schut (1996) found that the effects on depressive symptomatology resulting from the loss of spousal support (due to bereavement) were mediated by increases in emotional loneliness, whereas the support perceived to be available from family members and friends reduced social loneliness but had no significant impact on levels of depression. The second study examined mediation in the context of the frequently observed relationship between parental support and substance use among adolescents. Wills and Cleary (1996) found that the critical mechanisms through which parents' support operated had to do with the promotion of more effective coping through the parents' demonstration of problem-solving skills, discouragement of deviance-prone attitudes, and promotion of academic competence.

More generally, as revealed in the first two chapters of this book, there is abundant theory that can be invoked to identify and test specific pathways through which social support affects health outcomes, morale, quality of life, or role functioning. Chapter 2 sets out six theory-based models of social support's mechanisms of action on health. In addition, Cohen (1988), Stroebe and Stroebe (1996), and Wills and Filer (1999) have described several potential direct and indirect pathways through which social support may affect health. For example, the last authors identify physiological mechanisms, appraisal and reactivity mechanisms, and behavioral mechanisms of action. Stroebe and Stroebe (1996) also organize their discussion of social support's mechanisms of action in terms of their direct or main effects and their stress-buffering or indirect effects on health and morale. They maintain that the two mediators of social support's main effects on health are the network's influence on health attitudes and behaviors and its impact on loneliness, whereas the mediators of support's indirect effects concern the network's role in preventing exposure to stressful life events, moderating stress appraisals, attenuating stress responses, and improving individuals' motivation and ability to cope.

The important point is that these and other potential mediating processes are all candidates for change through the support interventions described in this section of the book. Intervention maneuvers that are informed by these models should be designed to impact the hypothesized mediating processes, and measures that are sensitive to change in these processes must also be included. If support interventions are found to have an effect that cannot be accounted for by one or more of these a priori mediating processes, then it is probable that the mediating processes were incompletely or incorrectly specified, calling for revision or further development of the theoretical model (Baranowski, Lin, Wetter, Resnicow, & Hearn, 1997). In short, the challenge is to design intervention maneuvers that can exert as much impact as possible on the hypothesized mediating processes, the most effective interventions being those that have the greatest impact on the mediating processes.

An example should help clarify this line of reasoning. In one of the most carefully designed and controlled community intervention studies, Heller et al. (1991) randomly assigned a sample of low-income elderly women to an intervention in which they received several weeks of friendly phone calls from a project staff member, followed by a second round of random assignment to weekly telephone support either from that staff member or from another elderly woman who had participated in the first series of telephone contacts. The proximal goal of the intervention was to establish peer telephone dyads, whereas the distal goal was to determine "whether such supportive contacts were effective in maintaining and enhancing health, activity, and morale" (p. 56). As for the mechanisms of action, Heller et al. placed primary emphasis on the psychological benefits that ensue from the bidirectional exchange of support, arguing that the elderly women's morale should improve as a result of their receipt *and donation* of support. Hence, in the second phase of their intervention, they tested the effects of a specific intervening process involving reciprocal peer support transactions and looked for any significant changes in support across each of the intervention periods. The important point of this example is that steps should be taken to examine the extent to which the intervention effects changes in the hypothesized mediating variables. Without doing this, it is impossible to determine why support interventions do or do not attain desired health and behavioral outcomes, much less contribute to emergent theory about social support's mechanisms of action.

A limitation of Heller et al.'s efforts to examine the mediating process is that they adopted what can only be presumed to be a proxy measure of support reciprocity—namely, perceived friendship support—instead of directly assessing the former. Presumably, perceived friend support is strongly correlated with the targeted mediating variable, with an increase in supportive exchanges reflected in heightened perceptions of the telephone partner as a source of support. The results, however, revealed neither an increase in perceived friendship support among any of the intervention groups, whether or not they had been assigned to the peer dyad condition, nor the addition of the peer partners to the study participants' lists of friends. In short, either the intervention failed to affect the hypothesized mediating process or the measures were not sensitive enough to register any effects. As one would expect, the intervention also had null effects on the participants' mental health.

A Framework for Planning Support Interventions: Critical Issue

Table 6.2 sets out a general framework for planning support interventions. It spotlights several of the issues already discussed and others yet to be elaborated. The chapter began by addressing considerations related to the first and third categories, support provider and supportive needs aroused by the stressor, followed by an explication of the importance of drawing on theory and empirical evidence to select and effect change in the mediating processes postulated to promote the health-related ends of the intervention. What remains to be considered are the characteristics of the support that is mobilized and of its recipients.

Characteristics of Support: Dosage

Program planners are faced with decisions about the intensity and duration of the support that is extended to or exchanged among the intended beneficiaries. To date, very little is known about the magnitude of support needed to bring about changes in the processes that mediate support's effects on health and

Table 6.2. A Framework for Planning Support Interventions

Support Provider
    Drawn from existing social network ties
    New ties grafted onto the social network
    Group, dyadic, or combined intervention format
Characteristics of Recipient of Support
    Coping style (receptiveness to support)
    Nature and extent of visible distress
    Relationships needs, skills, and motivation
    Cultural beliefs about and attitudes toward seeking help
Demands and Duration of Stressor
    Identification of specific adaptive challenges
    Changes in demands during different stages of the stress process
    Acute or chronic stressor exposure
Supportive Needs Aroused by the Stressor
    Emotional support
    Tangible support
    Esteem support
    Cognitive guidance
    Companionship and belonging
Processes Mediating Effects of Support
    Identify mediating processes hypothesized to affect health outcomes
    Design intervention component(s) to effect change in mediating processes
Characteristics of Support
    Duration (reliability, commitment, continuity)
    Dosage (quantity, frequency, intensity)
    Mutuality (unidirectional or bidirectional interpersonal process)
    Scope (coverage of supportive needs)
    Directedness (extent to which supportive activities are prescribed)
Intervention Goals
    Process: alter the social environment's structure or supportive transactions
    Proximal effects: demonstrate desired level of change in mediating processes
    Distal effects: demonstrate desired level of change in health status or behavior

whether support shows a dose-response relationship. For example, evidence from the support group literature (see chapter 7) shows that short-term groups, averaging 8 to 10 sessions, do not achieve outcomes comparable to those obtained by longer-term interventions, especially in contexts of chronic or continuing stress. In addition, support group participants consistently express their desire to extend the life of the group, and both those receiving and offering weekly support through home visits tend to express regret when the time comes to terminate their relationship. In fact, chapter 8 cites evidence that the larger the investment of support the visitor makes, the greater the impact on the beneficiary.

The very meaning of social support's dosage is uncertain. When support is defined in functional terms as coping assistance, it is not clear whether dosage means more intense support, such as a half-hour rather than a 10-minute weekly phone call from a nurse to cancer patients undergoing chemotherapy or daily interaction with a confidant, or whether it means a longer duration of support, such as a group for prostate cancer patients that meets for 1 year rather than 2 months. Similarly, when support is defined in terms of social integration or a sense of belonging, dosage may refer to the frequency of participation in voluntary associations, holding office in such associations, the diversity of social roles occupied, or the sheer amount of time spent interacting with network associates. Aside from this quandary, program planners are faced with questions about how much is enough, and the answers are complicated by the fact that individuals differ so much with respect to their supportive needs, their relationship skills, their coping styles, and a host of other personal and situational factors.

Ultimately, program planners need to test and progressively refine various dosages of support, with a criterion being their ability to effect sufficient change in the hypothesized mediating processes, whether they are psychological, emotional, physiological, or behavioral in nature. They also need to recognize that the duration and intensity of the support will differ, depending on the demands of the stressor and on the distal goals of the intervention. Some outcomes require more sustained provision of support than others. For example, a program designed to augment parental support for adolescents at risk of substance abuse is not likely to alter the mediating processes identified by Wills and Cleary (1996) unless it lasts for an extended period of time. After all, the parental support shown by these authors to have protective effects is likely to have developed over many years of interaction. In addition, some stressful life difficulties pose different demands at different stages in their evolution, calling for the intensification of different types of support at different times. Many chronic illnesses oscillate between periods of relative calm and periods of alarm, when extra support is required. Furthermore, there are likely to be major differences across and within target populations in the dosage of support required to effect change in the mediating pathways. For example, it may take a much heftier dose of support to improve the sense of mastery gained by a group of elderly caregivers of persons with dementia than to improve it among a sample of young mothers who are caring for premature babies. Similarly, it may take more persistent support to promote lifestyle changes for a member of a stroke club who has always lived a sedentary life than for a member who has a history of actively exercising.

A final issue concerning dosage applies to programs that introduce one or more new sources of support. In these programs, it is important to monitor the extent of contact that participants have outside the formally scheduled program because these contacts usually represent increased dosages of support that may bear on individual outcomes. Conversely, people who miss support group meetings, cancel scheduled appointments with their home visitor, or terminate their involvement with the program before it concludes will experience a diluted version of the intervention, which may bear on the extent of change they achieve in the mediating processes and distal outcomes. Indeed, selective attrition is one of the factors that complicates comparisons of the impacts of short-term and long-term support interventions. A related reason for the importance of collecting accurate information about dosage is that it allows one to discern whether and how dosage interacts with other personal and contextual variables to affect proximal and distal outcomes. For example, such analyses can disclose how outcomes differ for participants who came to the intervention with relatively high levels of perceived family support and then received relatively limited exposure to the intervention versus those who came with low levels of perceived family support and received full exposure.

Scope of Support

The scope of support is a second characteristic that deserves careful planning. Again, depending on their goals and their existing personal and social assets, candidates for support interventions may need only a single type of support or several types of support. For example, friendly visitors to elderly persons in nursing homes usually concentrate on providing companionship and social activities, whereas psychosocial support programs for people with chronic mental illness tend to provide multiple support functions, including emotional, instrumental, and informational support. Moreover, some initiatives have been designed to sequence different types of support from different sources over time, such as Silverman's (1986) widow-to-widow program, in which a confiding one-to-one relationship is first established between a veteran widow and a recently widowed woman, followed by their participation in a self-help, mutual aid group. Thus, in accordance with the widows' changing support needs, the more intense empathic understanding gained from interaction with the veteran widow is followed by the socially integrative and normalizing functions of the self-help group.

Characteristics of the Support Recipient

To date, relatively little is known about individual differences that predispose people to different types of support interventions or that distinguish between those who benefit most and least from any single intervention approach. For example, in this book's chapter on support groups, the authors observe that people who complete the full series of group meetings may differ in their personalities and coping styles from those who do not accept invitations to join a group and from those who drop out along the way. Similarly, in their critique of programs for the caregivers of persons with dementia, Bourgeois, Schulz, and Burgio (1996) cite a long list of factors that are likely to discriminate between caregivers who benefit more and less from supportive programs, including age, gender, racial and ethnic origin, socioeconomic and cultural status, relationship to the care recipient, type and severity of the patient's disability, and the support they have available in their natural networks.

The basic research on social support reveals that individual differences in the sense of control and self-efficacy, social competence, agreeableness, extraversion, and a generalized sense of acceptance by others that originates in early attachment processes distinguish individuals who tend to have stable and high levels of perceived support from those with consistently low levels of perceived support (Lakey & Lutz, 1996). Clearly, differences in extraversion and in the propensity to view others as responsive to one's emotional needs are likely to come into play in people's decisions about joining a support group and in the benefits they derive from such participation. Moreover, these same dispositional characteristics are likely to affect people's attractiveness to other group members, patterns of social interaction, and the nature and degree of attention received from the group leaders. In addition, in a series of laboratory studies, Lakey and his colleagues found that stable tendencies to view others as more or less supportive affect interpretations of the support rendered by new associates (Lakey & Cassady, 1990; Lakey, Moineau, & Drew, 1992); people who believe that others are not there for them tend to interpret supportive gestures and communications more negatively than people who believe they can count on others' support. Although it is unknown whether these findings generalize to individuals whose life difficulties make them more receptive to input from the environment, the implication is that people who have cognitive schemas of a social world as uncaring and unresponsive to their needs and people who do not have a network orientation to coping (Vaux, Burda, & Stewart, 1986) are unlikely to participate in or benefit from programs that depend on the formation of new supportive ties.

From the preceding, it follows that candidates for certain types of support programs should be screened or directly canvased regarding their preferences for involvement in different formats for obtaining or exchanging support. For example, in a study that exemplifies a careful process of drawing on theory and empirical data to design a support program for families in which a child was bereaved by the death of a parent, Sandler, Gersten, Reynolds, Kallgren, and Ramirez (1988) solicited the families' opinions regarding the acceptability of different potential components, including written and video material, discussions focusing on how to explain death to children and handle their grief, meetings with other bereaved families, face-to-face visits or telephone calls from a "family advisor," and information for parents about more general child socialization issues. They found that the families had distinct preferences; the children but not the parents endorsed the idea of meeting others in the same situation.

Short of directly soliciting the opinions of the intended beneficiaries, it may be feasible to collect baseline information about select personality characteristics and coping styles. For example, recognizing that education is a cornerstone of many intervention programs for patients with chronic diseases, Devins and Binik (1996b) suggest taking measures of their information-processing styles so that programs can be designed to harmonize with these styles. Accordingly, patients who are disposed to avoid threat-relevant information, known as *blunters*, would receive more structured, problem-focused behavioral training, whereas the *monitors*, who tend to seek out information as a way of controlling their anxiety, would receive more expert information about their disease and its treatment and exchange experiential knowledge about their illness with other patients. In sum, if individual differences play a significant role in shaping both perceptions and levels of support, then they are likely to affect both recruitment of people for support interventions and the benefits they derive from participating in such programs.

Creating a Hospitable Social Psychological Context

In discussing the protective effects of social support, Rutter (1987) made the simple yet often underappreciated observation that social support is not a variable but a process. This means that support is not a commodity or resource that can be dispensed by one party to another but an expression of a personal relationship that is characterized by a sense of attachment, intimacy, mutuality, and solidarity. It is relationships that give supportive meaning to behavior, a proposition that is reinforced in both basic and intervention research. For example, in their studies of the bereaved, Lieberman and Videka-Sherman (1986) found that the members of self-help groups who improved the most were those who formed new friendships that were characterized by mutual exchange. Similarly, in discussing why the previously described telephone intervention for elderly women showed no significant increase in perceived friendship support or inclusion of the telephone partners within the circle of friends, Heller et al. (1991) remark that "it is possible that telephone friendships were too limiting, and did not allow sufficient contact for the development of intimacy and mutual sharing" (p. 68). Moreover, the notion that relationships imbue gestures and communications with supportive meaning is verified by evidence of network members' specialization with respect to support (Coyne & DeLongis, 1986), variability in the evaluation of the helpfulness of the same behavior expressed by different categories of associates (Dakof & Taylor, 1990), and the fact that it is impossible to compensate for or replace the support of certain relationships with alternative sources of support (Brown, Andrews, Harris, Adler, & Bridge, 1986).

For those planning support interventions, especially programs that introduce new ties, this means fostering conditions that are hospitable to the development of relationships. It involves creating a program environment that is welcoming rather than stigmatizing, and shaping an interpersonal context that is psychologically attractive by creating opportunities for reciprocity and interdependence, and avoiding the damaging effects on self-esteem of casting one party exclusively and permanently in the roles of help seeker and recipient. Studies of people's reactions to offers of practical help and emotional support reveal that such aid is more likely to be rejected when it threatens the individual's self-esteem and sense of efficacy, when it is perceived to have strings attached to it that limit the individual's degrees of freedom, and when the individual believes that the acceptance of aid will incur a debt to the provider (Fisher, Nadler, & Whitcher-Alagna, 1982). Thus, programs that are universal, capitalize on people's experiential knowledge, and affirm and build on their capacity to be useful to others contain the social psychological preconditions for the formation of relationships.

A Final Caution: Do No Harm!

The literature contains numerous reports of social support that failed to materialize or was expressed in ways that nullified its beneficial effects or actually compounded the recipient's distress. For example, there is evidence that support providers are more likely to fall back on platitudes and self-centered responses and even blame and reject the help recipient when they are unprepared for and unsettled by the nature or intensity of the emotions the support recipient expresses (Howes & Hokanson, 1979; Lehman, Ellard, & Wortman, 1986; Notarius & Herrick, 1988). In addition, deteriorations in support can occur when one or more network members are called on to provide assistance over an extended period of time, to no apparent avail, and when the supporter actually reinforces sick role behavior or is so overprotective and overinvolved as to undermine the recipient's sense of autonomy and control (Coyne & Smith, 1994; Coyne, Wortman, & Lehman, 1988). In addition, research on the relationship between coping and social support reveals that offers of support are contingent on the would-be providers' interpretation and approval of the potential recipient's coping efforts (Dunkel-Schetter, Folkman, & Lazarus, 1987; Silver, Wortman, & Crofton, 1990).

These findings testify to the fragility and vulnerability of the support process and caution program planners to exercise prudence with respect to network members' endurance as support providers, their tolerance of distress, and their ability to resist imposing their own coping style on others. Similarly, when new sources of support are introduced, program planners are challenged to modulate the emotional climate and create a normative structure that minimizes threat and social distance. For example, support group facilitators have the responsibility of ensuring that no one monopolizes discussion, consistently uses the group as a forum to vent distress, or adopts a critical and hostile posture toward other members.

Support interventions can also have adverse consequences for members of the natural network who are not directly involved in the program. As Helgeson and Gottlieb point out in chapter 7, network members may perceive their associate's group participation as an implicit criticism or rejection of their own supportive efforts. This could result in sabotage of the intervention or a complete withdrawal of their support. It behooves program designers to monitor repercussions such as these and to try to avoid them by informing network members about the intervention and explaining the ways in which it complements rather than replaces the network's supportive functions.

Finally, program planners must watch for any negative rebound effects arising from the termination of the support intervention. This is especially important when new ties are grafted onto the network on a temporary basis and when the program beneficiaries are dealing with chronically stressful life difficulties, such as caring for an elderly relative or coping with arthritis. As the chapter on support groups reveals, the participants typically wish to continue meeting with one another after the final formal group session, suggesting that they have continuing needs for support and that more time is required to effect desired levels of change in the processes that mediate the support's effects. The programmatic implications are twofold: that efforts should be made to gauge the durability of intervention effects by taking at least one follow-up reading well after the program's termination and that booster sessions should be considered as a strategy of consolidating any program gains recorded immediately after the program terminates. One mechanism that has been used to prolong the benefits of support groups is to offer the members the opportunity to transform themselves into a self-help mutual aid group and shift the professional's role from facilitator to consultant and troubleshooter.

CONCLUSION

The task of selecting and designing interventions to augment, specialize, or prolong support on behalf of various populations at risk involves numerous decisions about the sources, types, dosage, and timing of the support. In addition, interventions must be guided by a blueprint that specifies how and why particular intervention tactics will alter particular mediating processes that are hypothesized to affect health and psychosocial functioning. In this respect, we are reminded of Lewin's dictum that there is nothing as practical as a good theory because progress toward achieving beneficial effects of support initiatives depends on a clear understanding of the provisions of social relationships that shore up the coping efforts of different people facing different life stressors in different social ecologies. More concerted efforts to compare different types of support strategies (e.g., Cunningham & Tocco, 1989; Telch & Telch, 1986) and to experiment with variations in the format, duration, and social composition of any single strategy are likely to disclose the conditions that optimize desired outcomes. Similarly, more effort needs to be invested in measuring the intervention process, not only to determine whether the maneuvers are faithful to the original script and whether the proposed mediating variables change as expected but also to capture the interpersonal dynamics that work to the detriment and benefit of the support process.

In the future, more thought should be given to ways of altering the structure and policies of community organizations and institutions, as well as work organizations in the private sector, to enhance the support their occupants receive or perceive to be available. For example, system-level changes that make flexible work arrangements available to employees as a way of helping them achieve a healthier balance between their job and family responsibilities have been found to mitigate stress, improve morale, and enhance job performance (Gottlieb, Kelloway, & Barham, 1998). Similarly, efforts to create a workplace culture in which management and coworkers alike exchange support in relation to both job and family demands have reaped considerable rewards (Cooper & Williams, 1994). In addition, by redefining the roles of school personnel such as homeroom teachers so that they develop a more personal relationship with their students and by creating smaller "schools within schools," supportive ties are more likely to be formed. In its report on the structure and functioning of middle schools in the United States, the Carnegie Commission on Adolescent Development emphasized the importance of every child being well known by at least one adult in the school.

Finally, if there is a single message in this and the three following chapters that bears reemphasis, it is that the tasks of selecting, planning, implementing, and evaluating support interventions require careful assessment of a host of personal, social, and contextual factors. As is the case for other intervention strategies, the question is not whether efforts to mobilize support promote health and well-being but whether particular support strategies are best suited to achieving particular health-related ends, given the social and cultural circumstances, needs, and preferences of the intended beneficiaries.

REFERENCES

Adelman, M. B., & Frey, L. R. (1994). The pilgrim must embark: Creating and sustaining community in a residential facility for people with AIDS. In L. R. Frey (Ed.), *Group communication in context: Studies of natural groups* (pp. 3–21). Hillsdale, NJ: Erlbaum.

Baranowski, T., Lin, L. S., Wetter, D. W., Resnicow, K., & Hearn, M. D. (1997). Theory as mediating variables: Why aren't community interventions working as desired? *Annals of Epidemiology, S7*, S89–S95.

Bourgeois, M. S., Schulz, R., & Burgio, L. (1996). Interventions for caregivers of patients with Alzheimer disease: A review and analysis of content, process, and outcomes. *International Journal of Aging and Human Development, 43*, 35–92.

Brown, G., Andrews, B., Harris, T., Adler, Z., & Bridge, L. (1986). Social support, self-esteem, and depression. *Psychological Medicine, 16*, 813–831.

Centre for Research and Education in Human Services. (1993). *Support clusters project: Evaluation report of a research demonstration project*. Waterloo, Ontario: Centre for Research and Education in Human Services.

Chowanek, G. D., & Binik, Y. M. (1982). End stage renal disease (ESRD) and the marital dyad: A literature review and critique. *Social Science and Medicine, 16*, 1551–1558.

Cohen, S. (1988). Psychosocial models of the role of social support in the etiology of physical disease. *Health Psychology, 7*, 269–297.

Cohen, S., Lichtenstein, E., Mermelstein, R., Kingsolver, K., Baer, J. S., & Kamarck, T. W. (1988). Social support interventions for smoking cessation. In B. H. Gottlieb (Ed.), *Social support strategies: Formats, processes, and effects* (pp. 211–240). Newbury Park, CA: Sage.

Cohen, S., & McKay, G. (1984). Social support, stress, and the buffering hypothesis: A theoretical analysis. In A. Baum, J. E. Singer, & S. E. Taylor (Eds.), *Handbook of psychology and health* (Vol. 4) (pp. 253–267). Hillsdale, NJ: Erlbaum.

Cooper, C. L., & Williams, S. (1994). *Creating healthy work organizations*. Chichester, UK: John Wiley.

Coyne, J. (1976). Depression and the response of others. *Journal of Abnormal Psychology, 85*, 186–193.

Coyne, J., & DeLongis, A. (1986). Going beyond social support: The role of social relationships in adaptation. *Journal of Consulting and Clinical Psychology, 54*, 454–460.

Coyne, J., & Smith, D. (1994). Couples coping with myocardial infarction: Contextual perspective on patient self-efficacy. *Journal of Family Psychology, 8*, 43–54.

Coyne, J., Wortman, C., & Lehman, D. (1988). The other side of support: Emotional overinvolvement and miscarried helping. In B. H. Gottlieb (Ed.), *Marshaling social support: Formats, processes, and effects* (pp. 305–330). Newbury Park, CA: Sage.

Crohan, S., & Antonucci, T. C. (1989). Friends as a source of social support in old age. In R. G. Adams & R. Blieszner (Eds.), *Older adult friendships: Structure and process* (pp. 129–146). Newbury Park, CA: Sage.

Cunningham, A. J., & Tocco, E. K. (1989). A randomized trial of group psychoeducational therapy for cancer patients. *Patient Education and Counseling, 14,* 101–114.

Cutrona, C. E., & Russell, D. W. (1990). Type of social support and specific stress: Toward a theory of optimal matching. In B. R. Sarason, I. G. Sarason, & G. R. Pierce (Eds,), *Social support: An interactional view* (pp. 319–366). New York: Wiley.

Dakof, G., & Taylor, S. E. (1990). Victims' perceptions of social support: What is helpful from whom? *Journal of Personality and Social Psychology, 58,* 80–89.

Devins, G. M., & Binik, Y. M. (1996a). Predialysis psychoeducational interventions: Establishing collaborative relationships between health service providers and recipients. *Seminars in Dialysis, 9* (1), 51–55.

Devins, G. M., & Binik, Y. M. (1996b). Facilitating coping with chronic physical illness. In M. Zeidner & N. S. Endler (Eds.), *Handbook of coping* (pp. 640–696). New York: Wiley.

Dunkel-Schetter, C., Folkman, S., & Lazarus, R. S. (1987). Social support received in stressful situations. *Journal of Personality and Social Psychology, 53,* 71–80.

Earp, J. A., & Ory, M. G. (1979). The effects of social support and health professionals' home visits on patients' adherence to hypertensive regimens. *Preventive Medicine, 8,* 155.

Felner, R., Ginter, M., & Primavera, J. (1982). Primary prevention during school transitions: Social support and environmental structure. *American Journal of Community Psychology, 10,* 277–290.

Fisher, J., Nadler, A., & Whitcher-Alagna, S. (1982). Recipient reactions to aid. *Psychological Bulletin, 91,* 27–54.

Folkman, S., Chesney, M., McKusick, L., Ironson, G., Johnson, D. S., & Coates, T. J. (1991). Translating coping theory into an intervention. In J. Eckenrode (Ed.), *The social context of coping* (pp. 239–260). New York: Plenum.

Garbarino. J. & Stocking, H. (1980). (Eds.). *Protecting children from abuse and neglect.* San Francisco, CA: Jossey-Bass.

Glidewell, J. C., Tucker, S., Todt, M., & Cox, S. (1983). Professional support systems. In A. Nadler, J. D. Fisher, & B. M. DePaulo (Eds.), *New directions in helping,* (vol. 3). New York: Academic Press.

Gottlieb, B. H. (1988). Support interventions: A typology and agenda for research. In S. Duck (Ed.), *Handbook of personal relationships* (pp. 519–542). Chichester, UK: John Wiley.

Gottlieb, B. H., Kelloway, E. K., & Barham, L. J. (1998). *Flexible work arrangements: Managing the work-family boundary.* Chichester, UK: Wiley.

Gottlieb, B. H. & Pancer, M. (1988). Social networks and the transition to parenthood. In G. Michaels and W. Goldberg (Eds.), *Current theory and research on the transition to parenthood.* New York: Cambridge University Press.

Granovetter, M. (1973). The strength of weak ties. *American Journal of Sociology, 78,* 1360–1380.

Helgeson, V., & Cohen, S. (1996). Social support and adjustment to cancer: Reconciling descriptive, correlational, and intervention research. *Health Psychology, 15,* 135–148.

Heller, K., Thompson, M. G., Trueba, P. E., Hogg, J. R., & Vlachos-Weber, I. (1991). Peer support telephone dyads for elderly women: Was this the wrong intervention? *American Journal of Community Psychology, 19,* 53–74.

Hirsch, B. J. (1980). Natural support systems and coping with major life changes. *American Journal of Community Psychology, 8,* 159–172.

Howes, M. J., & Hokanson, J. E. (1979). Conversational and social responses to depressive interpersonal behavior. *Journal of Abnormal Psychology, 88,* 625–634.

Humphreys, K., & Noke, J. M. (1997). The influence of posttreatment mutual help group participation on the friendship networks of substance abuse patients. *American Journal of Community Psychology, 25,* 1–16.

Lakey, B., & Cassady, P. B. (1990). Cognitive processes in perceived social support. *Journal of Personality and Social Psychology, 59,* 337–348.

Lakey, B., & Lutz, C. J. (1996). Social support and preventive and therapeutic interventions. In G. R. Pierce, B. R. Sarason, & I. G. Sarason (Eds.), *Handbook of social support and the family* (pp. 435–466). New York: Plenum.

Lakey, B., Moineau, S., & Drew, J. B. (1992). Perceived social support and individual differences in the interpretation and recall of supportive behaviors. *Journal of Social and Clinical Psychology, 11,* 336–348.

Lehman, D., Ellard, J., & Wortman, C. (1986). Social support for the bereaved: Recipients' and providers' perspectives on what is helpful. *Journal of Consulting and Clinical Psychology, 54,* 438–446.

Levine, D. M., Green, L. W., Deeds, S. G., Chualow, J., Russell, R. P., & Finlay, J. (1979). Health education for hypertensive patients. *Journal of the American Medical Association, 241,* 1700–1703.

Lieberman, M. A., & Videka-Sherman, L. (1986). The impact of self-help groups on the mental health of widows and widowers. *American Journal of Orthopsychiatry, 56* (3), 435–449.

Lowry, M. R., & Atcherson, E. (1984). Spouse-assistants adjustment to home hemodialysis. *Journal of Chronic Diseases, 37,* 293–300.

Neighbors, H. W., & Jackson, J. S. (1984). The use of informal and formal help: Four patterns of illness behavior in the black community. *American Journal of Community Psychology, 12,* 629–644.

Notarius, C. I., & Herrick, L. R. (1988). Listener response strategies to a distressed other. *Journal of Social and Personal Relationships, 5,* 97–108.

Olds, D., Eckenrode, J., Henderson, C., Kitzman, H., Power, J. Cole, R., Sidora, K., Morris, P., Pettitt, L., & Luckey, D., (1997). Long-term effects of home visitation on maternal life course and child abuse and neglect. *Journal of the American Medical Association, 278,* 637–643.

Rook, K. S., & Dooley, D. (1985). Applying social support research: Theoretical problems and future directions. *Journal of Social Issues, 41,* 5–28.

Rook, K. S., & Schuster, T. L. (1996). Compensatory processes in the social networks of older adults. In G. R. Pierce, B. R. Sarason, & I. G. Sarason (Eds.), *Handbook of social support and the family* (pp. 219–248). New York: Plenum.

Rutter, M. (1987). Psychosocial resilience and protective mechanisms. *American Journal of Orthopsychiatry, 57,* 316–331.

Sandler, I., Gersten, J. C., Reynolds, K., Kallgren, C. A., & Ramirez, R. (1988). Using theory and data to plan support interventions. In B. H. Gottlieb (Ed.), *Marshaling social support: Formats, processes, and effects* (pp. 53–83). Newbury Park, CA: Sage.

Schilling, R. F., Gilchrist, L. D., & Schinke, S. P. (1984). Coping and social support in families of developmentally disabled children. *Family Relations, 33,* 47–54.

Shope, J. T. (1980). Intervention to improve compliance with pediatric anticonvulsant therapy. *Patient Counseling and Health Education, 3,* 135–141.

Silver, R., Wortman, C., & Crofton, C. (1990). The role of coping in support provision: The self-presentational dilemma of victims of life crises. In B. R., Sarason, I. G. Sarason, & G. R. Pierce (Eds.), *Social support: An interactional view* (pp. 397–426). New York: Wiley.

Silverman, P. R. (1986). *Widow to widow.* New York: Springer.

Sobell, L. (1986). *Description of the social support study.* Unpublished manuscript, Addictions Research Foundation.

Stroebe, W., & Stroebe, M. (1996). The social psychology of social support. In E. T. Higgins & A. W. Kruglanski (Eds.), *Social psychology: Handbook of basic principles* (pp. 597–621). New York: Guilford.

Stroebe, W., Stroebe, M., Abakoumkin, G., & Schut, H. (1996). The role of loneliness and social support in adjustment to loss: A test of attachment versus stress theory. *Journal of Personality and Social Psychology, 70,* 1241–1249.

Suitor, J. J. (1987). Friendship networks in transition: Married mothers return to school. *Journal of Social and Personal Relationships, 4,* 445–461.

Suitor, J. J., Pillemer, K., & Keeton, S. (1995). When experience counts: The effects of experiential and structural similarity on patterns of support and interpersonal stress. *Social Forces, 73,* 1573–1588.

Telch, C. F., & Telch, M. J. (1986). Group coping skills instruction and supportive group therapy for cancer patients: A comparison of strategies. *Journal of Consulting and Clinical Psychology, 54,* 802–808.

Thoits, P. A. (1985). Social support and psychological well-being: Theoretical possibilities. In I. G. Sarason & B. R. Sarason (Eds.), *Social support: Theory, research, and applications* (pp. 51–72). The Hague: Martinus Nijhoff.

Valle, R., & Vega, W. (1980). *Hispanic natural support systems: Mental health promotion perspectives.* Sacramento: State of California Department of Mental Health.

Vaux, A. (1985). Variations in social support associated with gender, ethnicity, and age. *Journal of Social Issues, 41,* 89–110.

Vaux, A. (1988). *Social support: Theory, research, and intervention.* New York: Praeger.

Vaux, A., Burda, P., & Stewart, D. (1986). Orientation toward utilization of support resources. *Journal of Community Psychology, 14,* 159–170.

Weiss, R. S. (1974). The provisions of social relationships. In Z. Rubin (Ed.), *Doing unto others* (pp. 17–26). Englewood Cliffs, NJ: Prentice-Hall.

Wills, T. A., & Cleary, S. D. (1996). How are social support effects mediated? A test with parental support and adolescent substance use. *Journal of Personality and Social Psychology, 71,* 937–952.

Wills, T. A., & Filer, M. (1999). Social networks and social support. In A. Baum & T. Revenson (Eds.), *Handbook of health psychology.* Hillsdale, NJ: Erlbaum.

7

Support Groups

Vicki S. Helgeson
Benjamin H. Gottlieb

   I. What is a Support Group?
  II. Theories Underlying Peer Support Groups
 III. The Effectiveness of Peer Support Groups
  IV. Difficulties of Peer Pressure Groups
      A. Peers Are Expected to Provide Emotional Support
      B. It Is Expected That Expressing Negative Feelings Will Reduce Distress
      C. Peer Groups Provide Opportunities for Members to Help One Another,
         Which Should Enhance One's Own Self-esteem and Benefit Other Group
         Members
      D. Peers Are Expected to Be a Source of Positive Social Comparisons
      E. Identification with the Group Might Interfere with Existing Social Relations
      F. Support Groups May Not Last Long Enough
   V. Optimizing the Style and Effectiveness of Support Groups
      A. What Kind of Support Should Be Provided?
      B. Who Should Attend the Group?
      C. Addressing Specific Pitfalls of Peer Support Groups
         1. The Provision of Emotional Support
         2. The Expression of Feelings
         3. Helper-Therapy Principle
         4. Social Comparisons
         5. Increased Stigma and Adverse Effects on Natural Network Relations
  VI. Future Directions
      A. Outcome Assessment
      B. Alternative Forms of Support Groups
      C. Support Group Participants

In a recent article, Dreher (1997) called for the widespread implementation of psychosocial group interventions for people with cancer, suggesting that the benefits that have been documented are comparable to those observed from a strictly medical intervention, namely, chemotherapy. He also argued that, unlike chemotherapy, psychosocial interventions are at a minimum safe and nontoxic. However, just as one would not interchange two chemotherapeutic agents, one should not place all psychosocial group interventions into the same category. A closer examination of intervention studies for people with cancer, as well as for people facing other chronic and acute stressful life events and transitions, reveals that all intervention studies are not created from a single mold and all are not beneficial. Psychosocial group interventions can take several forms. As we show later, support groups can and should be designed differently for people in different stressful circumstances and for people with different coping styles.

WHAT IS A SUPPORT GROUP?

Peer support groups can be commonly found in the community for stressful life difficulties ranging from serious health conditions, such as cancer or diabetes, to major transitions, such as the death of a loved one, divorce, and new parenthood. Support groups can be distinguished from group therapy on the one hand and from self-help groups on the other hand. In fact, they are a hybrid of the two, employing professionals to impart information, possibly provide group skill training, and guide the group process. Unlike therapy groups, the support group leader does not engage in any clinical practices such as diagnostic assessment or psychological interpretation, nor are members assigned to a group on the basis of a common diagnostic category or prognosis. Support groups differ from self-help groups in that they have a closed membership, involve expert leader(s), usually have a fixed duration, and do not engage in advocacy activities. Support groups share with self-help groups the creation of a peer culture that is based on mutual disclosure, aid, and a sense of belonging that derives from mutual identification. We do not address self-help groups in this chapter for a variety of reasons. First, there is far less uniformity and structure among self-help groups than support groups, and it would be difficult to generalize across self-help groups. Second, from a practical standpoint, it is difficult to gain access to self-help groups because they are anonymous and exclude professionals who would be able to evaluate them from a research perspective.

Support groups capitalize on the similarity among participants' stressful experiences to foster the process of mutual aid. Support groups typically consist of 6 to 12 people who (1) share a similar life stressor, transition, affliction, or noxious habit and (2) receive expert information and/or training and engage in mutual aid to foster improved coping and adjustment (Gottlieb, 1998). Groups vary a great deal in the emphasis leaders place on providing information and guiding the group process, the extent of expert knowledge that is available for dissemination, the members' styles of relating to one another, and a host of other variables. Support groups typically combine education and peer support, although the lines between these two components tend to blur, and neither function is exclusively served by the leader(s) or the participants. For example, new information about the nature of the stressor, its sequelae, or the coping resources it calls for can be supplied by the leader or the participants, drawing on their respective expert and experiential knowledge (Borkman, 1976). Similarly, professionals are free to offer participants praise and encouragement, recognizing that it will have a different meaning and impact than the support offered by coparticipants. Perhaps the key differences between the contributions of the leader and those of the participants concern the extent to which their communications are personalized and affect-laden. Pitched to the group as a whole, the leader's messages tend to be more general and objective in nature, whereas the members' interactions are more personalized, dialogic, and emotionally colored.

Typically, support groups are called for when people find themselves in relatively novel stressful circumstances that occasion uncertainty about appropriate feelings, thoughts, and ways of behaving, and when they lack or desire contact with peers in similar stressful circumstances. The support group serves as a temporary, personal community that supplements or compensates for deficiencies in the participants' natural networks. Members of one's social network may not offer the appropriate support because they lack the experience with the stressful life event, are immersed in their own distress because of the stressor, or are uncomfortable dealing with the stressor. A support group is distinct from a single source of support in that it exposes people to varied ways of reacting to and coping with stressful demands, theoretically leading to a sense of belonging and validation of participants' needs and feelings. It is much more difficult to discount or dismiss collective opinion than the views or experiences of an individual.

From the practitioner's perspective, especially when staffing resources are tight, a group is a more efficient means of service delivery than one-to-one support. Although the "front-end" work of planning the educational material, composing the membership, and working out the logistical arrangements may be time-consuming, once the group is underway it can address the needs of several clients. If a fee for service is required, a group program can also generate more revenue than individual support services.

In this chapter, we examine support group interventions for adults. First, we examine the theories that explain why support groups are expected to be effective in reducing psychological distress and promoting well-being (see column 1 of Table 7.1). Next, we briefly review the literature on the effectiveness of support groups for a wide array of stressful life events, relying heavily on summary papers in several areas. Because these literatures do not provide unequivocal evidence for the benefits of support groups, we examine the difficulties and challenges these groups face (see column 2 of Table 7.1). Then, we suggest how these difficulties can be addressed (see column 3 of Table 7.1). We conclude by touching on several high priority topics for future research on the conduct and outcomes of support groups.

THEORIES UNDERLYING PEER SUPPORT GROUPS

Given the ubiquity of support groups, one would expect that there might be some theoretical basis for their design and intended benefits. Peer support interventions are rarely theoretically derived (Bourgeois & Schulz, 1996; Helgeson & Cohen,

Table 7.1. Why Peer Support Groups Are Expected to Be Effective, Difficulties These Groups Face, and Potential Solutions to Address Difficulties

Theories	Difficulties	Potential Solutions
Peers provide emotional support		
Share experiences	Members do not share experiences	Create homogeneous groups
Understanding		Facilitators draw out similarities
Validation	Members do not understand	
Reduce deviance	Feelings are not validated	Match to at least one member
	Group increases deviance	Screen out the most distressed
	Support is not "perceived"	
Expressing feelings (especially negative ones) is therapeutic	Expressing feelings (especially negative ones) could increase distress	Increased distress may not be a negative outcome
		Longer-term follow-ups
	Expressing feelings is not sufficient to alter distress	End groups on a positive note
		Do not force negative expressions
		Focus on construing meaning
		Focus on how to cope with negative feelings
Helper-therapy principle	The help provided may not be beneficial	Facilitators correct misinformation
	Helping others increases burden	Screen out people from group
Provides opportunities for social comparison	Comparisons are not positive	Monitor social comparisons
Lateral—normalize experience	Lateral—learn experience is unique	Facilitators model social comparisons
Upward—provide role models	Upward—leads to frustration	
Downward—enhance self-esteem	Downward—instill anxiety about own condition	
	Other problems	
	Adverse effects on existing social relations	Integrate network into group
	Duration too short	Lengthen group

1996). Instead, the theory usually follows the development of the intervention (Bourgeois & Schulz, 1996). This is problematic because it is difficult to discern the reasons for one group's positive effect and another group's null or negative effect without a theory that explains the group process.

There is, however, a rationale concerning why support groups should be helpful. The primary rationale is that peers—people facing a similar stressor—are able to understand one another's situation in a way that naturally occurring network members may not. There is evidence that in times of stress, members of one's social network do not always behave positively, partly from a lack of understanding of the stressful experience and partly from feelings of threat. Family members, friends, and other associates of people facing cancer or people who have been victimized by a traumatic event such as rape often discourage expression of feelings, try to distract the person from his or her problems, and force the person to be cheerful because they believe it is harmful for the person to talk about the experience (Coates & Winston, 1983; Dunkel-Schetter, 1984; Peters-Golden, 1982). Network members also withdraw out of fear, lack of knowledge, or discomfort with distress. Network members may minimize a person's difficulties or expect the person to return to normal functioning sooner than he or she is ready to do so (Coates & Winston, 1983), particularly in the case of bereavement (Silver & Wortman, 1980). In the context of family caregiving, network members may not be available to provide support because they are either afflicted with the same burden or they are the source of the stress (i.e., the one who needs care). Many of these problems with network members can be construed as a failure to provide emotional support.

The idea is that peers can compensate for emotional support deficits because they understand the situation and are less likely to behave in the ways just described. Thus, the basis of a peer support group is the shared experience. Because peers face similar challenges, it is assumed that they will understand the situation. Sharing experiences with other people facing a similar stressor is expected to lead to validation, normalization of the experience, a reduction in social and emotional isolation, and a sense of belonging (cancer: Lieberman, 1993; caregiving: Toseland & Rossiter, 1989; parenthood: Cowan & Cowan, 1986; general: Rosenberg, 1984).

The peer support group is distinguished from a strictly educational group by virtue of its emphasis on "experiential knowledge" rather than professional knowledge (Borkman, 1976). By sharing experiences with similar others, group members learn that their reactions are normal and appropriate (Coates & Winston, 1983), even though network members may have suggested otherwise. Many peer support groups exist for people who face a stigma (e.g., parents of special needs children, people with cancer or AIDS, people who have been raped). For these people, the validation provided by peers is thought to normalize the experience and reduce the stigma imposed by society. For example, a woman who has a child with Down syndrome may feel more comfortable when she is in a room with 10 other women who have children with special needs. There is evidence at least among rape victims that the peer support group reduces feelings of deviance (Coates & Winston, 1983). The commonality among group members provides each of them with a unique support system, a group with whom they can gain understanding and to whom they can feel an attachment and a sense of belonging.

An emphasis of the peer support group is sharing feelings and experiences. The assumption is that expressing feelings, particularly negative ones, is therapeutic. However, disclosing feelings about traumatic events must occur in a warm and accepting atmosphere for health benefits to appear (Lepore & Helgeson, 1999; Lepore, Silver, Wortman, & Wayment, 1996). The assumption that disclosure is therapeutic is supported by evidence that expressing feelings about a traumatic event through writing has health benefits. In a number of studies, Pennebaker (Pennebaker & Beall, 1986; Pennebaker, Colder, & Sharp, 1990) had people write about traumatic events, for as little as 20 minutes at a time over a few days, and observed subsequent physical health benefits.

The sharing of experiences and expression of feelings are expected to lead to emotional support. Emotional support involves expressions of caring, encouragement, and reassurance. In a warm and accepting atmosphere, group members are expected to respond to one another's disclosures and problems in positive ways. Group members should offer encouragement when others face difficult decisions and reassurance when others question the appropriateness of their feelings. Over time, personal disclosures should foster feelings of connection to one another. As members form attachments, expressions of caring and concern from the group become a source of emotional support.

Another process by which peer support groups are thought to influence well-being is captured by the helper-therapy principle (Riessman, 1965). By participating in the group, people not only receive help but also have the opportunity to help one another. Helping others instills a feeling of self-efficacy or competence. At a time when self-esteem may be challenged by the stressful event, the opportunity to help other people may increase positive feelings about the self. The expectation is that peers will be able to provide sound advice and useful ideas about ways of coping because they have first-hand experience with the stressor. A woman who is having nausea from chemotherapy may have come up with her own solution to the problem that she can share with the group. The group benefits from this knowledge, and the woman benefits from having helped the group.

Finally, support groups provide opportunities for social comparison. In times of uncertainty or in times of stress, people compare themselves with others to evaluate their feelings and abilities (Festinger, 1954). Comparisons to similar others, or lateral comparisons, may normalize the experience. One learns that others suffer the same problems and share the same hopes, fears, and concerns.

However, people engage in social comparison for reasons other than self-evaluation (Helgeson & Mickelson, 1995). For example, people may compare themselves to one another to improve their situations. Self-improvement is typically accomplished by comparing oneself to a better-off other, an "upward comparison." Upward comparisons, such as someone whose diabetes is better controlled than one's own or someone who begins to date after the loss of a spouse, can be a source of information about how to attain the desired state or a source of inspiration to move forward. Peers are expected to provide positive role models for one another.

People also may compare themselves to one another to make themselves feel better about their situation. Self-esteem enhancement is thought to be accomplished by comparisons to worse-off others, "downward comparisons." Downward comparisons enhance self-esteem by enabling one to feel lucky or fortunate about one's own circumstances in comparison with the worse-off other (Wills, 1981). Downward social comparisons are the most frequently made social comparison under conditions of threat (Bogart & Helgeson, in press; Buunk, Collins,

Taylor, Van Yperen, & Dakof, 1990). In a study of women with breast cancer, Taylor (1983) found that women were able to find some dimension on which they could compare themselves more favorably to other women. For example, a woman with a lumpectomy would compare herself to a woman with a mastectomy, a married woman would compare herself to a single woman, and a younger woman would compare herself to a less physically able older woman.

Thus, the support group provides multiple social comparison functions. Although there is a core of similarity within which group members can evaluate their situations and their responses, there are dimensions on which group members can compare upwardly to inspire self-improvement and downwardly to enhance self-esteem.

In summary, the defining characteristic of the peer support group is the shared experience. A group of people who face a similar stressor convene to share experiences and express feelings. These expressions are expected to reduce feelings of deviance, lead to validation, and provide opportunities for mutual aid. These expressions are also expected to foster a sense of connection so that the group becomes a place where one feels a sense of belonging and where one can receive emotional support. Within the group's core of similarity, the diversity among group members' functioning and experiences is thought to provide useful social comparison information. The information gained from better-off others may help one cope more effectively with the problem, the information gained from similar others may help to normalize the experience, and the information gained from worse-off others can boost self-esteem.

THE EFFECTIVENESS OF PEER SUPPORT GROUPS

Rather than review all of the individual studies that evaluate the effectiveness of a support group for each stressful life event, we rely heavily on the conclusions of literature reviews for some commonly studied stressors. When appropriate and available, we supplement the literature reviews with descriptions of instructive studies.

Helgeson and Cohen (1996) reviewed the literature on group support interventions for people with cancer. They concluded that there was more evidence for the effectiveness of educational interventions or peer discussion interventions that included a formal educational component than peer discussion interventions alone. However, they noted that two studies found positive effects of a peer discussion group on well-being (Kriss & Kraemer, 1986; Spiegel, Bloom, & Yalom, 1981). A noteworthy feature of both studies, which distinguishes them from much of the literature in this area, is the longer duration of the group. Both support groups convened for 1 year. In one of the studies, the effect was dramatic; the support group reduced mortality among women with metastatic breast cancer (Spiegel, Bloom, Kraemer, & Gottheil, 1989). It may not be fair to include this study in the present review, however, because the authors refer to their groups as psychotherapeutic in nature, not as support groups. The support groups may have been closer to group therapy. We return to this distinction later.

Recently, Helgeson, Cohen, Schulz, and Yasko (1999) compared the two components of group support interventions, education versus peer discussion, among women with stage I and II breast cancer. Women were randomly assigned to one of four conditions: education only, peer discussion only, education plus peer discussion, control group. Groups convened for 8 weeks. A major strength of this study is the large number of patients (n = 312) and the large number of groups (28 groups, 7 in each condition). Group education had positive effects on psychological and physical functioning immediately after the intervention ended, and these effects were maintained for 6 months. There were no short-term or longer-term benefits of peer discussion but some evidence of adverse effects of peer discussion, particularly with respect to increasing negative affect.

The educational intervention appeared to be effective because it enhanced self-esteem and body image, while reducing intrusive thoughts about the illness. Because the educational sessions took place in a group context, it is unclear which effects can be attributed to the information and which effects can be attributed to the presence of other women.

The authors speculated as to why peer discussion was not beneficial. First, 8 weeks may not have been long enough for a group of strangers to feel comfortable enough to share personal problems and have those problems addressed. Second, it is possible that the support offered by peer discussion did not match the participants' needs. The women in this study had a relatively good prognosis. People may benefit more from informational support when the stressor is relatively more controllable; people may benefit more from emotional support when the stressor is relatively uncontrollable, as in the case of metastatic disease. The Spiegel et al. (1981) study that found benefits for their peer support intervention involved women with metastatic breast cancer.

A study of men with HIV supports this latter conclusion. In contrast to early stage breast cancer, HIV has a poorer prognosis and may be conceived of as a relatively uncontrollable stressor. Kelly et al. (1993) randomly assigned 68 clinically depressed men with HIV to either an eight-session cognitive-behavioral therapy group where skills were taught, an eight-session social support group that emphasized sharing feelings and problems and encouraging group members to help one another, or a control group. Results showed stronger benefits of the support group intervention than the cognitive-behavioral intervention. Immediately after the groups convened, both interventions resulted in less psychological distress than the control group, but the effects were stronger for the support group than the cognitive behavioral group. At 3-month follow-up, improvements in the two interventions dissipated, but the support group had a larger positive effect than the cognitive-behavioral group. This is one of the few support group interventions to focus exclusively on men. It is not clear whether these findings generalize to heterosexual men.

Research in the caregiving literature also has tended to conclude that support groups are not very effective. This literature, however, rarely compares one kind of support group to another. Lavoie (1995) reviewed the literature on support groups for family caregivers, and Bourgeois and Schulz (1996) reviewed the literature on support groups for caregivers of persons with Alzheimer's disease. Both reviews concluded that the majority of studies show that support groups have little effect on objective measures, even though participants and practitioners typically evaluate the group favorably and report that the group has meaningful benefits. To be fair, many of these studies fail to include standardized instruments to measure objective outcomes. Instead, evaluations of groups are commonly made by the participants of the group and the group leaders; that is, benefits are documented by subjective reports of consumer and leader satisfaction. It is also difficult to evaluate the effectiveness of support groups in the caregiving literature because the studies are plagued by methodological flaws. The majority of studies evaluated in recent reviews do not contain a control group or randomize patients to conditions (Lavoie, 1995; Toseland & Rossiter, 1989).

One exceptionally well-controlled study in the caregiving literature illustrates the divergent findings from relying on objective versus subjective outcomes. Zarit, Anthony, and Boutselis (1987) randomly assigned caregivers of dementia patients to an individual/family counseling intervention, a support group intervention, or a wait-list control group. The goals of both interventions were to increase understanding of the disease, improve coping with problems, and increase use of support. The support group intervention used the group process to accomplish these goals. At the end of the 8-week interventions, all conditions showed improvements on measures of psychological distress and reductions in burden. However, the changes observed in the two intervention groups were not different from the changes observed in the wait-list control group. Group leaders reported that the support groups were more effective than the counseling intervention even though there was no evidence to support this claim. Leaders perceived the support groups to be effective because group members appeared to bond with one another through the sharing of experiences and emotions; that is, the leader took the process rather than the outcome of the group as evidence for its effectiveness.

In contrast, Mittelman et al. (1995) found beneficial effects of a multifaceted randomized intervention on depression among spouse caregivers of Alzheimer's patients. The intervention included six individual and family counseling sessions, followed by a support group that met for an unlimited number of weeks. Assessments were made at 4-month intervals during the first year. Results showed that the intervention group was less depressed than the control group, but the differences were not significant until 8 months after the study began. The authors attributed this positive outcome to the use of a lengthier intervention (i.e., one that matches the length of the stressor), the large number of subjects (n = 206), and the use of a homogeneous group of caregivers (all spouses). Because the intervention included multiple components, it is difficult to determine whether the support group meetings alone were beneficial.

One challenge in creating a peer support group based on the similarity principle is that participants may vary on a host of other dimensions, such as race, age, socioeconomic status, and personality. In the caregiving literature, participants vary on an important dimension—their relation to the patient. Spouses and children have different relationships to the patient and confront different problems.

Interventions that separate these two groups of caregivers have shown stronger benefits (Bourgeois & Schulz, 1996).

Like the caregiving literature, intervention research related to the transition to parenthood has shown that the participants—the parents—report benefits from the group, but there is little objective evidence for the group's effectiveness (Cowan & Cowan, 1986). For example, two studies of support groups for new parents that emphasized supportive exchanges and mutual aid found no differences in well-being among those who did and did not attend the support group (McGuire & Gottlieb, 1979; Wandersman, Wandersman, & Kahn, 1980). By contrast, Cowan and Cowan (1986) did find benefits of a support intervention for new parents, but only by including a longer follow-up assessment. They randomly assigned 24 couples to participate in a weekly group support intervention that lasted for 6 months (3 months before and 3 months after delivery) or a control group. Six months postpartum, they observed some increases in distress and areas of dissatisfaction among intervention participants compared with controls. By 18 months postpartum, however, intervention participants appeared to be better adjusted than controls.

Two other literature reviews lead to dismal conclusions about the benefits of peer support groups. Hughes (1988) reviewed the literature on support groups for those who recently divorced. The support groups were loosely structured and based on some of the informal helping processes that we previously discussed, but they did not include formal counseling or educational components. There was no clear evidence that these support groups facilitated adjustment to divorce. Coates and Winston (1983) reviewed the literature on peer support groups for victims, which included rape victims as well as some of the populations previously described, and found no particular benefits from participation in peer support groups.

When considering these studies and reviews of research, a number of limitations must be noted. First, many of the studies included in literature reviews suffer from serious methodological flaws. Studies fail to include a control group or randomize patients to conditions. Benefits of support groups documented by such studies should be interpreted with caution. Studies also do not always include objective measures of the group's effect. We should be careful not to rely on participants' reports of group satisfaction as the only measure of a group's success. Second, many studies are underpowered to obtain significant effects because of small sample sizes. Third, many studies include an immediate post-test after the groups end but fail to examine longer-term effects. We should also mention that participants in most support interventions are typically white and middle-class (Toseland & Rossiter, 1989) and frequently women, leaving questions unanswered about how to structure and conduct groups for men, minorities, and people of a lower socioeconomic status (Grych & Fincham, 1992). Thus, the extent to which findings generalize to other segments of the population is largely unknown. With these limitations in mind, we now turn to reasons for the relatively weak effects of peer support groups.

DIFFICULTIES OF PEER SUPPORT GROUPS

Given the mixed evidence for the benefits of peer support groups, we must evaluate the problems that such groups face. To do so, we return to the processes by which peer support groups are expected to provide benefits. We examine obstacles to each of these processes (see column 2 of Table 7.1). Then, we identify the conditions under which support groups could be more effective and ways to optimize positive outcomes.

Peers Are Expected to Provide Emotional Support

One particular kind of emotional support peers are expected to provide is validation. However, it is possible that peers will not provide validation. There are two kinds of validation, the validation of experiences and the validation of feelings. Validation of an experience requires that another group member has had the same experience and, hence, can understand it. The more heterogeneous the group, the more likely that the group will face divergent experiences. A person of low income with a health problem may report difficulties with insurance or childcare during physician visits, only to find that other group members do not have these same problems.

Validation of feelings does not require that the experience is shared but that the feelings can be understood. A higher-income person may not be able to validate the lower-income person's experience but can validate feelings by saying, "I understand—that must be really tough." If feelings can be validated, it may not be as important that experiences are not shared. However, it is not the case that feelings are always validated. A recently widowed person may share her difficulties with family members's accepting new dating behavior, only to find that other group members do not understand the person's feelings and side with the family! Thus, people may attend a support group expecting to have experiences and feelings validated, only to learn that group members do not share their experiences or understand their feelings.

One reason that validation may not occur is that all group members are unlikely to respond to the stressful life event with the same level of distress (Coates & Winston, 1983). One person may be having many difficulties and find that everyone else in the group reports few difficulties. Group members could withdraw from a member who is particularly distressed. Other group members may actually have fewer difficult experiences or may feel uncomfortable about disclosing difficulties. In either case, the person who admits difficulties has now had his or her experience and feelings invalidated. The person who is having few difficulties or many difficulties may actually feel more deviant by attending the group.

Peers may reduce the stigma associated with the stressful life event, but participation in the support group in and of itself could be stigmatizing. As group members come to identify with the group rather than with their social network, the group may replace one stigma with another (Coates & Winston, 1983).

Even if peers do provide emotional support, this support is not necessarily perceived by group members. This distinction is important because perceived support has been shown to be more strongly related to well-being than actual received support (Cohen & Wills, 1985; Wethington & Kessler, 1986). Gottlieb (1998) and Lakey and Lutz (1996) suggest that a fundamental flaw of support group interventions is that they are based on support provision rather than support perception. It may be that the structured atmosphere of the peer support group does not convey the same sense of naturally occurring support as do the informal support exchanges among family and friends. We need to consider the factors that influence support perceptions.

A strong determinant of support perceptions is the similarity in attitudes and values between the support provider and support recipient (Lakey, Ross, Butler, & Bentley, 1996). Because a support group is based on similarity, one would expect these groups to lead to perceived support. However, it is not clear which dimensions of similarity are important. Group members may share the same stressor but come from different backgrounds, have different coping styles, and have little else in common. Thus, support group interchanges may not always be perceived as supportive.

It Is Expected That Expressing Negative Feelings Will Reduce Distress

Support groups are supposed to provide a safe haven for the expression of negative feelings. However, expressing such feelings may increase rather than decrease distress, especially among group members who have not previously shared negative feelings. One group member's expression of negative feelings may lead other group members to feel compelled to express negative feelings. The expression of negative feelings could lead to a downward spiral whereby people become more comfortable talking about such feelings and more aware of them, both of which encourage greater discussion of negative feelings (Coates & Winston, 1983). The expression may lead people to perceive themselves to be more distressed than they initially thought they were. According to self-perception theory, we infer our attitudes from our behavior (Bem, 1967). If this process takes place, group members could report greater negative feelings at the end than at the beginning of the group.

It is also possible that expressing negative feelings could increase distress in the short term but decrease distress in the long term. Pennebaker and Beall (1986) showed in a study of college students that writing about a traumatic event for 15 minutes on 4 consecutive days led to an initial increase in blood pressure and distress. But, by 6 months, students who were assigned to the writing condition had fewer visits to the health care center and reported fewer physical health problems than the control group. Recall that Cowan and Cowan (1986) found adverse effects of their couples support group intervention in the first few months but benefits a year later. They suggested that discussing problems may have initially made them more salient but that this initial disequilibrium may have been necessary for long-term benefits to accrue.

Another reason that expressing negative feelings may not reduce distress is that expression of feelings alone is not sufficient to produce the changes in thinking, feeling, or coping with the stressor that are required to influence quality-of-life outcomes. The mere expression of negative feelings might sustain a focus on the problem rather than the solution. Carkhuff (1973) examined the group helping process and noted that convening a group of people to share similar problems, with an occasional insight from a group leader, will leave people with their same problems. He further noted that group members may be disappointed because they expected the group to improve their outcomes. Carkhuff (1973) suggests that support groups will be helpful only to the extent that participants develop skills to cope with the problem for which they are seeking help. The distinction here may be between a support group and group therapy or cognitive-behavioral skills training. According to Rosenberg (1984), the focus of a support group is cohesion and enhancement of self-esteem, whereas the focus of group therapy is problem-solving, an increase in self-insight, and making changes in personality. Thus, it is possible that sharing experiences and feelings is not sufficient to reduce people's distress; in some cases, more intensive therapeutic intervention is needed.

Peer Groups Provide Opportunities for Members to Help One Another, Which Should Enhance One's Own Self-Esteem and Benefit Other Group Members

First, the help a group member provides may not be beneficial; that is, group members may suggest ineffective ways of coping with the stressor or even harmful ways of coping. Although knowledgeable facilitators should be able to prevent group members from exchanging inaccurate information, it is always possible that a group member will prefer a peer's experience over a professional's expertise. Second, helping a group member may boost self-esteem but perhaps at the expense of other personal resources. Helping other people is not without its costs. People who attend a support group may feel burdened by other people's problems, especially if placed in the role of having to provide support.

Peers Are Expected to Be a Source of Positive Social Comparisons

It is likely that peers compare themselves with each other, but these comparisons are not necessarily positive or predictive of positive affect. For example, group members could learn through comparison with similar others that their experience is unique rather than shared. Group members also could discover that they are coping less well than they originally thought. Seeing people in better psychological or physical states may leave participants feeling frustrated rather than inspired. Exposure to people whose situation is worse (i.e., downward comparison) is expected to enhance self-esteem but may instill anxiety and concern over the potential for deterioration. This kind of negative downward comparison was observed in the Helgeson et al. (1999) peer support intervention and partly explained its adverse effect. Thus, not all social comparisons are positive, nor do they all necessarily lead to positive affect.

In addition to the intended peer support group processes going awry, there are other reasons that peer support groups may appear ineffective. We describe two potential problems.

Identification with the Group Might Interfere with Existing Social Relations

One of the premises of the peer support group is that peers compensate for emotional support that is unavailable from network members. The extent to which participation in a peer support group affects relations with the naturally occurring support network is an understudied issue. In a study of women with breast cancer (Helgeson et al., 1999), people who participated in the peer discussion intervention reported an increase in negative interactions with natural network members after the group ended. It is not clear from this finding, however, whether the support group altered women's perceptions of their network or their actual interactions with network members. Support group discussions about relationships with family and friends may have led women to perceive network relations as less supportive than they initially thought them to be, or the group could have adversely affected interactions with network members by excluding network members from the support group. The privacy of the peer group discussions may make family and friends feel more emotionally isolated from the person. Support group participants may turn to the group rather than their family and friends for help. In addition, information obtained from the group may conflict with information from one's social network (Wandersman, 1982). Network members may feel that they are being cast aside in favor of the support group.

Support Groups May Not Last Long Enough

One reason for the lack of effectiveness of peer support groups may be their short duration (Hughes, 1988; Lavoie, 1995). It may be wishful thinking to expect six to eight weekly meetings to change established behavior patterns and lasting psychological states (e.g., anxiety, depression; Lavoie, 1995; Wandersman, 1982). Wandersman (1982) has suggested that a small number of sessions with peers is trivial compared with the duration of past and future interactions with network members. She argues that it is unreasonable to expect peers to replace the existing network or even diminish its influence. Zarit et al. (1987) cited evidence of the need for interventions of longer duration when they observed that half of the participants in their 8-week caregiving intervention study were involved in support groups or receiving counseling 1 year later. Many of the successful peer support groups lasted at least a year (Mittelman et al., 1995; Spiegel et al., 1981). The short-term nature of the support group may be especially problematic in the case of chronic stressors, such as caregiving. Short-term support groups may be more effective for addressing acute stressors or coming to terms with life crises and turning points.

OPTIMIZING THE STYLE AND EFFECTIVENESS OF SUPPORT GROUPS

In this section, we first make some general remarks about the kinds of issues that need to be taken into consideration when designing a support group. Specifically, we address how to decide what kinds of support should be provided in a group context. Then, we discuss who might benefit most from different kinds of support groups. Finally, we make specific suggestions about how to avoid the previously identified pitfalls of support groups.

What Kind of Support Should Be Provided?

Before designing a support group, one should take into consideration the nature of the stressor. Researchers have shown that the most beneficial kind of support must match the needs associated with the stressor (Cohen & McKay, 1984; Cutrona, 1990). Some stressors may be best addressed with informational support, whereas other stressors may be best addressed with emotional support. The severity of the stressor or the phase of the stressor may influence the kind of support needed. For example, women recently diagnosed with breast cancer facing radiation and chemotherapy may benefit most from informational support in the form of coping skills that enable them to deal with the treatment. After the treatment ends, however, women who remain distressed may benefit most from emotional support to help them accept their diagnosis and the uncertainty of the future. Whether the stressor is chronic or acute also should determine the nature of the support intervention. A short-term intervention might be well-suited to an acute problem or to the acute phases of a problem. For example, a short series of sessions could be offered to people with cancer undergoing treatment with the goal of managing treatment-related side effects. After treatment has ended, a longer-duration support group might be offered for people who need to integrate the cancer experience into their lives.

The controllability of the stressor may influence which kind of support is effective and what the emphasis of a support group should be. According to Folkman (1984), problem-focused coping (i.e., trying to alter the stressor) is most effective when the stressor is controllable, and emotion-focused coping (i.e., trying to manage one's emotional reactions to the stressor) is most effective when the stressor is uncontrollable. Support groups that emphasize education and coping skills address problem-focused coping, whereas support groups that emphasize sharing experiences and feelings address emotion-focused coping.

This conceptual distinction is not so easily implemented in practice. Stressors cannot always be divided into "controllable" versus "uncontrollable." There may be multiple dimensions to a given stressor. For example, on the surface, bereavement would seem to be an uncontrollable stressor, meaning that one cannot change the fact that a loved one is lost. However, the loss of a loved one may affect other life domains that are controllable. Financial difficulties or household responsibilities that one faces after losing a spouse may be amenable to control.

Thus, even within a given stressor, one might need to know what aspects of the stressor are the most troublesome before deciding which kind of support would be more beneficial.

Collectively, the studies we have considered prompt some general advice about the content of peer support groups. In general, it would seem best to design support groups that involve informational support provided by experts along with peer support rather than peer support alone. There is very little evidence for the effectiveness of unstructured peer discussion groups that rely on mutual aid, sharing of experiences, and expressions of feelings alone. There is more consistent evidence for benefits of educational groups. At a minimum, one would at least want to combine peer discussion with information.

The chances that peer discussion groups could be effective are increased under one of two conditions. First, peer support groups are more likely to be effective if the duration is long-lasting. Short-term peer discussion groups may only serve to raise issues that are then left unresolved. Longer-term groups not only have the opportunity to resolve issues but also have the opportunity to create lasting bonds among group members. Group members need time to develop the trust and mutual identification required to form the kind of personal relationships that have supportive meaning. With a longer-duration group, the nature of the relationship among group members is more likely to change from peers facing a common stressor to friends; that is, the peers in the group become integrated into one's natural network. Second, peer discussion groups may be more effective when more structure is imposed or when leaders take more active roles in directing the group.

Who Should Attend the Group?

It is important to take into consideration individual difference variables when referring someone to a particular kind of support group. Some people seek information and will respond well to support groups that provide information. Other people avoid information and are distressed when faced with a lot of information; these people may become more distressed if provided with detailed information about their illness, for example (Miller, 1995). Thus, it may be best to turn to the particular individual and ascertain whether he or she is interested in obtaining information, learning coping skills, or listening to other people share similar experiences.

Another variable that may determine whether someone benefits from a support group is the existing support from the natural environment. People who lack support from their existing social network may be more likely to benefit from peer support groups. People who lack emotional support from family and friends may benefit from peer group discussions. People who lack informational support regarding the nature of the stressor (i.e., people with cancer who lack information about their illness, new parents who lack information about how to cope with childcare) may be more likely to benefit from support provided by experts rather than peers.

Support groups, in general, may be most beneficial to people who are most distressed. Wandersman (1982) suggested that support groups for new parents appear to be ineffective because most of the participants are satisfied with their family's functioning at the start of the group. Helgeson, Cohen, Schulz, and Yasko (2000) found that women with breast cancer who had more difficulties were more likely to benefit from any kind of support group—peer discussion or education—than women with fewer difficulties.

Addressing Specific Pitfalls of Peer Support Groups

We now identify ways to avoid some of the previously identified problems with support groups (see column 3 of Table 7.1).

The Provision of Emotional Support

We mentioned that peers are expected to validate one another's feelings and experiences and to provide emotional support, but neither may occur. The opportunity for validation is more likely to occur when group members are homogeneous on key dimensions. The more homogeneous the group, the more likely that peer discussion will lead to understanding, empathy, and mutual help. Research also has shown that homogeneity increases the chances that support is perceived. However, the literature is unclear as to what the key comparison dimensions are. Demographic variables, such as socioeconomic status, age, and gender, bear on the communication style of group members and the rapport established in the group. The nature of the stressor and the time since the onset of the stressor also bear on whether group members can share similar experiences. However, people also may come to the group with quite different backgrounds and situations and find that the group provides a basis for commonality that supercedes all other differences. People of different ages and different races may find that the life stressor they face levels their differences and normalizes their experience.

The fact of the matter is that it is not always practical to design homogeneous groups. For example, it is probably true that younger women who face breast cancer have different needs than older women, and that black women facing breast cancer have different needs than white women, but how likely is it that a community can organize a group for young black women with breast cancer? If group members vary on important dimensions (e.g., severity of their illness, time since the onset of the stressor, relationship to family member), it may be the task of the facilitator to highlight the similarities among group members. It also may be that groups should be constructed so that there is at least one person in the group with whom each member can relate—with whom the person shares key background characteristics (e.g., race, socioeconomic status, severity of disease). This is an issue that has been understudied and deserves more research.

One obstacle to validation is a group in which one member is more or less distressed than everyone else in the group. In the case of more distress, one might consider screening group members ahead of time. Highly distressed individuals should be referred to individual counseling before—or in place of—taking part in the group. Those who are in the midst of an emotional crisis, such as people who have just learned that their cancer has metastasized or people who have unexpectedly lost a loved one, are not in a state of mind that allows them to hear others or render support to them. By the same token, their presence in the group is likely to be distressing to others. A highly distressed individual will not be consoled by the group and may raise other group members' distress levels. In the case of an individual who is relatively less distressed than other group members, one would have to evaluate whether this group member can provide a role model to other members or would detract from the group by negating other members' experiences. Again, a trained facilitator can integrate people's divergent experiences into the group context and provide validation.

The Expression of Feelings

One of the major activities that occurs during a peer support group is the expression of feelings. Concerns have been raised that the expression of negative feelings may be just as likely to increase distress as to decrease distress. First, one might want to consider the possibility that increased distress is not always a negative outcome. One should consider what the goal of the group is and how best to accomplish it. Perhaps the goal of the group is treatment compliance, and increased distress about a problem will motivate compliance. Perhaps the goal of the group is to maintain Alzheimer's patients at home as long as possible, and increasing distress among caretakers is a side effect of this goal. Second, it is also possible that increased distress will be temporary. Longer-term groups and/or longer-term follow-ups of the group will determine whether a temporary increase in distress is offset by a long-term decrease in distress.

There are other precautions to take against raising group members' distress levels. The facilitator could make sure that the group always ends on a positive note so that distress is dealt with in the context of the group and not always taken home as a residual of the group experience. Some group members will be bothered more by the expression of negative feelings than others. The group leader should make sure that people do not feel forced to express negative feelings and allow for expressions of positive feelings. Pennebaker (1993) showed that it is not mere expression of feelings that led to better health outcomes but the making sense of the experience. Thus, a more directive leader could help group members to construe meaning from their experiences rather than just let group members voice expression after expression of negative feelings. The latter kind of group can deteriorate into a series of complaining sessions. The group leader should help group members construe something positive from the experience or to find effective ways of coping with negative feelings.

Helper-Therapy Principle

Peer support groups are supposed to be beneficial because they foster a process of mutual aid and helping can be a source of self-esteem. We identified two difficulties with this process. First, group members may provide information to one another that is harmful. In this instance, it is up to the facilitator to make sure the information is corrected promptly. The facilitator also should follow up with group members to make sure that the correction was understood. Facilitators should have access to resources outside the group, such as other experts who can attend the group or who can contact specific individuals to address areas of concern. Second, helping other people can be a burden to some group members. This may be a case where someone does not belong in a group. The individual who is so distressed that he or she is unable to help other group members may not benefit from a peer support group and may require individual counseling. The group may raise the person's feelings of distress and lead to guilt over witnessing others' distress without being able to offer support. Such a situation should be avoided.

Social Comparisons

We mentioned that peer groups may be a source of negative as well as positive social comparisons. This is a difficult issue to address in any kind of standardized fashion because social comparisons are private cognitions and people may construe the same information differently. However, there may be some people who can be expected to construe social comparisons negatively. For example, Bogart and Helgeson (in press) showed that people with low self-esteem and people with low perceived control report more negative comparisons during the course of a support group. Thus, facilitators might pay extra attention to how those kinds of people are responding to the group process and to other people's experiences.

One way to guard against this problem is to monitor people's social comparisons; that is, find out how group members are responding to one another. Someone, such as a staff psychologist, could be designated as a consultant to the group. Group members would be introduced to this person and told that they can confide concerns about the group to him or her on a regular basis. Better yet, this consultant could periodically solicit feedback from participants about aspects of the group experience. Another solution is to have the facilitator model positive social comparisons in the group, if this does not already occur spontaneously by group members; that is, the facilitator would point out how someone adjusting well to the stressor can be a source of inspiration or point out how people should feel fortunate when seeing someone who is having more severe problems.

Increased Stigma and Adverse Effects on Natural Network Relations

We raised two other difficulties with peer support groups: that peer groups may increase stigma and social isolation and that peer groups may adversely affect interactions with natural network members. The best way to avoid both of these problems is to integrate the natural support network into the group by inviting network members to participate in selected aspects of the group experience. Particularly when the group involves education, the presence of a close family member or friend could be mutually beneficial; there will be two people to absorb and discuss the information. It is not clear whether it is beneficial to invite friends and family members to confidential group discussions. The presence of outsiders might inhibit participants from bringing up distressing experiences, especially if they implicate the family. A study in which cardiac patients were randomly assigned to a patient group, a patient-spouse group, or a control group, found that only the patient group had a significant improvement in self-esteem compared with the control group (Dracup, 1985). The authors found that the presence of spouses altered the nature of the group's discussions. An alternative arrangement is being tested by Lepore, Helgeson, and Schulz (1998) in a study of support groups for men with prostate cancer. Couples listen to an educational lecture together, but husbands and wives convene separately for group discussions. Without violating the confidentiality of the peer group's discussion, group members could share the kinds of issues raised and their thoughts about the group's discussion with network members.

There are, however, circumstances when it may be more prudent to maintain a relatively sharp boundary between the support group and the natural network. In fact, there are stressful contexts in which the goal is to loosen the tight grip of a central figure in the participants' social network. One example is a support group for young adults who have schizophrenia and are enmeshed with a household member who is emotionally overinvolved and highly critical. Another example is a teenager with diabetes whose overprotective parents are unwilling to allow their child to exercise any control over the illness. In these kinds of circumstances, it may be more adaptive for all parties to segregate rather than link the natural and created networks.

FUTURE DIRECTIONS

As mentioned earlier, there are abundant variations in the design, duration, and emphases of support groups that need to be systematically compared in terms of their impact on both the support process and its outcomes. Program planners are advised to more carefully consider and evaluate alternative ways of composing the group, including screening tools to assign people to groups on the basis of their information-processing styles, coping abilities, problem severity, and current distress. There are three other directions for future research that we discuss. First, we should pay greater attention to the outcomes assessed, making sure the outcomes are consistent with the goals of the group. Second, researchers should consider alternative forms of support groups for use when face-to-face contact is difficult. Third, researchers should gather more information on who selects in and who selects out of support groups.

Outcome Assessment

In future research, more attention should be paid to the identification of relevant and realistic outcomes of support groups. More effort needs to be invested in soliciting the input of the intended beneficiaries of support groups regarding outcomes that matter to them. For example, if the voices of family caregivers of persons with dementia were heard, they might hone in on outcomes that bear on the quality of their relationship with their relatives and on their sense that they are doing right by them rather than on outcomes that reflect only their own mental health. In addition, assessment should focus on realistic outcomes. For example, the outcomes that have been adopted in studies of family caregivers of persons with dementia have centered on some combination of depressive affect, anxiety, and anger, with the aim of reducing these emotions. However, from a normative, human perspective, it is entirely appropriate for persons who are losing their loved ones to a pernicious disease to experience depressive affect, anxiety, and a sense of loss. Hence, it is reasonable to ask whether the yardstick for assessing the group's success should be calibrated in units of reduced distress or gauge the extent to which the caregivers are able to understand and accept their distress, as long as it is within a normative range for that stressor and not disabling.

Group processes also need to be measured. Ideally, one could capture them on video or audiotape and then code such features as the nature and degree of emotionality, disclosure, and productive problem solving. The goal of such monitoring and scoring procedures is not only to determine whether the support group was implemented in a manner that is faithful to its blueprint (program fidelity), but also to relate proximal and distal outcomes to these group processes. At the level of individual group members, it would be instructive to relate these processes to their actual exchanges of support as well as their perceptions of support. In this way, we can begin to learn which group processes give rise to the psychological sense of support.

The social comparison process is integral to support groups but rarely assessed. Little is known about its operation over the course of the group. It would be particularly illuminating to conduct periodic assessments of the extent to which members perceive themselves to be in similar stressful predicaments, the extent to which contact reduces uncertainty about feelings and cognitions, and the extent to which contact with others is fear arousing versus inspiring. Because social comparison is largely a private process, observation cannot substitute for direct canvasing of group members' views of these processes.

Alternative Forms of Support Groups

Recognizing the logistical impossibility of convening a support group for people who are geographically distant or who face mobility barriers, some investigators have experimented with telephone and computer-based support groups. For example, Dunham, et al. (1998) created a computer-mediated support network for 50 poor, young, single mothers, aimed to reduce the stress they experienced during the first year as mothers. The were given modem-equipped terminals or microcomputers that had been donated by local businesses. They were given access to a network server that was available 24 hours a day and taught how to use a bulletin board system that allowed them to post messages to one another in a public forum, send private e-mail messages to one another, and hold a real-time, text-based teleconference with up to eight mothers. After establishing a set of ground rules for their communication (e.g., no one could send a personal threat to another person), Dunham et al. (1998) operated the support network for 6 months and then tallied the number of times the participants accessed the system, the extent and kinds of support that were communicated, and the impact of the program on maternal parenting stress. He found extensive use of the network, characterized predominantly by expressions of emotional support, and a significant pretest to post-test decrease in parenting stress among those mothers who participated consistently over the 6-month period. Equally interesting, content analysis of the communications revealed that this medium allowed the expression of emotionally sensitive material and fostered the development of close relationships and a strong sense of psychological community among many of the mothers.

Other studies have reported beneficial effects of computer-mediated support for children with chronic medical conditions (Ellerton, Stewart, & Ritchie, in press) and of telephone support groups for caregivers of persons with dementia (Goodman & Pynoos, 1990), for persons infected with HIV (Stewart, Hart, & Mann, in press), and for parents of children with chronic medical ailments (Ritchie et al., in press). However, because none of these studies was designed as a randomized, controlled trial, and none had a sufficient sample size to determine whether statistically meaningful effects were obtained, they must be interpreted with caution.

Support Group Participants

A third and final direction for future research lies in the investigation of factors that determine who benefits, who does not, and who—if anyone—is adversely affected by the support group experience. Relatively little is known about the characteristics of those who are most and least likely to be attracted to and benefit from a support group. Data on the characteristics of those who refuse to participate and those who drop out are rarely gathered and never reported in the published literature. Indeed, the widespread implementation of support groups by many community agencies suggests that this is a universally attractive, relevant, and beneficial helping approach. In addition, the reports from these groups leave the impression that everyone embraces this type of social program and cannot get enough of its good medicine. What is forgotten is that those clamoring for more of the same may be a highly self-selected set of individuals who survived the group and who may differ in important ways from those who refused to participate and from those who dropped out along the way.

REFERENCES

Bem, D. J. (1967). Self-perception: An alternative interpretation of cognitive dissonance phenomena. *Psychological Review, 74*, 183–200.
Bogart, L. M., & Helgeson, V. S. (in press). Social comparison among women with breast cancer: A longitudinal investigation. *Journal of Applied Social Psychology.*
Borkman, T. (1976). Experiential knowledge: A new concept for the analysis of self-help groups. *Social Service Review 50*, 445–456.

Bourgeois, M. S., & Schulz, R. (1996). Interventions for caregivers of patients with Alzheimer's disease: A review and analysis of content, process, and outcomes. *International Journal of Aging and Human Development, 43*(1), 35–92.

Buunk, B. P., Collins, R. L., Taylor, S. E., Van Yperen, N. W., & Dakof, G. A. (1990). The affective consequence of social comparison: Either direction has its ups and downs. *Journal of Personality and Social Psychology, 59*, 1238–1249.

Carkhuff, R. R. (1973). A human technology for group helping processes. *Educational Technology, 13*, 31–38.

Coates, D., & Winston, T. (1983). Counteracting the deviance of depression: Peer support groups for victims. *Journal of Social Issues, 39*, 169–194.

Cohen, S., & McKay, G. (1984). Social support, stress, and the buffering hypothesis: A theoretical analysis. In A. Baum, J. E. Singer, & S. E. Taylor (Eds.), *Handbook of psychology and health* (pp. 253–267). Hillsdale, NJ: Erlbaum.

Cohen, S., & Wills, T. A. (1985). Stress, social support, and the buffering hypothesis. *Psychological Bulletin, 98*, 310–357.

Cowan, C. P., & Cowan, P. A. (1986). A preventive intervention for couples becoming parents. In C. F. Z. Boukydis (Ed.), *Research on support for parents and infants in the postnatal period.* New York: Ablex.

Cutrona, C. E. (1990). Stress and social support: In search of optimal matching. *Journal of Social and Clinical Psychology, 9*, 3–14.

Dracup, K. (1985). A controlled trial of couples group counseling in cardiac rehabilitation. *Journal of Cardiopulmonary Rehabilitation, 5*, 436–442.

Dreher, H. (1997). The scientific and moral imperative for broad-based psychosocial interventions for cancer. *Journal of Mind-Body Health, 13*(3), 38–49.

Dunham, P. J., Hurshman, A., Litwin, E., Gusella, J., Ellsworth, C., & Dodd, P. W. (1998). Computer-mediated social support: Single young mothers as a model system. *American Journal of Community Psychology, 26*, 281–306.

Dunkel-Schetter, C. (1984). Social support and cancer: Findings based on patient interviews and their implications. *Journal of Social Issues, 40* 77–98.

Ellerton, M.-L., Stewart, M., & Ritchie, J. (in press). Social support for children with a chronic condition. In M. Stewart (Ed.), *Chronic conditions and caregiving: Does support help?* Toronto, Ontario: University of Toronto Press.

Festinger, L. (1954). A theory of social comparison processes. *Human Relations, 7*, 117–140.

Folkman, S. (1984). Personal control and stress and coping processes: A theoretical analysis. *Journal of Personality and Social Psychology, 46*(4), 839–852.

Goodman, C., & Pynoos, J. (1990). A model telephone information and support program for caregivers of Alzheimer's patients. *Gerontologist, 30*, 399–404.

Gottlieb, B. H. (1998). Support groups. In H. S. Friedman (Ed.), *Encyclopedia of mental health.* San Diego: Academic Press.

Grych, J. H., & Fincham, F. D. (1992). Interventions for children of divorce: Toward a greater integration of research and action. *Psychological Bulletin, 111*, 434–454.

Helgeson, V. S., & Cohen, S. (1996). Social support and adjustment to cancer: Reconciling descriptive, correlational, and intervention research. *Health Psychology, 15*, 135–148.

Helgeson, V. S., Cohen, S., Schulz, R., & Yasko, J. (1999). Effects of education and peer discussion group interventions on 6-month adjustment to breast cancer. *Archives of General Psychiatry, 56*, 340–347.

Helgeson, V. S., Cohen, S., Schulz, R., & Yasko, J. (2000). Group support interventions for people with cancer: Who benefits from what? *Health Psychology 19*, 107–114.

Helgeson, V. S., & Mickelson, K. D. (1995). Motives for social comparison. *Personality and Social Psychology Bulletin, 21*, 1200–1209.

Hughes, R. J. (1988). Divorce and social support: A review. *Journal of Divorce, 11* (3/4), 123–145.

Kelly, J. A., Murphy, D. A., Bahr, R., Kalichman, S. C., Morgan, M. G., Stevenson, Y., Koob, J. J., Brasfield, T. L., & Bernstein, B. M. (1993). Outcome of cognitive-behavioral and support group brief therapies for depressed, HIV-infected persons. *American Journal of Psychiatry, 150*(11), 1679–1686.

Kriss, R. T., & Kraemer, H. C. (1986). Efficacy of group therapy for problems with postmastectomy self-perception, body image, and sexuality. *Journal of Sex Research, 22*, 438–451.

Lakey, B., & Lutz, C. J. (1996). Social support and preventive and therapeutic interventions. In G. R. Pierce, B. R. Sarason, & I. G. Sarason (Eds.), *Handbook of social support and the family.* New York: Plenum.

Lakey, B., Ross, L. T., Butler, C., & Bentley, K. (1996). Making social support judgements: The role of similarity and conscientiousness. *Journal of Social and Clinical Psychology, 15*, 283–304.

Lavoie, J.-P. (1995). Support groups for informal caregivers don't work! Refocus the groups or the evaluations? *Canadian Journal of Aging, 14*(3), 580–595.

Lepore, S. J., & Helgeson, V. S. (1999). Psychoeducational support group enhances quality of life after prostate cancer. *Cancer Research, Therapy and Control, 8*, 81–92.

Lepore, S. J., Helgeson, V. S., & Schulz, R. (1998). *Adjustment to prostate cancer.* Unpublished data.

Lepore, S. J., Silver, R. C., Wortman, C. B., & Wayment, H. A. (1996). Social constraints, intrusive thoughts, and depressive symptoms among bereaved mothers. *Journal of Personality and Social Psychology, 70*, 271–282.

Lieberman, M. A. (1993). Self-help groups. In H. I. Kaplan & B. J. Sadock (Eds.), *Comprehensive group psychotherapy.* Baltimore: Williams & Wilkins.

McGuire, J. C., & Gottlieb, B. H. (1979). Social support groups among new patients: An experimental study in primary prevention. *Journal of Clinical Child Psychology, 8*, 111–116.

Miller, S. M. (1995). Monitoring versus blunting styles of coping with cancer influence the information patients want and need about their disease. *Cancer, 76*, 167–177.

Mittelman, M. S., Ferris, S. H., Shulman, E., Steinberg, G., Ambinder, A., Mackell, J. A., & Cohen, J. (1995). A comprehensive support program: Effect on depression in spouse-caregivers of AD patients. *Gerontologist, 35*(6), 792–802.

Pennebaker, J. W. (1993). Putting stress into words: Health, linguistic and therapeutic implications. *Behavioral Research and Therapy, 31*, 539–548.

Pennebaker, J. W., & Beall, S. K. (1986). Confronting a traumatic event: Toward an understanding of inhibition and disease. *Journal of Abnormal Psychology, 95*, 274–281.

Pennebaker, J. W., Colder, M., & Sharp, L. K. (1990). Accelerating the coping process. *Journal of Personality and Social Psychology, 58*, 528–537.

Peters-Golden, H. (1982). Breast cancer: Varied perceptions of social support in the illness experience. *Social Science and Medicine, 16*, 483–491.

Riessman, F. (1965). The helper therapy principle. *Social Work, 10*, 29–38.

Ritchie, J., Stewart, M., Thompson, D., Ellerton, M.-K., Sullivan, M., & Salisbury, S. (in press). Parents of children with chronic conditions: Fostering competence through telephone support groups. In M. Stewart (Ed.), *Chronic conditions and caregiving: Does support help?* Toronto, Ontario: University of Toronto Press.

Rosenberg, P. P. (1984). Support groups: A special therapeutic entity. *Small Group Behavior, 15*(2), 173–186.

Silver, R. L., & Wortman, C. B. (1980). Coping with undesirable life events. In J. Garber & M. E. P. Seligman (Eds.), *Human helplessness: Theory and applications* (pp. 279–340). New York: Academic Press.

Spiegel, D., Bloom, J., & Yalom, I. (1981). Group support for patients with metastatic cancer: A prospective randomized outcome study. *Archives of General Psychiatry, 38*, 527–533.

Spiegel, D., Bloom, J. R., Kraemer, H. C., & Gottheil, E. (1989). Effect of psychosocial treatment on survival of patients with metastatic breast cancer. *Lancet, 2*, 888–891.

Stewart, M., Hart, G., & Mann, K. (in press). Overcoming loneliness of hemophiliacs with AIDS and their caregivers through telephone support. In M. Stewart (Ed.), *Chronic conditions and caregiving: Does support help?* Toronto, Ontario: University of Toronto Press.

Taylor, S. E. (1983). Adjustment to threatening events: A theory of cognitive adaptation. *American Psychologist, 38*, 1161–1173.

Toseland, R. W., & Rossiter, C. M. (1989). Group interventions to support family caregivers: A review and analysis. *Gerontologist, 29*(4), 438–448.

Wandersman, L. P. (1982). An analysis of the effectiveness of parent-infant support groups. *Journal of Primary Prevention, 3*(2), 99–115.

Wandersman, L. P., Wandersman, A., & Kahn, S. (1980). Social support in the transition to parenthood. *Journal of Community Psychology, 8*, 332–342.

Wethington, E., & Kessler, R. C. (1986). Perceived support, received support, and adjustment to stressful life events. *Journal of Health and Social Behavior, 27*(1), 78–89.

Wills, T. A. (1981). Downward comparison principles in social psychology. *Psychological Bulletin, 90*, 245–271.

Zarit, S. H., Anthony, C. R., & Boutselis, M. (1987). Interventions with caregivers of dementia patients: Comparison of two approaches. *Psychology and Aging, 2*(3), 225–232.

8

One-to-One Support Interventions
Home Visitation and Mentoring

John Eckenrode
Stephen Hamilton

I. Characteristics of One-to-One Support Interventions
   A. The Support Provider
   B. The Support Recipient
   C. The Support Need
   D. The Goal of the Support Program
   E. The Type and Method of Support
   F. The Location of the Intervention
II. Conceptual Framework for One-to-One Support Interventions
III. Home Visitation Programs
   A. The Effectiveness of Home Visitation Programs
   B. Mediating Mechanisms
   C. Limitations and Challenges of Home Visitation Programs
      1. Scope of the Program
      2. Selecting Home Visitors
      3. Training and Supervision
      4. Privacy and Safety Concerns
      5. Dependency
   D. Future Directions
IV. Mentoring Adolescents
   A. The Effectiveness of Social Mentoring Programs
   B. Mentoring Adolescents at Work
   C. Mentoring Program Design Issues
   D. The Future of Mentoring
V. Conclusions

Acknowledgments—We would like to thank Julie Heim and Allison Ludwig for their help with this chapter. The thoughtful comments on earlier drafts by Benjamin Gottlieb, Sheldon Cohen, Alan Vaux, Karen Rook, and James House are also very much appreciated. Work on this chapter was aided by support to John Eckenrode from the Children's Bureau, Office of Child Abuse and Neglect (Grant #90CA-1631).

This chapter discusses social support interventions that seek to temporarily graft a relationship onto a person's existing social network (Gottlieb, 1988). Typically, such programs identify persons who are seen as having a social support deficit because they have lost one or more important relationships (e.g., through death or divorce), they never had what is normatively considered an important social relationship (e.g., children with absent fathers), or their support needs at least temporarily exceed the capacity of their existing social network because of stressful life events or the demands of a life transition (e.g., birth of a first child). Although distinguished from professional helping relationships, these support interventions are often sponsored by community organizations such as hospitals, school districts, nonprofit social service agencies, or county departments of health or social services. Indeed, some support interventions employ professional support providers such as teachers or nurses. In these instances, however, the role of the professional is expanded to include the provision of informal types of social support in the context of a more personal relationship. These interventions are also distinguished from programs that focus on assisting existing network members to provide more effective support to a person in need, such as a spouse, child, parent, or friend. Such programs are the focus of chapter 9.

CHARACTERISTICS OF ONE-TO-ONE SUPPORT INTERVENTIONS

It is useful to distinguish the relationships encompassed by these interventions from other one-to-one relationships in which social provisions are exchanged. Although these relationships may have some of the characteristics of both informal social ties and professional client-provider relationships, they should be distinguished from each (Lenrow & Burch, 1981). Generally, the social relationships formed in one-to-one support interventions have most, if not all, of the following characteristics:

- No fees are involved.
- The relationship is not one of client or patient.
- The relationship is introduced from the outside; it is a new social tie.
- The supporter usually (but not always) has experience with the issue or problem being addressed (e.g., a parent, skilled worker, a former addict, recovered patient).
- Encounters extend over a period of time (vs. one or two interactions).
- Interactions occur outside formal service delivery settings (e.g., at home, in the community, at the workplace).
- The process of forming a relationship between the supporter and the beneficiary is part of the intervention.
- The relationship typically ends after a period of time, with independence, ties to the recipient's informal social network, or other community resources being encouraged.

Of course, not all one-to-one support interventions have all of these characteristics. For example, telephone "warm lines" may offer advice from trained peers but do not involve face-to-face contact and do not extend over time. Likewise, some support interventions may involve fees, at least indirectly, as a result of being an extension of health or educational services. Indeed, determining the critical elements necessary for the success of these forms of support interventions is an important research agenda.

There are several aspects of one-to-one support interventions, a consideration of which serves to characterize the variety of programs that fall within this broad type of support interventions and also to reflect decision points in the design of such interventions (see Table 8.1 for a summary).

The Support Provider

The supporters may be trained professionals such as nurses or social workers, paraprofessionals, or lay persons who share some of the life experiences of the beneficiaries (e.g., were parents themselves or had the disease) or are seen as respected role models in the community (e.g., mentors for at-risk youth).

Another important distinction involves the age of the supporter relative to the support recipient. Some programs match recipients to persons of the same age (e.g., peer support programs); others are intergenerational (e.g., mentoring pro-

Table 8.1. Characteristics of One-to-One Support Interventions

Characteristics	Some Program Variations
Support provider	Professional vs. nonprofessional May possess experiences similar to the support recipient Role model
Support recipient	At-risk subgroups vs. universal Child, adolescent, or adult
Support need	General support deficit, social isolation Coping with stressful event Aid with life course transition Behavior change
Goal of program	Narrow vs. broad Specific vs. comprehensive goals
Support strategy or method	Compansionship Emotional support Instruction Advising Modeling Referral
Location of program	Home Centers, clinics, or agencies Schools Workplaces Community settings

grams). Important programmatic issues concern how to recruit, select, train, and support the support providers.

The Support Recipient

Most one-to-one support programs aim to serve specific subgroups in the population (e.g., at-risk teen mothers, homebound elderly, bereaved children), although there is not always consensus within the research or clinical communities regarding the populations that should be served. For example, some advocates of home visiting argue for making support services available to all new mothers regardless of the presence of "risk" characteristics (Gomby, Larson, Lewit, & Behrman, 1993); others argue that research supports targeting such programs on high-risk groups, such as poor, teen mothers (Olds & Kitzman, 1993). Important programmatic issues include how to identify, recruit, and orient the support recipient and how to match recipients with providers, for example, through self-selection or predetermined on the basis of mutual interests, age, gender, race, or geographical proximity.

The Support Need

One-to-one support interventions are intended to address either a long-term support deficit, such as social isolation; bolster the coping resources of persons experiencing stressful life events, such as the loss of a spouse; aid in behavior changes that may prevent disease or promote health, such as reducing cigarette smoking or substance use; or aid in normative life course transitions, such as moving from school to work or having a first child.

The Goal of the Support Program

Given the diversity of problems or issues that lead to the need for a support intervention, it follows that the goals of such programs vary considerably (e.g., healing, coping, making a successful transition, learning). Although some programs address a limited number of very specific goals, others seek to address multiple needs. In this sense, support programs can be compared in terms of their comprehensiveness.

The Type and Method of Support

One-to-one support programs vary in terms of the range of support provided. Many seek to provide informational support through direct instruction or the modeling of new skills or by providing written information or referrals to community resources. Others may provide emotional support through the use of more unstructured activities reflective of companionship and friendship. The more comprehensive the program, the more likely it is that a combination of approaches will be used. Programs also vary in terms of the degree to which the provider's role and the methods employed are specific or prescribed. Some have highly specific protocols to guide the activities of the support provider. Others have specific objectives, but the methods vary. Still others have broad goals and considerable latitude in terms of activities and methods.

The Location of the Intervention

Some one-to-one programs are defined in terms of where the support interactions occur, for example, home visiting programs in the home, apprenticeship programs in the workplace. Others are not tied to one setting but can vary, depending on the needs of the support provider and the support recipient.

Each of these characteristics helps to differentiate one-to-one support programs and also represents crucial issues in the design and implementation of these programs. In discussing specific types of support programs later in this chapter, we return to these distinctions, which help to distinguish the programs that have been shown to be more or less successful.

CONCEPTUAL FRAMEWORK FOR ONE-TO-ONE SUPPORT INTERVENTIONS

Although there is not a unified theory of support interventions, it is clear that there are various theoretical foundations of the specific one-to-one programs considered in this chapter. Each theory emphasizes certain aspects of the process and content of one-to-one support relationships, while ignoring or deemphasizing others. A well-designed one-to-one support program is likely to draw on multiple theoretical traditions that cross disciplinary boundaries.

Several theoretical perspectives in social psychology, developmental psychology, and sociology have been called on to guide the design of support interventions (Heller & Rook, 1997; see also chapters 1 and 6). Table 8.2 provides a summary of our discussion. Some of the theoretical and empirical underpinnings of one-to-one support interventions arise from research on the health-protective effects of social relationships, especially under conditions of stress (Cohen & Wills, 1985; Vaux, 1988). Recognizing that social relationships may buffer stress or promote health in several ways, researchers have found it useful to distinguish among various functions of social relationships. Such insights may be equally useful in the design, implementation, and evaluation of one-to-one support interventions.

Heller and Rook (1997) review several attempts to categorize support functions. For example, Weiss (1974) discussed six "social provisions" that characterize social relationships: attachment, social integration, nurturance, reassurance of worth, reliable alliances, and guidance. Thoits (1985) described a set of functions that overlap partially with this list: social integration, development and maintenance of identity and self-esteem, affect regulation, coping assistance, and social control. Recognizing that social relationships can have negative as well as positive effects (Rook, 1984), each of these functions can be further distinguished by po-

Table 8.2. Some Theories and Concepts Relevant to the Design and
Evaluation of One-to-One Support Interventions

Theory or Concept	Intervention Implications
Social provisions framework	Approach to identifying specific support needs addressed by the intervention Relationships are seen as source of stress as well as support
Ecology of human development theory	Emphasis on the larger social context of the intervention such as community and culture Attention to process issues, especially reciprocal dyadic relationships
Self-efficacy theory	Importance of efficacy beliefs and sense of mastery in behavior change Need for intervention to help support recipient to achieve a series of small successes and be fortified against setbacks
Attachment theory	Emphasis on the importance of early relationships and the continuity of attachment themes throughout the life course Influence of significant social losses or unmet attachment needs may influence intervention success Focus on the special relationship that exists between support provider and support recipient

tentially positive and negative features. For example, network members may provide coping assistance that is unhelpful as well as helpful; they may bolster as well as undermine self-esteem.

Distinguishing among the functions performed by social relationships is important in the design and evaluation of one-to-one support interventions for several reasons. First, it underscores the fact that social relationships are complex and may have multiple effects. Hence, it is useful to determine what functions the support intervention is attempting to supplement or change. Second, multiple functions mean that there may be one or more specific deficits that the intervention is designed to address. Assessing specific support needs that are present is more useful than conceptualizing an intervention as more globally focused on "social support." Third, it alerts us to the fact that the impact (positive or negative) of a specific social provision may depend on the presence or absence of other social provisions. For example, attempts to bolster self-esteem (one social provision) through a support intervention may fail when the person being helped is embedded in a social network that encourages drug and alcohol use as a means of affect regulation (another social provision). Therefore, it may be necessary to assess multiple dimensions of the social field when designing a support interven-tion to address even quite specific support needs.

Although reviewing each support function or social provision would seem to be an important step in the design of one-to-one interventions, other theoretical perspectives from social and developmental psychology also provide useful guidelines for the design and implementation of such programs. Indeed, behind each support function (e.g., social integration) is a theoretical and empirical lit-erature that may provide more specific guidance to program planners seeking to incorporate that support function into a one-to-one support intervention. For ex-ample, Olds, Kitzman, Cole, and Robinson (1997) discuss three theoretical foun-dations of a program of research involving the implementation and evaluation of prenatal and early childhood home visitation services to new mothers: (1) ecology of human development theory (Bronfenbrenner, 1979, 1995), (2) attachment the-ory (Bowlby, 1969), and self-efficacy theory (Bandura, 1977). Although Olds, Kitz-man, et al. (1997) discuss each of these theoretical frameworks in relation to one type of support intervention, these frameworks are equally useful for understand-ing one-to-one support interventions generally.

Ecology of human development theory is perhaps best known for its emphasis on the social context of human development. Persons are seen as embedded in a series of interconnected social fields, including the family, informal social net-works, neighborhoods and communities, and the larger culture. In the present context, this perspective sensitizes the program planner to the role of these varied social contexts and the connections among them in the success of one-to-one support interventions. For example, Cole, Kitzman, Olds, and Sidora (1998) doc-ument the influence (including active resistance) that household members had in determining the success of a nurse home visitation program for young first-time mothers in Memphis. Of course, the informal social network can be an explicit focus of support interventions as well, as discussed in chapter 9 of this volume. But interventions that seek to temporarily graft a new tie onto a person's network also need to be sensitive to the influence of other network members and to the neighborhood and community in which the support recipient lives (Slaughter-Defoe, 1993). Some one-to-one support interventions also make explicit attempts to work with the other members of the support recipient's social network (e.g., spouses, grandmothers) or have as one goal support recipients' more effective use of their social networks. When they do so, these programs may be best viewed as focused on the entire family or social network rather than on one individual. For example, in their intervention with bereaved children, Sandler, Gersten, Reynolds, Kallgren, and Ramirez (1988) describe a program of support for be-reaved children and their families that involved linking a "family advisor" to the family.

Bronfenbrenner's (1995) more recent elaboration of ecology of human devel-opment theory adds social and developmental processes (e.g., reciprocal parent-child interactions) and individual differences (e.g., past experiences, mental health) to the previous focus on context. Attention to process issues underscores the need to identify mechanisms that underlie support interventions (Gottlieb, 1988). Person factors alert us to individual characteristics, such as psychological resources, that may influence the design of specific program components or may account for variability in program effects. For example, Kitzman, Olds et al. (1997) report that a program of home visitation for young mothers reduced their children's health care encounters more for women with fewer, compared with more, psychological resources (IQ, psychological well-being, active coping style). Lakey and Lutz (1996) also review evidence that social support can be viewed, in part, as a personality characteristic. Individual differences in beliefs related to social relationships are reflected in the psychological literature by research on such constructs as network orientation or help-seeking beliefs (Eckenrode, 1983; Vaux, 1988), interpersonal sensitivity (Leadbeater, Blatt, & Quinlan, 1995), or rejection sensitivity (Downey, Lebolt, Rincon, & Freitas, 1998). These theoretical perspectives and empirical findings have implications for the selection of persons needing one-to-one support interventions and for the content of the interventions. For example, one goal of an intervention may be to identify and change perceptual biases that prevent a person from accurately assessing the potential supportiveness of the existing social relationships.

Self-efficacy theory (Bandura, 1977) connects people's cognitions (i.e., expectations) to their motivation to enact certain behaviors. This is particularly relevant to one-to-one interventions that seek to change existing behavior patterns, such as quitting smoking or decreasing alcohol use, or to add new behaviors, such as beginning contraceptive use or starting to use a community-based service. The support recipients' efficacy beliefs about their ability to perform a behavior or accomplish a goal are directly tied to the initiation and persistence of the relevant behaviors. Successes and failures in performing the desired behavior have a particularly strong effect on a person's level of expectations and sense of mastery, compared to other forms of feedback, such as persuasive messages from others. Olds, Kitzman et al. (1997) used these theoretical insights to design a series of home-visiting interventions that included a focus on helping new mothers set and reach small, achievable objectives, thereby gradually increasing their sense of mastery and ability to cope with future problems. In this instance, program designers identified a psychological need (bolstering self-confidence and esteem), concluded that one of the support provisions communicated by the support provider would be the development and maintenance of positive self-esteem, and used the theoretical insights from self-efficacy theory to help design the specific activities that would lead to this outcome.

Attachment theory (Bowlby, 1969) has been frequently called on in writings about the role of social support in promoting health and buffering stress and in the design of one-to-one support interventions. Attachment theory directs our attention to the importance of early relationship histories in shaping the support recipient's receptivity to a support intervention, mediated through perceived trust in relationships, confidence in forming new ties, and beliefs about help giving and receiving (Sarason, Pierce, & Sarason, 1990). These issues are often missing from discussions of support provisions or functions. A history of unmet needs for secure attachment relationships or an experience with neglectful or abusive relationships may be implicated in current support deficits and represents a challenge to establishing a new tie as part of a support intervention. Attachment history may also underlie a support recipient's difficulties in building, maintaining, and mobilizing an existing social network. In such a case, the support intervention may need to focus on building social skills or addressing perceptions or beliefs about relationships (the "internal working model") that may interfere with the establishment of sensitive and caring relationships.

The need for a support intervention may also directly result from the loss of a primary attachment relationship. Sandler et al.'s (1988) program for bereaved children represents one example; Silverman's widow-to-widow program (1986) represents another. The theoretical literature on loss and grieving (Bowlby, 1969) provides guidance for the design and evaluation of such interventions. Insights from attachment theory are also useful in thinking about the nature of the relationship between the support provider and the support recipient. An explicit goal of many one-to-one support programs is the establishment of a close, relatively long-term relationship with the support recipient. Olds, Kitzman, et al. (1997), use the term *therapeutic alliance* to describe the relationship between nurses and young mothers in their home visitation program. This term is perhaps more apt to this situation, where the nurses serve as teachers and mentors as well as health professionals, than in interventions involving peers or other nonprofessionals, where the roles may be more of friend, companion, or "fellow sufferer" (Gottlieb, 1988). In each case, the close, confiding nature of the relationship distinguishes these relationships from other professional-client relationships. Such a relationship may also be a vivid contrast to the harsh or neglectful histories of some support recipients and be a precondition for learning new social skills, as reflected in outcomes such as improved parent-child relationships or less conflictual relations with peers.

Each of these theoretical perspectives emphasizes one set of issues over others, which reinforces the need for multiple perspectives. For example, focusing on social support provisions or functions is most relevant to the content of the relationship once it is established. If the primary need is determined to be the lack of social integration, the intervention might work with the person to establish meaningful community roles (Heller, Thompson, Trueba, Hogg, & Vlachos-Weber 1991). But other important issues not directly addressed by the "support functions" perspective have to do with the initial establishment of the support relationship: What are the processes that affect whether the grafted tie takes or is rejected (to use an organ transplant analogy)? Here, theory and research related to the development and maintenance of new relationships, especially friendship formation (see Hays, 1988), is perhaps most useful because the grafted tie does not involve kin. For example, the self-disclosure literature in social psychology can provide guidance to the processes that facilitate or inhibit the establishment of informal reciprocal ties (Derlega, Metts, Petronio, & Margulis, 1993). Whether the supporter is encouraged to gradually disclose personal information depends on the goals of the program with regard to the desired closeness and stability of the relationship. For example, if the desired role of the supporter is one of "teacher" as opposed to "friend," then disclosure processes may be more limited. The literature on "social penetration" processes (Altman & Taylor, 1973) also directs our attention to the stages of relationship formation, especially the gradual process of increasing the breadth (the content areas of the exchange) and the depth (the intimacy level of the exchange) of the relationship.

One-to-one support programs vary in the length of time the relationship is expected to last, although few view the relationship as permanent. As such, theoretical perspectives relevant to the ending of relationships are also relevant to the planning of such programs. The social support literature is more focused on the establishment of social bonds and their functions than with processes that lead to the planned ending of generally positive social relationships (vs. ending through unplanned losses or conflictual processes). This is a particularly important issue in designing one-to-one interventions in that many of the resulting relationships take on friendship or confidant qualities. Hence, ending such programs may result in a sense of loss on the part of the recipient of support. Such an unintended consequence has been reported by Schulz and Hanusa (1978), who found that a program of friendly visiting by college students to elderly retirement home residents was unexpectedly associated with a decline in well-being when assessments were made 2 to 3 years after the program ended. Although these authors hypothesized that factors other than the loss of these relationships were responsible for the declines, their data do not rule out such an explanation.

In the remainder of this chapter, we review the characteristics of two general types of one-to-one support interventions: (1) home visiting programs and (2) mentoring programs. Although not exhaustive of all one-to-one support programs, there is considerable variability across these programs in terms of the characteristics of support providers and recipients, needs addressed, and content of the support program. Therefore, these programs encompass the problems and prospects of implementing and evaluating one-to-one support interventions more generally. Each of these types of interventions has also enjoyed increased popularity among practitioners, policy makers, and the research community in recent years.

HOME VISITATION PROGRAMS

Visiting individuals and families in their homes to provide emotional support, information, health care, or educational services is not new (Wasik, 1993). In the United States, this mode of intervention has occurred since at least the 1890s, when "friendly visitors" from charitable organizations visited poor urban families. However, in recent years there has been a considerable renewal of interest among clinicians and policy makers in home visitation programs, with some claiming that home visiting represents a "new profession" (Klass, 1996). A number of expert commissions and advisory panels have called for more federal funding for home visitation programs. For example, the National Commission to Prevent Infant Mortality (1989) has recommended increased federal support for home visiting programs for low-income pregnant women (see also American Academy of Pediatrics, 1998). The U.S. Advisory Board on Child Abuse and Neglect (1991) similarly urged the federal government to begin phasing in a national program of home visitation for all new parents as part of a comprehensive strategy for the prevention of child maltreatment. The renewed interest in home visitation has also resulted in numerous efforts at the state and local levels by nongovernmental organizations to institute such programs, as well as attempts to coordinate and support these efforts. For example, the National Committee to Prevent Child Abuse has supported the establishment of postnatal home visitation programs in many states under the Healthy Families America program, based on Hawaii's Health Start program (Breakey & Pratt, 1991).

Some home visitation programs are stand alone in the sense that home visitation is the only mode of intervention with the support recipient. In other cases, home visitation represents an extension of services based in hospitals, schools, preschool centers, or human services agencies. Home visitation programs also vary along a number of dimensions, including the population served (e.g., young mothers, elderly), the background of the home visitor (professional, paraprofessional, lay volunteer), the content of the visits, and the length and frequency of visits. The support needs addressed by these programs also vary considerably. Some programs attempt to generally increase the fund of support resources because the underlying need is social isolation or loneliness; many others seek to establish a supportive relationship for the purpose of affecting other outcomes, such as improved parenting, increased employability, or changes in health behaviors such as increased well-child visits. Given this diversity, it is not possible to talk about a single home visitation intervention. However, some of the key elements of the social support interactions that take place in the home that distinguish them from agency- or clinic-based encounters include (Weiss, 1993):

- Visiting in the home meets individuals on their own turf, thereby increasing their sense of control over the interaction and balancing the power between the visitor and the person(s) being visited (when the visits are voluntary in nature).
- Visits are less formal and structured and, as such, tend to promote a friendlier atmosphere.
- Home visitors can assess the home and neighborhood environment as a source of stress or support for parents and children and thereby modify the goals and approach of the visits accordingly.
- Home visiting can lower barriers to access to services where transportation or mistrust of professional settings is an issue.

Perhaps most important, home visiting programs assume that visits over a long enough period of time can promote the development of an enduring and trusting relationship between the visitor and the support recipient. This special relationship, in turn, can be an effective vehicle for the transmission of various forms of social support, for influencing behavior change, for learning new skills, and for linkages to broader community resources and service systems.

In recent years, most research and demonstration activity, as well as policy initiatives, have centered on home visitation programs that seek to improve the health and development of infants and preschool-age children and their parents, particularly young and low-income families. It is here that the most rigorous evaluations have been conducted with randomized trials.

From the 1960s to the 1990s, the nature of home visitation with families of young children has shifted from a focus that was almost exclusively on the child to a focus on the family as the context for the healthy development of the child (Wasik, 1993). It is now common for home visiting programs to focus on the broader support needs of the parent(s) in addition to the developmental needs of the child, hence the term *two-generation* programs (Smith, Blank, & Bond, 1990; St. Pierre, Layzer, & Barnes, 1995). This is consistent with the theoretical underpinnings of these programs, principally ecology of human development theory, a perspective that places child development in the context of the family and the broader social network (Cochran & Brassard, 1979). The role of the support provider has likewise changed from "problem-solver, expert, and decision-maker to negotiator, collaborator, and facilitator" (Wasik, 1993, p. 143). Supporting parents to achieve broad life course goals, such as educational achievement and economic self-sufficiency, has thus become part of many home visiting programs, along with the dissemination of information about the child's physical, psychological, and social development (Ramey & Ramey, 1993). Stress and coping theorists might see these as attempts to bolster coping resources; economists might refer to these programs as building social and human capital.

Strong advocacy efforts have led to the widespread adoption of a variety of home visitation programs in communities. Although home visitation seems to have an intuitive appeal, especially for hard-to-reach, stressed, and young families, the current level of enthusiasm must be tempered by a realistic assessment of the evidence for effectiveness. Some home visiting efforts have undoubtedly worked well to the benefit of parents and children, but others have clearly failed to achieve their goals.

The Effectiveness of Home Visitation Programs

Of the many evaluations of home visitation programs, there are relatively few randomized trials, but their number is now sufficient to allow some general conclusions and to isolate program characteristics that are more likely to lead to positive outcomes. Olds and Kitzman (1993) have conducted the most comprehensive review of experimental studies focused on parents and young children. Their review of 31 studies concentrates on evaluations that permit the isolation of effects attributable to home visitation; that is, one of the experimental conditions involves only home visitation. Some experimental studies not reviewed by Olds and Kitzman include treatment conditions that combine home visitation with clinic- or agency-based services, such as the Infant Health and Development Program (The Infant Health and Development Program, 1990) and the High/Scope Perry Preschool Program (Weikert & Schweinhart, 1997). In such studies, it is difficult to tease apart the unique effects of home visitation.

The outcomes addressed by the programs reviewed by Olds and Kitzman (1993) include preterm delivery and low-birth weight, health-related behaviors (e.g., cigarette smoking), economic self-sufficiency, parental caregiving (e.g., home environment, child abuse and neglect), and children's physical and mental development. Some programs had goals limited to one or a few such outcomes, and others adopted a more comprehensive approach that addressed multiple goals. The content of these programs also varied considerably and could include health education, parenting education, parental cognitive stimulation of the child, emotional support to mothers and the family, linkage to community services, and maternal life course development (e.g., family planning, educational achievement, employment).

The evidence for effectiveness varies by outcome assessed and program characteristics. For example, Olds and Kitzman (1993) report that none of seven trials designed to reduce preterm delivery and low birth weight was effective in showing positive effects on birth outcomes, perhaps because they failed to concentrate their efforts on women most at risk or to have explicit strategies to help women change behaviors known to be associated with poor pregnancy outcomes (e.g., smoking, alcohol, and drug use). By contrast, all four studies of home visiting for parents of preterm and low-birth-weight infants showed promising outcomes in terms of child development and maternal caregiving. Between these extremes are a group of 19 programs that aimed to improve the health and well-being of children born to low-income families. These have had mixed success. For example, of 15 programs that emphasized the promotion of children's cognitive development, only 6 showed significant treatment effects. However, some of these 19 programs have clear evidence of success. For example, Olds and his colleagues conducted a widely cited program, the Prenatal/Early Infancy Program, in Elmira, New York, in the late 1970s and early 1980s. Four hundred women, considered at risk because of young age, unmarried status, and low incomes, were recruited during pregnancy. Half of the women were randomly assigned to control conditions, and the other half received home visitation by nurses (half of these had visits only during pregnancy, the other half through the child's second birthday). The nurses provided health education, emotional and instrumental support, assistance to the mothers with issues of life course development, and linkages to other community services.

Results showed that home visitation until the child's second birthday resulted in less smoking during pregnancy, fewer preterm deliveries (among the young adolescents), fewer child maltreatment reports in the first 2 years, fewer emergency room visits for injuries and ingestions through the child's fourth birthday, fewer subsequent pregnancies, a longer interval to subsequent pregnancies, and greater participation in the work force by the mothers (Olds, Henderson, Chamberlin, & Tatelbaum, 1986; Olds, Henderson, & Kitzman,; Olds, Henderson, Tatelbaum, & Chamberlin, 1988). Most of these results were concentrated in the higher risk subgroups of women (i.e., poor and unmarried). A recent follow-up study of these families around the child's fifteenth birthday (Olds, Eckenrode et al., 1997) showed that these early results endured, with significant reductions in child maltreatment reports over this time period, as well as reductions in welfare use, fewer subsequent births, fewer impairments due to substance use, and fewer arrests among the mothers.

Overall, Olds and Kitzman (1993) come to several conclusions regarding program characteristics that appear to be associated with positive treatment effects. First, programs that were designed to be more comprehensive—that is, address a number of needs and issues in the family—were more likely to succeed than programs that were more narrowly focused (see also Ramey & Ramey, 1993). The success of the more comprehensive programs is not simply a function of more outcomes measured and therefore more chances for significant effects. Rather, a positive impact on a specific outcome such as parental caregiving was more likely if the support for positive parenting was embedded in a comprehensive program that addressed other concerns (e.g., health, education, employment) than if the program was more narrowly focused on parent education.

Second, positive outcomes were more likely for parents and children that were assessed as more vulnerable or at risk at the beginning of the study. This may reflect the greater support needs in these families. Multiproblem families require the comprehensive approach reflected in the most successful home visitation programs, in which emotional and instrumental support is combined with links to other formal services such as child care and therapy (Thompson, 1995). Olds and Kitzman (1993) also suggest that families need to see a reason for being visited for the relationship with the home visitor to develop and be sustained. Dunst and Trivette (1990) make a similar point in addressing social support in the context of early intervention programs: "We have repeatedly found that an *indicated need* is a necessary condition for support to have positive influences on family functioning. In contrast, support has minimal and in some cases negative effects when it is offered to a family that has not indicated a need for that particular type of aid or assistance" (p. 327, emphasis in original). Home visiting for home visiting's sake, however supportive and friendly, may not be enough to engage families and motivate them to change behaviors or more effectively promote their children's development. Evidence to date does not suggest that universal home visitation services for all new parents, irrespective of need, would be an effective social policy.

Third, programs where home visitors were professionals (e.g., registered nurses) were generally more effective than those with paraprofessionals. This result may in part be due to the fact that these programs targeted a life course transition that involves numerous health-related needs and issues (pregnancy, birth, and the physical development of infants and young children). Nurses have expertise and legitimacy in these areas that are difficult to achieve with paraprofessionals. Some authors (e.g., Powell, 1993; Wasik, 1993) suggest that, with adequate training and supervision, paraprofessionals can be as effective as professionals with most families, but this conclusion needs to be confirmed with additional experimental data. Some popular programs, such as the Hawaii Healthy Start program, employ paraprofessionals with high school diplomas, but results from two randomized trials that evaluated this program have yet to be published.

Fourth, families that received more visits benefited most. For example, in a home visitation program for poor urban children in Jamaica, Powell and Grantham-McGregory (1989) showed that weekly visits by health aides over 2 years were related to small but significant increased in young children's cognitive development, but no such gains were observed for a similar group who were visited only monthly. In part, this "dose-response" relationship may reflect the fact that families with greater needs received more visits, because some programs, such as the Prenatal/Early Infancy Program (Olds & Korfmacher, 1998) and the Parents as Teachers program (Winter & McDonald, 1997), allow visitors to adjust the number of visits to the needs of the families. But these findings also begin to suggest a minimum number of visits or length of time over which visits need to occur for positive outcomes for parents and children to occur. For instance, the failure of some home visitation programs to prevent child maltreatment and other adverse child outcomes is likely to be due in part to the short duration of these programs (e.g., 3 months for Siegel, Bauman, Schaefer, Saunders, & Ingram, 1980; 6 months for Barth, 1991). The more effective programs with high-risk families begin during pregnancy or birth of the child and visit at least once a month for at least 2 years to achieve significant and lasting outcomes (Weiss, 1993; Wekerle & Wolfe, 1993).

Mediating Mechanisms

The types of home visitation programs we have discussed generally view the supportive relationship between the home visitor and the person being visited, although critical, as a means to other ends (e.g., improving parenting skills). Viewed from the "support intervention" lens, it would be useful to know if these interventions had an impact on social support processes and if program effects vary as a function of changes in these support processes. Although most home visiting programs assume that support of various forms offered by the home visitor in part accounts for the effectiveness of these programs, the actual support process is infrequently measured and analyzed. Qualitative data collected as part of randomized home visitation trials, however, have begun to shed some light on these issues. For example, as part of the New Mothers Study in Memphis (a replication of the Prenatal/Early Infancy Project in Elmira), a record-keeping system was instituted to track the process of delivering the intervention (what nurse home visitors did during the home visits). In addition, mothers were asked to report on aspects of their relationship with the nurses. For example, at 24 months, their perception of the helping relationship was assessed with items dealing with the mother's perception of trust, understanding, acceptance, and sensitivity from the nurse, summarized as a "nurse empathy" scale (Korfmacher, Kitzman, & Olds, 1998). There were mixed results when the amount of nurse empathy was related to program outcomes, with nurse empathy predicting quality of the home environment, but not to the amount of mother's empathy toward her child or the child's responsiveness to the mother (an important focus of this program was on the quality of the parent-child relationship). Other process variables, such as amount of contact time with the home visitor, did predict these child outcomes. This suggests that building a trusting and sensitive relationship between home visitors and mothers may be a necessary but not sufficient condition to produce program effects. This is consistent with the conclusion reached by Olds and Kitzman (1993), who, when reviewing randomized trials of home visiting programs aimed at reducing preterm deliveries and low birth weight, concluded that the provision of emotional support alone, in the absence of instrumental assistance in changing behaviors, is unlikely to change birth outcomes.

As home visiting programs have generally evolved from an individual focus to a family focus (Wasik, 1993), home visitors in contemporary programs may be seen as providing family support as well as individual support. Two-generation and family support programs typically adopt this expanded focus. They may take the form of working with family members to attain family-level goals (e.g., economic self-sufficiency) but may also involve assistance with the mobilization of support resources within the family unit to provide additional support to a family member in need of support. With some exceptions, home visiting evaluations generally do not document the success of such efforts and link them to the program outcomes.

Limitations and Challenges of Home Visitation Programs

Despite the recent enthusiasm for home visitation programs, program administrators often face or must address a number of challenges to run successful programs.

Scope of the Program

There seems to be little question that home visiting programs that address a range of support needs are more successful than those that are more narrowly focused. More comprehensive programs, however, also mean lengthier and costlier programs (e.g., training and supervision costs). These up-front costs are often difficult for local communities to absorb. But a recent Rand Corporation economic analysis of early intervention programs, including the Elmira Prenatal/Early Infancy Project and the Perry Preschool Program, (Karoly et al., 1998) shows that the costs of running effective programs are more than recovered in future years in terms of reduced costs in health care, child welfare services, public assistance benefits, and criminal justice services (see also Barnett, 1993). These types of benefits are unlikely in programs that, in an effort to cut costs, hire less qualified home visitors, provide them with less training and supervision, and reduce the number of visits.

It is also important to determine when home visitation services, by themselves, can be effective in meeting the support needs of the recipient(s) and when home visits need to be combined with other services, such as clinic-based or school-based programs. Research evidence provides some, although not as yet definitive, guidance on this question. The effectiveness of one strategy over another depends, in part, on the goals of the program. In a review of early childhood programs, Yoshikawa (1995) compared child and parent outcomes in programs that were center focused (mostly, enriched preschool programs), family-support programs that generally involved home visiting only, and programs that combined both approaches. For outcomes centered on early cognitive ability (e.g., IQ, school achievement, language development), interventions that combined center-based programs with family support produced the most positive findings, followed by programs that were center-based. Programs that focused on home visitation alone (family support) produced mixed results. For outcomes focused on parenting (e.g., mother-child interaction, parenting behavior) and maternal life course (e.g., education, employment, childbearing), stand-alone family support programs were generally as successful as programs combining center-based programs (focused on the child) and home-based family support. Then again, in the few studies that examined long-term program effects on children's social development, such as antisocial and delinquent behavior, the combined programs were clearly superior to either center-based or family support programs alone in producing positive effects. The lesson appears to be that, at least with programs whose goals include the long-term development of young children, instituting home visits as part of a coordinated and continuous set of community-based services is likely to be more fruitful than home visiting alone; that is, home visits may be "necessary but not sufficient" (Larner & Halpern, 1987; Weiss, 1993).

Selecting Home Visitors

As we noted before, there is some evidence that interventions employing professionals, such as nurses, lead to more efficacious outcomes for parents and children in randomized trials (Olds & Kitzman, 1993). However, qualitative studies also suggest that personal qualities of the home visitor, such as sensitivity, warmth, communication skills, flexibility, and respect for cultural differences, may be important in determining level of participation and program impact (McCurdy, 1996; Wasik, 1993). Future research is needed to determine if the use of paraprofessional home visitors carefully selected on personal qualities can, with adequate training and supervision, produce the same program outcomes that have been achieved with professionally trained home visitors.

Training and Supervision

Few studies have carefully examined the amount of training and types of supervision needed for successful home visiting programs, but those administering home visiting programs agree that adequate training and supervision are key to successful programs, particularly when the home visitors are paraprofessionals (Halpern, 1992; Wasik, 1993). Training can take the form of classroom sessions, independent study, working with "pilot" families, and shadowing experienced home visitors (Hiatt, Sampson & Baird, 1997). Curricula specific to home visitors have been developed (Wasik, 1993). Adhering to a consistent training schedule often becomes difficult, however, in the face of high staff turnover.

A successful supervisor in these programs serves multiple roles: administrator, teacher, and supportive therapist (Hiatt et al., 1997; Wasik, 1993). Because home visitors often work alone with multiproblem families, they need considerable emotional support and feedback to contain their stress levels and reduce the chances of burnout.

Privacy and Safety Concerns

One of the major advantages of home visiting programs is also a source of potential problems. Those being visited are letting another person into their home and, as such, are agreeing to give up some of their personal privacy. Some localities where the benefits of home visiting are perhaps the greatest (e.g., rural, isolated communities) may also have the most ingrained attitudes about "private property" that represent an obstacle to starting a home visitation program. In such cases, establishing initial trust levels with the individual or family in a school, office, or agency setting may need to precede the first home visit.

A home visit, by its very nature, is not under the total control of the visitor. As such, home visitors observe things that they normally would not in encounters outside the home. This includes observing abusive behaviors between spouses or parenting behaviors and home conditions that might raise concerns for a child's well-being or safety. Although the role of home visitor is not one of "spy" or agent of social control, they do need to be trained with regard to the child protection and spouse abuse laws in their state and given protocols to follow in case they observe home environments that represent a danger to someone in the household. Home visitors may also be asked to enter isolated or high-crime areas that pose real or perceived danger to the home visitor. Some programs have addressed this concern by having visitors travel in pairs, employing escorts, or restricting visiting to certain hours (Wasik, 1993).

Dependency

Establishing a close, trusting relationship between the home visitor and the person being visited is assumed to be a crucial component to successful home visiting programs (Wasik, 1993). There are two potential challenges that this generally positive program characteristic poses. First, because home visitors often become "friends" as well as helpers, maintaining a balance between these roles is often difficult. Problems with role ambiguity are especially relevant for paraprofessional home visitors because of the diminished social distance between the client and the visitor (Hiatt, et al., 1997) but is also an issue for professional home visitors such as nurses (Kitzman, Cole, Yoos, & Olds, 1997). The more similar the home visitor's experiences are to those of the person being visited, the greater the likelihood that painful personal experiences in the life of the home visitor (e.g., financial hardship, child or spouse abuse) will be reflected in the lives of the adults or children being supported. This will be an asset for many home visitors who have successfully resolved those issues in their own lives; at other times, it may be a source of stress and potential burnout. Home visitors need training and supervision specific to these issues.

Second, encouraging an emotional bond between the parent and the home visitor, although beneficial in the short run, may be problematic in the long term. Interventions that achieve the development of the support recipient's mastery, self-esteem, and increased self-sufficiency lessen the chances of overdependence by the end of the program. In cases where these goals are not met, the termination of the relationship may be stressful for the client and the home visitor. Staff turnover may also lead to the sudden termination of a relationship or the substitution of another home visitor. Relatively high turnover rates are not uncommon in home visiting programs that extend over 2 or more years, especially among paraprofessionals. For example, in a home visitation program for new mothers now taking place in Denver, there was a 50% turnover rate among paraprofessionals over a 2-year period (Hiatt et al., 1997). For the support recipients, these changes may represent unanticipated and significant social losses. Planning for termination, therefore, becomes an important training and supervision issue. Planned terminations at the end of the program may also be redefined in positive terms (e.g., as a "graduation") to reduce their stressfulness (Hiatt et al., 1997).

Future Directions

There is no question that home visiting programs will continue to grow in the United States, given the current policy and advocacy environment. The question is whether program models that have solid empirical evidence of the effectiveness will be the ones that are chosen for large-scale efforts. Many factors go into deciding about program design and implementation, in addition to what the best research suggests. Ideological beliefs, anecdotal evidence, or concerns over cost, for example, might result in the exclusive choice of paraprofessionals as home visitors, even though the research evidence, at least with programs for new parents and young children, does not justify such a decision. It is important that additional research be conducted that systematically varies program components (e.g., frequency of visits, program content) so that program planning can proceed with a strong empirical base.

Equally important, it is crucial that evaluation efforts do not focus exclusively on outcomes but that they also measure and analyze process variables that reflect the mechanisms underlying the intervention. In doing so, these evaluations should test the "small theory" of the intervention (Lipsky, 1990). For example, it is important to know what forms of social support were actually exchanged in the home visits, how the client perceived those exchanges, and whether these interactions had an impact on the broader social network of the individual. In multicomponent home visitation programs, it is often difficult to determine what processes led to positive outcomes when they do occur. Hence, it is difficult, when replicating the program, to know what program components need to be revised, expanded, or dropped.

There is also a critical need for more long-term studies of the effects of home visitation. A recent long-term follow-up of the Elmira Prenatal Early Infancy Project (Olds, Eckenrode et al., 1997; Olds, Henderson et al., 1998) suggests that benefits of home visiting seen in childhood may continue in adolescence in some cases and for some outcomes. But this one study should not suggest that a few years of home visitation provides at-risk families with a lifetime inoculation against future negative outcomes. More studies are needed to determine those conditions that lead to long-term effects and to document the pathways through which such effects occurred.

Finally, more explicit attention needs to be given to the promises and pitfalls of scaling up successful demonstration programs. There are many obstacles to having strong research-based home visitation programs influence broader public policies and large-scale program implementation (Olds, O'Brien, Racine, Glazner,

& Kitzman, 1998). Effective diffusion of the scientific knowledge regarding home visiting will require researchers to step outside academic walls and traditional scholarly channels of communication to engage policy makers, administrators, and community leaders in an effective partnership.

MENTORING ADOLESCENTS

The terms *mentor* and *mentoring* have gained currency in recent years to describe a one-to-one support intervention in which a person, usually one without professional training as a counselor, explicitly assumes a role as advisor and also as teacher and friend or companion. Although many different people can perform these different roles, the etymology of the word suggests an unrelated person who acts as a quasi-parent. The original Mentor was Odysseus' friend, in whose care he left his son Telemachus when he went off to fight against Troy.

We next discuss mentoring of adolescents and distinguish two different contexts and purposes. The first, social mentoring, aims at a broad range of adolescent functioning. The second, mentoring at work, is more narrowly focused on career preparation. We begin with a definition and a brief look at the rationale for mentoring.

Urie Bronfenbrenner has defined the term *mentor* as follows:

> A mentor is an older, more experienced person who seeks to further the development of character and competence in a younger person by guiding the latter in acquiring mastery of progressively more complex skills and tasks in which the mentor is already proficient. The guidance is accomplished through demonstration, instruction, challenge, and encouragement on a more or less regular basis over an extended period of time. In the course of this process, the mentor and the young person develop a special bond of mutual commitment. In addition, the young person's relationship to the mentor takes on an emotional character of respect, loyalty, and identification. (Personal communication)

According to this definition, a mentor performs an instrumental support function, teaching specific knowledge and skills, within the context of a close and enduring personal relationship. The implication is that mentoring by this definition offers something special, something different from what parents, teachers, professional counselors, and even older kin can provide. Setting aside this implication, which, not surprisingly, remains untested, mentoring programs can provide information and advice to young people whose families and communities do not afford many opportunities for supportive relations with adults.

Mentoring has been widely hailed as a means of reducing the risks facing children and youth. One of the major themes of the President's Summit for America's Future in April 1997 was the need to recruit more mentors for young people. One source of this enthusiasm is the remarkable story of Eugene Lang's I Have a Dream program (Berger, 1989). Lang, a New York City entrepreneur and philanthropist, was invited to give a commencement address to sixth-graders at P.S. 121, the school he had attended. Facing a low-income African American and Hispanic audience, he felt the hollowness of the usual rhetoric of opportunity and spontaneously set aside his prepared speech to promise to pay for the college education of every student who graduated from high school. The result was immediate, enduring, encouraging, and instructive.

Eight years later, 34 of the 61 "dreamers" were enrolled in college at least part-time. Most of the rest were employed. Aside from 8 who left the neighborhood and the program, only 4 were lost souls who were unlikely to benefit from Lang's generosity. One young man was incarcerated, but taking college courses. Ironically, the money to pay for college, which had originally motivated the students and their parents, proved not to be the critical ingredient. Low-income high school graduates who have done reasonably well in high school can usually get financial aid to pay for college. What mattered was the hope instilled by the promise of aid and the personal attention given the students both by Lang himself and by the person he hired to work full-time to support the young people. Together they advised, cajoled, encouraged, and helped solve problems. And many of the problems were severe. The dreamers experienced pregnancy, delinquency, lack of money, family difficulties, and the entire array of issues that make it difficult for poor and minority youth to succeed. But they had two people to turn to who had access to money, knowledge, and contacts to help them overcome those barriers.

Another source of enthusiasm for mentoring has been research on young people who not only survived but also became productive and well-adjusted adults despite being reared in conditions known to predict multiple problems. One factor those studies have found to be associated with "resilience" is the presence of a strong parent or a nonparental adult who gives guidance and encouragement (Garmezy, 1987; Lefkowitz, 1987; Rutter, 1987; Werner & Smith, 1982; Wilson, 1987). More recently, analysis of data from the National Longitudinal Survey of Adolescent Health has found that the factor that was most protective against behaviors associated with poor health was "connectedness" with parents and family and with school (Resnick et al., 1997). A logical inference is that introducing a caring adult into the life of a young person living in oppressive circumstances can improve her or his life chances. Note, however, that a leap is required, first because young people who have mentors may differ in critical ways from those who do not and second because natural mentors may differ from those whose presence is programmatically contrived. Designing empirical studies of these issues will require enormous creativity. In the meantime, program designs need not assume that only one choice is possible. Hobbs (1982) described an intervention program that identified adults already in a young person's social network and provided them with various forms of support in assuming a mentoring role.

The Effectiveness of Social Mentoring Programs

An experimental study of Big Brothers/Big Sisters provides strong empirical support for the efficacy of mentoring programs (Tierney & Grossman, with Resch,

1995). Taking advantage of the delay applicants experience before being assigned a mentor, the investigators had applicants randomly assigned to either a treatment or a control group. Applicants ranged in age from 5 to 18 years with a mean of 12 (most were between 11 and 14); almost all were from single-parent families. Those in the treatment group were eligible for a match immediately; those in the control group were not matched with a mentor for 18 months, the standard amount of time on the waiting list. Initially 1,138 youth were randomly assigned. After sample attrition for various reasons, including nonresponse and errors in implementation, analyses were performed on 487 subjects who received the treatment and 472 control subjects. Standard measures were used for self-concept, peer relations, and family relations. Academic performance, social and cultural enrichment, and antisocial activities were assessed by a few standard measures but mostly by items developed for the study. No statistically significant differences were found between the treatment and control groups at the time of the baseline survey in the fall of 1991. The comparison was conservative because matches could not be made immediately for all members of the treatment group; 22% were not matched with a mentor during the study period.

After 18 months, subjects in the treatment group demonstrated several advantages over the control group. They were less likely to have begun using drugs and alcohol or to have hit others; their attitudes and behavior toward school improved, as did their relations with peers and family members. The results of this study are impressive because they come from a true experiment and because they demonstrate differences between the treatment and control groups of socially significant magnitude; for example, young people in the treatment group skipped 52% fewer days of school and were 46% less likely to begin using drugs than those in the control group. The authors point out that effects of this nature and magnitude are not guaranteed simply by providing mentors. Big Brothers/Big Sisters attracts well-educated young professionals as volunteers and subjects them to an elaborate selection, training, and supervision process that surely contributes to its effectiveness.

No other studies of mentoring programs have employed experimental designs to assess outcomes, but other studies by Public/Private Ventures (summarized by Sipe, 1996) reveal how difficult it is to operate mentoring programs. The initial step of establishing and maintaining mentoring relationships is quite challenging. A study by Hamilton and Hamilton (1992) found that many matched pairs failed to meet on a regular basis, suggesting a paradox of mentoring. Mentoring programs are designed to synthesize what is ideally a naturally occurring relationship between a young person and a caring older person who is not part of the family and is not professionally responsible. When teachers and other professionals become mentors, they are going beyond their professional responsibilities. Programs are created to synthesize the relationship because the opportunities for such relationships to occur naturally have grown ever more restricted. Neighborhoods are segregated by social class even when they are racially integrated, and they are often age-segregated as well. Voluntary organizations also tend to attract members from the same class and age groups.

Adults are busy with their own careers and family responsibilities. Young people spend time in their schools, neighborhoods, peer groups, and other activities. Paradoxically, barriers to natural mentoring, which make mentoring programs necessary, also constrain the programs' viability and effectiveness. Scheduling times to meet is a challenge, as are orchestrating transportation and allowing sufficient travel time. Then, when an adult-youth pair meet, they have to work out why they are together and what they will do, which is something couples on a blind date may have to negotiate but not a topic of discussion in the normal course of human interaction.

Hamilton and Hamilton (1992) found that mentors who succeeded in meeting regularly with middle-school students began with an instrumental focus. They saw themselves as fostering competence and character in their mentees, and they proposed engagement in purposeful activities and tasks. For example, one mentor proposed taking a long bicycle ride together, which entailed repairing an old bicycle, planning a route, and preparing food for the trip. In contrast, would-be mentors who were unable to establish a relationship were more likely to see themselves as potential friends or confidants and to propose more social interactions, like going to a movie.

The Big Brothers/Big Sisters research (Tierney et al., 1995) found that a mentor's emotional commitment to the mentee was associated with effectiveness more than a mentor's desire to improve the mentee, in contrast to Hamilton and Hamilton's finding, which suggests that a different kind of relationship may be appropriate and effective for adolescents than for school-age children and that programs for the different age groups must be designed differently. If this is correct, it would be useful to know at what age the emphasis should shift from primarily social-emotional toward more instrumental mentoring, recalling from Bronfenbrenner's definition that they are mutually reinforcing. It appears that the early teenage years are a turning point. This is also the time when young people begin to spend more time with and pay more attention to their peers, reducing their interest in a new quasi-parental relationship. But more research is needed to substantiate such a general rule, especially research on possible differences in the nature of mentoring relationships by gender and other personal characteristics.

Mentoring Adolescents at Work

If older adolescents are not as open as younger children to social mentoring, then workplaces may be especially appropriate contexts for the development of mentoring relationships with adolescents. Adolescents tend to take work seriously, even when it seems routine to adults. The awkward question of what to do together is answered by the press of daily tasks. To help get things done in an adult workplace, young people need to learn some technical skills that are challenging and satisfying, including how to operate computers.

Because work by itself does not necessarily place adolescents in close contact with caring adults (Greenberger & Steinberg, 1986), the optimal way in which adolescents can be mentored at work is as apprentices. Apprentices by definition are worker-learners. They are expected to accomplish real work, but they are also authorized to take extra time to learn how to do the work. They are paid for the work they accomplish but not at the rate of regular workers. Apprenticeship thrives in the German-speaking countries and Denmark as an institution for vocational education and for socializing youth to adult roles. Many American observers have admired those systems and seen in them approaches that could be adapted to this country, where formal apprenticeship is both very small and predominantly an institution for young adults rather than youth (Hamilton, 1990). As a result, the idea of youth apprenticeship was written into the School-to-Work Opportunities Act of 1994, along with federal support for less intensive types of work-based learning.

Work-based teaching or mentoring is an essential component of work-based learning programs. According to the principles for high-quality work-based learning derived from an early demonstration of youth apprenticeship (Hamilton & Hamilton, 1997), mentoring at work is more complicated than matching one youth with one adult. In the first place, young people need to experience a wide range of work tasks; they do not remain in one department. Second, while it is relatively easy to assign a skilled worker to teach a young person how to perform work tasks, it is a stretch to assign a person to teach personal and social competence and to develop a close personal relationship of respect and affection. A mentoring relationship is more likely to develop from a mutual selection process rather than assignment.

It appears that when adults and youth spend time together, they naturally talk about careers. A study of career mentoring in a hospital (McClanahan, 1998) found that the amount of career mentoring done in a relationship did not vary according to the degree to which the program emphasized careers. Youth in mentoring programs emphasizing social activities actually received as much career mentoring as those in programs that more narrowly emphasized career advising.

Mentoring Program Design Issues

As the long waiting period for Big Brothers/Big Sisters suggests, there is a shortage of mentors. Recruiting mentors is, therefore, a key program issue. But selecting from among willing recruits those who are likely to be most effective poses a serious challenge. Legally, screening is required to rule out volunteers with criminal pasts and especially those with a history of child abuse. Mentors need orientation and training before they are matched, and continued support afterward.

Among mentoring program staff, the question of matching looms large. Some programs have developed elaborate criteria and processes for matching. The two characteristics that are most universally used in matching are gender and race. To the extent that mentors serve as role models and that these characteristics are central to identity, matching by gender and race makes sense. Interestingly, the careful research by Public/Private Ventures has found no empirical basis for such matching. Indeed, the principal finding is that matching is less critical than screening prospective mentors and providing them with orientation, training, and continuing supervision and support (Sipe, 1996).

The need to recruit, screen, train, and match mentors entails a substantial programmatic infrastructure. This point is crucial because it contrasts with one of mentoring's strongest attractions, especially to those who doubt the efficacy of social spending, which is that it is a voluntary, nonbureaucratic, and inexpensive response to social problems. Compared to professional services and especially to residential treatment, mentoring is quite inexpensive. But there is no basis for believing that it can be provided on a large scale and sustained without professional staffing. Big Brothers/Big Sisters, by far the largest mentoring program, makes about 75,000 matches annually at a cost of about $1,000 per match (Tierney et al., 1995).

Another issue that has not yet been explored systematically is the time horizon for mentoring programs. Typically, programs ask for a mutual commitment of 1 year, with the option of terminating early if either party chooses. Extending the term by mutual agreement is also an option. Little is known about the conditions associated with maintaining relationships beyond the term or the consequences of early termination.

Freedman (1993) made a point related to time limits by distinguishing mentoring relationships as either primary or secondary. A secondary mentoring relationship has clear boundaries in time, frequency of interaction, location, and content. By definition, a primary relationship is open-ended. Mentees may move in and live with their mentor's families. Their relationship may achieve the same depth and duration as kin relationships. Although such devotion by mentors is laudable, programs must be designed to support and honor secondary relationships, because primary relationships are unlikely to evolve in most cases, and the effectiveness of a program cannot depend on that level of mutual commitment.

The Future of Mentoring

Despite the uncertainties and limitations just noted, mentoring has much to recommend it, beginning with the compelling claim that adolescents are better off if someone older and wiser cares about and advises them. Its reliance on volunteerism appeals to both ends of the political spectrum. One benefit offered by mentoring that distinguishes it from other social support interventions is that it enables nonprofessionals to play a role in the lives of disadvantaged youth. Personal bonding across the barriers of age, class, and race can help to close social divisions, and it can enhance the knowledge of middle-class voters about the conditions facing disadvantaged adolescents and bolster their commitment to ameliorating those conditions.

CONCLUSIONS

Although there are many variations of one-to-one support interventions, they all share the common goal of seeking to temporarily add a new tie to the social network of someone who has a need for support because of loss, stressful events, life course transitions, or a perceived social support deficit. We have reviewed some common issues in establishing one-to-one interventions, while focusing in more depth on two forms of one-to-one interventions. Home visitation and mentoring have grown in popularity in recent years and attracted the attention, and occasionally the funding, of federal, of federal and state policy makers seeking new ways to provide support and guidance to vulnerable populations, especially poor children and their parents.

In concentrating on these two types of programs, we have inevitably left out of our discussion many examples of one-to-one interventions. A few such programs deserve brief mention here because each involved a rigorous experimental evaluation and because each failed to achieve positive outcomes. As such, they are instructive in highlighting the challenges associated with mounting successful support interventions (see also chapters 7 and 9). Heller et al. (1991), for example, randomly assigned low-income elderly with low perceived support to one of several conditions that involved phone contracts once or twice a week for several weeks for a staff person or a peer. These contacts did not result in improvements in perceived support or mental health. Although no treatment effects were found, this research is exemplary because of the care with which the authors and other researchers in the social support field extracted lessons from the study (see *American Journal of Community Psychology*, vol. 9, no. 1). The authors discuss the difficulties of establishing peer relationships and suggest that doing so may have been the wrong focus, given the needs of these women. They suggest that building competent role performance in the context of family-like relationships may have been a more effective goal, one common, for example, to intergenerational mentoring programs.

There is also the question of whether interventions restricted to telephone contacts are sufficiently robust to result in new relationships, as measured by changes in perceived support. For instance, in a study by Weinberger, Tierney, Booher, and Katz (1991), osteoarthritis patients were randomly assigned to receive regular care or care supplemented with phone calls from trained nonclinical staff who reviewed patients' medications, the presence of symptoms, and ways to best use their medical provider. The intervention had no effect on perceived social support, morale, satisfaction with care, or compliance with medications. In this case, the authors speculate that the telephone contacts were possibly viewed by patients as an extension of the clinic-based services and as such did not engender an increase in support perceptions.

Finally, we mention a large-scale randomized clinical trail involving home visits and phone calls by nurses to patients upon hospital discharge following a myocardial infarction (MI) (Frasure-Smith et al., 1997). This trial was a larger (1,376 patients) and better designed follow-up to an earlier trial that had shown some positive benefits (fewer MI recurrences, deaths) of nurses providing a combination of emotional support, reassurance, education, practical advice, and referral to male patients who had displayed elevated signs of stress (Frasure-Smith & Prince, 1985, 1989). The more recent trial, however, failed to replicate the earlier results with male patients; for women, the intervention was actually associated with worse outcomes. The authors point to advances in post-MI medical management that leave little room for improvements based on such psychosocial

interventions. They also raise the possibility that the interventions served to increase, rather than decrease, stress among some patients because the home visits
may have "revealed family and social strains that usually remain hidden in outpatient settings, and raised expectations for the resolution of longstanding difficulties that were beyond the programmed's scope" (Frasure-Smith et al., 1997,
p. 478).

These examples and our previous discussion suggest a number of areas where
program designers' empirical base for decision making is rather scant. For example, there is a clear need for a better understanding of the characteristics of
home visitors, mentors, and others recruited into support programs that lead to
the successful establishment of a relationship to the person in need. Many programs screen potential supporters and attempt some form of matching with support recipients. However, we do not have good information on which specific
characteristics make for a good supporter of how many characteristics need to be
included in a matching process. For example, is race a crucial characteristics in
matching young people to mentors, or is social class origin more critical? Compared to lay volunteers or paid paraprofessional staff, does professional training
in medicine, nursing, teaching, or social work convey to the supporter competencies that lessen the importance of personal qualities in predicting a successful
one-to-one relationship? It is likely that the answers to such questions will need
to be context and population-specific (Powell, 1993). What makes for a good mentor to a 10-year-old inner city youth is probably not exactly the same as what
makes for an excellent nurse home visitor to a rural teen mother.

There is also a need for more research on the actual content of the interactions
between support providers and recipients. Program evaluations need to include
more assessments of what occurred during the interactions, in addition to the
number or average length of time of the interactions. More detailed record keeping by support providers is one approach, but innovative ways to engage support
recipients also need more experimentation. In addition to periodic surveys of
support recipients, program evaluations might include diaries or similar methods
of assessing individual interactions. A considerable literature discusses the benefits and challenges of such methods (Eckenrode & Bolger, 1995).

We also have very little systematic information about how social context mod-
erates the effects of one-to-one support programs. Although many program designers are sensitive to the roles of family members, peers, and the larger community in the success of their individual one-to-one relationships, there has not
been much attention to measuring such influences and analyzing these effects as
part of program evaluation (see Cole et al., 1998, for an exception). How do family
members help or undermine home visiting or mentoring programs? What are the
most effective ways for support providers to engage family or peers in supporting
the goals of the intervention? Such questions need to become a routine part of
the evaluation of these programs.

As certain forms of one-to-one support interventions become ever more popular, it is incumbent on the research community to address such questions, and
on government agencies and foundations to demand more rigorous evaluations
of these programs.

REFERENCES

Altman, I., & Taylor, D. (1973). *Social penetration: The development of interpersonal relationships.* New York: Holt, Rinehart, & Winston.

American Academy of Pediatrics. (1998). The role of home-visitation programs in improving health outcomes for children and families. *Pediatrics, 101,* 486–489.

Bandura, A. (1977). Self-efficacy: Toward a unifying theory of behavioral change. *Psychological Review, 84,* 191–215.

Barnett, W. S. (1993). Economic evaluation of home visiting programs. *The Future of Children, 3,* 93–112.

Barth, R. P. (1991). An experimental evaluation of in-home child abuse prevention services. *Child Abuse and Neglect, 15,* 363–375.

Berger, J. (1989). East Harlem students clutch a college dream. *New York Times,* August 27, A1, 28.

Bowlby, J. (1969). *Attachment and loss:* vol. 1. *Attachment.* New York: Basic Books.

Breakey, G., & Pratt, B. (1991). Healthy growth for Hawaii's "Healthy Start": Toward a systematic statewide approach to the prevention of child abuse and neglect. *Zero to Three, 11,* 16–22.

Bronfenbrenner, U. (1979). *The ecology of human development: Experiments by nature and design.* Cambridge: Harvard University Press.

Bronfenbrenner, U. (1995). Development ecology through space and time: A future perspective. In P. Moen, G. H. Elder Jr., & K. Luscher (Eds.), *Examining lives in context* (pp. 619–647). Washington, DC: American Psychological Association.

Cochran, M., & Brassard, J. (1979). Social networks and child development. *Child Development, 50,* 601–616.

Cohen, S., & Wills, T. (1985). Stress, social support, and the buffering hypothesis. *Psychological Bulletin, 98,* 310–357.

Cole, R., Kitzman, H., Olds, D., & Sidora, K. (1998). Family context as a moderator of program effects in prenatal and early childhood home visitation. *Journal of Community Psychology, 26,* 37–48.

Derlega, V. J., Metts, S., Petronio, S., & Margulis, S. (1993). *Self-disclosure.* Newbury Park, CA: Sage.

Downey, G., Lebolt, A., Rincon, C., & Freitas, A. L. (1998). Rejection sensitivity and children's interpersonal difficulties. *Child Development, 69,* 1074–1091.

Dunst, C. J., & Trivette, C. M. (1990). Assessment of social support in early intervention programs. In S. J. Meisels & J. P. Skonkoff (Eds.), *Handbook of early childhood intervention* (pp. 326–349). New York: Cambridge University Press.

Eckenrode, J. (1983). The mobilization of social support: Some individual constraints. *American Journal of Community Psychology, 11,* 509–520.

Eckenrode, J., & Bolger, N. (1995). Daily and within-day event measurement. In S. Cohen, R. Kessler, & L. Gordon (Eds.), *Measuring stress: A guide for health and social scientists* (pp. 80–101). New York: Oxford University Press.

Frasure-Smith, N., Lesperance, F., Prince, R. H., Verrier, P, Garber, R. A., Juneau, M., Wolfson, C., & Bourassa, M. G. (1997). Randomised trial of home-based psychosocial nursing intervention for patients recovering from myocardial infarction. *Lancet, 350,* 473–479.

Frasure-Smith, N., & Prince, R. (1985). The ischemic heart disease life stress monitoring program: Impact on mortality. *Psychosomatic Medicine, 47,* 431–445.

Frasure-Smith, N., & Prince, R. (1989). Long-term follow-up of the ischemic heart disease life stress monitoring program. *Psychosomatic Medicine, 51* 485–513.

Freedman, M. (1993). *The kindness of strangers: Reflections on the mentoring movement.* San Francisco: Jossey-Bass.

Garmezy, N. (1987). Stress, competence, and development: Continuities in the study of schizophrenic adults, children vulnerable to psychopathology, and the search for stress-resistant children. *American Journal of Orthopsychiatry, 57* (2), 159–174.

Gomby, D. S., Larson, C. S., Lewit, E. M., & Behrman, R. E. (1993). Home visiting: Analysis and recommendations. *The Future of Children, 3,* 6–22.

Gottlieb, B. H. (1988). Support interventions: A typology and agenda for research. In S. W. Duck (Ed.), *Handbook of personal relationships* (pp. 519–541). New York: Wiley.

Greenberger, E., & Steinberg, L. (1986). *When teenagers work: The psychological and social costs of adolescent employment.* New York: Basic Books.

Halpern, R. (1992). Issues of program design and implementation. In M. Larner, R. Halpern, & O. Harkavy (Eds.), *Fair start for children: Lessons learned from seven demonstration programs* (pp. 179–197). New Haven: Yale University Press.

Hamilton, M. A., and Hamilton, S. F. (1997). *Learning well at work: Choices for quality.* Washington, DC: U.S. Government Printing Office.

Hamilton S. F. (1990). *Apprenticeship for adulthood: Preparing youth for the future.* New York: Free Press.

Hamilton, S. F., & Hamilton, M. A. (1992). Mentoring programs: Promise and paradox. *Phi Delta Kaplan, 73,* 546–550.

Hays, R. B. (1988). Friendship. In S. W. Duck (Ed.), *Handbook of personal relationships* (pp. 391–408). New York: Wiley.

Heller, K., & Rook, K. S. (1997). Distinguishing the theoretical functions of social ties: Implications for social support. In S. Duck (Ed.). *Handbook of personal relationships,* 2nd ed. (pp. 649–670), New York: Wiley.

Heller, K., Thompson, M. G., Trueba, P. E., Hogg, J. R., & Vlachos-Weber, I. (1991). Peer support telephone dyads for elderly women: Was this the wrong intervention? *American Journal of Community Psychology, 19,* 53–74.

Hiatt, S. W., Sampson, D. & Baird, D. (1997). Paraprofessional home visitation: Conceptual and pragmatic considerations. *Journal of Community Psychology, 25,* 77–93.

Hobbs, N. (1982). *The troubled and troubling child.* San Francisco: Jossey-Bass.

Infant Health and Development Program. (1990). Enhancing the outcomes of low-birth-weight, premature infants. *Journal of the American Medical Association, 263,* 3035–3042.

Karoly, L. A., Greenwood, P. W., Everingham, S. S., Hoube, J., Kilburn, M. R., Rydell, C. P., Sanders, M., & Chiesa, J. (1998). *Investing in our children: What we know and don't know about the costs and benefits of early childhood interventions.* Santa Monica, CA: Rand.

Kitzman, H., Olds, D., Henderson, C. H. Jr., Hanks, C., Cole, R., Tatelbaum, R., McConnochie, K. M., Sidors, K., Luckey, D. W., Shaver, D., Engelhardt, K., James, D., & Barnard, K. (1997). Randomized trial of prenatal and infancy home visitation by nurses on pregnancy outcomes. *Journal of the American Medical Association, 278*, 644–652.

Kitzman, H. J., Cole, R., Yoos, H. L., & Olds, D. (1997). Challenges experienced by home visitors: A qualitative study of program implementation. *Journal of Community Psychology, 25*, 95–109.

Klass, C. S. (1996). *Home visiting: Promoting healthy parent and child development*. Baltimore: P. H. Brooks.

Korfmacher, J., Kitzman, H., & Olds, D. (1998). Intervention processes as predictors of outcomes in a preventive home-visitation program. *Journal of Community Psychology, 26*, 49–64.

Lakey, B., & Lutz, C. J. (1996). Social support and preventive and therapeutic interventions. In G. R. Pierce, B. S. Sarason, & I. G. Sarason (Eds.), *Handbook of social support and the family* (pp. 435–465). New York: Plenum.

Larner, M., & Halpern, R. (1987). Lay home visiting programs: Strengths, tensions, and challenges. *Zero to Three 8*, 1–7.

Leadbeater, B., Blatt, S., & Quinlan, D. M. (1995). Gender-linked vulnerabilities to depressive symptoms, stress, and problem behaviors in adolescents. *Journal of Research in Adolescence, 5*, 1–29.

Lefkowitz, B. (1987). *Tough change: Growing up on your own in America*. New York: Free Press.

Lenrow, P. B., & Burch, R. W. (1981). Mutual aid and professional services: Opposing or complimentary. In B. H. Gottlieb (Ed.), *Social networks and social support* (pp. 233–257). Beverly Hills, CA: Sage.

Lipsky, M. W. (1990). Theory as method: Small theories of treatments. In L. Sechrest, E. Perrin, & J. Bunker (Eds.), *Research methodology: Strengthening causal interpretations of nonexperimental data*. Washington, DC: U.S. Department of Health and Human Services, Agency for Health Care Policy and Research.

McClanahan, W. S. (1998). *Relationships in a career mentoring program: Lessons learned form the Hospital Youth Mentoring Program*. Philadelphia: Public/Private Ventures.

McCurdy, K. (1996). *Home visiting*. Washington, DC: National Center on Child Abuse and Neglect.

National Commission to Prevent Infant Mortality. (1989). *Home visiting: Opening doors for America's pregnant women and children*. Washington, DC: National Commission to Prevent Infant Mortality.

Olds, D., Eckenrode, J., Henderson, C. R. Jr., Kitzman, H., Powers, J., Cole, R., Sidora, K, Morris, P., Pettitt, L., & Luckey, D. (1997). Long-term effects of home visitation on maternal life course and child abuse and neglect: 15-year follow-up of a randomized trial. *Journal of the American Medical Association, 278*, 637–643.

Olds, D., Henderson, C., Chamberlin, R., & Tatelbaum, R. (1986). Preventing child abuse and neglect: A randomized trial of nurse home visitation. *Pediatrics, 78*, 65–78.

Olds, D., Henderson, C., Cole, R., Eckenrode, J., Kitzman, H., Pettitt, L., Sidora, K., Luckey, D., Morris, P., & Powers, J. (1998). Long-term effects of nurse home visitation on children's criminal and antisocial behavior: 15-year follow-up of a randomized trial. *Journal of the American Medical Association, 280*, 1238–1244.

Olds, D., Henderson, C., & Kitzman, H. (1994). Does prenatal and infancy nurse home visitation have enduring effects on qualities of parental caregiving and child health at 25 to 50 months of life? *Pediatrics, 93,* 89–98.

Olds, D., Henderson, C., Tatelbaum, R., & Chamberlin, R. (1988). Improving the life-course development of socially disadvantaged mothers: A randomized trail of nurse home visitation. *American Journal of Public Health, 78,* 1436–1445.

Olds, D., & Kitzman, H. (1993). Review of research on home visiting. *The Future of Children, 3,* 51–92.

Olds, D., Kitzman, H., Cole, R., & Robinson, J. (1997). Theoretical foundations of home visitation for pregnant women and parents of young children. *Journal of Community Psychology, 25,* 9–25.

Olds, D., & Korfmacher, J. (1998). Maternal psychological characteristics as influences on home visitation contact. *Journal of Community Psychology, 26,* 23–36.

Olds, D., O'Brien, R. A., Racine, D., Glazner, J., & Kitzman, H. (1998). Increasing the policy and program relevance of results from randomized trials of home visitation. *Journal of Community Psychology, 26,* 85–100.

Powell, C., & Grantham-McGregory, S. (1989). Home visiting of varying frequencies and child development. *Pediatrics, 84,* 157–164.

Powell, D. R. (1993). Inside home visiting programs. *The Future of Children, 3,* 23–38.

Ramey, C. T., & Ramey, S. L. (1993). Home visiting programs and the health and development of young children. *The Future of Children, 3,* 129–139.

Resnick, M. D., Bearman, P. S., Blum, R. W., Bauman, K. E., Harris, K. M., Jones, J., Tabor, J., Beuhring, T., Sieving, R. E., Shew, M., Ireland, M., Bearinger, L. H., & Udry, J. R. (1997). Protecting adolescents from harm: Findings from the National Longitudinal Survey on Adolescent Health. *Journal of the American Medical Association, 278,* 823–832.

Rook, K. S. (1984). The negative side of social interaction: Impact on psychological well-being. *Journal of Personality and Social Psychology, 46,* 109–118.

Rutter, M. (1987). Psychosocial resilience and protective mechanisms. *American Journal of Orthopsychiatry, 57*(3), 316–331.

Sandler, I., Gersten, J. C., Reynolds, K., Kallgren, C. A., & Ramirez, R. (1988). Using theory and data to plan support interventions: Design of a program for bereaved children. In B. H. Gottlieb (Ed.), *Marshalling social support: Formats, processes, and effects.* Newbury Park, CA: Sage.

Sarason, B. R., Pierce, G. R., & Sarason, I. G. (1990). Social support: The sense of acceptance and the role of relationships. In B. R. Sarason, G. R. Pierce, & I. G. Sarason (Eds.), *Social support: An interactional view* (pp. 97–128). New York: Wiley.

Schulz, R., & Hanusa, B. H. (1978). Long-term effects of control and predictability-enhancing interventions: Findings and ethical issues. *Journal of Personality and Social Psychology, 36,* 1194–1201.

Siegel, E., Bauman, K. E., Schaefer, E. S., Saunders, M. M., & Ingram, D. D. (1980). Hospital and home support during infancy: Impact on maternal attachment, child abuse and neglect, and health care utilization. *Pediatrics, 66,* 183–190.

Silverman, P. (1986). *Widow to widow.* New York: Springer.

Sipe, C. L. (1996). *Mentoring: A synthesis of P/PV s research: 1988–1995.* Philadelphia: Public/Private Ventures.

Slaughter-Defoe, D. T. (1993). Home visiting with families in poverty: Introducing the concept of culture. *The Future of Children, 3,* 172–183.

Smith, S., Blank, S., & Bond, J. T. (1990). *One program, two generations.* New York: Foundation for Child Development.

St. Pierre, R. G., Layzer, J. I., & Barnes, H. V. (1995). Two-generation programs: Design, cost, and short-term effectiveness. *The Future of Children, 5,* 76–93.

Thoits, P. A. (1985). Social support and psychological well-being: Theoretical possibilities. In I. Sarason & B. Sarason (Eds.), *Social support: Theory, research, and application* (pp. 51–72). Dordrecht: Martinus Nijhoff.

Thompson, R. A. (1995). *Preventing child maltreatment through social support.* Thousand Oaks, CA: Sage.

Tierney, P., & Grossman, J. B., with Resch, N. L. (1995). *Making a difference: An impact study of Big Brothers/Big Sisters.* Philadelphia: Public/Private Ventures.

U.S. Advisory Board on Child Abuse and Neglect. *Creating caring communities: Blueprint for an effective federal policy on child abuse and neglect.* Washington, DC: U.S. Government Printing Office, 1991.

Vaux, A. (1988). *Social support: Theory, research, and intervention.* New York: Praeger.

Wasik, B. H. (1993). Staffing issues for home visiting programs. *The Future of Children, 3,* 140–157.

Weikert, D. P., & Schweinhart, L. J. (1997). High/Scope Perry preschool program. In G. W. Albee & T. P. Gullotta (Eds.), *Primary prevention works* (pp. 146–166). Thousand Oaks, CA: Sage.

Weinberger, M., Tierney, W. M., Booher, P., & Katz, B. P. (1991). The impact of increased contact on psychosocial outcomes in patients with osteoarthritis: A randomized controlled trial. *Journal of Rheumatology, 18,* 849–854.

Weiss, H. B. (1993). Home visiting: Necessary but not sufficient. *The Future of Children, 3,* 113–128.

Weiss, R. S. (1974). The provisions of social relationships. In Z. Rubin (Ed.), *Doing unto others* (pp. 17–26). Englewood Cliffs, NJ: Prentice-Hall.

Wekerle, C., & Wolfe, D. (1993). Prevention of physical abuse and neglect: Promising new directions. *Clinical Psychology Review, 13,* 501–540.

Werner, E. E.. & Smith, R. S. (1982). *Vulnerable but invincible: A longitudinal study of resilient children and youth.* New York: McGraw-Hill.

Wilson, W. J. (1987). *The truly disadvantaged: The inner city, the underclass, and public policy.* Chicago: University of Chicago Press.

Winter, M. M., & McDonald, D. S. (1997). Parents as teachers: Investing in good beginnings for children. In G. W. Albee & T. P. Gullotta (Eds.), *Primary prevention works* (pp. 119–145). Thousand Oaks, CA: Sage.

Yoshikawa, H. (1995). Long-term effects of early childhood programs on social outcomes and delinquency. *The Future of Children, 5,* 51–75.

9

Optimizing Support in the Natural Network

Carolyn E. Cutrona
Valerie Cole

I. Advantages of Interventions in the Natural Network
II. Characteristics of Interventions to Enhance Support in the Natural Network
III. Dimensions along Which Interventions Differ
    A. Intervention Goals
    B. Mechanisms and Techniques
    C. Agents of Change
IV. Underlying Theoretical Frameworks
    A. Mobilization of Network Resources
        1. The Empathy-Altruism Hypothesis
        2. Diffusion of Responsibility
        3. Attribution Theory
        4. Social Learning Theory
        5. Family Systems Theory
V. The Effectiveness of Network Enhancement Interventions
    A. Training Individuals to Solicit and Use Support
    B. Mobilizing the Support of One Key Network Member
    C. Mobilizing Support in the Social Network
    D. Interventions That Focus on Neighborhoods or Organizational Networks
VI. Lessons from Controlled Intervention Studies
VII. Cautions about Network Interventions
VIII. Future Research Directions
IX. Conclusions

Interventions to enhance the supportiveness of existing networks are the most heterogeneous type of social support intervention. They differ widely along a number of dimensions, including the ultimate goal of the intervention, the support processes that are targeted for change to attain the intervention goal, the techniques used to bring about change, and the agent(s) of change within the natural network. Nevertheless, they share several important characteristics. Their aim is to enrich and improve the quality of support provided by friends, relatives, coworkers, and neighbors, not to introduce new persons into stressed individuals' lives. The assumption is that needed support resources exist in people's social networks but that their quality, frequency, appropriateness to current circumstances, predictability, and coordination can be improved to the benefit of the stressed individual.

This chapter begins by addressing the advantages inherent in interventions that strive to increase the flow of support from the natural social network. Next, characteristics that distinguish this family of interventions from other kinds of preventive and therapeutic interventions are highlighted. This discussion is followed by a description of four dimensions along which network enhancement interventions vary. The final sections of the chapter are devoted to in-depth descriptions of rigorously evaluated interventions to increase support in the natural network and the conclusions that can be drawn from them. Cautions regarding the implementation of interventions and suggestions for future research follow.

ADVANTAGES OF INTERVENTIONS IN THE NATURAL NETWORK

Arguably, the most important advantage of utilizing the natural network for support is that there is a long-term commitment from family members and friends that is unmatched by other sources of support. In a review of studies linking social support to adjustment among cancer patients, Helgeson and Cohen (1996) concluded that "emotional support from existing network members—friends and family and physicians—has a greater influence on adjustment than does emotional support from other cancer patients" (p. 145). Further support for this notion that "real friends" provide more effective support than those "grafted on" to the social network comes from an intervention designed to prevent relapse among recovering alcoholics (Barber & Crisp, 1995). Participants were assigned to either a befriender group, in which they were given opportunities to socialize with other recovering alcoholics, or to a control condition in which they were instructed to keep records of the amount of alcohol they consumed. Participants in the befriender group condition did not show lower rates of relapse than those in the control condition. However, for participants in both conditions, social support from the natural network—friends, family, and coworkers—predicted relapse rates better than any other variable.

Cultural relevance is an advantage of interventions that enhance support in the natural network. Even when professional helpers are well educated about the particular problems being faced, members of the natural network have a more complete understanding of the cultural context in which the individual defines and strives to cope with his or her difficulties (Gottlieb, 1983, 1988a, 1988b). Thus, input from network members is more likely to align with the individual's values and beliefs and less likely to pose threats to the person's sense of dignity and place in the community (Thoits, 1986). There is some evidence to support the superiority of interventions enacted by members of the natural network. For instance, in a Latino community in Southern California, lay community workers were found to be more effective in increasing the use of cancer screening tests than a professionally led living skills class (Navarro et al., 1998).

Members of the natural network also have access to populations who are unlikely to seek professional assistance. For example, an ethnographic study in London, England, found that key informal opinion leaders existed in a drug-using network (Power, Jones, Kearns, Ward, & Perera, 1995). These leaders spread information about HIV prevention and influenced users in the network to use clean syringes. They also distributed clean syringes and disseminated information about services related to HIV prevention that professional health workers had been unable to transmit effectively.

An important benefit to members of the natural network is the sense of empowerment that results from many interventions that focus on the natural network (Gottlieb, 1983). Individuals prefer to solve their own problems, without intensive professional intervention. Sometimes, the empowerment is simply a result of education about the problem, such as educating cancer patients and their families about treatment options. Training in problem-solving strategies also results in empowerment. Sisson and Azrin (1986) showed that teaching family members how to assist an alcoholic to maintain sobriety resulted in substantial psychological gains for both the alcoholic and the family members.

CHARACTERISTICS OF INTERVENTIONS TO ENHANCE SUPPORT IN THE NATURAL NETWORK

Interventions that enhance support in the natural network share some of the goals and methods of psychotherapy, especially family therapy, but they differ in several ways. Unlike psychotherapy, little in-depth exploration of problem etiology or personal history occurs. Interventions to enhance the natural network focus on current relationships and how they can be encouraged to function more effectively. With the possible exception of network therapy, natural network interventions are not designed to treat psychopathology. Some network interventions are designed to maintain positive behavior changes that were achieved through more intensive therapeutic interventions, such as maintaining sobriety after treatment for alcoholism. Others assist people in dealing with chronic stressors, such as caring for a multiply handicapped child or a dementia patient. Some interventions increase the caring and concern people receive when they face traumatic events, such as the diagnosis and treatment of cancer. At the community level, network interventions facilitate communication and the pursuit of common goals among people who live in the same neighborhood or work in the same industry.

Like other support strategies, the effects of interventions to enhance support in the natural network may be therapeutic, but the benefits are not conferred by a therapist. Rather, it is network members whose increased commitment and caring provide relief from suffering. The role of the professional is to motivate and educate family, friends, and neighbors to maximize the quality of care they provide to one another.

Interventions to enhance support in the natural network are often, although not always, preventive rather than remedial. For example, a social support skills intervention was offered to children after surgery for brain tumors, to prevent social rejection and isolation after they returned to school (Die-Trill et al., 1996). Natural network enhancement interventions also deemphasize skills required to initiate new relationships, instead emphasizing skills required to enrich existing relationships. Natural network interventions concentrate on increasing positive input from others and on preventing or managing aversive input that blocks the flow of support.

DIMENSIONS ALONG WHICH INTERVENTIONS DIFFER

Network interventions to enhance support in the natural network vary along four dimensions. The first concerns the ultimate goal of the intervention, for example, to enhance mental and/or physical health. A second dimension concerns the support processes that are targeted for change to attain the intervention goal. The third concerns the techniques employed to mobilize support in the natural network, and the fourth concerns the agent of change—who actually receives input or training from the professional who is implementing the intervention.

Intervention Goals

Although many different goals have been articulated for interventions that enhance support in the natural network, three general types of goals can be identified. The first is to enhance or prevent the deterioration of the psychological and physical health of individuals who are facing severe chronic or acute stress, such as a diagnosis of breast cancer or the loss of a child. The second is to promote and sustain positive behavior change, such as smoking cessation, abstinence from drug or alcohol use, weight loss, or engaging in safer sex practices. The third is to maximize the natural social network's capacity to care for ill or incapacitated members outside institutional settings, for example, a spouse afflicted with Alzheimer's disease or a multiply handicapped child (Table 9.1).

Mechanisms and Techniques

The support-related processes thought to facilitate the attainment of intervention goals vary across interventions. Examples of techniques that have been used to

Table 9.1. The Most Common Long-Term Goals of Interventions to Enhance Support in the Natural Network

- To enhance or prevent the stress-related deterioration of mental or physical health
- To promote and sustain positive health behavior, such as smoking cessation or weight loss
- To maximize the natural network's capacity to care for its members outside institutional settings

influence these processes are discussed along with each process. A summary of mediating support processes and techniques is given in Table 9.2.

One process through which the flow of support can be influenced is education. When an individual suffers from a disease or stigmatizing condition, family and friends often lack understanding of the individual's disorder. They may have incorrect beliefs and assumptions about the disorder that prevent them from offering effective support. Their beliefs may lead them to engage in destructive behaviors that interfere with recovery, such as criticizing a schizophrenic relative for his or her difficulties in maintaining steady employment. Many network interventions include an educational or didactic component. For example, educa-

Table 9.2. Mechanisms and Examples of Techniques for Increasing Support in the Natural Network

Mechanisms	Techniques
Increase understanding	Provide educational programming on the specific disease or problem faced by the stressed individual
Change attitudes	Use cognitive modification techniques to alter dysfunctional attitudes that interfere with giving and receiving social support
Improve interaction skills	Model, rehearse, and provide constructive feedback on behavioral skills related to giving and receiving emotional and instrumental social support
Increase communication	Provide opportunities for network members to meet as a group and facilitate open communication and problem solving among network members
Coordinate responsibilities	Encourage network members to commit to specific support responsibilities to avoid diffusion of responsibility
Strengthen bonds with positive network members	Encourage and facilitate enjoyable interactions with positive network members
Weaken bonds with destructive network members	Discourage interaction with destructive network members, and teach methods to minimize harm that results from contact with them
Remove structural barriers to support	Facilitate interaction and communication between network members who have been kept apart by rigid subsystem boundaries and alliances
Provide support to network members	Provide emotionally supportive counseling to members of the natural network to sustain them in their efforts to support other members of the network

tion for network members on the symptoms, course, and demands imposed on caregivers by Alzheimer's disease was included in an intervention to assist caregivers of spouses afflicted with Alzheimer's disease (Mittelman, Ferris, Shulman, Steinberg, & Levin, 1996).

A second process through which support may be increased is attitude change. Both the recipients and providers of support may have maladaptive beliefs that interfere with the support process. Recipients may believe that requesting assistance from others is a sign of weakness and hide their needs from family and friends. They may further believe that they are not worthy of assistance from others. Network members may believe that providing support undermines the independence or dignity of the recipient, or they may believe that there is nothing they can do to be helpful. Techniques from cognitive therapy are often used to help people overcome such maladaptive beliefs. For example, among lonely adults, Brand, Lakey, and Berman (1995) used cognitive therapy techniques to modify self-deprecating beliefs that interfered with accepting, perceiving, and benefiting from social support.

Many interventions to enhance support from the natural network are built on the assumption that support resources can be enhanced through improving the support-related interaction skills of both recipients and providers of support. Recipients receive more support if they learn how to request assistance from others appropriately and how to reinforce others for offering assistance. Network members are more effective sources of support if they know how to offer a wide range of support types in a manner that is sensitive to the feelings and needs of the recipient. Network members are also more effective if they refrain from well-intentioned but harmful behaviors, such as nagging. With respect to techniques, the first step for the professional is to model or demonstrate effective ways to request or provide support by a professional. Often conducted in group settings, participants then take turns practicing the skills that were demonstrated through role playing. Other participants and the group leader provide constructive feedback on performances, which are repeated until the individual feels confident that he or she has mastered the specific skill. An example is a skill-building intervention implemented by El-Bassel and colleagues for incarcerated women who were scheduled for release in the near future (El-Bassel, Ivanoff, Schilling, Borne, & Gilbert, 1997; El-Bassel et al., 1995).

One mechanism for increasing the flow of support to stressed individuals is to increase communication among network members. Increased communication among network members may be beneficial in several ways. It provides the opportunity for spontaneous exchanges of support. It heightens people's sense of community and belonging. It also provides opportunities to work together to solve problems that face individuals in the network. Techniques to promote communication among network members typically involve gathering together family, friends, and neighbors of the stressed individual for meetings. Professionals model and facilitate open communication and constructive problem solving. Family meetings are frequently included in interventions to enhance support in the families of chronically mentally ill individuals (e.g., Gottlieb & Coppard, 1987).

Sometimes, family and friends are aware that a member of their network needs help, but they do not know how to intervene. Alternatively, individuals may assume that other members of the network are providing all of the assistance that is needed. Coordination of support efforts may be needed to clarify who will perform needed tasks. In an intervention to support foster families of children with multiple disabilities, monthly meetings or phone contacts were held between the social worker who implemented the intervention and each network member to write specific contracts regarding services to be provided to the foster family in the upcoming month (Barsh, Moore, & Hamerlynck, 1983).

Not all members of a stressed individual's social network are positive influences. Some are destructive, such as drug users in the network of an individual who is struggling to overcome addiction. In some interventions, stressed individuals are encouraged to strengthen ties to prosocial members of their network and to weaken bonds to destructive or antisocial members of their network. Interventions facilitate opportunities for interaction with positive network members. For example, in a school-based intervention for adolescents at high risk for dropping out of school, opportunities for positive interactions with teachers and prosocial peers were scheduled into the students' school day (Eggert, Thompson, Herting, Nicholas, & Dicker, 1994). Participants were discouraged from interacting with drug-using or delinquent members of their social network.

Sometimes, family members and friends form alliances and rivalries within the larger network. Individuals involved in such factions may block the stressed individual's access to members of the network. For example, in a distressed marriage, the mother may form an alliance with her children against her husband. When one of the children develops a problem, the mother may try to prevent the child access to his or her father and to the potential support resources he could provide. Network therapy interventions strive to break down structural barriers within families to promote the free flow of communication and caring across boundaries. A variety of family therapy techniques are used to alter the structure of the social network, such as raising awareness of destructive factions, assigning tasks to increase the interaction between members of estranged factions, blocking interaction between overly enmeshed members of the network, and facilitating free communication about family problems. Examples of network therapy with families of chronically mentally ill members are described by Speck and Attneave (1973). Although network therapy began with families in which there was a schizophrenic member, it has since been expanded to families with many types of illnesses (e.g., Sirkin & Rueveni, 1992).

Family and friends who are striving to provide support can become emotionally and physically depleted. To sustain their efforts, some interventions include emotionally supportive counseling for support providers. For example, Goldberg and Wool (1985) provided supportive psychotherapy to the spouses of lung cancer patients. One goal of psychotherapy was to bolster the spouse's emotional strength so that he or she could provide effective support to the patient. The other goal was to aid the spouse in mobilizing the support of the wider network, rather than taking on the entire burden of support.

Agents of Change

The intervention's agents of change may be the stressed individual or members of his or her social network (Table 9.3). When members of the social network are involved, interventions may marshal the support of a single network member, multiple members of the personal network, or groups beyond the personal network (Gottlieb, 1988a). The personal network consists of the individuals with whom the individual interacts regularly, shares an emotional bond, and identifies as family or friends. Persons beyond the personal network include people who live or work in proximity to the individual but with whom the individual does not share an emotional bond, for example, neighbors or coworkers.

UNDERLYING THEORETICAL FRAMEWORKS

Interventions that enhance support in the natural network operate through two sets of mechanisms, one pertaining to the challenge of motivating the network to intensify its supportive efforts and the other pertaining to the process that links the receipt of support to health outcomes. Because the latter set of mechanisms is addressed in the first two chapters of this book, here we concentrate on theories of human motivation that are relevant to the mechanisms entailed in the mobilization of the social network's support (Table 9.4).

Mobilization of Network Resources

The task of mobilizing a stressed individual's social network calls for strategies for motivating people to increase the support they provide and to sustain their support efforts over time. Thus, theories of motivation are germane. We have identified five theoretical frameworks that are relevant to the mobilization of helping behaviors: empathy-altruism theory, diffusion of responsibility theory, attribution theory, social learning theory, and general systems theory.

Table 9.3. Agent(s) of Change

The stressed individual
  The individual gains skills for effectively eliciting and using support.
One key network member
  The spouse or a close friend gains skills for providing support, promoting behavior change, and/or mobilizing the social network.
Multiple members of the personal network
  Family, friends, and neighbors are convened to learn support skills, coordinate support efforts, and facilitate communication among network members.
Organization or community group beyond the personal network
  People who live or work in proximity to each other, such as neighbors or coworkers, are given opportunities to build supportive connections with each other through emphasizing common goals and training key network members to promote a more supportive social environment.

Table 9.4. Underlying Theoretical Frameworks for Mobilizing the Natural Network

- Empathy-altruism theory
- Diffusion of responsibility theory
- Attribution theory
- Social learning theory
- General systems theory

The Empathy-Altruism Hypothesis

According to the empathy-altruism hypothesis proposed by Batson (Batson, 1987; Batson, Fultz, & Schoenrade, 1987), people experience some combination of two emotional responses when they witness someone in need of assistance: personal distress and empathic concern. Personal distress refers to feeling alarmed, troubled, upset, or worried. Empathic concern is centered more on the other person, involving sympathy and compassion. Batson maintains that if personal distress predominates in reaction to a person in need, people are egoistically motivated to reduce their own distress. The motive to reduce one's own distress can be satisfied either by helping the other person or by avoiding contact with the stressed individual. If, however, empathic concern predominates, people are altruistically motivated to reduce the other person's distress. According to Batson, if escape is easy, such that one can avoid having further contact with the needy person, those who are egoistically motivated often choose to leave the scene rather than help. By contrast, those who are altruistically motivated do not leave, even if escape is easy. For these individuals, the motive to reduce the other person's distress can be satisfied only by helping. Thus, increasing empathy for the stressed individual among his or her network members should increase the probability of helping efforts.

Empathy is based on understanding another's circumstances, difficulties, and emotions. It is also heightened by perceptions of similarity between oneself and the stressed individual (Batson, Duncan, Acherman, Buckley, & Birch, 1981). Most efforts to elicit support from the peer network include an educational component, which may serve to boost empathy. For example, if the stressor is a disease, information is provided to network members regarding the disease's symptoms, course, and treatments and the challenges it poses to victims and their caregivers. Research by Batson et al. (1981) suggests that these informational presentations should also highlight *similarities* between the stressed individuals and their network members, because perceived similarity enhances empathy.

Diffusion of Responsibility

Another consideration in motivating network members to come to the aid of a stressed associate is the diffusion of responsibility phenomenon. The more people who are available to provide help, the less likely any one person is to take action (Latané & Nida, 1981). Thus, it is important that all members of the network know exactly what helping behaviors are expected of them and that they feel a sense of personal responsibility for completing their assignments.

Attribution Theory

An attributional analysis of helping behavior points to the importance that people place on the causes of other people's misfortunes. Weiner (1980) demonstrated that people are least likely to help others when they believe that stressed individuals brought their troubles on themselves. When people make causal attributions for a person's misfortunes that are internal to and controllable by the victim, they are less likely to offer assistance than when the person's misfortunes are attributed to factors that are external to or uncontrollable by the victim. For example, when a man collapses in a subway station because he is drunk, people are much less likely to offer assistance than when a man collapses because he has been mugged or has suffered a heart attack. In the first case, the collapse is attributed to the victim's controllable dispositions and behaviors. In the second, the collapse is attributable to factors outside the victim's control. An important task in mobilizing a person's social support network may be educating its members regarding the causes of the person's misfortune. It is important to frame such causal explanations in a way that minimizes blame, for example, emphasizing biological causes of schizophrenia rather than poor parenting by the mother of a psychotic child.

Attributions also figure prominently in the reactions of support recipients to assistance. Interventions must anticipate issues related to recipients' causal attributions for received support. If recipients believe that family and friends are increasing their help efforts only out of a sense of obligation imposed on them by the intervention, they do not value the assistance as much as if they believe that it was volunteered out of genuine caring and desire to help. Thus, interventions should be designed to present *ideas* to network members about how best to help, not as ways to coerce others to assist. An added benefit is that when support recipients attribute helping efforts to the genuine concern of their associates, they are more likely to behave in ways that reinforce the provider. For example, they are more likely to say thank you, show pleasure, and report ways that the other's efforts lightened their load. As described later, reinforcement is a powerful but often overlooked mechanism in eliciting and sustaining support efforts.

Social Learning Theory

A highly developed and effective technology for bringing about behavior change is based on reinforcement theory (Skinner, 1974) and, more broadly, on social learning theory (Bandura, 1977, 1986). The most effective applications of behavior modification are in settings that allow a high degree of control over people's reinforcement contingencies, such as classrooms or hospital wards. Such control is generally not possible in the natural environment. However, reinforcement and social learning principles can be part of network enhancement interventions, both in achieving or maintaining increased support efforts among network members and in effecting and sustaining behavior change in the target individual.

Some network interventions teach effective support behaviors to a partner of the individual whose current life difficulties are the focus of the intervention. Network interventions directed at behavior change, such as smoking cessation and weight loss programs, train the partner to use selective reinforcement techniques (Cohen et al., 1988; Gruder et al., 1983). An important principle is that positive reinforcement for desired behaviors is more effective than punishment for negative behaviors (Patterson & Reid, 1982).

Modeling (learning through observing another perform a skill) is used in the social skills training components of many social network interventions. Techniques for providing effective support are demonstrated by a coach and then practiced by network members, often in role-play situations. Modeling is incorporated in a somewhat different way into interventions to maintain behavior change, such as weight loss. In these interventions, the spouse or partner of the individual who is striving to acquire better health habits is encouraged to engage in the same new healthful behaviors as the target of the intervention, thus modeling adaptive habit change.

Interventions to enhance support in the natural network often seek to change the behavior of network members and to maintain these changes for a long time. Social learning principles have broad but largely unrecognized applicability in efforts to shape, increase, and sustain the support behaviors of network members. One program that explicitly recognized the need to reinforce people for their ongoing support efforts was the Foster Extended Family Service model (Barsh et al., 1983). The purpose of the program was to provide practical and emotional support to foster parents of difficult-to-place multiply handicapped children. Friends, neighbors, and relatives of the foster family were provided with extensive training on various aspects of the foster child's care. Each was given a special role in relation to the child and family, including the provision of respite care to the parents, transportation, simple physical therapy for the child, and construction of special equipment needed to care for the child at home. Monthly contracts were written, in which specific responsibilities were assigned to each participating network member, including the foster parents. All participants were paid $100 for participating in the training and $3.50 an hour for performing their assigned support services. Each family was allotted up to $200 a month for support services. This system of payment used money as a tangible reinforcer for support services provided. It elevated support services to the status of paid employment, thus cutting down on missed appointments and shirked responsibilities. As noted previously, difficulties could develop if the foster families attribute the support they receive entirely to the payment, but if such "wages" are relatively low, attributions to genuine concern and a desire to help are more likely.

Of course, few intervention programs can afford to pay network members. Furthermore, only interventions that focus on the provision of tangible assistance could reasonably use a payment system. One would not want to pay a network member for "emotional support time" for obvious reasons. Other kinds of reinforcements are possible. Ideally, the direct results of support provision prove to be reinforcing, such as watching the stressed individual gradually overcome difficulties. Family meetings in which individuals discuss the progress they have made may highlight the value of their efforts. Parties to celebrate milestones, such as a year of sobriety, or gains in performance by a handicapped child may also enhance reinforcements for sustained support efforts. In short, there is much room for the creative incorporation of social learning principles into network interventions.

Family Systems Theory

General systems theory grew out of evolutionary biology and has been applied to the functioning of families, especially those with a mentally ill member. Von Bertalanffy was the first to describe the features of a system: an entity that is maintained by the mutual interaction of its parts (Nichols & Schwartz, 1998). The distinctive feature of systems theory is that the illness of the identified patient is seen as a function of the entire network rather than as a symptom of the individual. Therefore, from a systems perspective, interventions to enhance support from the natural network are a logical choice because the target of intervention (the network itself) is the locus of the problem, and change will last because of its structural character (Speck & Attneave, 1973). That a schizophrenic patient may have a chemical brain disturbance and need long-term medication is acknowledged, but the family is seen as the crucial factor in the recovery process after hospitalization. Network therapy encompasses the notion that coalitions have been formed and that family rules have developed around the identified patient that prevent both the family and the patient from receiving the support necessary to cope effectively and adapt successfully to a chronic illness (Speck & Attneave, 1973). Dysfunctional family patterns are targeted for change, which frees the family to develop new, more adaptive coping strategies and methods of communication. Therapist participation can then be gradually removed as the network itself takes over the caregiving and coping responsibilities.

THE EFFECTIVENESS OF NETWORK ENHANCEMENT INTERVENTIONS

A relatively small number of network enhancement interventions have been rigorously evaluated with randomized experimental designs. In the 1970s and 1980s, when most network interventions were attempted, many interventions were not evaluated or employed very weak assessment procedures, such as asking participants how satisfied they were with the program.

This section emphasizes findings from a handful of controlled evaluation studies. Because network enhancement interventions are very heterogeneous, outcomes are considered separately by agent of change: (1) interventions that train stressed individuals to elicit and use support from their social network, (2) interventions that mobilize the support of one key network member (e.g., smoking cessation or weight loss), (3) interventions that involve multiple members of the individual's personal network, and (4) interventions that attempt to enhance support-related functioning in organizations or community groups beyond the personal network. Many different goals were pursued in these interventions. Unfortunately, few studies that conceptualized social support as an intermediate or mediating factor in the attainment of the intervention goal included actual tests of mediation. Those that performed such analyses are highlighted.

Training Individuals to Solicit and Use Support

In light of research documenting that people with better social skills report higher levels of social support (Sarason, Sarason, Hacker, & Basher, 1985), some network enhancement interventions have focused on training stressed individuals to elicit more frequent and higher quality support from their networks.

This intervention strategy has been used to address a wide range of problems. Five controlled interventions were located, allowing some assessment of the overall effectiveness of this approach. A carefully designed study tested the effectiveness of a support boosting intervention on levels of stress, coping, and social support among caregivers of children with HIV/AIDS (Hansell et al., 1998). Caregivers ($N = 70$) were stratified with respect to their own HIV/AIDS status (positive vs. negative) and then randomly assigned to the social support intervention or the control condition. The intervention consisted of monthly meetings over a 12-month period between the investigator and the caregiver, aimed at helping caregivers identify and access network resources that could provide emotional, informational, and material support. At each meeting, progress was evaluated, and plans for increasing network support were revised as needed. The intervention was evaluated 6 months after completion. Results showed that the caregiver's own HIV status was a key factor in the intervention's effectiveness. The intervention resulted in positive results only for HIV-negative caregivers, who showed a significant increase in perceived social support. Neither coping nor perceived stress was significantly affected by the intervention in any group.

In a second study, 145 incarcerated female drug users who were scheduled for release within 3 months were randomly assigned to either a social support intervention or a standard HIV/AIDS information group (El-Bassel et al., 1995, 1997). The goal of the intervention was to increase women's social support and network involvement to promote safer sex practices, sexual self-efficacy, AIDS knowledge, and coping skills. Those in the social support condition participated in 16 2-hour group sessions in jail and an additional 6 monthly booster sessions after release. Skills for eliciting social support were modeled by the group facilitator and rehearsed during group sessions. While in jail, women were encouraged to make contact with members of their non–drug-using network and to identify individuals who might harm their recovery. Project staff offered advice and encouragement when the women placed phone calls or sent letters to reestablish connections with prosocial network members prior to release. Postrelease sessions focused on the transfer and application of the skills learned in the jail group to real-world high-risk situations. Postintervention evaluation revealed that participants in the intervention group showed significantly greater gains in safer sex behaviors, coping skills, and perceived emotional support.

Community adults with low perceived social support were recruited from singles organizations and divorce and bereavement support groups for participation in a psychoeducational intervention designed to increase perceived social support (Brand et al., 1995). Participants ($N = 51$) were randomly assigned to the intervention or a wait-list control condition. Intervention participants attended 13 weekly 3-hour group sessions. The program targeted both cognitive and behavioral barriers to rewarding interpersonal relationships. Maladaptive beliefs about the self, experiences with family of origin, and ongoing social interactions were specifically targeted with techniques adopted from cognitive-behavioral therapy. Approximately half of the sessions targeted maladaptive cognitions, and half focused on building social skills. Participants in the intervention experienced a significantly greater increase than controls in perceived family support, self-esteem, and frequency of self-reinforcement. Neither perceived support from friends nor anxiety and depression was significantly affected by the intervention. Analyses also revealed that changes in perceived family support were mediated by changes in self-esteem and self-reinforcement. The authors concluded that cognitions about the self are a critical factor in efforts to change levels of perceived social support.

Two school-based interventions sought to improve the support resources of at-risk adolescents. Barth and Schinke (1984) sought to strengthen family relationships among childbearing adolescent girls. Based on earlier pilot work, the investigators identified conflict between adolescent mothers and their families as a central impediment to a supportive home atmosphere. Thus, the intervention taught adolescent parents social and cognitive skills for maintaining harmonious family and social relationships. Adolescent mothers met twice weekly for 10 sessions with intervention staff members. Those in the intervention ($N = 33$) and a comparable group of adolescents from the same school who were not involved in the intervention ($N = 37$) were assessed at two time points, before the intervention and after its completion (although assignment to condition was not specified as random). Girls who had completed the intervention performed significantly better on verbal skills, cognitive problem solving, and self-reinforcement. In addition, girls in the intervention showed significantly higher perceived social support than those in the control group (controlling for pretest levels).

Another school-based intervention tried to strengthen the prosocial network ties of youth at risk for dropping out of high school (Eggert et al., 1994). The intervention sought to strengthen ties to school, especially to teachers, and to weaken ties to deviant peers. It was hoped that this would facilitate decreased drug involvement and improved school performance and attendance. Eligible students ($N = 259$) were randomly assigned to the network intervention or control condition. Those in the network intervention enrolled in a semester-long personal growth class, taught within the regular curriculum at each of four high schools. The social network component of the class consisted of group support, friendship development, and school bonding fostered through positive teacher-student and peer group relationships within the class. Support behaviors were modeled and practiced in discussions of students' personal problems. In addition, students were trained in self-esteem enhancement, decision making, personal control, and interpersonal communication. Data on drug use, school attendance, and school performance were collected before and after the intervention and 5 months post-intervention. Participants in the network intervention condition showed a near-significant decrease in drug use and a significant decrease in drug-related problems, in contrast with the control subjects. Intervention participants increased their grade point average significantly, whereas the controls showed no change. School attendance remained steady for the intervention participants and decreased among the controls. Intervention subjects increased significantly more than controls in self-esteem and in school bonding (i.e., positive relationships with teachers and other students in the personal growth class). For girls only, bonding with deviant peers significantly decreased as a function of the intervention.

Helping stressed individuals learn behavioral and cognitive skills that promote supportive interactions with others is a promising strategy for increasing social support from the natural social network. Both maladaptive behaviors, such as hiding one's distress from others, and maladaptive cognitions, such as the belief that asking for help is a sign of weakness, can impede the efforts of concerned network members to provide comfort and assistance. Interventions that increase both skill in eliciting support and comfort in accepting support have been successful in a wide range of settings and with a variety of populations. In addition, studies suggest that important behavioral changes can be achieved by helping stressed individuals strengthen prosocial and weaken antisocial network ties.

Mobilizing the Support of One Key Network Member

There is evidence that support from people with whom we share an intimate relationship is most effective in buffering the effects of stressful life events (e.g., Brown & Harris, 1978). Interventions to mobilize the support of one key network member have been designed to achieve two kinds of long-term goals. Some interventions seek to increase the flow of support to stressed individuals to ease their suffering and prevent stress-related deterioration in mental and physical health. Others seek to increase the flow of support to assist an individual who is striving to make health-related behavior changes, such as smoking cessation or weight loss.

A controlled intervention to enhance the psychological and physical health of lung cancer patients and their spouses was implemented by Goldberg and Wool (1985). In this study, the spouses of newly diagnosed lung cancer patients were randomly assigned to a social support condition ($N = 28$) or a control condition ($N = 25$). Those assigned to the social support condition were provided with 12 sessions of individual social support counseling. The counseling sessions were designed to help the spouse fulfill five support functions: (1) to maintain and strengthen the patient's social support system, (2) to promote the patient's sense of autonomy, (3) to be an advocate in the medical system for the patient when necessary, (4) to encourage communication between the patient and those around him or her, and (5) to facilitate the mutual expression of feelings between spouse and patient. Patients and spouses in both conditions were assessed within 6 weeks of diagnosis, 8 weeks later, and 16 weeks later. Measures included physical functioning, psychological well-being, and perceived network support. The intervention did not show any significant effects for either patients or spouses. The authors reported that one reason the intervention had no effect was that most of the patients and their spouses were functioning quite well before the intervention, and there was little room for improvement in scores on the measures that were administered. They speculated that those who were having the most difficulty in coping with the patient's illness might not have volunteered for participation. The authors argued for careful screening of potential participants so that individuals who are not functioning well can be targeted for assistance.

A number of controlled studies examined the extent to which involving one key network member, typically the spouse, enhanced the effectiveness of programs to enhance positive health behaviors. These programs targeted either smoking cessation or weight loss. Turning first to smoking cessation, Cohen et al. (1988) randomly assigned 64 smokers with spouses who were willing to cooperate to the smoker-only or spouse-involved condition. In both conditions, the intervention consisted of six 2-hour group sessions on how to quit smoking (e.g., nicotine fading, self-management training, relapse prevention). In the spouse-involved condition, the spouse was urged to attend all sessions and received training on specific supportive and nonsupportive behaviors related to smoking cessation. Guided group discussions and homework exercises were used to encourage couple problem solving. Spouses were encouraged to reward their partners and to participate in prescribed program activities. Multiple follow-up assessments of smoking were conducted after treatment concluded. Rates of abstinence did not differ significantly as a function of condition at any assessment, although they approached significance immediately after treatment and always favored the spouse-involved condition. Cohen et al. (1988) reported similar nonsignificant results in an unpublished replication study (Lichtenstein, Mermelstein, Kamarck, & Baer, 1985) and two additional smoking cessation programs (described in Lichtenstein, Glasgow, & Abrams, 1986).

Somewhat more positive results were reported in a smoking cessation intervention reported by Gruder et al. (1993). Reasoning that most smokers do not want intensive professional help in their attempts to quit smoking, Gruder and colleagues implemented a minimalist smoking cessation intervention. A 20-part series on how to quit smoking was aired on local television newscasts. Participants were solicited to augment this televised self-help intervention. To be eligible, applicants had to indicate that they were interested in attending group sessions and had a nonsmoking buddy who was also willing to attend. Participants ($N = 793$) were randomly assigned to one of three conditions. In the no-contact condition, they were simply mailed a manual on smoking cessation. Those in the other two conditions were given the manual and participated in three 90-minute group sessions. Their nonsmoking buddies attended a separate group session scheduled at the same time as the second smoker group session. In the social support condition, buddies received explicit training on how to support the smoker's efforts to quit, including a "Buddy Manual." In the discussion condition, buddies were given general information about the program but no explicit training. Follow-up phone calls from the investigator to provide encouragement to both ex-smokers and buddies were provided 1 and 2 months postintervention. These phone calls focused on support issues in the social support condition. In the discussion condition, only general encouragement was provided.

Immediately following the intervention, significantly more smokers were abstinent in the social support condition than in the discussion condition. In addition, the ratio of positive to negative interactions with the buddy was significantly higher in the social support condition than in the discussion condition. Although positive interactions did not increase, negative interactions decreased. Analyses showed that the superior outcome of the social support group was mediated by the change in the ratio of positive to negative interactions with the buddy. Follow-up assessments were conducted over the 12-month period following the intervention. Unfortunately, the effects of the social support intervention no longer exceeded those of the other conditions at any subsequent time point. It should be noted that more than 200 people participated in each of the three conditions in the Gruder et al. (1993) study. Thus, the power to detect differences between conditions was much greater than in other studies.

Similar intervention techniques were applied to the problem of weight control in a controlled intervention conducted by Brownell, Heckerman, Westlake, Hayes, and Monti: (1978). Twenty-nine married overweight individuals were enrolled in a weight loss program. Those whose spouses were willing to participate were randomly assigned to either the cooperative-spouse, subject-alone condition or the cooperative-spouse, spouse-involved condition. Those with a noncooperative spouse were considered as a separate group in the analyses. Participants in all conditions attended weekly 90-minute group sessions for 10 weeks, followed by monthly maintenance sessions for an additional 6 months. In the subject-alone condition, the spouse was not included in any of the training sessions. In the couples-training condition, the spouse attended all sessions with the subject. These sessions included training for spouses on modeling, monitoring, and reinforcing adaptive eating habits. The spouses were encouraged to change their own eating habits along with the subjects. Subject and spouse monitored both their own and their partner's adaptive eating behaviors. The couple, rather than the individual, was reinforced for habit change to foster a spirit of cooperation and mutuality.

Follow-up assessments were conducted immediately after the 10-week intervention and 3 and 6 months postintervention. Weight loss did not differ as a function of condition at the immediate posttest. However, at both the 3- and 6-month follow-ups, those in the couples-training condition showed significantly greater weight loss than those in either of the other groups. The other two groups (cooperative-spouse subject-alone and noncooperative-spouse) did not differ significantly from each other. The authors noted that the mean weight loss in the couples-training condition was higher than that reported in most weight loss intervention studies: 66% lost more than 20 pounds, and 22% lost more than 40 pounds. One notable feature of this intervention was that monthly maintenance sessions continued for 6 months after the conclusion of the core 10-week module. Unfortunately, no measures of perceived spouse supportiveness were obtained, precluding a determination of whether change in spousal support was the underlying mechanism in successful weight loss.

In sum, findings are mixed regarding the effectiveness of programs to mobilize the support of one key network member. The intervention to bolster the support available from the spouses of lung cancer patients had no significant effects on either spouses or patients. Regarding behavior-change interventions, findings are less encouraging for smoking cessation interventions than for weight loss interventions. It may be that smoking cessation is more difficult than weight loss. Alternatively, there may have been features of the weight loss program reported by Brownell et al. (1978) that account for its success. The duration of the program was its most notable difference from the smoking cessation interventions. Brownell et al. offered 10 weeks of intensive weekly intervention plus monthly maintenance meetings for another 6 months. By contrast, the smoking cessation interventions were typically completed within about 2 months. Of course, the more sessions, the higher the cost of the intervention. However, more widely spaced follow-up ("booster") sessions have been found to increase maintenance of behavior change programs in other contexts (Patterson & Reid, 1982) and should be considered in the design of future programs.

Mobilizing Support in the Social Network

We located few controlled studies of efforts to mobilize support among multiple members of the support network. A particularly regrettable gap is the absence of controlled evaluations of network interventions to mobilize the family and friends of chronically mentally ill patients, although good descriptions of uncontrolled network interventions can be found in the literature (e.g., Biegel, Tracy, & Corvo, 1994; Gottlieb & Coppard, 1987; Morin & Seidman, 1986; Speck, 1998; Speak & Attneave, 1973). Social work interventions to assist the families of physically or cognitively handicapped children also abound in the literature (e.g., Barsh et al., 1983; Gabel & Kotsch, 1981; Moore, Hamerlynck, Barsh, Spieker, & Jones, 1982; Schilling, Gilchrist, & Schinke, 1984; Tracy & Whittaker, 1987) but were not generally subjected to rigorous evaluation. Two controlled natural network mobilization studies that were located are described next.

A family intervention to delay nursing home placement of patients with Alzheimer's disease by increasing support for their caregivers was implemented by Mittelman and colleagues (1996). Spouse caregivers for Alzheimer's patients (N = 99) were randomly assigned to a support intervention or standard case management services. Those in the intervention group were provided four family sessions and two individual counseling sessions for the caregiver. Family sessions focused on (1) educating the family about dementia and (2) teaching network members how to provide appropriate emotional and tangible support to the caregiver. In addition, family sessions were used to increase communication among family members to facilitate exchanges of support. Individual sessions with the caregiver bolstered the caregiver's skills in solving problems and in eliciting support from others. After the first 4 months of the intervention, caregivers and families were given unlimited access to counselors for consultation and support, and caregivers were instructed to join an ongoing caregiver support group. Researchers discovered that not all intervention subjects participated in a support group and that almost half of the control group participated in a support group on their own. Thus, when analyzing results, support group participation was entered as a variable in the prediction of outcomes.

Participants were followed for up to 8 years. The key outcome measure was length of time the patient was maintained at home, prior to placement in a nursing home. Those in the intervention group delayed institutionalization significantly longer than those in the control group (approximately 12 months), especially those whose relatives were in the mild to moderate stage of the illness. At these stages of the illness, rates of institutionalization were 2.5 to 5 times lower among intervention families. Participation in a support group was not a significant predictor of time to institutionalization. It must be noted, however, that the researchers did not assess the mediating role of perceived family support, so it cannot be determined whether the delay in institutionalization was attributable to increased support from members of the natural network.

A controlled intervention designed to increase the psychological well-being of stroke survivors was reported by Friedland and McColl (1992). Participants ($N =$ 88) had all completed a course of inpatient and outpatient rehabilitation and were an average of 11 months poststroke. Patients were randomly assigned to a social support intervention or a control group. The social support intervention consisted of 6 to 12 sessions. Patients attended the first 3 sessions alone and were assisted by their therapist in conducting an intensive assessment of their social network resources. Subsequent sessions involved members of the patient's social network, with whom the therapist worked to improve the quality and frequency of support provided to the patient.

Follow-up assessments were conducted 3 and 6 months postintervention. Contrary to prediction, no significant differences between intervention and control participants were found on measures of social support or psychosocial adjustment. The investigators proposed a variety of explanations for the intervention's failure. First, the timing may not have been optimal. Eleven months after their strokes, patients may have passed through their original crisis stage, when social support may be most beneficial (Cwikel & Israel, 1987). For a substantial number of patients, depression had already set in by the time the intervention began. The authors speculated that an earlier intervention might have prevented such depression. They also conjectured that by providing the intervention at the completion of patients' rehabilitation program, participants may have seen the program as prolonging the sick role. In addition, perceived social support was high among most patients prior to the intervention, so a ceiling effect may have precluded significant gains.

Interventions to enhance support through mobilizing the resources of multiple social network members may be effective only under specific circumstances and for specific problems. Of the two controlled interventions we found, one was successful and one was not. Although a number of creative interventions have been implemented, few have been rigorously evaluated. More controlled outcome studies are needed to identify the parameters that are associated with positive outcomes.

Interventions That Focus on Neighborhood or Organizational Networks

Interventions that focus on neighborhood or organizational networks seek to enhance the functioning of people in these networks through facilitating supportive connections, emphasizing common goals, and training key network members to promote a more supportive social environment. Many creative programs have been implemented, although few were subjected to rigorous assessment. For example, the Community Helpers Project (D'Augelli, Vallance, Danish, Young, & Gerdes, 1981) offered training to enrich the support skills of natural helpers in the community, including clergy, hairdressers, merchants, housewives, and teachers. The Day Care Neighbor Service (Collins, Emlen, & Watson, 1969) enhanced the support skills and childcare knowledge of local women who served as informal advisors on childcare to their friends and neighbors. Projects to strengthen the informal helping networks of elderly residents of urban neighborhoods were implemented by Chapman and Pancoast (1985).

We found a single controlled neighborhood-based support intervention in the literature. In addition, we found two controlled interventions designed to increase support in the workplace.

The Neighborhood Participation Project was implemented in urban Nashville, Tennessee, to rehabilitate housing and living conditions (Unger & Wandersman, 1982, 1983). It was hoped that by facilitating the development of block organizations, residents would become better acquainted, engage in more social activities, and work together to improve conditions in their neighborhood. Community organizers went door to door in a seven-block area and interviewed people about their needs, interests, and concerns. They found a resident to host an initial block meeting and helped notify residents of the meeting. They offered assistance with future meetings as well. Residents in an adjacent four-block area served as the control group. Residents in the intervention blocks and the control blocks were interviewed once before the organizational efforts and again 6 months later. At the 6-month follow-up, individuals who had joined a block organization had increased significantly more on frequency of meaningful interaction with neighbors than those who lived in the intervention blocks but had not joined a block organization and those in the control blocks.

Turning next to workplace interventions, one well-designed study focused on staff members of group homes for developmentally delayed or chronically mentally ill adults (Heaney, Price, & Rafferty, 1995). Fifty-five agencies participated. Half of the group homes within each agency were randomly assigned to receive the intervention program. The program's goals were to teach employees about the value of social support and to build skills in mobilizing support at work. In the intervention condition, the manager and one direct service worker from each group home were invited to participate in a series of six half-day workshops. In turn, they were expected to hold training sessions for their coworkers back at their home sites. Training sessions included analyzing social support resources at work, refining interpersonal skills relevant to support, and developing plans for increasing support at each individual site.

A variety of issues arose in implementing the intervention. Some agencies did not send any staff members to training sessions. Some employees who attended the workshops did not hold any training sessions in their group home. These agencies were nevertheless included as intervention sites in the outcome evaluations. Results showed that those at the intervention sites increased significantly more than those at control sites in the amount of supportive feedback they received on the job and the quality of the work team climate. There were no significant intervention effects for perceived supervisor support, positive work team functioning, or personal mental health.

A second workplace intervention was designed to promote employee weight loss (Cohen, 1988). Employees of three light manufacturing firms and three banks were assigned to one of three conditions. In all three conditions, participants were provided with written instructions on how to lose weight and were weighed weekly by a member of the research team. Cash rewards for weight loss were distributed in different ways in the three conditions. In the individual competition program, employees competed against each other. Those who lost the most weight won cash rewards. In the pure cooperative condition, the amount of the cash reward was determined by the percentage of people who reached their weight loss goal. The more people who were successful, the greater the reward for all. In the team-competitive, group-cooperative condition, participants were assigned to teams. The cash rewards went to the team that showed the greatest weight loss. The latter two conditions were designed to build supportive relationships among employees. Support was expected to assist persons in their efforts to lose weight. As predicted, weight loss was significantly greater in the two conditions that promoted support than in the individual competition condition. A replication showed that support from coworkers and from employers were significant predictors of amount of weight lost, confirming the mediational role of support in successful weight reduction.

Results of these studies suggest that interventions to increase the level of support within neighborhoods and in the workplace can be effective. However, the challenge remains of motivating people to participate in such interventions. In all three interventions, participation rates were relatively low. In addition, methods are needed to maintain changes in neighborhoods and workplaces after the interventions end.

LESSONS FROM CONTROLLED INTERVENTION STUDIES

In general, interventions that lasted longer appeared to be more effective than very brief interventions. A particularly good strategy appears to be the inclusion of "booster sessions," which reinforce skill and knowledge acquisition from the main intervention, especially when they are spaced further apart than the initial intervention sessions.

A second conclusion is that teaching the stressed individual skills relevant to the mobilization and use of support resources is a worthwhile investment of resources. Several programs demonstrated that training stressed individuals strategies for eliciting support resulted in significant increases in the support they perceived from others (e.g., Barth & Schinke, 1984; Brand et al., 1995; El-Bassel et al., 1995). People can alter many dimensions of their interactions with others, including the frequency, content, and emotional tone of their social transactions (Heller & Swindle, 1983). Social skills can be improved through modeling, feedback, and practice, with an associated improvement in social support (Barth & Schinke, 1984).

Different target populations undoubtedly require different specific skills to improve the social support resources they gain from their networks. One notable characteristic of some interventions was meticulous preparatory research on the specific interpersonal barriers to successful relationships faced by the target group. For example, Barth conducted research on correlates of perceived social support among adolescent mothers before he designed the support intervention (Barth, 1988). He found that global social skills did not predict perceived social support as strongly as the possession of specific conflict-resolution skills. Thus, the intervention focused on teaching adolescent mothers to decrease the frequency and intensity of conflict with their parents as a means to facilitate the flow of social support. Similarly, before designing their support-based HIV/AIDS intervention for incarcerated women, El-Bassel and colleagues conducted focus groups with inmates and former offenders (El-Bassel, et al., 1997). Participants emphasized that feeling supported by and responsible to their families, children, and communities was essential in their motivation to seek drug treatment and reduce their HIV/AIDS risk. Thus, a major component of the intervention was strengthening links to their families, which frequently required mending long-neglected or damaged relationships. The need for preparatory research on the actual support needs of targeted populations cannot be overemphasized.

A characteristic of several successful intervention programs was a focus on cognitions that are relevant to social support and successful relationships (Brand et al., 1995; El-Bassel et al., 1995; Schilling et al., 1984). Brand et al. (1995) based their intervention for divorced and widowed adults on the belief that perceived social support is primarily a cognitive phenomenon, which reflects a variety of perceptual and interpretive processes. According to this view, increasing the frequency and quality of support received from other people does not necessarily increase the level of perceived support availability. People's support assessments are strongly biased by their past experiences, especially in their family of origin. The tendency to mistrust others as sources of support and the related tendency to view oneself as unworthy of support were explicitly targeted for change in the intervention. Changes in cognitions about the self mediated changes in perceived social support, thus bolstering the argument that beliefs about the self influence beliefs about support. Interventions that seek to bolster network support may be most successful if they include an explicit focus on overcoming attitudinal barriers operating among the recipients of support.

Interventions to enhance support from the natural network may not be appropriate for all populations. Several interventions have attempted to strengthen the existing network ties of abusive mothers, based on the research finding that those who abuse their children are often socially isolated (Lovell & Hawkins, 1988). An intensive 26-week network enhancement intervention in which abusive mothers of preschoolers were taught interpersonal skills failed to yield significant changes on any network parameter (Lovell & Hawkins, 1988). Similarly, Lovell & Richey (1997) failed to achieve significant gains in the social interactions of parents at risk for child maltreatment. Perhaps the setting, a court-mandated social service intervention, contributed to participants' lack of engagement. However, the intervention's lack of success was probably attributable in part to individual personality factors that made it difficult for participants to change their relationships with members of their social networks. In a separate study of young mothers who maltreated their children, Egeland and colleagues reported that the abusive mothers had little social support because they had alienated kin and friends, not because no kin or friends were nearby (Egeland, Brietenbacher, & Rosenberg, 1980). Clearly, some people benefit less from social support interventions than others. For persons who have long-standing patterns of social isolation, more than a brief skill-building intervention is required. Among those with evidence of serious difficulties, such as those with a history of child maltreatment, long-term educational and therapeutic interventions may be more appropriate.

Ironically, individuals who are facing overwhelming life stress may be poorly suited for network enhancement interventions. As reported previously, among caregivers for HIV-positive children, a network enhancement intervention was beneficial only to caregivers who were not themselves infected with the HIV virus (El-Bassel et al., 1995, 1997). Infected caregivers, who faced debilitating physical symptoms and realistic anxiety over their own survival, may have lacked the personal resources required to implement the skills that were taught in the intervention. When the stressed individual is incapacitated, network members should be approached directly and encouraged to increase their support efforts.

Timing can also be a crucial factor in the design of social support interventions. There is some evidence that people are most receptive to interventions when they are in the midst of a crisis. Waiting until the crisis has resolved (positively or negatively) may mean that an opportunity to intervene at a time of optimal receptivity will be missed.

CAUTIONS ABOUT NETWORK INTERVENTIONS

Network members tend to specialize in certain types of support. A study of very low-income mothers revealed that different relationships were used for different kinds of resources (Baxter & Kahn, 1996). Friends provided babysitting and talk about the child but did not provide input on or assist in discipline. Similarly, in a review of correlational studies on social support among cancer patients, it was determined that patients needed emotional support from family and friends and informational support from professionals (Blanchard, Albrecht, Ruckdeschel, Grant, & Hemmick, 1995). In short, intervention planners should assign support functions in a way that is normative for different categories of relationships.

Other issues that may impede progress in a network intervention include resistance of the immediate family to outside intervention. Especially if the illness is stigmatized, such as alcoholism or schizophrenia, family members may actively resist efforts to include other members of the extended family in a therapeutic approach. Efforts must be made by program designers to develop a strong therapeutic alliance with the nuclear family first and then invite the participation of others.

Sometimes network members become overly involved in one another's lives. For example, spouses of cardiac patients may feel that it is their responsibility to assure that the patient adheres exactly to all medical regimens (Coyne, Wortman, & Lehman, 1988). They may be highly critical and express anger when they believe that the patient is engaging in health-threatening behavior. The patient, exasperated by the spouse's intrusiveness, may actually engage in less health-promoting behavior as a means of asserting independence (Coyne et al., 1988). The designers of interventions to enhance support from the natural network must be sensitive to signs of overinvolvement and strive to communicate the need to respect the stressed individual's autonomy.

Network members may also become discouraged if their efforts at providing support do not yield the expected improvements in the individual's mental or physical condition (Coyne et al., 1988). They may blame the patient for ignoring their advice or not trying hard enough. To avoid disapproval, the patient may hide discomfort and portray a false picture of recovery. This perceived need to hide suffering may lead the patient to experience feelings of strain and isolation. Interventions should include educational components to communicate realistic expectations to both stressed individuals and members of their network regarding the course and process of recovery.

Conflict in relationships with network members may be a significant factor in maladaptive coping. Chapman and Pancoast (1985) point out that some interpersonal relations are simply nonsupportive. Hurd, Pattison, and Llamas (1981) emphasized that networks have stress-mediating functions that may be supportive, destructive, insignificant, or merely innocuous and that such dynamics need to be taken into account before an intervention is planned. When the natural network is destructive, the most effective interventions may assist the individual in disentangling himself or herself from the network and seeking new relationships elsewhere (Gottlieb & Coppard, 1987).

The effect of psychosocial interventions is often quite small. In a meta-analysis of randomized experiments that included support groups as well as family interventions, Meyer and Mark (1995) found that the effect size for emotional adjustment was −.23, and the effect size for functional adjustment was only −.08. Thus, studies using small samples may fail to attain significance because of to a lack of statistical power. Furthermore, even a statistically significant effect can fail to meet the more rigorous standard of clinical significance—making a difference in a person's social and emotional life.

FUTURE RESEARCH DIRECTIONS

Given the limited number of controlled intervention studies on the effectiveness of programs that seek to enhance the supportiveness of natural networks, such evaluation research must be considered a priority. When the stressed individuals are too incapacitated to act on their own behalf to increase support, direct work with family, friends, and neighbors to increase and coordinate their support efforts is sometimes the only option. However, little is known about parameters of such interventions that are associated with success.

The integration of direct network mobilization with efforts to increase the social skills and decrease the attitudinal barriers of support recipients should be investigated. Ideally, the skills recipients attain will allow them to accept and utilize support resources to their maximal effectiveness. In addition, recipients may learn to respond to support efforts in a way that reinforces network members, thus maximizing the likelihood that they will continue to provide support. If recipients learn support-related skills, they may eventually be able to reciprocate, once their own personal crises resolve. In this way, network interventions may have a radiating influence throughout the network.

Interventions reported in the literature frequently include both techniques to foster social support and techniques to build other skills, such as decision making or problem solving. Thus, we cannot determine the extent to which positive results were due to social support enhancement. Two kinds of studies can address this issue. Study designs are needed that permit components of multifaceted interventions to be tested individually and in combination to determine which components are the "active ingredient(s)" (West, Aiken, & Todd, 1993). In addition, more studies are needed in which theoretically identified mediators of intervention effects are tested. Interventions designed to improve well-being through increasing the frequency and quality of social interactions should include measures of the mediating social variables. Formal tests of mediation should be performed to see if the intervention's success can be attributed to changes in the presumed mediators, such as increased social interaction.

Research is needed on how to maximize participation and retention rates in interventions to enhance support in the natural network. Low volunteer rates and poor attendance are often issues in group-based interventions. Techniques developed for maximizing participation in other kinds of interventions should be tested in the context of natural network interventions (Spoth & Redmond, 1994; Spoth, Redmond, Hockaday, & Shin, 1996).

Methods for assessing the support needs of specific populations should also be a focus of research. Innovative methods may produce information that extends beyond self-report questionnaires. For example, Bryant (1985) developed the neighborhood walk, a method for obtaining information on the social support resources of children in middle childhood. Children are actually taken for a walk around their neighborhood to elicit cues and reminders of people who play supportive roles in the children's lives. In general, interventions should be built upon a solid foundation of knowledge about support resources and processes in the specific group for whom the intervention is designed.

CONCLUSIONS

Interventions to enhance support in the natural network are built on the assumption that untapped potential exists within people's circle of family, friends, and neighbors. A wide variety of approaches have been developed to transform this potential into effective sustained support. Some approaches focus on the stressed individual as the agent of change. The underlying premise of such approaches is that people whose support resources are not sufficient can learn how to mobilize their network and increase their supply of support. Furthermore, it is assumed that stressed individuals may not recognize, appreciate, or benefit from support without the kind of preparation provided by the intervention. Dysfunctional attitudes may interfere with the support process as much as dysfunctional behaviors.

Other approaches assign the role of change agent to the network that surrounds the stressed individual. The underlying premise of such approaches is that networks can best be mobilized through direct contact with potential support providers. It is assumed that people who care about a stressed individual can be motivated to increase the social support they provide and can be trained to improve the quality of their support efforts.

Three considerations seem primary in determining whether the stressed individual or the network is selected as the agent of change. First, the capabilities of the stressed individual must be evaluated. Those who are severely incapacitated, through physical or mental illness, may not be able to participate in an intervention. In this case, the network is the logical agent of change. Second, access to the network must be evaluated. If the network is not accessible, either because of geographical location or discomfort with psychological interventions, the individual is the logical agent of change. Third, others' receptivity to support of the stressed individual must be evaluated. If the stressed person demonstrates attitudes and behaviors that reject or undermine assistance from others, these issues must be addressed or help from others will fail.

Although many interventions to enhance support in the natural network have not received rigorous evaluation and not all controlled interventions have been successful, we should continue to investigate the potential of this type of intervention. When individuals work together to solve their own problems, the solutions will be congruent with the personalities of the people involved and with the larger cultural context in which they reside. A sense of empowerment may be gained that is not easily derived from interventions that stress the expertise of an outside professional. Most important, when assistance is provided by people who are significant in the individual's life, the bonds between recipient and supporter are strengthened and can serve as an important psychological resource for both in times of need.

REFERENCES

Bandura, A. (1977). *Social learning theory.* Englewood Cliffs, NJ: Prentice Hall.

Bandura, A. (1986). *Social foundations of thought and action: A social cognitive theory.* Englewood Cliffs, NJ: Prentice-Hall.

Barber, J. G., & Crisp, B. R. (1995). Social support and prevention of relapse following treatment for alcohol abuse. *Research on Social Work Practice, 5,* 283–296.

Barsh, E. T., Moore, J. A., & Hamerlynck, L. A. (1983). The foster extended family: A support network for handicapped foster children. *Child Welfare, 62*(4), 349–359.

Barth, R. P. (1988). Social skill and social support among young mothers. *Journal of Community Psychology, 16,* 132–143.

Barth, R. P., & Schinke, S. P. (1984). Enhancing the social supports of teenage mothers. *Social Casework: The Journal of Contemporary Social Work, 65,* 523–531.

Batson, C. D. (1987). Prosocial motivation: Is it ever truly altruistic? In L. Berkowitz (Ed.), *Advances in experimental social psychology* (vol. 20, pp. 65–122). Orlando: Academic Press.

Batson, C. D., Duncan, B. D., Acherman, P., Buckley, T., & Birch, K. (1981). Is empathic emotion a source of altruistic motivation? *Journal of Personality and Social Psychology, 40,* 290–302.

Batson, C. D., Fultz, J., & Schoenrade, P. A. (1987). Distress and empathy: Two qualitatively distinct vicarious emotions with different motivational consequences. *Journal of Personality, 55,* 19–39.

Baxter, A., & Kahn, J. V. (1996). Effective early intervention for inner-city infants and toddlers: Assessing social supports, needs, and stress. *Infant-Toddler Intervention, 6*(3), 197–211.

Biegel, D. E., Tracy, E. M., & Corvo, K. N. (1994). Strengthening social networks: Intervention strategies for mental health care case managers. *Health and Social Work, 19,* 206–216.

Blanchard, C. G., Albrecht, T. L., Ruckdeschel, J. C., Grant, C. H., & Hemmick, R. M. (1995). The role of social support in adaptation to cancer and to survival. *Journal of Psychosocial Oncology, 13,* 75–95.

Brand, E. F., Lakey, B., & Berman, S. (1995). A preventive, psychoeducational approach to increase perceived social support. *American Journal of Community Psychology, 23*(1), 117–135.

Brown, G. W., & Harris, T. (1978). *Social origins of depression.* New York: Free Press.

Brownell, K. D., Heckerman, C. L., Westlake, R. J., Hayes, S. C., & Monti, P. M. (1978). The effect of couples training and partner co-operativeness in the behavioral treatment of obesity. *Behavior Research and Therapy, 16*, 323–333.

Bryant, B. K. (1985). The neighborhood walk: Sources of support in middle childhood. *Monographs of the Society for Research in Child Development, 50*(3).

Chapman, N. J., & Pancoast, D. L. (1985). Working with the informal helping networks of the elderly: The experiences of three programs. *Journal of Social Issues, 41*, 47–63.

Cohen, R. Y. (1988). Mobilizing support for weight loss through work-site competitions. In B. H. Gottlieb (Ed.), *Marshaling social support: Formats, processes, and effects* (pp. 241–264). Newbury Park, CA: Sage.

Cohen, S., Lichtenstein, E., Mermelstein, R., Kingsolver, K., Baer, J. S., & Kamarck, T. W. (1988). Social support intervention for smoking cessation. In B. H. Gottlieb (Ed.), *Marshaling social support: Formats, processes, and effects* (pp. 211–240). Newbury Park, CA: Sage.

Collins, A. H., Emlen, A. C., & Watson, E. L. (1969). The day care neighbor service: An intervention experiment. *Community and Mental Health Journal, 5*, 219–224.

Coyne, J. C., Wortman, C. B., & Lehman, D. R. (1988). The other side of support. Emotional overinvolvement and miscarried helping. In B. H. Gottlieb (Ed.), *Marshaling social support: Formats, processes, and effects* (pp. 305–330). Newbury Park, CA: Sage.

Cwikel, J., & Israel, B. (1987). Examining mechanisms of social support and social networks: A review of health-related intervention studies. *Public Health Review, 15*, 159–193.

D'Augelli, A. R., Vallance, T. R., Danish, S. J., Young, C. E., & Gerdes, J. L. (1981). The community helpers project: A description of a prevention strategy for rural communities. *Journal of Prevention, 1*, 209–224.

Die-Trill, M., Bromberg, J., LaVally, B., Portales, L. A., SanFeliz, A., & Patenaude, A. F. (1996). Development of social skills in boys with brain tumors: A group approach. *Journal of Psychosocial Oncology, 14*(2), 23–41.

Egeland, B., Brietenbacher, M., & Rosenberg, D. (1980). A prospective study of the significance of life stress in the etiology of child abuse. *Journal of Consulting and Clinical Psychology, 48*, 195–205.

Eggert, L. L., Thompson, E. A., Herting, J. R., Nicholas, L. J., & Dicker, B. G. (1994). Preventing adolescent drug abuse and high school dropout through an intensive school-based social network development program. *American Journal of Health Promotion, 8*, 202–215.

El-Bassel, N., Ivanoff, A., Schilling, R. F., Borne, D., & Gilbert, L. (1997). Skills building and social support enhancement to reduce HIV risk among women in jail. *Criminal Justice and Behavior, 24*(2), 205–223.

El-Bassel, N., Ivanoff, A., Schilling, R. F., Gilbert, L., Borne, D., & Chen, D.-R. (1995). Preventing HIV/AIDS in drug abusing incarcerated women through skills building and social support enhancement: Preliminary outcomes. *Social Work Research, 19*(3), 131–141.

Friedland, J. F., & McColl, M. A. (1992). Social support intervention after stroke: Results of a randomized trial. *Archives of Physical Medicine Rehabilitation, 73*, 573–581.

Furstenberg, F. F. Jr., & Crawford, A. G. (1978). Family support: Helping teenage mothers to cope. *Family Planning Perspectives, 10*, 322–333.

Gabel, H., & Kotsch, L. S. (1981). Extended families and young handicapped children. *Topics in Early Childhood Special Education, 1*(3), 29–35.

Garrison, J. E. (1981). Clinical construction of action social networks. *International Journal of Family Therapy, 3*, 258–267.

Goldberg, R. J., & Wool, M. S. (1985). Psychotherapy for the spouses of lung cancer patients: Assessment of an intervention. *Psychotherapy and Psychosomatics, 43*, 141–150.

Gottleib, B. H. (1983). *Social support strategies.* Beverly Hills, CA: Sage.

Gottlieb, B. H. (1988a). Marshaling social support: The state of the art in research and practice. In B. H. Gottlieb (Ed.), *Marshaling social support: Formats, processes, and effects* (pp. 11–51). Newbury Park, CA: Sage.

Gottlieb, B. H. (1988b). Support interventions: A typology and agenda for research. In S. W. Duck (Ed.), *Handbook of Personal Relationships* (pp. 519–541). New York: Wiley.

Gottlieb, B. H., & Coppard, A. (1987). Using social network therapy to create support systems for the chronically mentally disabled. *Canadian Journal of Community Mental Health, 6*, 117–132.

Gruder, C. L., Mermelstein, R. J., Kirkendol, S., Hedeker, D., Wong, S. C., Schreckengost, J., Warnecke, R. B., Burzette, R., & Miller, T. Q. (1993). Effects of social support and relapse prevention training as adjuncts to a televised smoking-cessation intervention. *Journal of Consulting and Clinical Psychology, 61*(1), 113–120.

Hansell, P. S., Hughes, C. B., Caliandro, G., Russo, P., Budin, W. C., Hartman, B., & Hernandez, O. C. (1998). The effect of a social support boosting intervention on stress, coping, and social support in caregivers of children with HIV/AIDS. *Nursing Research, 47*(2), 79–86.

Heaney, C. A., Price, R. H., & Rafferty, J. (1995). Increasing coping resources at work: A field experiment to increase social support, improve team functioning, and enhance employee mental health. *Journal of Organizational Behavior, 16*, 335–352.

Helgeson, V. S., & Cohen, S. (1996). Social support and adjustment to cancer: Reconciling descriptive, correlational, and interventional research. *Health Psychology, 15*, 135–148.

Heller, K., & Swindle, R. W. Jr. (1983). Social networks, perceived social support and coping with stress. *Journal of Consulting and Clinical Psychology, 54*, 461–465.

Hurd, G. S., Pattison, E. M., & Llamas, R. (1981). Models of social network intervention. *International Journal of Family Therapy, 3*, 246–257.

Latané, B., & Nida, S. (1981). Ten years of research on group size and helping. *Psychological Bulletin, 89*, 308–324.

Lichtenstein, E., Glasgow, R., & Abrams, D. A. (1986). Social support in smoking cessation: In search of effective interventions. *Behavior Therapy, 17*, 607–619.

Lichtenstein, E., Mermelstein, R. J., Kamarck, T. W., & Baer, J. S. (1985). *Partner support and smoking cessation: Replication and extension* (unpublished manuscript). Eugene: Oregon Research Institute.

Lovell, M. L., & Hawkins, J. D. (1988). An evaluation of a group intervention to increase the personal social networks of abusive mothers. *Children and Youth Services, 10*, 175–188.

Lovell, M. L., & Richey, C. A. (1997). The impact of social support skill training on daily interactions among parents at risk for child maltreatment. *Children and Youth Services Review, 19*(4), 221–251.

Meyer, T. J., & Mark, M. M. (1995). Effects of psychosocial interventions with adult cancer patients: A meta-analysis of randomized experiments. *Health Psychology, 14,* 101–108.

Mittelman, M. S., Ferris, S. H., Shulman, E., Steinberg, G., & Levin, B. (1996). A family intervention to delay nursing home placement of patients with Alzheimer disease. *Journal of the American Medical Association, 276,* 1725–1731.

Moore, J. A., Hamerlynck, L. A., Barsh, E. T., Spieker, S., & Jones, R. R. (1982). *Extending Family Resources.* Seattle: Children's Clinic and Preschool.

Morin, R. C., & Seidman, E. (1986). A social network approach and the revolving door patient. *Schizophrenia Bulletin, 12,* 262–273.

Navarro, A. M., Senn, K. L., McNicholas, L. J., Kaplan, R. M., Roppe, B., & Campo, M. C. (1998). *Por La Vida* model intervention enhances use of cancer screening tests among Latinas. *American Journal of Preventive Medicine, 15,* 32–41.

Nichols, N. P., & Schwartz, R. C. (1998). *Family therapy: Concepts and methods.* Needham Heights, MA: Allyn & Bacon.

Patterson, G. R., & Reid, J. B. (1982). *A social learning approach to family intervention.* Eugene, OR: Castalia.

Power, R., Jones, S., Kearns, G., Ward, J., & Perera, J. (1995). Drug user networks, coping strategies, and HIV prevention in the community. *Journal of Drug Issues, 25,* 565–581.

Sarason, B. R., Sarason, I. G., Hacker, T. A., & Basher, R. B. (1985). Concomitants of social support: Social skills, attractiveness, and gender. *Journal of Personality and Social Psychology, 49,* 469–480.

Schilling, R. F., Gilchrist, L. D., & Schinke, S. P. (1984). Coping and social support in families of developmentally disabled children. *Family Relations, 33,* 47–54.

Sirkin, M. I., & Rueveni, U. (1992). The role of network therapy in the treatment of relational disorders: Cults and folie a deus. *Contemporary Family Therapy, 14,* 211–224.

Sisson, R. W., & Azrin, N. H. (1986). Family-member involvement to initiate and promote treatment of problem drinkers. *Journal of Behavioral Therapy and Experimental Psychiatry, 17,* 15–21.

Skinner, B. F. (1974). *About behaviorism.* New York: Knopf.

Speck, R. V. (1998). Network therapy. *Marriage and Family Review, 27,* 51–69.

Speck, R. V., & Attneave, C. (1973). *Family networks.* New York: Vintage.

Spoth, R., & Redmond, C. (1994). Effective recruitment of parents into family-focused prevention research: A comparison of two strategies. *Psychology and Health: An International Journal, 9,* 353–370.

Spoth, R., Redmond, C., Hockaday, C., & Shin, C. (1996). Barriers to participation in family skills preventive interventions and their evaluations: A replication and extension. *Family Relations, 45,* 247–254.

Stewart, M. J. (1989). Social support intervention studies: A review and prospectus of nursing contributions. *International Journal of Nursing Studies, 26*(2), 93–114.

Thoits, P. A. (1986). Social support as coping assistance. *Journal of Consulting and Clinical Psychology, 54,* 416–423.

Tracy, E. M., & Whittaker, J. K. (1987). The evidence base for social support interventions in child and family practice: Emerging issues for research and practice. *Child and Youth Services Review, 9,* 249–270.

Unger, D. G., & Wandersman, A. (1982). Neighboring in an urban environment. *American Journal of Community Psychology, 10,* 493–509.

Unger, D. G., & Wandersman, A. (1983). Neighboring and its role in block organizations: An exploratory report. *American Journal of Community Psychology, 11,* 291–300.

Watkins, E. L., Harlan, C., Eng, E., Ganasky, S. A., Gehan, D., & Larson, K. (1994). Assessing the effectiveness of lay health advisors with migrant farmworkers. *Family Community Health, 16*(4), 72–87.

Weiner, B. (1980). May I borrow your class notes? An attributional analysis of judgments of help giving in an achievement-related context. *Journal of Educational Psychology, 72,* 676–681.

West, S., Aiken, L., & Todd, M. (1993). Probing the effects of individual components in multiple component prevention programs. *American Journal of Community Psychology, 21,* 571–605.

PART IV

Implications

10

Social Support Measurement and Interventions

Comments and Future Directions

Karen S. Rook
Lynn G. Underwood

I. Delineating the Health-Related Functions of Social Relationships
  A. Companionship as a Health-Related Function of Social Ties
  B. Social Control as a Health-Related Function of Social Ties
  C. Joint Effects of Different Health-Related Functions of Social Relationships
II. Investigating the Health-Related Functions of Social Relationships
  A. Global versus Specific Effects
  B. Measures of Health-Related Functions in the Context of Intervention Planning and Evaluation
III. Social Support as a Stable Personality Trait versus Dynamic Interpersonal Process
IV. Contexts of Social Support
V. The Gradient or Dosage of Social Support
VI. Support Processes and Effects over Time
VII. Conclusion

It is a pleasure to have the opportunity to comment on a book that will undoubtedly help to lay the foundation for the next generation of research on the health effects of social support. The preceding chapters provide an exceptionally thorough, yet compact, treatment of approaches to measurement and intervention in the social support field. Researchers who seek guidance in the selection of measures or the design of interventions will find a wealth of ideas and suggestions in this book. The authors offer their suggestions in the context of rich conceptual frameworks that embed social support phenomena in a network of antecedents, outcomes, mediating processes, and moderating conditions. The authors take great care to delimit the scope of their analyses, while also suggesting places where the boundaries between the social support literature and related literatures could be made more permeable They are consistently careful, moreover, to avoid overstating the promise of social support either as an explanatory variable in understanding human health or as a means of intervening to bring about improvements in health and adaptive functioning.

The material in these chapters is encyclopedic, and each of the chapters contains excellent summaries and suggestions for future research. Our goal, therefore, is not to reiterate key points from the chapters but, rather, to highlight a number of important themes that recur across the chapters. In doing so, we also raise for consideration some additional issues that received more limited attention in this volume but that may suggest possibilities for assessment or intervention approaches.

DELINEATING THE HEALTH-RELATED FUNCTIONS
OF SOCIAL RELATIONSHIPS

Conceptualizations of the basic health-related functions of social relationships have clear implications for measurement and intervention approaches, as emphasized by many of the contributors to this volume (Cohen, Gottlieb, & Underwood, chapter 1; Eckenrode & Hamilton, chapter 8; Wills & Shinar, chapter 4). Exactly what constitutes a health-related "function" is somewhat ambiguous (see Lawton & Moss, 1987, for a discussion), although most definitions emphasize the material, psychological, and symbolic resources that are derived from social relationships and that are believed to confer specific health-related benefits. The health-related functions of social relationships, accordingly, can be distinguished from the properties of persons (Cohen, Gottlieb, & Underwood, chapter 1; Gottlieb, chapter 6) or relationships (Reis & Collins, chapter 5) that facilitate the provision or receipt of such resources.

An important issue raised by several authors (Lakey & Cohen, chapter 2; Reis & Collins, chapter 5) is the extent to which relationship properties that foster the exchange of health-enhancing forms of support confer similar health-enhancing effects in their own right. For example, does the sense of intimacy or trust in a relationship, which is presumably distilled from a relational history in which personal concerns and vulnerabilities could be disclosed safely, yield health benefits independent of those produced by the ongoing opportunities to engage in such disclosures? Similarly, does the sense that one belongs to a social group (Cohen, Gottlieb, & Underwood, chapter 1) confer health benefits apart from the set of ongoing interpersonal transactions (e.g., group gatherings) from which the sense of belonging is distilled? These questions may be difficult to resolve, and the answers may vary at different points in the developmental course of the relationship. As Reis and Collins (chapter 5) observed, "Supportive processes are not functionally independent of processes such as intimacy and satisfaction . . . and these processes may be difficult to untangle in real relationships." Nonetheless, wrestling with these distinctions has value because they suggest somewhat different foci and levels of analysis in our efforts to "locate" the health-enhancing dimensions of social relationships.

Delineation of a comprehensive, but manageable, list of the key health-related functions of social ties represents a basic point of departure for efforts to understand the causal pathways by which supportive social ties enhance health (Cohen, 1988; Weiss, 1974; Wills, 1985). The importance of this level of analysis is highlighted in several of the chapters (Cohen, Gottlieb, & Underwood, chapter 1; Eckenrode & Hamilton, chapter 8; Wills & Shinar, chapter 4) and in other reviews of the literature (e.g., Cutrona & Russell, 1987; Heller & Rook, 1997; House, 1981; House, Umberson, & Landis, 1988; Stroebe & Stroebe, 1996).

Drawing on the tradition in the stress literature of theorizing about the role of social support in facilitating adaptation to stressful life events (Cohen & Wills, 1985), most researchers have emphasized the various types of aid that people provide to friends and family members in times of need (e.g, Cobb, 1976; Cohen & McKay, 1984; House, 1981; Kahn & Antonucci, 1980; Wills, 1985). For example, an early taxonomy offered by House (1981) included emotional support (empathy, reassurance, liking, respect), appraisal support (feedback relevant to self-evaluation), informational support (problem-solving advice and information), and instrumental support (services and other forms of tangible aid). In this book, Wills and Shinar (chapter 4) offer a slightly different categorization that includes companionship (participation in social and leisure activities). Cohen, Gottlieb, and Underwood (chapter 1) emphasize social integration (a sense of belonging), information, tangible goods and services, social influence (pressure to exhibit normative health behavior), and perceived interpersonal resources (resources perceived to be available if needed) that affect appraisals of or responses to stressful events and experiences.

The helpfulness of each type of support is believed to vary across stressors (Cohen & McKay, 1984; Cutrona & Russell, 1987; Wills, 1985), and this hypothesized specificity is the cornerstone of matching theories of social support (Cohen & McKay, 1984; Cutrona, 1990; see Litwak & Szelinyi, 1969, for an early version). The loss of a job, for example, may create needs for informational and instrumental support, whereas the loss of a loved one may create a pressing need for emotional support. The matching hypothesis suggests that the support that most closely matches the needs aroused by particular stressors will yield the greatest health benefits. Different types of support are also believed to vary in importance across phases of the stress-adaptation process (Jacobson, 1986). For example, this is illustrated in research indicating that the support needs of widowed individuals change over time, as they move from the acute stages of grief to the long-term process of reconstituting their lives (Stylianos & Vachon, 1993).

Some researchers have suggested, however, that emotional support is singularly important to well-being (Antonucci, 1985; House, 1981; Sarason, Pierce, & Sarason, 1990, Uchino, Cacioppo, & Kiecolt-Glaser, 1996; Wills & Shinar, chapter 4), both because a wide variety of stressors arouse needs for reassurance of self-worth (Wills, 1985) and because intimacy represents an existential human need (House, 1981). Because of this broad importance in many life contexts (Wills & Shinar, chapter 4), some researchers believe that measures of social support should typically include an assessment of emotional support.

Companionship as a Health-Related Function
of Social Ties

A potentially important health-related function of social network ties that has received more limited attention in the literature is companionship, or leisure and recreational activity shared with others (Rook, 1987; Wills & Shinar, chapter 4). Stress researchers understandably have paid less attention to companionship than to support, given their interest in relationship processes and resources that aid adaptation to life stress. Yet most people desire social bonds not only for the aid and security they afford (Bowlby, 1977) but also for the opportunities they afford for enjoyable interaction and camaraderie (Gordon & Gaitz, 1976; Simmel, 1949). Wright (1989, p. 218) noted in this regard that researchers tend to ascribe so much importance to emotional supportiveness in social relationships that they often overlook the "plain, unvarnished camaraderie—the joking, griping, teasing, story-swapping, interest-sharing, hobby-sharing, note-comparing, kind of interaction" that lies at the heart of many friendships.

According to Sullivan (1953), the need for companionship first emerges in childhood in the form of a desire for adult interest and participation in the child's play. This need continues throughout life as a desire to be involved with others in mutually interesting and enjoyable activities.

The motivations for seeking companionship may differ from those underlying support, with companionship motivated by the desire to experience hedonic rewards (e.g., positive affect, stimulation) and support motivated by the desire to reduce emotional distress and obtain assistance with personal problems (cf. Thoits, 1985). Companionship and support may differ, as well, in their importance across different life contexts (Rook, 1987). Companionship sustains mood and well-being in the course of everyday life, whereas support assumes singular importance in times of stress. Companionship and support may also influence different dimensions of well-being or health (Bolger & Eckenrode, 1991; Buunk, 1990; Haines & Hurlbert, 1992; Rook, 1987). If social support is particularly important when an individual's equilibrium has been disrupted by stressful life experiences, then it may contribute to well-being primarily by restoring equilibrium (by restoring the individual to a previous "baseline" level of functioning). It may do little, however, to elevate the individual's psychological state beyond this baseline level. Shared recreation and other forms of companionship, in contrast, help to boost well-being above the customary baseline level. The "cultivation of the social environment" to produce positive affect accordingly represents a central motive for social interaction (Carstensen, 1991). Weiss (1974, p. 23) argued in this regard that friendships "offer a base for social events and happenings" and "in the absence of such ties life becomes dull, perhaps painfully so." Other theorists similarly have argued that mental health involves more than the absence of pathology; it requires stimulation, challenge, and uplifting experiences as well (e.g., Diener, 1984; Lawton, 1983). Thus, social support may be particularly effective in preventing threats to health and well-being, whereas companionship may be particularly effective in fostering psychological states that promote enhanced well-being.

Recognition of the potentially important and distinctive contributions of companionship is evident among the contributors to this volume (e.g., Cohen, Gottlieb, & Underwood, chapter 1; Wills & Shinar, chapter 4; see also Barrera, Sandler, & Ramsay, 1991; Cohen & Hoberman, 1983, Cutrona & Russell, 1987). This is less true of the broader literature on support, however, where multidimensional measures of support often emphasize specific forms of support (such as emotional, informational, and instrumental support) but omit companionship. Because the enjoyable, hedonic forms of social interaction (companionship) appear to make independent contributions to health and well-being (e.g., Bolger & Eckenrode, 1991; Buunk, 1990; Rook, 1987; Thompson, Futterman, Gallagher-Thompson, Rose, & Lovett, 1993), they warrant greater attention in analyses of the health-sustaining effects of social relationships (Rook, 1987, 1994).

Social Control as a Health-Related Function of Social Ties

Social relationships represent a source not only of support and companionship but also of social control (Cohen, Gottlieb, & Underwood, chapter 1; Lakey & Cohen, chapter 2; Rook, 1990; Umberson, 1987). Sociologists, in particular, have long argued that social relationships serve an important regulatory or control function in the lives of most people (e.g., Durkheim, 1897/1951); that is, people who are embedded in a cohesive network of social ties are likely to be deterred from engaging in risky or deviant behavior.

This idea is sometimes represented in taxonomies of social support that include social influence (e.g., cohen, Gottlieb, & Underwood, Chapter 1; House et al., 1988) or health-related support (e.g., Cohen, 1988). The theoretical underpinnings of the social influence construct in such taxonomies tend to differ in subtle but important respects from those reflected in sociological discussions of social control, (see Hirschi, 1969, for a criminological perspective on social control).

Social support theorists typically argue that social support must be affirming to be helpful (e.g., Kahn, 1979), but social control theorists argue that others' regulatory actions may be helpful even when they are not affirming. For example, intervening to stop a family member from excessive drinking may help to preserve his or her physical health but also may arouse resentment. In this vein, Hughes and Gove (1981) hypothesized that others' regulatory actions may provoke psychological distress even though they lead to less risk taking and more stable functioning: "Constraint may be the source of considerable frustration; at the same time it tends to reduce the probability of problematic or maladaptive behaviors" (p. 71). Thus, efforts by network members to exercise social control may have dual effects (Lewis & Rook, 1999).

Two basic mechanisms of restraint appear in the writings of Durkheim (1897/1951) and other social control theorists (e.g., Hirschi, 1969; Hughes & Gove, 1981). First, many close relationships, such as those involving marriage and parenting, entail enduring responsibilities or obligations (Umberson, 1987). Such responsibilities, or social role obligations, presumably exert a stabilizing influence on behavior. Compared with individuals who lack significant responsibilities to others, those who have such responsibilities should experience greater motivation to exhibit stable behavior and, perhaps, to engage in better self-care (e.g., Hughes & Gove, 1981; Leventhal, Prohaska, & Hirschman, 1985). Social role obligations likewise should serve to inhibit deviant or self-destructive behavior. For example, individuals with significant caregiving responsibilities to others (such as parents or spouses) may be motivated to refrain from excessive drinking or reckless driving to avoid jeopardizing performance of their role obligations.

This mechanism of social control is largely indirect (Umberson, 1987). Even if families rarely offered explicit positive or negative feedback for the purpose of shaping a family member's behavior, the mere existence of familial responsibilities and commitments would serve to encourage the family member to engage in appropriate self-care and to minimize risky or deviant behavior.

Social control also occurs through more direct means, such as explicitly urging someone to engage in sound health practices and to avoid unsound or risky practices (Hughes & Gove, 1981; Umberson, 1987). These attempts at social control may incorporate negative sanctions or threatened sanctions (Umberson, 1987), as well as persuasive appeals. Thus, social control operates through network members' efforts to monitor, persuade, and reward or punish a focal person, as well as through a focal person's self-restraint of risky behavior.

Social control is believed to affect behavioral outcomes (e.g., deviance, risk taking) and psychological states (e.g., irritation, distress). With respect to health practices, social control may influence routine self-care, preventive health behaviors, adherence to prescribed medical regimens, and the utilization of health care services. Through its impact on such health practices, social control is believed to affect health status and, ultimately, the risk of mortality (Umberson, 1987). Psychological outcomes may be affected, as well, with possible reactions to others' social control attempts including irritation, resentment, and guilt (e.g., Lewis & Rook, 1999); positive outcomes have been discussed less often but could include appreciation or gratitude (Lewis & Rook, 1999).

This discussion has emphasized the hypothesized risk-detering and health-promoting role of social control in personal relationships. Yet abundant evidence also indicates that social networks can operate to encourage undesirable, rather than desirable, health practices (Cohen, 1988; Gottlieb, chapter 6). This is apparent, for example, in the literature on adolescent substance use and other risk behavior (e.g., Jessor, Donovan, & Costa, 1991; Wills, 1990). Recognition of such negative forms of social influence provides a rationale for support interventions designed to counter the effect of social network members who may be reinforcing behaviors that compromise health (Gottlieb, chapter 6).

Joint Effects of Different Health-Related Functions of Social Relationships

Most discussions of the health effects of different functions of social relationships implicitly reflect an additive model, with each function viewed as making unique and largely independent contributions to the health outcome of interest. Yet the health-related functions studied by social support researchers have the potential to interact in complex ways that may magnify, dampen, cancel, or reverse their separate effects on health. Such interactions have received only modest attention in the literature, in part because of the difficulties associated with detecting interaction effects in nonexperimental studies (McClelland & Judd, 1993). Nonetheless, social exchanges in most people's daily lives very likely unfold in ways that reflect the simultaneous or sequential expression of several of the functions discussed in this volume. For example, a concerned spouse who is worried about her husband's escalating alcohol intake following a job layoff may alternate between communicating emotional support, as a means of helping him deal with his distress, and exerting social control, to pressure him to curtail his drinking. Given that many social relationships (and social interactions) are likely to entail just such a mix of different functions, it becomes important to grapple with ways to conceptualize and investigate their joint health effects. One example, involving the possible joint effects of social control and social support, is considered here to illustrate the kinds of questions that might arise in investigating interactions among different health-related relationship functions.

Social control and social support in a personal relationship could be hypothesized to have opposing effects, with efforts by others to exercise control (e.g., efforts to dissuade a partner from abusing alcohol) eroding the sense of support in the relationship (Ryan & Solky, 1996). Miller and Boster (1988, p. 283) observed in this regard that people who wish to induce change in a significant other's behavior face a dilemma because influence tactics that bring about such change may succeed at the expense of relational solidarity, whereas influence tactics that preserve solidarity may fail to induce change. Dillard and Fitzpatrick (1985, p. 420) termed a social control attempt that succeeds in prompting behavioral compliance while simultaneously provoking resentment a "pyrrhic victory." Consistent with this, Dillard and Fitzpatrick (1985) found in a study of married couples engaged in a compliance-gaining task that many of the persuasive strategies the participants used were associated with marital dissatisfaction and unhappiness.

Alternatively, social control and social support could be hypothesized to have compatible, rather than contradictory, effects. A prior history of supportive and companionate exchanges in a relationship may make a partner's efforts to exercise control more palatable and, perhaps, more effective. Thus, social control attempts may not detract from relationship quality when they occur in a relationship that, at other times, functions as a source of support and companionship (Rook, 1990). Coordinated investigation of the dynamics of social control and social support— and other relationship functions—is needed to shed light on how these distinctive functions of social ties jointly influence health and well-being.

INVESTIGATING THE HEALTH-RELATED FUNCTIONS OF SOCIAL RELATIONSHIPS

Differentiating among key health-related functions of social relationships helps to provide a conceptual framework for the selection of measurement strategies and for the design of interventions (though see Lakey & Cohen, chapter 2; Sarason, Sarason, & Pierce, 1990, for a dissenting view). Yet the translation of these conceptual distinctions into viable empirical distinctions has met with some difficulties, most notably the problem of high intercorrelations among indices of different kinds of social support (Wills & Shinar, chapter 4; House & Kahn, 1985; Sarason, Sarason, & Pierce, 1990; Sarason, Shearin, Pierce, & Sarason, 1987). Factor analyses of items believed to represent five or six conceptually distinct forms of support have often yielded evidence of fewer factors (e.g., Levitt, Weber, & Guacci, 1993; Sherbourne & Hays, 1990; though see Mancini & Blieszner, 1992). Emotional support has been distinguished most reliably from instrumental support and, to a lesser extent, from informational support (Anderson & McCulloch, 1993; see reviews by Krause, 1989; Orth-Gomer & Unden, 1987; Oxman & Berkman, 1990). It has been difficult to substantiate theoretical distinctions among more closely related constructs, such as emotional support and appraisal support.

Much social interaction is organized around multiple simultaneous goals (Tracy & Coupland, 1990), and people in close relationships often exchange multiple forms of social support (and companionship and control) (e.g., Hirsch, 1980). Moreover, for socially integrated individuals, the multiple support functions performed by one member of the network are often replicated by other network members (Heller & Rook, 1997). Because of this bundling of support functions within a given relationship and the duplication across relationships, disentangling the distinctive effects of different relationship functions is necessarily challenging.

Global versus Specific Effects

The challenge posed by high intercorrelations among indices of different kinds of social support need not be regarded as a mere statistical nuisance. In fact, some of the solutions to this problem that researchers have pursued invite new ways of thinking about the level at which social support operates to affect health and well-being. Some researchers have made use of analytic methods that permit examination of a higher order, global support factor, as well as specific, intercorrelated support factors (e.g., Brookings & Bolton, 1988; Newcomb, 1990; Russell & Cutrona, 1991). Such approaches may yield greater evidence of the unique effects of conceptually distinct health-related functions of social relationships. Yet the emergence in some of this work of a global support factor may warrant further consideration in its own right. The health effects of social bonds may reflect, in part, the extent to which these ties are broadly or diffusely supportive. The earliest epidemiological work on the links between social network involvement and health outcomes (reviewed by Berkman & Breslow, 1983; Brissette, Cohen, & Seeman, chapter 3; Cohen, 1988; House et al., 1988) revealed that even fairly crude indicators of such network involvement often exhibited strong associations with morbidity and mortality, controlling for rival explanatory factors. Such findings have been replicated in well-controlled prospective studies conducted in the United States and other countries (Cohen, 1988; House et al., 1988). The robustness of these findings appears to be consistent with the existence of a higher order social support factor that reflects powerful but diffuse effects of social relationships.

Some theorists have argued for the existence of such a general social support factor that transcends specific relationship functions, but they have suggested, further, that support is a perceptual factor—that the benefits of social support derive largely from people's global evaluations of their social network members as supportive and caring (Lakey & Drew, 1997; Sarason, Pierce, & Sarason, 1990). From this perspective (discussed in a subsequent section), social support is a stable, trait like variable, and it is the stable, global perception of the social surround as caring and dependable that accounts for its beneficial effect on health outcomes. This may be the means by which such a global support factor operates, but it may also operate through physiological effects (Cohen & Herbert, 1996; Uchino et al., 1996; Wills & Shinar, Chapter 4) and biobehavioral processes that motivate people to find the formation and maintenance of social bonds gratifying and to experience the absence of social bonds as distressing (Baumeister & Leary, 1995). Regardless of the interpretation, it may be useful for support researchers to devote more attention to the possible coexistence of global effects of social bonds and specific (albeit intercorrelated) effects of the various health-related functions that have been discussed in the literature (cf. Cohen, Gottlieb, & Underwood, chapter 1; Brissette, Cohen, & Seeman, chapter 3).

Measures of Health-Related Functions in the Context of Intervention Planning and Evaluation

Efforts to apply theory and research on social support to the design and evaluation of interventions necessarily sharpen our thinking and often expose limitations in the existing knowledge base as a guide for interventions (Gottlieb, 1992). This is both the attraction and the frustration of cross-fertilization between the theoretical and applied traditions of research on social support (e.g., Rook & Dooley, 1985). The theoretical literature has inspired the development of multidimensional measures that capture many different health-related functions of social relationships, as discussed in detail in the first five chapters of this volume, but it offers little guidance about the suitability of such measures for determining the need for an intervention or screening prospective candidates for participation. Low scores on a measure of support could presumably be used in such screening, but we generally lack knowledge about the appropriateness of alternative cutpoints for defining "low" support. Moreover, low scores per se do not necessarily reflect a perceived need for greater support or receptivity to potential support interventions on the part of prospective intervention participants. Several chapter writers proposed in this regard that explicit assessment of prospective participants' perceived need for additional support may provide a stronger foundation for the decision to initiate an intervention and a more viable way of identifying intervention candidates (Gottlieb, chapter 6; Eckenrode & Hamilton, chapter 8). Cutrona and Cole (chapter 9) urge the development of screening tools that go beyond simple self-reports, such as the neighborhood walk method for assessing the support resources and needs of children.

Similar questions arise about the usefulness of existing measures of support in evaluating the effectiveness of support interventions. For example, if an intervention is designed, in part, to increase participants' access to emotional support (as an intermediate step toward improving their health status), then it is reasonable to include a measure of emotional support as an outcome. Many existing measures of support were not developed, however, with sensitivity to change as a key consideration. Failure to find evidence of changes in emotional support following an intervention designed to effect such changes could reflect either a weak intervention or use of a measure with limited sensitivity to change. To reduce such potential ambiguities, care should be exercised in efforts to import into intervention work measures that were developed for purposes of theory testing in basic research. More generally, however, as greater articulation occurs between the basic and applied traditions of research on social support, a more substantial knowledge base should emerge regarding the appropriateness of alternative assessment strategies for intervention screening and evaluation (Wills & Shinar, chapter 4). The dual emphases of this book on measurement and intervention should help to foster this articulation between the two research traditions.

SOCIAL SUPPORT AS A STABLE PERSONALITY TRAIT VERSUS DYNAMIC INTERPERSONAL PROCESS

A debate exists in the social support literature, with echoes present in this book, regarding the conceptualization of support as an intrapersonal or interpersonal phenomenon. Some researchers believe that the greatest gains in understanding the health effects of social support will come from examining it as a perceptual variable; they argue that perceptions of the extent to which one's social network members are available to provide support reflect stable, internal working models of self and others that stem from early attachment experiences with parents and other caregivers (Lakey & Cohen, chapter 2; Reis & Collins, chapter 5). From this perspective, social support represents a stable set of beliefs about the social environment, and it is this belief system, rather than actual exchanges of support with others, that accounts for the beneficial effects of support on health (e.g., Lakey & Drew, 1997; Sarason et al., 1987, Sarason, Pierce, & Sarason, 1990; Turner, 1992). Turner (1992, p. 219) argued, for example, "Perceived support is . . . what matters for health and well-being and the central tool for identifying the most promising targets toward which . . . intervention efforts might be aimed." Other researchers favor efforts to document and evaluate the behavioral aspects of social support, arguing that it is the actual supportive interactions that occur between network members that influence health outcomes, although they acknowledge that support perceptions may mediate the effects of such interactions (e.g., Dunkel-Schetter & Bennett, 1990; Vaux, 1988).

Proponents of the intrapersonal perspective base their argument about the critical importance of perceived social support on several kinds of empirical evidence. First, perceptions of available social support have been found to correlate only weakly with the amount of support received in a particular period of time (see review by Dunkel-Schetter & Bennett, 1990). Second, in studies that have examined both subjective and objective indicators of social support in relation to health outcomes, the subjective indicators often have exhibited stronger associations (e.g., Antonucci & Akiyama, 1987; Ward, Sherman, & LaGory, 1984). Research suggests, for example, that perceived social support more reliably buffers the adverse effects of life stress on psychological health than does received support (see reviews by Cohen & Wills, 1985; Kessler, 1992). Third, measures of perceived social support show impressive stability over time (Costa, Zonderman, & McCrae, 1985; Field & Minkler, 1988; Sarason et al., 1987), which should not be the case if such perceptions derive from dynamic, changing transactions with social network members (Vaux, 1992). This apparent traitlike stability has led some researchers to infer that perceived social support (particularly the sense of being accepted and cared for by others) more closely resembles an enduring personality trait than a mirror of transactions occurring in the social environment (Lakey & Cohen, chapter 2; Lakey & Drew, 1997; Sarason, Pierce, & Sarason, 1990).

Interpretations of these empirical findings vary, however, and some researchers reject the inference that measures of received or enacted social support have limited utility (e.g., Dunkel-Schetter & Bennett, 1990; Vaux, 1992). Many of the studies that have found measures of perceived and received support to correlate weakly have failed to determine the extent to which stress or other factors created needs for support (Dunkel-Schetter & Bennett, 1990; Ensel, 1991). It is doubtful that people attempt to access the full range of support perceived to be available through their social networks in the absence of a compelling reason to do so, such as the need to cope with an exceptionally disruptive life event. Moreover, even in the context of a highly stressful situation, people may not seek to mobilize an entire network to assist with their coping efforts; rather, they may seek help selectively from a subset of their network ties, broadening their help-seeking efforts over time only as needed. Evidence for just such a hierarchical model of support seeking has emerged in studies of older adults (Cantor, 1979). From this perspective, measures of perceived support and received support would be expected to correlate only modestly in many life contexts.

Additional research challenges the view that received (enacted) support rarely buffers people from the adverse effects of life stress. Studies in which large samples have been disaggregated to identify subsamples of people who are experiencing relatively homogeneous stressors have demonstrated that received support does buffer certain categories of stressors (e.g., Krause, 1986). Clear evidence of a buffering effect of received support emerged in a study that distinguished health-related from other stressors and that further distinguished support needed from support received (Ensel, 1991); received support by itself did not predict well-being, but received support did predict well-being when considered in conjunction with the degree of need reported. In addition, stress-buffering studies that contrast baseline levels of perceived support and received support as predictors of subsequent adjustment to a stressor may not provide a fair test of the relative importance of the two types of support because baseline measures of received support fail to capture the support that may be mobilized once a stressor occurs (Alloway & Bebbington, 1987; Barrera, 1986).

Moreover, the stability over time of measures of perceived social support need not necessarily be interpreted as evidence that perceived support is a traitlike intrapersonal phenomenon. Such stability could reflect a highly stable social environment, rather than a stable personality trait (Cohen, Sherrod, & Clark, 1986). Thus, some of the evidence that has been mustered to buttress the argument that support is largely a perceptual phenomenon, and that measures of perceived support are superior to measures of received support, may not bear up under close scrutiny.

One possible resolution of this debate is to make use of research designs and analytic methods that examine both trait and state aspects of social support simultaneously. Daily diary approaches, described by Reis and Collins (chapter 5), are well suited for this purpose. In such approaches, both social support and a health outcome (e.g., physical health symptoms) are assessed on a daily basis for a period of several weeks or longer. With such repeated assessments, researchers can investigate the extent to which a person's symptoms covary with occurrences of social support. These within-person analyses estimate the extent of covariation relative to the person's own average level of symptoms, irrespective of whether this average level is higher or lower than that of other people in the study. Thus, even individuals who experience many physical symptoms on a chronic basis may experience better days and worse days, and some of this covariation may be attributable to day-to-day fluctuations in the quality of their social interactions. Similarly, individuals who rarely report physical symptoms may likewise experience better days and worse days, and this variability, too, may reflect variations in the degree of support provided by others.

Relatively new statistical methods (e.g., hierarchical linear modeling, Bryk & Raudenbush, 1992; Schwartz & Stone, 1998) allow researchers, moreover, to create person-specific estimates of the degree of covariation between social interactions and an outcome of interest (e.g., physical symptoms) and to treat these estimates as dependent variables to be modeled as a function of between-person differences. A researcher could examine, for example, whether the covariation between daily mood and daily experiences of supportive or stressful social interactions can be explained by neuroticism (e.g., Bolger & Zuckerman, 1995) or other individual differences. Other dependent variables that exhibit variation over time could, of course, be examined with this approach. For example, daily variations in pain experience among people coping with a chronic disability or recovering from an acute health problem might be partly attributable to the supportiveness of their daily interactions with others.

The value of such an approach in disentangling the role of relatively stable (traitlike) between-person factors and more dynamic (statelike) within-person processes was illustrated in a recent study of work stress and social support conducted by Buunk and his colleagues (Buunk, 1990; Buunk & Verhoeven, 1991). In this study, police officers kept daily records for several weeks of their emotional distress, job stress, and the social support they received from various work colleagues. Between-person analyses that collapsed across days indicated that the officers were more distressed on days when they received more social support. Within-person analyses that examined covariation across days, in contrast, took into account differences between the officers in mean levels of distress; these analyses revealed that, relative to their own average levels of distress, the officers were less distressed on days when they received social support and more distressed on days when they did not receive support. Thus, what initially appeared to be a "reverse-buffering" effect (Barrera, 1986) in the between-person (aggregated) analyses was more accurately viewed as a support-mobilization effect, as revealed through the within-person analyses; officers who experienced more distress also received more support over the course of the study, but the support that was mobilized appeared to be beneficial (rather than harmful) because their distress was lower on those days that they received support.

Analytic approaches such as these allow researchers to examine both trait and state components of the complex web of causal factors that link social support to health. Such approaches seem likely to reveal that the health-related effects of social support reside both in the perception of others as supportive and caring and in the actual behaviors of others that either succeed or fail to convey such care.

CONTEXTS OF SOCIAL SUPPORT

Another unifying theme across the chapters in this book is the idea that the health effects of support depend not only on the specific kinds of support that people receive from others but also on features of the contexts in which support transactions take place. Characteristics of support providers, support recipients, and their relationship influence the likelihood that supportive exchanges occur, as well as the effectiveness of such exchanges (e.g., Gottlieb, chapter 6; Lakey & Cohen, chapter 2; Reis & Collins, chapter 5). With respect to support providers, for example, the capacity for empathy and interpersonal sensitivity may influence the quality of the support provided (e.g., Reis & Collins, chapter 6). Social norms also create preferences or expectations for certain members of a social network to provide particular kinds of support (Gottlieb, chapter 6). In later life, kin are preferred as sources of instrumental support, whereas friends tend to be preferred as sources of emotional support and day-to-day companionship (Rook & Schuster, 1996). Departures from these normative preferences or patterns may dilute the impact of the support provided (Felton & Berry, 1992). In designing interventions, the supportive capacities of potential participants, as well as these normative considerations, must be taken into account to optimize the delivery of support. Moreover, in interventions that bring together "strangers" for the purpose of exchanging support, careful thought must be giving to the conditions that are conducive to relationship formation, including the degree of similarity among participants and the specific kinds of interactions that foster friendship and trust (Cohen, Gottlieb, & Underwood, chapter 1; Cutrona & Cole, chapter 9; Gottlieb, chapter 6; Helgeson & Gottlieb, chapter 7).

With respect to characteristics of support recipients, several authors noted that support is unlikely to have beneficial effects unless the intended recipient expresses a willingness to receive assistance from others (Cutrona & Cole, chapter

9; Eckenrode & Hamilton, chapter 8). Similarly, the level of emotional distress a prospective support recipient exhibits may influence the occurrence and outcome of support transactions (Helgeson & Gottlieb, chapter 7). Intense or persistent distress may be disturbing to would-be support providers, leading them disengage from or communicate disapproval of the distressed individual (e.g., Coyne, Ellard, & Smith, 1990; Dunkel-Schetter, 1984; Wortman & Lehman, 1985). In planning intervention programs, it may be necessary to screen out potential participants whose lack of receptivity to support or whose level of distress may make them poor candidates for the program (Cutrona & Cole, Chapter 9; Helgeson & Gottlieb, chapter 7).

Characteristics of the relationship between a support provider and recipient (whether well established or just emerging) represent other defining features of the context in which support transactions occur, as noted throughout the chapters in this volume. Reis and Collins (chapter 5) discussed these relationship properties, such as intimacy and trust, in detail, and additional candidates for investigation were discussed in other chapters (Lakey & Cohen, chapter 2).

Efforts to investigate or to engineer optimal matches between the characteristics of support providers and recipients represent an extension of matching theories of support (Gottlieb, chapter 6), which have more often focused on the match between the needs created by stressful life events and the particular kinds of support that best meet these needs (Cohen, Gottlieb, & Underwood, chapter 1; Lakey & Cohen, chapter 2; Wills & Shinar, chapter 4). Further extensions involve efforts to tailor support interventions to the sociocultural background and life stage of participants (Cutrona & Cole, chapter 9; Eckenrode & Hamilton, chapter 8; Gottlieb, chapter 6; Helgeson & Gottlieb, chapter 7). The limits of existing theory and research as a guide for achieving such complex matches are reached quickly in actual practice (Eckenrode & Hamilton, chapter 8; Gottlieb, 1992), and this is further complicated by constraints on the resources and options available to program planners (Eckenrode & Hamilton, chapter 8; Helgeson & Gottlieb, chapter 7). Nevertheless, despite these complexities, efforts to optimize the match between the support rendered and the individuals providing support, the unique needs created by stressful life transitions, and characteristics of support recipients would seem to be a worthwhile goal. Moreover, several authors noted that the "guesswork" in this process can be reduced by careful assessment of prospective participants' needs, existing social ties, and life circumstances in the planning stages of an intervention (Cutrona & Cole, chapter 9; Eckenrode & Hamilton, chapter 8; Gottlieb, chapter 6; Helgeson & Gottlieb, chapter 7; Wills & Shinar, chapter 4; see also Heller, Thompson, Trueba, Hogg, & Vlachos-Weber, 1991).

THE GRADIENT OR DOSAGE OF SOCIAL SUPPORT

Several contributors to this book raised questions about how much social support is required to produce health benefits (Cohen, Gottlieb, & Underwood, chapter 1; Gottlieb, chapter 6). Does a critical threshold exist beyond which additional support adds little to a person's health, or do the effects of support tend to be linear, such that increases in support are reliably associated with further improvements in health (Brissette, Cohen, & Seeman, chapter 3)? It has often been suggested that the effects of social support should be most pronounced when individuals who lack any confidants or other support providers are compared with individuals who have at least one such support provider (House, 1981). In planning support programs, parallel questions arise about the appropriate dosage of social support (Gottlieb, chapter 6). Moreover, as Gottlieb (chapter 6) noted, varied meanings of "dosage" exist; the dosage of social support could refer to the number of people providing support, the frequency with which support is provided, the duration of support provision over time, the intensity with which support is provided, and so forth.

In the literature on naturally occurring social ties, questions about the gradient of support effects have most often been framed in terms of the number of support providers, the frequency of support provision, or the diversity of network members (e.g., Cohen, Doyle, Skoner, Rabin, & Gwaltney, 1997), with less attention given to duration, intensity, or other dimensions of social support. Determining whether the benefits of social support in such correlational studies are best characterized by threshold effects or by a linear gradient requires statistical procedures that can detect nonlinear associations, although formal tests of nonlinearity have been rare in actual practice (Veiel, 1992). Sampling procedures may also influence the conclusions derived because truly isolated individuals tend to be difficult to recruit to research studies, and their omission from the resulting samples reduces the likelihood of detecting a critical threshold for support.

Different challenges arise in intervention studies, where it is often necessary to make judgments in advance about the optimal level of social support and to incorporate such judgments into the design of the intervention. This planning is complicated by the possibility that different dosages and different forms of social support may be optimal at different points in the course of the intervention (Cutrona & Cole, chapter 9; Eckenrode & Hamilton, chapter 8; Gottlieb, chapter 6; Helgeson & Gottlieb, chapter 7). Moreover, even in the context of support programs designed to administer a particular dose of support, the actual dose delivered may vary across participants because of variations in attendance at support group meetings, in the rates and timing of attrition, and other factors. This underscores the importance of tracking the support dosage over time for each participant to provide a more sensitive test of dose-response relationships (Gottlieb, chapter 6).

Additionally, in intervention programs that do not involve efforts to strengthen existing network ties or to foster the development of permanent new ties, unique issues arise that concern the discontinuation of support (Eckenrode & Hamilton, chapter 8). Thus, a reverse version of the dosage question becomes centrally important: How can the support program be phased out or the interim support provider (e.g., mentor) withdrawn without doing harm (Eckenrode & Hamilton, chapter 8; Gottlieb, chapter 6)? An early warning about the potentially harmful effects of withdrawing support emerged in an experimental evaluation of a friendly visiting program for older adults conducted by Schulz and Hanusa (1978), as noted by Eckenrode and Hamilton (chapter 8). Elderly residents of a retirement home who received these visits initially fared better on indicators of health and well-being than did residents who did not receive visits, but a follow-up assessment conducted 2 years later, after the termination of the program, revealed that the residents who had been visited exhibited significantly worse health outcomes than did residents who had not been visited. Thus, great care must be taken in phasing out support in interventions that create time-limited support structures. This is an especially significant challenge in interventions that involve peer support groups, network enhancement, or home visitations, because the available evidence suggests these interventions have more beneficial effects when they are of longer duration (Cutrona & Cole, chapter 9; Eckenrode & Hamilton, chapter 8; Helgeson & Cohen, 1996; Helgeson & Gottlieb, chapter 7).

SUPPORT PROCESSES AND EFFECTS OVER TIME

The contributors to this book generally agree that social support processes and effects change over time, with important implications for the sequencing of assessments and for the selection of intervention strategies. As noted earlier, different supportive resources appear to be important at different stages in the course of adapting to a significant life change or disruption. In addition, support processes and effects may change over time even when support needs remain relatively constant. For example, chronic illnesses or disabilities that require members of a social network to render support over extended periods may create network strains that can kindle conflict and resurrect dormant resentments (e.g., Johnson, 1983; Johnson & Catalano, 1983; Lyons, Sullivan, & Ritvo, with Coyne, 1995). Evidence of such support deterioration has been documented in studies of adaptation to stressors that create long-term needs for support (e.g., Kaniasty & Norris, 1993). The psychological costs of the care provided in such cases sometimes exceeds the benefits (Johnson, 1983).

The meaning of social support may also vary at different points in the course of clinical disorders, such as depression, that follow distinctive trajectories of onset, development, exacerbation, remission, and possible recurrence (Monroe & Johnson, 1992). Yet researchers may overlook these variations if they use research designs that indiscriminately mix together newly symptomatic and consistently symptomatic individuals (Monroe & Johnson, 1992). A given score on a measure of psychological health could potentially indicate, for different people, any of several qualitatively different states. For example, a score above 16 on a widely used measure of depressive symptoms, such as the Center for Epidemiological Studies Depression Scale (Radloff, 1977), is often regarded as suggesting the presence of clinical depression, but it is impossible to know from such a score alone whether it represents the first onset of the disorder, a recurrence of the disorder, or an improving or deteriorating trajectory in an already established disorder. Different kinds of social support may be differentially important in the onset versus maintenance of clinical disorders, but this is difficult to evaluate in the absence of systematic attention to the chronicity, or stability, of the emotional health outcomes under study and to the meaning of shifts in psychological functioning over time.

Cohen (1988) has urged attention to a similar set of issues regarding the role of support processes at different stages in the course of physical illness. The role of support in influencing the development of cardiovascular disease over a period of many years undoubtedly differs, for example, from the role of support in influencing behavior change and emotional adjustment following a myocardial infarction or bypass surgery.

CONCLUSION

A book such as this that lays bare the many complexities that surround efforts to assess social support and to design and evaluate support interventions can be a kind of projective test for readers. For researchers who are immersed in this literature, the book identifies gaps in knowledge and intriguing but unresolved conceptual and methodological issues that can invigorate research agendas. For readers who are new to this literature, the challenges laid out can seem more daunting than inspiring. The ambiguities and complexities that exist in the social support literature, however, are no greater than those that exist in many other literatures on human behavior and human disease, once one scratches the surface. Impressive strides have been made in our understanding of social support processes and outcomes, and the pursuit of an expanded knowledge base that will extend our understanding even further is well justified by the very centrality of supportive relationships to human health and well-being.

Personal relationships form a central part of our lives. These relationships have multiple and complex qualities, with varying valences and impacts on health, but it is clear that they matter greatly to most people. In studies in which people have been asked what gives their lives the greatest sense of meaning, the majority respond with references to their family relationships and friendships (Klinger, 1977). Research on the perceived quality of life indicates that the quality of people's social lives is a powerful predictor of their happiness and life satisfaction, second in importance only to physical health (Argyle, 1987; Campbell, Converse, & Rodgers, 1976). Moreover, as emphasized throughout this book, supportive relationships help to limit the toll that stressful life events can take on emotional and physical health. Studies of loneliness and bereavement clearly document the anguish, longing, and despair experienced by people who either lack or have lost close relationships (Peplau & Perlman, 1982; Stroebe, Stroebe, & Hansson, 1993).

It is also apparent, however, as one examines the literature, that some issues have received only limited attention. The chapters offer a wealth of suggestions for applying the growing knowledge base to the design of interventions, but further work may be needed on aspects of social relationships that have been neglected to date and that offer strong theoretical possibilities. For example, perspectives on religiousness and spirituality may suggest avenues for extending research on support by directing attention to the conditions on which support is based and the motivations of support providers. One of the key factors in a variety of religious and spiritual traditions is the concept of unconditional love: caring deeply for another person and expecting nothing in return. Expressions of such unconditional care may constitute a particularly potent form of support, as suggested by research on marital interaction. Investigations of spouses' perceptions of giving and receiving support have found that support is most beneficial when one spouse has engaged in a number of supportive acts on the partner's behalf, but the partner is largely unaware of the specific acts; the benefits of such support exceed the benefits of support that is perceived and acknowledged by the recipient (Clark & Brissette, in press). Such noncontingent giving that is woven into the day-to-day fabric of intimate relationships, and that does not compel attention to itself, may be a uniquely potent form of support that warrants further investigation (cf. Coyne & Bolger 1990). In addition, support that is anchored in feelings of love and commitment to another person may be less taxing than support that arises from other motivations, thereby limiting the emotional and physical toll that support provision sometimes takes.

Recognition of the significance of close relationships in the lives of most people, and of the consequences for those who lack such relationships, provides a valuable backdrop for efforts to build a broader base of knowledge regarding social support. The chapters in this book have laid out some of the most effective ways scientists have found of quantifying these relationships, which makes possible basic research on the health effects of personal relationships. The chapters also offer rich suggestions for applying this growing knowledge base to the design of interventions to enhance the health and well-being of individuals who lack adequate social support. Support interventions have often been initiated without reference to the theoretical and empirical literature on support. Greater links are needed between basic and applied research on social support, so that support interventions are grounded in the scientific literature and scientific hypotheses about support processes and effects are put to the test in intervention studies. This book should help to achieve exactly such a productive synergy.

REFERENCES

Alloway, R., & Bebbington, P. (1987). The buffer theory of social support: A review of the literature. *Psychological Medicine, 17*, 91–108.

Anderson, T. B., & McCulloch, B. J. (1993). Conjugal support: Factor structure for husbands and wives. *Journal of Gerontology: Social Sciences, 48*, S133–S142.

Antonucci, T. C. (1985). Personal characteristics, social support, and social behavior. In R. H. Binstock & E. Shanas (Eds.), *Handbook of aging and the social sciences* (pp. 94–128). New York: Van Nostrand-Reinhold.

Antonucci, T. C., & Akiyama, H. (1987). Social networks in adult life and a preliminary examination of the convoy model. *Journal of Gerontology, 42*, 519–527.

Argyle, M. (1987). *The psychology of happiness.* London: Methuen.

Barrera, M. (1986). Distinctions between social support concepts, measures, and models. *American Journal of Community Psychology, 14*, 413–446.

Barrera, M., Sandler, I. N., & Ramsay, T. B. (1986). Preliminary develoment of a scale of social support. *American Journal of Community Psychology, 9*, 435–447.

Baumeister, R. F., & Leary, M. R. (1995). The need to belong: Desire for interpersonal attachments as a fundamental human motivation. *Psychological Bulletin, 117*, 497–529.

Berkman, L., & Breslow, L. (1983). *Health and ways of living.* New York: Oxford University Press.

Bolger, N., & Eckenrode, J. (1991). Social relationships, personality, and anxiety during a major stressful event. *Journal of Personality and Social Psychology, 61*, 440–449.

Bolger, N., & Zuckerman, A. (1995). A framework for studying personality in the stress process. *Journal of Personality and Social Psychology, 69*, 890–902.

Bowlby, J. (1977). The making and breaking of affectional bonds. I. Aetiology and psychopathology in the light of attachment theory. *British Journal of Psychiatry, 130*, 201–210.

Brookings, J. B., & Bolton, B. (1988). Confirmatory factor analysis of the Interpersonal Support Evaluation List. *American Journal of Community Psychology, 16*, 137–147.

Bryk, A. S., & Raudenbush, S. W. (1992). *Hierarchical linear models: Applications and data analysis methods.* Newbury Park, CA: Sage.

Buunk, B. (1990). Affiliation and helping interactions within organizations: A critical analysis of the role of social support with regard to occupational stress. In W. Stroebe & M. Hewstone (Eds.), *European review of social psychology* (vol. 1, pp. 293–322). Chichester, England: Wiley.

Buunk, B. P., & Verhoeven, K. (1991). Companionship and support at work: A microanalysis of the stress-reducing features of social interaction. *Basic and Applied Social Psychology, 12*, 243–258.

Campbell, A., Converse, P. E., & Rodgers, W. L. (1976). *The quality of American life.* New York: Russell Sage.

Cantor, M. H. (1979). Neighbors and friends: An overlooked resource in the informal support system. *Research on Aging, 1*, 434–463.

Carstensen, L. (1991). Selectivity theory: Social activity in life-span context. In M. P. Lawton (Ed.), *Annual review of gerontology and geriatrics* (vol. 11, pp. 195–217). New York: Springer.

Clark, M. S., and Brissette, I. (in press). Relationship beliefs and experiencing and expressing emotions: Reciprocal effects. In N. Frijda, A. Manstead, & G. Semin (Eds.), *Emotions and beliefs.* London: Cambridge University Press.

Cobb, S. (1976). Social support as a moderator of life stress. *Psychosomatic Medicine, 38*, 300–314.

Cohen, S. (1988). Psychosocial models of the role of social support in the etiology of physical disease. *Health Psychology, 7*, 269–297.

Cohen, S., Doyle, W. J., Skoner, D. P., Rabin, B., & Gwaltney, J. M. (1997). Social ties and susceptibility to the common cold. *Journal of the American Medical Association, 277*, 1940–1944.

Cohen, S., & Herbert, T. B. (1996). Health psychology: Psychological factors and physical disease from the perspective of human psychoneuroimmunology. *Annual Review of Psychology, 47*, 113–142.

Cohen, S., & Hoberman, H. M. (1983). Positive events and social supports as buffers of life change stress. *Journal of Applied Social Psychology, 13*, 99–125.

Cohen, S., & McKay, G. (1984). Social support, stress and the buffering hypothesis: A theoretical analysis. In A. Baum, S. E. Taylor, & J. E. Singer (Eds.), *Handbook of psychology and health* (pp. 253–267). Hillsdale, NJ: Lawrence Erlbaum.

Cohen, S., Sherrod, D. R., & Clark, M. S. (1986). Social skills and the stress-protective role of social support. *Journal of Personality and Social Psychology, 50*, 963–973.

Cohen, S., & Wills, T. A. (1985). Stress, social support, and the buffering hypothesis. *Psychological Bulletin, 98*, 310–357.

Costa, P. T., Zonderman, A. B., & McCrae, R. R. (1985). Longitudinal course of social support among men in the Baltimore Longitudinal Study of Aging. In I. G. Sarason & B. R. Sarason (Eds.), *Social support: Theory, research, and applications* (pp. 136–154). Dordrecht: Martinus Nijhoff.

Coyne, J. (1976). Depression and the response of others. *Journal of Abnormal Psychology, 85*, 186–193.

Coyne, J., & Bolger, N. (1990). Doing without social support as an explanatory construct. *Journal of Social and Clinical Psychology, 9*, 148–158.

Coyne, J. C., Ellard, J. H., & Smith, D. (1990). Social support, interdependence, and the dilemmas of helping. In B. R. Sarason & I. G. Sarason (Eds.), *Social support: An interactional view* (pp. 129–149). New York: Wiley.

Cutrona, C. E. (1990). Stress and social support: In search of optimal matching. *Journal of Social and Clinical Psychology, 9*, 3–14.

Cutrona, C. E., & Russell, D. W. (1987). The provisions of social relationships and adaptation to stress. In W. H. Jones & D. Perlman (Eds.), *Advances in personal relationships* (vol. 1, pp. 37–67). Greenwich, CT: JAI Press.

Diener, E. (1984). Subjective well-being. *Psychological Bulletin, 95*, 542–575.

Dillard, J. P., & Fitzpatrick, M. A. (1985). Compliance-gaining in marital interaction. *Personality and Social Psychology Bulletin, 11*, 419–433.

Dunkel-Schetter, C. (1984). Social support and cancer: Findings based on patient interviews and their implications. *Journal of Social Issues, 40*, 77–98.

Dunkel-Schetter, C., & Bennett, T. L. (1990). Differentiating the cognitive and behavioral aspects of social support. In B. R. Sarason, I. G. Sarason, & G. R. Pierce (Eds.), *Social support: An interactional view* (pp. 267–296). New York: Wiley.

Durkheim, E. (1951). *Suicide: A study in sociology*, J. Spaulding & G. Simpson (Trans.). New York: Free Press. (Originally published 1897).

Ensel, W. M. (1991). "Important" life events and depression among older adults: The role of psychological and social resources. *Journal of Aging and Health, 3*, 546–566.

Felton, B. J. & Berry, C. A. (1992). Do the sources of the urban elderly's social support determine its psychological consequences? *Psychology and Aging, 7*, 89–97.

Field, D., & Minkler, M. (1988). Continuity and change in social support between young-old and old-old or very-old age. *Journal of Gerontology: Psychological Sciences, 43* P100–P106.

Gordon, C., & Gaitz, C. M. (1976). Leisure and lives: Personal expressivity across the life span. In R. H. Binstock & E. Shanas (Eds.), *Handbook of aging and the social sciences* (pp. 310–341). New York: Van Nostrand Reinhold.

Gottlieb, B. H. (1992). Quandaries in translating support concepts to intervention. In H. O. F. Veiel & U. Baumann (Eds.), *The meaning and measurement of social support* (pp. 293–309). New York: Hemisphere.

Haines, V. A., & Hurlbert, J. S. (1992). Network range and health. *Journal of Health and Social Behavior, 33*, 254–266.

Helgeson, V., & Cohen, S. (1996). Social support and adjustment to cancer: Reconciling descriptive, correlational, and intervention research. *Health Psychology, 15*, 135–148.

Heller, K., & Rook, K. S. (1997). Distinguishing the theoretical functions of social ties: Implications for support interventions. In S. Duck (Ed.), *Handbook of personal relationships: Theory, research, and interventions*, 2nd ed. (pp. 649–670). Chichester, England: Wiley.

Heller, K., Thompson, M. G., Trueba, P. E., Hogg, J. R., & Vlachos-Weber, I. (1991). Peer support telephone dyads for elderly women: Was this the wrong intervention? *American Journal of Community Psychology, 19*, 53–74.

Hirsch, B. J. (1980). Natural support systems and coping with major life changes. *American Journal of Community Psychology, 8*, 159–172.

Hirschi, T. (1969). *Causes of delinquency*. Berkeley: University of California, Berkeley.

House, J. S. (1981). *Work stress and social support*. Reading, MA: Addison-Wesley.

House, J. S., & Kahn, R. L. (1985). Measures and concepts of social support. In S. Cohen & S. L. Syme (Eds.), *Social support and health* (pp. 83–108). Orlando: Academic Press.

House, J. S., Umberson, D., & Landis, K. (1988). Structures and processes of social support. *Annual Review of Sociology, 14*, 293–318.

Hughes, M., & Gove, W. R. (1981). Living alone, social integration, and mental health. *American Journal of Sociology, 87*, 48–74.

Jacobson, D. E. (1986). Types and timing of social support. *Journal of Health and Social Behavior, 27*, 250–264.

Jessor, R., Donovan, J. E., & Costa, F. M. (1991). *Beyond adolescence: Problem behavior and young adult development* (pp. 17–38). Cambridge: Cambridge University Press.

Johnson, C. L. (1983). Dyadic family relations and social support. *Gerontologist, 23*, 377–383.

Johnson, C. L., & Catalano, D. J. (1983). A longitudinal study of family supports to impaired elderly. *Gerontologist, 23*, 612–625.

Kahn, R. L. (1979). Aging and social support. In M. W. Riley (Ed.), *Aging from birth to death: Interdisciplinary perspectives* (pp. 77–91). Boulder, CO: Westview Press.

Kahn, R. L., & Antonucci, T. C. (1980). Convoys over the life course: Attachment, roles, and social support. In P. B. Baltes & O. G. Brim (Eds.), *Life-span development and behavior* (pp. 253–286). New York: Academic Press.

Kaniasty, K., & Norris, F. H. (1993). A test of the social support deterioration model in the context of natural disaster. *Journal of Personality and Social Psychology, 64*, 395–408.

Kessler, R. (1992). Perceived support and adjustment to stress: Methodological considerations. In H. O. F. Veiel & U. Baumann (Eds.), *The meaning and measurement of social support* (pp. 259–271). Washington, DC: Hemisphere.

Klinger, E. (1977). *Meaning and void: Inner experiences and the incentives in people's lives*. Minneapolis: University of Minnesota Press.

Krause, N. (1986). Social support, stress, and well-being among older adults. *Journal of Gerontology, 41*, 512–519.

332   Implications

Krause, N. (1989). Issues of measurement and analysis in studies of social support, aging and health. In K. S. Markides & C. L. Cooper (Eds.), *Aging, stress and health* (pp. 43–66). Chichester, England: Wiley.

Lakey, B., & Drew, J. (1997). A social-cognitive perspective on social support. In G. R. Pierce, B. Lakey, I. B. Sarason, & B. R. Sarason (Eds.), *Sourcebook of social support and personality* (pp. 107–140). New York: Plenum.

Lawton, M. P. (1983). The varieties of well-being. *Experimental Aging Research, 9,* 65–72.

Lawton, M. P., & Moss, M. (1987). The social relationships of older adults. In E. F. Borgatta & R. J. V. Montgomery (Eds.), *Critical issues in aging policy: Linking research and values* (pp. 92–126). Newbury Park, CA: Sage.

Leventhal, H., Prohaska, T. R., & Hirschman, R. S. (1985). Preventive health behavior across the life span. In J. C. Rosen & L. J. Solomon (Eds.), *Prevention in health psychology* (pp. 191–235). Hanover, NH: University Press of New England.

Levitt, M. J., Weber, R. A., & Guacci, N. (1993). Convoys of social support: An intergenerational analysis. *Psychology and Aging, 8,* 323–326.

Lewis, M. A., & Rook, K. S. (1999). Social control in personal relationships: Impact on health behaviors and psychological distress. *Health Psychology, 18,* 63–71.

Litwak, E., & Szelinyi, I. (1969). Primary group structures and their functions. *American Sociological Review, 34,* 54–64.

Lyons, R. F., Sullivan, M. J. L, & Ritvo, P. G., with J. C. Coyne. (1995). *Relationships in chronic illness and disability.* Thousand Oaks, CA: Sage.

Mancini, J. A., & Blieszner, R. (1992). Social provisions in adulthood: Concept and measurement in close relationships. *Journal of Gerontology: Psychological Sciences, 47,* P14–P20.

McClelland, G. H., & Judd, C. M. (1993). Statistical difficulties of detecting interactions and moderator effects. *Psychological Bulletin, 114,* 376–390.

Miller, G. R., & Boster, F. (1988). Persuasion in personal relationships. In S. Duck (Ed.), *Handbook of personal relationships: Theory, research and interventions* (pp. 275–288). Chichester, England: Wiley.

Monroe, S. M., & Johnson, S. L. (1992). Social support, depression, and other mental disorders: In retrospect and toward future prospects. In H. O. F. Veiel & U. Baumann (Eds.), *The meaning and measurement of social support* (pp. 93–105). Washington, DC: Hemisphere.

Newcomb, M. D. (1990). What structural equation modeling can tell us about social support. In B. R. Sarason, I. G. Sarason, & G. R. Pierce (Eds.), *Social support: An interactional view* (pp. 26–63). New York: Wiley.

Orth-Gomer, K., & Unden, A. L. (1987). The measurement of social support in population surveys. *Social Science and Medicine, 24,* 83–94.

Oxman, T. E., & Berkman, L. F. (1990). Assessments of social relationships in the elderly. *International Journal of Psychiatry in Medicine, 21,* 65–84.

Peplau, L. A., & Perlman, D. (Eds.). (1982). *Loneliness: A sourcebook of current theory, research and therapy.* New York: Wiley.

Radloff, L. S. (1977). The CES-D scale: A self-report depression scale for research in the general population. *Applied Psychology and Measurement, 1,* 385–401.

Rook, K. S. (1987). Social support versus companionship: Effects on life stress, loneliness, and evaluations by others. *Journal of Personality and Social Psychology, 52,* 1132–1147.

Rook, K. S. (1990). Social networks as a source of social control in older adults' lives. In H. Giles, N. Coupland, & J. Wiemann (Eds.), *Communication, health, and the elderly* (pp. 157–169). Manchester, England: University of Manchester Press.

Rook, K. S. (1994). Assessing the health-related dimensions of older adults' social relationships. In M. P. Lawton & J. A. Teresi (Eds.), *Annual review of gerontology and geriatrics* (vol. 14, pp. 142–181). New York: Springer.

Rook, K. S., & Dooley, D. (1985). Applying social support research: Theoretical problems and future directions. *Journal of Social Issues, 41,* 5–28.

Rook, K. S., & Schuster, T. L. (1996). Compensatory processes in the social networks of older adults. In G. Pierce, B. R. Sarason, & I. G. Sarason (Eds.), *The handbook of social support and family relationships* (pp. 219–248). New York: Plenum.

Russell, D. W., & Cutrona, C. (1991). Social support, stress, and depressive symptoms among the elderly: Test of a process model. *Psychology and Aging, 6,* 190–201.

Ryan, R. M., & Solky, J. A. (1996). What is supportive about social support? On the psychological needs for autonomy and relatedness. In G. Pierce, B. R. Sarason, & I. G. Sarason (Eds.), *The handbook of social support and family relationships* (pp. 249–267). New York: Plenum.

Sarason, B. R., Pierce, G. R., & Sarason, I. G. (1990). Social support: The sense of acceptance and the role of relationships. In B. R. Sarason, I. G. Sarason, & G. R. Pierce (Eds.), *Social support: An interactional view* (pp. 97–128). New York: Wiley.

Sarason, B. R., Sarason, I. G., & Pierce, G. R. (1990). Traditional views of social support and their impact on assessment. In B. R. Sarason, I. G. Sarason, & G. R. Pierce (Eds.), *Social support: An interactional view* (pp. 9–25). New York: Wiley.

Sarason, B. R., Shearin, E. N., Pierce, G. R., & Sarason, I. G. (1987). Interrelations of social support measures: Theoretical and practical implications. *Journal of Personality and Social Psychology, 52,* 813–832.

Schulz, R., & Hanusa, B. H. (1978). Long-term effects of control and predictability-enhancing interventions: Findings and ethical issues. *Journal of Personality and Social Psychology, 36,* 1194–1201.

Schwartz, J. E., & Stone, A. A. (1998). Strategies for analyzing ecological momentary assessment data. *Health Psychology, 17,* 6–16.

Sherbourne, C. D., & Hays, R. D. (1990). Martial status, social support, and health transitions in chronic disease patients. *Journal of Health and Social Behavior, 31,* 328–343.

Simmel, G. (1949). The sociology of sociability. *American Journal of Sociology, 55,* 254–261.

Stroebe, M., Stroebe, W., & Hansson, R. (Eds.). (1993). *Handbook of bereavement: Theory, research, and intervention.* Cambridge: Cambridge University Press.

Stroebe, W., & Stroebe, M. (1996). The social psychology of social support. In E. T. Higgins & A. W. Kruglanski (Eds.), *Social psychology: Handbook of basic principles* (pp. 597–621). New York: Guilford.

Stylianos, S. K., & Vachon, M. L. S. (1993). The role of social support in bereavement. In M. S. Stroebe, W. Stroebe, & R. O. Hansson (Eds.), *Handbook of bereavement: Theory, research, and intervention* (pp. 397–410). New York: Cambridge University Press.

Sullivan, H. S. (1953). *The interpersonal theory of psychiatry*. New York: Norton.

Thoits, P. A. (1985). Social support and psychological well being: Theoretical possibilities. In I. Sarason & B. Sarason (Eds.), *Social support: Theory, research, and application* (pp. 51–72). Dordrecht: Martinus Nijhoff.

Thompson, E. H., Futterman, A. M., Gallagher-Thompson, D., Rose, J. M. & Lovett, S. B. (1993). Social support and caregiving burden in family caregivers of frail elders. *Journal of Gerontology: Social Sciences, 48*, S245–S254.

Tracy, K., & Coupland, N. (1990). *Multiple goals in discourse*. Clevedon, UK: Multilingual Matters.

Turner, R. J. (1992). Measuring social support: Issues of concept and method. In H. O. F. Veiel & U. Baumann (Eds.), *The meaning and measurement of social support* (pp. 217–233). New York: Hemisphere.

Uchino, B. N., Cacioppo, J. T., & Kiecolt-Glaser, J. K. (1996). The relationship between social support and physiological processes: A review with emphasis on underlying mechanisms and implications for health. *Psychological Bulletin, 119*, 488–531.

Umberson, D. (1987). Family status and health behaviors: social control as a dimension of social integration. *Journal of Health and Social Behavior, 28*, 306–319.

Vaux, A. (1988). *Social support: Theory, research, and intervention*. New York: Praeger.

Vaux, A. (1992). Assessment of social support. In H. O. F. Veiel & U. Baumann (Eds.), *The meaning and measurement of social support* (pp. 193–216). Washington, DC: Hemisphere.

Veiel, H. O. F. (1992). Some cautionary notes on buffer effects. In H. O. F. Veiel & U. Baumann (Eds.), *The meaning and measurement of social support* (pp. 272–289). New York: Hemisphere.

Ward, R. A., Sherman, S. R., & LaGory, M. (1984). Subjective network assessments and subjective well-being. *Journal of Gerontology, 39*, 93–101.

Weiss, R. S. (1974). The provisions of social relationships. In Z. Rubin (Ed.), *Doing unto others: Joining, molding, conforming, helping, loving* (pp. 17–26). Englewood Cliffs, NJ: Prentice-Hall.

Wills, T. A. (1985). Supportive functions of interpersonal relationships. In S. Cohen & S. L. Syme (Eds.), *Social support and health* (pp. 61–82). New York: Academic Press.

Wills, T. A. (1990). Multiple networks and substance use. *Journal of Social and Clinical Psychology, 9*, 78–90.

Wortman, C., & Lehman, D. (1985). Reactions to victims of life crises: Support attempts that fail. In I. G. Sarason & B. R. Sarason (Eds.), *Social theory, research, and applications* (pp. 463–489). Dordrecht: Martinus Nijhoff.

Wright, P. H. (1989). Gender differences in adults' same- and cross-gender friendship. In R. B. Adams & R. Blieszner (Eds.), *Older adult friendship* (pp. 222–242). Newbury Park, CA: Sage.

Index

Acceptance, 143
Adult Attachment Interview, 163
Adult Romantic Attachment Measure, 162–163
Affect, positive and negative, on social integration, 68
Agnew, C. R., 152
Akiyama, H., 75
Alateen, 200
Alcoholics Anonymous, 16, 200
Alexander, J. F., 175
Alzheimer's disease, caregivers for, 16, 197, 203, 229, 283, 295–296
Ambivalence over Emotional Expressiveness Questionnaire (AEQ), 160–161
Anan, R. M., 45
Anthony, C. R., 229
Antonovsky, A., 67
Antonucci, T. C., 75
Applegate, J. L., 170
Arizona Social Support Interview Schedule (ASSIS), 106, 110
Armsden, G. C., 163
Attachment
  in perceived partner responsiveness, 143
  theory, 103, 104, 161–163, 207–208, 252, 253–254
Attachment styles, 162
Attneave, C., 284
Attribution theory, 287
Available support, 87
Azrin, N. H., 280

Barbee, A. P., 8, 169
Barnett, D. B., 45
Barrera, M., Jr., 7
Barrera Social Support Scale (BSSS), 109

Barth, R. P., 291, 299
Bartholomew, K., 163
Batson, C. D., 159, 286
Beach, S., 153
Beall, S. K., 232
Berkeley Expressivity Questionnaire, 161
Berkman, Lisa F., 5–6, 62, 98
Berman, S., 283
Big Brothers/Big Sisters, 9, 266–267, 268, 269
Binik, Y. M., 213
Bivariate and bipolar models, relationship sentiment as, 152
Blascovich, J., 38
Blunters, 213
Bogart, L. M., 239
Bolger, N., 178
Booher, P., 271
Boster, F., 317
Bourgeois, M. S., 212, 228–229
Boutselis, M., 229
Bowlby, J., 103, 104, 161
Bradbury, T. N., 170
Brand, E. F., 283, 299
Brennan, K. A., 162
Breslow, L., 62
Brewer, M. B., 138
Bromet, E. J., 152
Bronfenbrenner, Urie, 252, 265, 268
Brownell, K. D., 294, 295
Buckner, J. S., 69
Buhrmester, D., 109
Burgio, L., 212
Burleson, B. R., 170, 171
Burton, R. P. D., 67
Buunk, B., 322

Campbell, D. T., 138, 165
Cantor, N., 178

Caregivers
  for Alzheimer's disease, 16, 197, 203,
    229, 283, 295–296
  support groups for family, 16–17
Caregiving scale, 163
Carkhuff, R. R., 233
Carlson, C. I., 174
Carnegie Commission on Adolescent
    Development, 216
Caspi, A., 178
Cassel, John, 6, 9, 102, 105
Center for Epidemiological Studies
    Depression Scale, 326
Chapman, N. J., 297, 301
Children and adolescents
  measures for, 107–110, 175
  See also Mentoring adolescents
Children's Inventory of Social Support
    (CISS), 109–110
Christensen, A., 155
Clark, C. L., 162
Clark, M. S., 151, 164
Cleary, S. D., 208, 211
Closeness, close relationships, 150–151
Clusters, 72
Coates, D., 230
Cobb, Sidney, 6, 9, 87, 102, 105
Coding systems, 167–171, 172–174, 175
Cognitive tradition, the, 6–7
Cohen, S. 3, 4, 5, 6–7, 10–13, 33–36, 56,
    57–59, 66, 74, 88–89, 105, 139, 164,
    201, 202, 208, 227, 228, 279, 293,
    313
Colby, P. M., 177
Cole, R., 252
Collectivism, 138
Collins, N. L., 162
Commitment Level Scale, 152
Commitment in relationships, 151–152
Communal Orientation Scale, 151
Communication Patterns Questionnaire
    (CPQ), 156–157
Community Helpers Project, 297
Companionship, 314–315
Companionship support, 88
Computer-mediated support network,
    241–242
Conflict in relationships, 64, 155–157
Conflicts and Problem-Solving Scales
    (CPS)., 155–156

Connell, M. M., 152
Convoy measure, 75
Coopersmith, S., 67
Cowan, C. P., 230, 232
Cowan, P. A., 230, 232
Cox, S., 204
Cronbach alpha statistic, 98
Cunningham, M. R., 169
Cutrona, C. E., 7–8, 167, 179, 206

Danish, S., 9
D'Augelli, A., 9
Davis, M. H., 140
Day Care Neighbor Service, 297
Defensive and Supportive
    Communication Interaction System,
    175
Dempster-Mcclain, D., 57
Density, network, 72–73
Devins, G. M., 213
Diary studies, 167, 176–177, 180–181
Dillard, J. P., 317
Discriminant validity, 165–166
Donald, C. A., 63
Downward social comparisons, 226–227
Dreher, H., 221
Dunham, P. J., 241–242
Dunst, C. J., 259
Durkheim, E., 5, 54, 315
Dyadic Adjustment Scale (DAS), 153

Earls, F., 69
Eckenrode, J. E., 8, 178, 201
Ecological Momentary Assessment
    (EMA), 178
Ecology of human development theory,
    252–253
Eddy, J. M., 172
Edwards, J. R., 33
Egeland, B., 300
El-Bassel, N., 283, 299
Elmira Prenatal/Early Infancy Program,
    258, 260, 261, 264
Emmons, R. A., 160–161, 177
Emotional expressiveness, 143, 160–161
Emotional Expressiveness Questionnaire
    (EEQ), 160–161
Emotional support, 88, 237–238, 318
Empathy, 143, 158–160
Empathy-altruism hypothesis, 286

Event-contingent methods, 179–180
Exchange Orientation Scale, 151
Experience Sampling Method (ESM), 178
Experiential knowledge, 225

Family Adaptability and Cohesion Scale (FACES), 157–158
Family Assessment Measure, 158
Family Emotional Involvement and Conflict Scale (FEICS), 156
Family Environment Scale (FES), 104, 157
Family environment, relationships within the, 157–158
Family interaction, 174–176
Family Relationship Index (FRI), 104–105
Family systems theory, 289
Faris, R. E. L., 54–55
Filer, M., 208
Fincham, F., 153, 154
Fischer, C. S., 106
Fiske, A. P., 41
Fiske, D. W., 165
Fitzpatrick, M. A., 317
Folkman, S., 235
Foster Extended Family Service model, 288
Franks, P., 45, 148
Freedman, M., 270
French, J. R. P., 102
Friedland, J. F., 296
Functional congruence, 144, 145
Functional support measures, 87–119
Furman, W., 109

Gable, S. L., 177
Gerdes, J., 9
Gersten, J. C., 213
Glidewell, J. C., 204
Global integrative meaning scale, 67
Global satisfaction scales, 154
Goldberg, R. J., 292
Goode, W. J., 55
Gottlieb, B. H., 7, 8, 215, 232, 313
Gove, W. R., 315
Grantham-McGregory, S., 259
Greenberg, M. T., 163
Grotevant, H. D., 174

Gruder, C. L., 293, 294
Gurung, R., 140

Hamilton, M. A., 267–268
Hamilton, S. F., 201, 267–268
Hanson, B. S., 61
Hanusa, B. H., 255, 325
Harlow, R. E., 178
Hatfield, E., 154
Hawaii Healthy Start program, 256, 259
Hayes, S. C., 294
Hazan, C., 161, 162
Health. See Social relationships and health
Healthy Families America program, 256
Heckerman, C. L., 294
Heidrich, S. M., 61
Helgeson, V. S., 110, 279
    support groups, 227, 228, 233, 239, 240
    support interventions, 201, 215
Heller, K., 205, 208–209, 214, 250, 271
Helper-therapy principle, 226, 238–239
Heyman, R. E., 172
Hierarchical coding system for sensitivity of comforting messages, 170–171
Hierarchical linear modeling, 177
Higgins, E. T., 39, 68
High-density networks, 71, 72
High/Scope Perry Preschool Program, 257, 261
Hirsch, B. J., 71, 72
HIV/AIDS
    caregivers for, 290
    support interventions for, 299
Hoberman, H. M., 34
Hobfoll, S. E., 102, 148
Hogg, J. R., 205
Holmes, J. G., 148–149
Home visitation programs, 255–257
    dependency, 263–264
    effectiveness of, 257–260
    future directions, 264–265
    limitations and challenges of, 261–264
    mediating mechanisms, 260–261
    privacy and safety concerns, 262–263
    scope of the program, 261–262
    selecting home visitors, 262
    training and supervision, 262

Hong, J., 59
Horowitz, L. M., 163
House, J. S., 60, 102, 313
Hughes, M., 315
Hughes, R. J., 230
Hurd, G. S., 301

I Have a Dream program, 265–266
Ickes, W., 160
Identity accumulation hypothesis, 56
Inclusion of Other in the Self Scale, 150–151
Infant Health and Development Program, 257
Informational support, 88
Instrumental support, 88–89, 318
Interactive coping, 169
Interactive Coping Behavior Coding System (ICBCS), 169
Interdependence processes in relationships, 143–146
Internal consistency, 98
International Network for Social Network Analysis (INSNA), 73
Interpersonal Competence Questionnaire (ICQ), 164–165
Interpersonal process tradition, 7–8
Interpersonal Reactivity Index (IRI), 159–160
Interpersonal Support Evaluation, 35
Interpersonal Support Evaluation List (ISEL), 105, 106, 156
Interval-contingent methods, 177–178
Intervention tradition, the, 8–10
Interview Schedule for Social Interaction (ISSI), 103
Intimacy in relationships, 145, 146, 148
Intimate Friendship Scale, 148
Inventory of Parent and Peer Attachment, 163
Inventory of Social Supportive Behaviors (ISSB), 110
Inventory of Socially Supportive Behaviors, 7

Johnson, R. J., 148

Kallgren, C. A., 213
Kaplan, G. A., 62
Katz, B. P., 271

Kaul, M., 45
Kawachi, I., 70
Keeton, S., 200
Kelly, J. A., 228
Kemp-Fincham, S., 153
Kennedy, B. P., 70
Kessler, R. C., 66
King, L. A., 160–161
Kitzman, H., 252, 253, 254, 257–259, 260
Kraus, L. A., 140
Kunce, L. J., 163
Kuo, W. H., 71

Lakey, B., 38–39, 45, 139, 213, 232, 253, 283
Lang, Eugene, 265–266
LaRocco, J. M., 102
Lavoie, J.-P., 228
Lazarus, R. S., 34, 35
Leiberman, J. R., 102
Lepore, S. J., 240
Lerman, M., 102
Levy, L. H., 7
Lieberman, M. A., 18, 214
Life Events and Difficulties Schedule (LEDS), 105
Linfield, K. J., 154
Linville, P. W., 39, 68
Llamas, R., 301
Lochner, K., 70
Locus of control measure, 66
Love in relationships, 154–155
Lovell, M. L., 300
Low-density networks, 71–72
Lutz, C. J., 232, 253

McColl, M. A., 296
McKay, G., 7
Main effect model, 11–13
Malmö Influence, Contact, and Anchorage Measure (MICAM), 61–62
Marital Adjustment Scale, 153
Marital interaction, 171–174
Marital Interaction Coding System (MICS), 172
Mark, M. M., 302
Marks, S., 55
Martz, J. M., 152

Matching hypothesis, 88–89
Mead, G. H., 40, 66
Meaning and Purpose in Life scales, 67
Measuring perceived and received social
    support, 86
  brief unidimensional scales, 98–102
  broadly based scales of close and
    diffuse support, 103–105
  buffering effects, 94
  conceptual and theoretical basis for
    these measures, 87–90
  confounders, 95
  generality vs. specificity, 96
  intervention research, 96–97
  length, 94
  measures for children and
    adolescents, 107–110
  measures of perceived support, 97–
    110
  measures of received support, 110–
    112
  multidimensional inventories, 105–
    106
  negative interactions, 95–96
  network-based inventories, 106–107
  perceived or received support, 93–94
  questions and issues for using
    functional measures, 90–119
  relevance, 93
  selecting and using a support
    measure, 112–119
  structural and functional measures, 96
  subscale correlations, 95
Measuring relationship properties and
    interactions relevant to social
    support, 136–138, 181–182
  measures of relationship properties
    relevant to perceiving and providing
    social support assessed in
    dispositional terms, 158–166
  measures of relationship properties
    relevant to perceiving and providing
    social support in particular
    relationships, 146–158
  measures of supportive interaction,
    166–181
  the relationship processes perspective,
    138–146
Measuring social integration and social
    networks, 53

future directions, 76–77
issues in the measurement of social
    integration, 63–70
social integration, 54–63
using social network analysis to
    measure social integration, 70–76
Mentor and mentoring, 265
Mentoring adolescents, 265–266
  effectiveness of social mentoring
    programs, 266–268
  future of mentoring, 270
  mentoring adolescents at work, 268–
    269
  mentoring program design issues, 269–
    270
Mentoring and coaching programs,
    one-to-one, 9–10
Meyer, T. J., 302
Mikulincer, M., 39
Miller, G. R., 317
Miller Social Intimacy Scale, 148
Mills, J., 151
Mittelman, M. S., 229
Modeling, 288
Moen, P., 57
Monitors, 213
Monroe, S. M., 152
Monti, P. M., 294
Morris, M. M., 140
Multilevel modeling, 177
Multiple operationalism, 138
Multiple pathways to health, concept of,
    91
Mutual aid self-help (MASH) groups, 7
My Family and Friends (MFF) measure,
    108

Nagle, L. C., 39
National Commission to Prevent Infant
    Mortality, 255
National Committee to Prevent Child
    Abuse, 256
Natural network. See Optimizing
    support in the natural network
Neighborhood Cohesion Instrument
    (NCI), 69–70
Neighborhood networks, 297–298
Neighborhood Participation Project, 297
Network interventions. See Optimizing
    support in the natural network

Network and support assessment, 205–
    216
New Mothers Study, 260
Newcomb Loneliness and Support
    Inventory (NLSI), 109
Nowlis Mood Adjective, 68
Nurse empathy, 260

Older Americans and Resources
    Inventory (OARS), 102
Olds, D., 202, 252, 253, 254, 257–259,
    260
One-to-one support interventions, 246–
    247, 270–272
    characteristics of, 247–250
    conceptual framework for, 250–255
    goal of the support program, 249
    home visitation programs, 255–265
    location of the intervention, 250
    mentoring adolescents, 265–270
    the support need, 249
    the support provider, 248–249
    the support recipient, 249
    type of method of support, 249–250
Optimizing support in the natural
    network, 278–279, 303–304
    advantages of interventions in the
        natural network, 279–280
    agents of change, 285
    attribution theory, 287
    cautions about network interventions,
        301–302
    characteristics of interventions to
        enhance support in the natural
        network, 280–281
    diffusion of responsibility, 286–287
    dimensions along which interventions
        differ, 281–285
    effectiveness of network enhancement
        interventions, 289–298
    empathy-altruism hypothesis, 286
    family systems theory, 289
    future research directions, 302–303
    intervention goals, 281
    interventions that focus on
        neighborhood or organizational
        networks, 297–298
    lessons from controlled intervention
        studies, 299–300

    mechanisms and techniques, 281–
        284
    mobilization of network resources,
        285
    mobilizing the support of one key
        network member, 292–295
    mobilizing support in the social
        network, 295–297
    social learning theory, 287–289
    training individuals to solicit and use
        support, 290–292
    underlying theoretical frameworks,
        285–289
Organizational networks, 297–298
Ormel, J., 74

Pancoast, D. L., 297, 301
Parent-Adolescent Interaction Coding
    System (PAICS), 175
Parents as Teachers program, 260
Participation-based social integration
    measures, 76–77
Partner Interaction Questionnaire (PIQ),
    112, 202
Partner support manuals, 16
Pasch, L. A., 170
Passionate Love Scale, 154
Pattison, E. M., 301
Paulhus, D. L., 66–67
Peer support groups
    difficulties of, 231–234
    duration of, 234
    effectiveness of, 227–230
    emotional support peers, 231–232
    expression of negative feelings, 232–
        233
    identification with the group and
        existing social relations, 234
    opportunities for members, 233
    optimizing the style and effectiveness
        of, 235–240
    pitfalls of, 237–240
    as source of positive social
        comparisons, 233–234
    theories underlying, 223–227
Pennebaker, J. W., 232, 238
Perceived acceptance, in relationships,
    149–150, 164
Perceived Acceptance Scale, 149–150
Perceived integration measures, 61–62

Perceived partner responsiveness, 142–143, 146, 148–150

Perceived support. *See* Measuring perceived and received social support

Perceived Support from Family and Friends, 103–104

Perry Preschool Program, 257, 261

Personal Assessment of Intimacy in Relationships, 148

Personality systems, perceived support and, 92

Pierce, G. R., 39, 140

Pillemer, K., 200

Powell, C., 259

Prager, K. J., 148

Prenatal/Early Infancy Program, 258, 260, 261, 264

President's Summit for America's Future, 265

Primary appraisals, stress and, 34, 35

Professional knowledge, 225

Profile of Mood States, 68

Prothrow-Stith, D., 70

Public/Private Ventures, 267, 269

Purpose in Life scale, 67

Q-sort, 68

Quality of Relationship Index (QRI), 156

Quality of Relationship Inventory, 39

Ramirez, R., 213

Ramsay, T. B., 7

Rand Corporation, 261

Rand Health Insurance Experiment (HIE), 63, 64

Rapid Couples Interaction Scoring System (RCISS), 172–174

Raudenbush, S. W., 69

Read, S. J., 162

Received support. *See* Measuring perceived and received social support

Reference subscale, 61

Reis, H. T., 45, 148, 177, 179–180

Rejection Sensitivity Questionnaire (RSQ), 164

Relationship Assessment Scale (RAS), 153–154

Relationship Closeness Inventory (RCI), 150

Relationship perspective, the, 42–45, 181–182

attachment, 161–163

closeness, 150–151

coding systems, 169–171, 172–174, 176

commitment, 151–152

conflict, 155–157

daily experience reports of social support, 176–181

differentiating relationship processes from social support, 145–146

emotional expressiveness, 160–161

empathy, 158–160

family environment, 157–158

family interaction, 174–176

interdependence orientation, 151

intimacy, 145, 146, 148

love, 154–155

marital interaction, 171–174

measures of relationship properties relevant to perceiving and providing social support assessed in dispositional terms, 158–166

measures of relationship properties relevant to perceiving and providing social support in particular relationships, 146–158

measures of supportive interaction, 166–181

microanalytic behavioral observations of supportive interaction, 167–169

nature and extent of interdependence, 143, 150–158

observational methods, 175–176

perceived acceptance, 149–150, 164

perceived partner responsiveness, 142–143, 146, 148–150

relationship processes perspective, 138–146

relationship processes and social support, 141–142

satisfaction, 153–154

sentiment, 143–145, 152–153

social competence, 164–165

trust, 143, 148–149

Reliability indices, 101

Repetti, R. L., 178

Reverse-buffering effect, 323
Reynolds, K., 213
Reynolds, P., 62
Richey, C. A., 300
Robinson, J., 252
Rochester Interaction Record (RIR), 179
Role accumulation theory, 55, 58–59
Role strain, 55
Roles subscale, 61
Rook, K. S., 44–45, 64, 250
Rosenberg, M., 67
Rosenberg, P. P., 233
Ross, L., 38–39
Rotter, J. B., 66
Rusbult, C. E., 152
Russell, D. W., 206
Rutter, M., 17, 214
Ryff, C. D., 61, 67

Sampson, R. J., 69
Sandler, I., 7, 213, 254
Sarason, B. R., 39, 140
Sarason, I. G., 39, 140
Satisfaction Level Scale (SLS), 153–154
Satisfaction, relationship, 153–154
Scale of Available Behaviors (SAB), 112
Schinke, S. P., 291
Schoenbach, V. J., 62
School-to-Work Opportunities Act of
    1994, 269
Schultz, R., 212, 228, 240, 255, 325
Schwartz, R. D., 138
Sechrest, L., 138, 166
Secondary appraisals, stress and, 34–35
Seeman, T. E., 62, 67, 98
Selecting and planning support
    interventions, 195–197
  characteristics of support: dosage, 209–
    212
  characteristics of the support
    recipient, 212–213
  conditions hospitable to the
    introduction of new ties, 198–202
  conditions warranting intervention
    within the natural network, 202–205
  creating a hospitable social
    psychological context, 214
  do no harm!, 214–216
  framework for planning support
    interventions, 209–212

  identifying and changing processes
    that mediate support's effects, 206–
    209
  network and support assessment, 205–
    216
  scope of support, 212
  selecting appropriate support
    strategies, 197–198
  when the attainment of health goals
    strongly depends on the behavior
    of one or more network members,
    202
  when the existing network lacks
    experiential knowledge, 200–201
  when the existing network needs
    strengthening to meet long-term,
    continuing support needs, 203
  when the existing social network is
    impoverished, drained, or
    conflictual, 198–199
  when the existing social network
    reinforces undesirable behaviors or
    identities, 199–200
  when the presenting problem or
    outside intervention is highly
    stigmatizing, 203–204
  when specialized knowledge and
    expert opinion are required, 201–
    202
  when there is a cultural gap between the
    support recipient and external
    providers, 204–205
Self-concept, 67–68
Self-criticism, 40
Self-efficacy theory, 250, 253
Self-esteem, 67, 226
Self-Esteem Inventory, 67
Self-Esteem Scale, 67
Self-Evaluation and Social Support
    Schedule (SESS), 105
Self-Expressiveness in the Family
    Questionnaire (SEFQ), 161
Self-help groups, 222
Self-improvement, 226
Self-perception theory, 232
Self-Referent Encoding Task, 40–41
Seltzer, M. M., 59
Sense of Coherence scale, 67
Sentiment override hypothesis, 152–153,
    166

Sentiment, relationship, 143–145, 152–153

Sharabany, R., 148

Shaver, P. R., 161, 162, 163, 179–180

Sherrod, D. R., 164

Short-term support groups, 234, 236

Sibling Relationship Questionnaire, 158

Sidora, K., 252

Sieber, S. D., 55

Signal-contingent methods, 178

Silverman, P. R., 212, 254

Simulated Social Interaction Test (SSIT), 165

Sisson, R. W., 280

Sobell, L., 202

Social cognition, 36–39

Social comparisons, 88, 233–234, 239

Social competence, 164–165

Social conflict, 43

Social Connections Index (SCI), 62–63

Social constructions, 36–42

Social controls, 68–69, 315–316

Social integration, 54
    affect, 68
    assessing pathways linking social integration and health, 66–68
    complex indicators, 56, 62–63
    conflict, 64
    functional support and, 92
    meaning and purpose, 67
    measuring, 56–63
    perceived integration measures, 56, 61–62
    personal control, 66
    role of social ties in, 5–6
    role-based integration measures, 56–59
    scale components, 64
    selecting appropriate integration measures, 65–66
    self-concept, 67–68
    self-esteem, 67
    social controls, 68–69
    social isolation, 64–65
    social participation measures, 56, 59–61
    social support, 69
    socially integrated communities, 69–70
    theories, 54–56

using social network analysis to measure, 70–76

weighting, 63–64

Social isolation, 64–65

Social learning theory, 287–289

Social network, 70–76, 295–297

Social Network Index (SNI), 57–59, 62, 74

Social Network List (SNL), 72

Social Networks in Adult Life questionnaire (SNAL), 75

Social participation measures, 59–61

Social Participation Scale (SPS), 60

Social penetration processes, 254–255

Social Provisions Scale (SPS), 39, 106, 179

Social Relations Model, 160

Social relationships and health, 3–5
    the cognitive tradition and stress-buffering hypothesis, 6–7
    companionship as a health-related function of social ties, 314–315
    delineating the health-related functions of social relationships, 312–317
    goals and organization, 19–20
    how social relationships influence health, 10–14
    the interpersonal process tradition, 7–8
    the intervention tradition, 8–10
    investigating the health related functions of social relationships, 317–320
    joint effects of different health-related functions of social relationships, 316–317
    research directions, 14–19
    social control as a health-related function of social ties, 315–316
    the sociological tradition, 5–6

Social Skills Inventory (SSI), 165

Social Support Behavior Code (SSBC), 167–169

Social Support Behaviors Scale (SS-B), 105–106, 112

Social Support Interaction Coding System (SSICS), 170

Social support measurement and interventions, 311–312, 327–328

Social support measurement and
  interventions (*continued*)
  companionship as a health-related
    function of social ties, 314–315
  contexts of social support, 323–324
  delineating the health-related
    functions of social relationships,
    312–317
  global vs. specific effects, 318–319
  gradient or dosage of social support,
    324–326
  investigating the health-related
    functions of social relationships,
    317–320
  joint effects of different health-related
    functions of social relationships,
    316–317
  measures of health-related functions
    in the context of intervention
    planning and evaluation, 319–320
  social control as a health-related
    function of social ties, 315–316
  social support as a stable personality
    trait vs. dynamic interpersonal
    process, 320–323
  support processes and effects over
    time, 326–327
Social Support Questionnaire, 104
Social support theory and measurement,
  29–30
  the relationship perspective, 42–45
  the social constructionist perspective,
    36–42
  the stress and coping perspective, 30–
    36
Socially integrated communities, 69–
  70
Sociological tradition, the, 5–6
Sociomatrix, 73
Solky-Butzel, J. A., 39
Specific Affect Coding System (SPAFF),
  174
Speck, R. V., 284
Spheres of Control (SOC) scale, 66
Spiegel, D., 228
Sprecher, S., 154
Steinberg, M., 8
Steiner, S. C., 152
Stokes, J. P., 72
Stone, A. A., 68

Stress and coping perspective, the, 30–
  31
  appraisal, 34–35
  appropriate measures of social
    support, 31–32, 35
  hypothesized mediators and analytic
    issues, 32–33, 35
  supportive actions, 31
  unresolved research issues, 33–34, 35–
    36
Stress-buffering hypothesis, 6–7
  in functional support, 88
  perceived support measures and stress-
    buffering effects, 91, 94
  stress-buffering model in social
    support, 11, 13–14, 321, 323
Stressors, support groups and, 235–236
Stroebe, M., 208
Stroebe, W., 208
Stroop Task, 41
Stryker, S., 40
Suhr, J. A., 167
Suicides, social ties and, 5
Suitor, J. J., 200
Sullivan, H. S., 314
Sullivan, K. T., 170
Support Activation Behavioral Coding
  System (SABCS), 169–170
Support Clusters program, 203
Support groups, 16–17, 197, 221–222
  alternative forms of, 241–242
  creation of, 9
  difficulties of peer support groups,
    231–234
  effectiveness of peer support groups,
    227–230
  the expression of feelings, 238
  future directions, 240–242
  helper-therapy principle, 238–239
  increased stigma and adverse effects
    on natural network relations, 239–
    240
  optimizing the style and effectiveness
    of, 235–240
  outcome assessment, 240–241
  the provision of emotional support,
    237–238
  social comparisons, 239
  support group participants, 242
  support interventions, 16–17

theories underlying peer support
    groups, 223–227
what are, 222–223
what kind of support should be
    provided?, 235–236
who should attend the group?, 236–
    237
Support interventions. *See* Selecting and
    planning support interventions
Support-intended behaviors, categories
    of, 7
Supportive functions, 87–90
Survey of Children's Social Support
    (SCSS), 108–109, 112
Symbolic interactionism, 40–42
Syme, S. L., 5–6, 62
Synchronization and desynchronization
    of human biological rhythms, social
    interaction and, 12

Taylor, S. E., 227
Telephone "warm lines," 247–248
Test-retest reliability, 98, 107
Therapeutic alliance, 254
Thoits, P. A., 55–56, 57, 66, 250
Thompson, M. G., 205
Tidwell, M. O., 179–180
Tierney, W. M., 271
Todt, M., 204
Tomaka, J., 38
Triangular Love Scale (TLS), 154–155
Trivette, C. M., 259
Trueba, P. E., 205
Trust, relationship, 143, 148–149
Trust Scale, 149
Tsai, Y., 71
Tucker, S., 204
Twenty Statements Test (TST), 68
Two-generation programs, 257

UCLA Social Support Interview (UCLA-
    SSI), 107, 110, 112
Underwood-Gordon, L., 66
Unstructured Interaction Paradigm, 160
U.S. Advisory Board on Child Abuse
    and Neglect, 255

Validity, 138
    discriminant, 165–166
Vallance, T., 9
Van Groenou, M. B., 74
Van Lange, P. A., 149
Van Sonderen, E., 74
Vanfossen, B. L., 102
Videka-Sherman, L., 18, 214
Vivian, D., 172
Vlachos-Weber, I., 205

Walczynski, P. T., 155
Wandersman, L. P., 234, 237
Ware, J. E., 63
Waring Intimacy Interview, 148
Webb, E. J., 138
Weighting, 63–64
Weinberger, M., 271
Weiner, B., 287
Weis, H. M., 9
Weisenfeld, A. R., 9
Weiss, R. L., 166, 172
Weiss, R. S., 103, 109, 250, 314
Welin Activity Scale (WAS), 60
Westlake, R. J., 294
Wethington, E., 8
Wheeler, L., 177
Widow-to-widow program, 212, 254
Williams, R. B., 98–102
Williams, R. M., J., 57
Wills Parental Support Scale (WPSS),
    100
Wills, T. A., 6–7, 33, 208, 211
Winston, T., 230
Wool, M. S., 292
Work Environment Scales, 104
Work Relationship Index (WRI), 104–105
Work-based teaching/work-based
    learning programs, 269
Wright, P. H., 314

Yasko, J., 228
Yoshikawa, H., 261
Young, P., 9

Zalcberg-Linetzy, A., 148
Zarit, S. H., 229, 234